1991

TEXT AND MATTER

TEXT AND MATTER
NEW CRITICAL PERSPECTIVES
OF THE *PEARL*-POET

EDITED BY

ROBERT J. BLANCH
MIRIAM YOUNGERMAN MILLER
JULIAN N. WASSERMAN

THE WHITSTON PUBLISHING COMPANY
TROY, NEW YORK
1991

"Fyrst telle me þe tyxte of þe tede lettres,
And syþen þe mater of þe mode mene me þereafter…"

Purity, 1634-35

CONTENTS

CONTRIBUTORS

Ross G. Arthur, Associate Professor of Humanities at York University in Toronto, Canada, is author of *Medieval Sign Theory and* Sir Gawain and the Green Knight (1987) and has published articles on *Pearl*, Chrétien de Troyes, the *Chanson de Roland*, Chaucer's *Parliament of Fowls*, the *Reeve's Tale*, the *Wife of Bath's Tale*, and Mallarmé as well as a feminist morphology of the Catalan adjective. He is currently working on the social context of extra-canonical French and Provençal *lais* and romances.

Kathleen Ashley, Professor of English at the University of Southern Maine, has published widely on medieval literature and is editor of two forth-coming volumes, *St. Anne in Late Medieval Culture* (co-edited by Pamela Sheingorn) and *Between Literature and Anthropology: Victor Turner and the Construction of Cultural Criticism.* She is currently completing a book on the cycle drama and is researching women owners of early modern conduct books.

Robert J. Blanch, Professor of English at Northeastern University, is editor of Sir Gawain *and* Pearl: *Critical Essays* (1966), author of Sir Gawain and the Green Knight: *A Reference Guide* (1984), and co-editor of *Chaucer in the Eighties* (1986). He has published extensively on *Sir Gawain and the Green Knight.*

Jane Chance, Professor of English at Rice University, is author of *The Genius Figure in Antiquity and the Middle Ages* (1975), *Tolkien's Art: A 'Mythology for England'* (1979), and *Woman as Hero in Old English Literature* (1986). Her edited and co-edited collections include *Approaches to Teaching* Sir Gawain and the Green Knight (1985) and *The Mythographic Art: Classical Fable and the Rise of the Vernacular in Early France and England* (1990). She is editor of a new series of translations, the Focus Library of Medieval Women, for which she has recently published a translation of Christine de Pizan's *The Letter of Othea.*

Charlotte Gross, Assistant Professor of English at North Carolina State University, Raleigh, has published essays on twelfth-century cosmology and the Provençal lyric and is presently at work on an interdisciplinary study of medieval philosophy and poetry, *Troubadours and Time*.

Britton J. Harwood, Professor of English at Miami University, is author of articles on Middle English poetry that have appeared in *ELH, JEGP, Medium Ævum, Modern Language Quarterly, Modern Philology, Philological Quarterly, PMLA, Review of English Studies*, and other journals. *PMLA* will also publish his recently completed essay, "*Gawain* and the Gift." He is currently writing a Marxist analysis of *Piers Plowman* for *Speaking Two Languages: Traditional Disciplines and Contemporary Theory in Medieval Studies*.

Lynn Staley Johnson, Professor of English at Colgate University, has published many articles on medieval and renaissance literature and is author of *The Voice of the* Gawain-*Poet* (1984) and *Spenser's* Shepheardes Calender: *An Introduction* (1990).

Miriam Youngerman Miller, Associate Professor of English at the University of New Orleans, is co-editor of *Approaches to Teaching* Sir Gawain and the Green Knight (1986) and has published articles on fantasy and science fiction, the Middle Ages in children's literature, Tolkien, and Updike. She is currently preparing an annotated bibliography of children's literature with medieval subject matter.

John F. Plummer, Associate Professor of English at Vanderbilt University, has written on the romances of Chrétien de Troyes and Sir Thomas Malory, medieval lyrics, medieval drama, and Chaucer. He has recently completed the Variorum Chaucer edition of *The Summoner's Tale*.

Paul F. Reichardt, Professor of English and Comparative Literature and Chair of the Department of Literature and Language at Northern Kentucky University, teaches medieval and classical literature and has published on Old English poetry, *Gawain*, Milton, and Umberto Eco's *Name of the Rose*. He is presently at work on topics in Dante's *Inferno*.

Gary D. Schmidt, Associate Professor of English at Calvin College, has contributed articles on medieval art and literature to *Mediævalia, Journal of the Rocky Mountain Medieval and Renaissance Association*, and *Concerning Poetry*. He has recently co-edited *The Voice of the Narrator* *in Children's Literature* and is currently working on a study of mystical journeys in medieval literature, focusing on the *Vision to the Monk of Evesham*.

Sarah Stanbury, English Lecturer at Tufts University, has published articles on the *Pearl*-Poet in *The Chaucer Review, Mediævalia,* and *Medievalia et Humanistica*. She is author of *Visual Poetics: The Viewer's Gaze in the Works of the* Pearl-*Poet* and is currently at work on a book-length study, *The Woman's Gaze: Transgression and Taboo in Medieval Devotional Literature*.

Lorraine Kochanske Stock, Associate Professor of English at the University of Houston, has published on a variety of medieval literary topics including Dante, Chaucer, Langland, and medieval drama. She is currently writing a book interpreting Langland's final revisions of *Piers Plowman* to be titled, *Wheat and Tares: Parable, Allegory, and History in* Piers Plowman C Text and is editing the *Tale of Melibee* for the Chaucer Variorum project.

Michael W. Twomey, Associate Professor of English at Ithaca College, has published articles on Old and Middle English texts such as *Bede's Death Song*, the Alliterative *Morte Arthure*, and *Cleanness*. A collaborator in R. E. Kaske's *Sources for Interpreting Medieval Christian Literary Imagery*, he is currently at work on a book-length study of *Cleanness* and on an edition of the Old and Middle English fragments of the *Elucidarium*. He is also a contributor to the forthcoming reference works *Fontes Anglo-Saxonici, Sources of Anglo-Saxon Literary Culture*, and *Medieval England: An Encyclopedia*.

David Wallace, Associate Professor, Department of English at the University of Texas at Austin, has recently contributed to an anthology of medieval literary theory and edited a collection of essays on the Beatrice-Dante relationship. He is currently writing a short book on Boccaccio's *Decameron* as well as a longer study of the place of literature (Chaucer, Boccaccio, Dante, Petrarch) in the passage from associational forms of medieval polity to the absolute state.

Julian N. Wasserman, Professor of English at Loyola University/ New Orleans, is co-author of *The Poetics of Conversion* (1977) and *Thomas Hardy and the Tristan Legend* (1983) as well as co-editor of *Edward Albee: An Interview and Essays* (1983), *Chaucer in the Eighties* (1986), and *Sign, Sentence, Discourse* (1989). He has published widely on the *Pearl*-Poet.

Victoria L. Weiss, Professor of English at Oglethorpe University, has published a number of articles on *Sir Gawain and the Green Knight* as well as other subjects, and her work on early forms of court entertainment and their relationship to narrative has been funded by the National Endowment for the Humanities and the American Council of Learned Societies. Her essay in this volume is part of an anticipated book-length study of the subject.

INTRODUCTION

Although overshadowed by their sister poems in the Cotton Nero A.x. manuscript—*Sir Gawain and the Green Knight* and *Pearl* — *Cleanness* (or *Purity*) and *Patience* have recently become objects of critical scrutiny. Within the last ten years, for instance, *Cleanness* scholars have examined the influence of Biblical paraphrases and fourteenth-century *artes praedicandi* upon the poem or have explored important narrative and symbolic patterns, particularly the employment of a homiletic structure. Still other studies of *Cleanness* have focused upon the scriptural underpinnings of concepts (*Kynde*) or episodes (Sodom and Gomorrah), have called attention to vessel, threshold, and city imagery, have explored enclosed space as a reference point for optical perspective, have concentrated upon the function and meaning of significant themes (*daunger* and judgment), or have illuminated the hierarchical design in and the "festive decorum" of the work. Finally, in some analyses of *Cleanness*, the traditional concern with questions of style and authorship has been revived. For a few scholars, at least, stylistic variables—especially disparate syntactic patterns—may be amassed in order to refute the argument for common authorship of the Cotton Nero poems, whereas other critics have provided evidence identifying John Mascy of Sale with the *Pearl*-Poet.

Both the number and variety of interpretations of *Cleanness* are reflected in current *Patience* range from genre studies (sermon and missal), discussions of symbolic patterns and narrative perspectives, and investigations of figural typology (Jonah as Christ or the whale as Hell) to more untraditional treatments—the application of Saussure's theories to the poem and the thematic significance of *poynt* (*punctus*), a geometric figure rooted in scholastic background. Other useful studies examine the work's sources, particularly the questions of how and why the Beatitudes and the *Book of Psalms* shape the theme and narrative of *Patience*; the emergence of important patterns (cosmic space and visual perspective), symbols (heart), or themes (suffering); the key images (*munster dor*, the cities) woven into the poem; the narrative roles of Jonah and God; and the links between poetic style and authorship identification.

Mirroring current scholarly interest in *Cleanness* and *Patience*, then, this anthology of criticism represents the first collection of essays to explore all four works commonly attributed to the anonymous fourteenth-century *Pearl*-Poet. While previous anthologies of the late 1960s and early 1970s—devoted exclusively to *Sir Gawain*, *Pearl*, or both poems—offer reprints of articles from scholarly journals and excerpts from books, this collection provides fifteen original essays, articles delivered initially as papers at various medieval conferences or written specifically for this volume. Addressing ourselves, in part, to the question of a traditional imbalance in *Pearl*-Poet scholarship, an overriding concern with *Gawain* and *Pearl*, we thus include in this book three essays on *Cleanness* and three on *Patience*—critical studies which may spark future interest in these biblical homilies. The remaining nine essays, however, are designed to appeal to a wider audience, both medievalists who teach the *Pearl* poems at the advanced level and non-specialists who teach *Sir Gawain* (or *Pearl*) as part of the traditional "Survey of British Literature" or "Introduction to Literature" courses.

That this anthology of criticism devoted to the *Pearl*-Poet's works appears at an important juncture is demonstrated by recent scholarly activity. The most significant effort, perhaps, is William Vantuono's two-volume edition, *The* Pearl *Poems: An Omnibus Edition* (New York: Garland, 1984. Representing the only work to provide Middle English texts supported by variant readings as well as complete literal translations on pages facing the texts, the Vantuono edition, likewise, contains two unique features—extensive variorum commentary (1:213—351, 2:205—371) and comprehensive bibliographies. Such exhaustive annotation makes previous interpretations of the Cotton Nero poems more accessible to modern readers, thereby fueling critical interest in these four works. Equally important, especially for those instructors and students who are approaching *Gawain* for the first time, is the new pedagogical text, *Approaches to Teaching* Sir Gawain and the Green Knight, edited by Miriam Youngerman Miller and Jane Chance (New York: Modern Language Association, 1986). The first part of this volume, compiled by Professor Miller, is devoted to the materials needed for teaching *Gawain*, including editions, translations, background studies, critical works, reference guides, and audiovisual aids. In the second major section ("Approaches"), however, Professor Chance pilots instructors through a survey of the teaching of *Gawain*; the remainder of this section focuses on important background materials (romance, chivalry, courtly love, religion and law, and medieval aesthetics) as well as on specific classroom approaches to the work. This splendid MLA volume concludes with Miller's extensive bibliography (pp. 215-47) of primary sources, second-ary sources, and audiovisual materials cited throughout the text.

At least two recent critical studies cover all four Cotton Nero poems. In Lynn Staley Johnson's *The Voice of the* Gawain-*Poet* (Madison: University of Wisconsin Press, 1984, for instance, the author examines the works "not only individually but as a group and in the context of medieval literary, social, and religious views," particularly "within the context of the spiritual life of the Middle Ages" (p. ix). Thus, in the course of her study, Johnson perceives the Jonah of *Patience* as a type of Everyman and Christ; identifies the threefold pattern of *Cleanness*, the three scriptural episodes, with the three temptations noted by John (1 John 2.16); links the garden setting of *Pearl* with the *noli me tangere* incident, Mary Magdalene's dialogue with Christ, depicted in the New Testament (John 20. 11-18); and examines three potential time patterns in *Gawain*—cyclic, degenerative, and regenerative (a time scheme grounded in the liturgical calendar). In *The Matter of Courtesy, Medieval Courtesy Books and the* Gawain-*Poet* (Woodbridge, Eng.: D. S. Brewer, 1985), however, J. W. Nicholls explores the role of courtesy books in medieval intellectual and religious life and relates the social ideals embodied in those books to important themes pervading the *Pearl* poems.

While only two recent scholarly books are devoted to all four Cotton Nero poems, five works published in the 1980s—one edition, one annotated bibliography, and three critical studies—focus on *Gawain*. Theodore Silverstein's Sir Gawain and the Green Knight: *A New Critical Edition* (Chicago: University of Chicago Press, 1984) offers a Middle English text of the poem; a full Introduction covering sources and analogues, literary conventions, poetic form, manuscript history, authorship meter, diction and style, and language and dialect; lengthy explanatory notes, particularly lexical annotations, rhetorical traditions (Seneca and Cicero) and tropes, and key terms (*fides, trawth,* and *clannesse*); and a full glossary. Robert J. Blanch's Sir Gawain and the Green Knight: *A Reference Guide* (Troy, N.Y.: Whitston, 1984), however, provides an annotated bibliography (objective abstracts) of critical or interpretive treatments of *Gawain*, ranging from the early nineteenth century to the late 1970s. Employing chronologically arranged entries in order to trace the evolution of *Gawain* scholarship from nineteenth-century explorations of sources, analogues, and authorship problems to the more specifically literary concerns of the twentieth century, Blanch outlines in some detail the scope and contents of each bibliographical item. His book includes, likewise, a subject and author index as well as a critical introduction reviewing *Gawain* scholarship (1969-77) and offering desiderata for future research.

Although the Silverstein edition and the Blanch reference guide may be placed safely in the vein of traditional scholarship, the three critical studies of *Gawain* offer innovative approaches to this elusive Middle English romance. In *The Poem as Green Girdle: Commercium in Sir Gawain and the Green Knight* (Gainesville: University Presses of Florida, 1984), for instance, R. A. Shoaf employs contemporary critical theories (poststructuralism and semiotics) in order to illuminate "the conflict in late fourteenth-century England...between chivalry and commerce as two systems of value" (p. vii). Then, attempting to prove that commercial vocabulary in *Gawain* serves as an instrument of reconciliation between chivalric and mercantile values, Shoaf proceeds to investigate commercial motifs (exchanges and covenants) in scripture, fourteenth-century poetry, and medieval social history. In the remaining chapters of his monograph, Shoaf examines the economic and religious implications of the Green Chapel scene—an episode which takes place on New Year's Day, the feast of the Circumcision of Christ; evaluates Gawain's pride as well as commercial diction (temptation and hunting scenes); links covetousness with idolatry (Gawain's inordinate attachment to the pentangle and its ideals); and underscores both the knotting of the *luf-lace* as sign and the poem itself as sign. Wendy Clein's *Concepts of Chivalry in* Sir Gawain and the Green Knight (Norman: Pilgrim Books, 1987), however, provides a discussion of the "open" structure of *Gawain*. Furthermore, in order to quell the conflict between courtly and moralist views of the poem, she explores *Gawain* in terms of fourteenth-century perspectives of chivalry and of death. In the final *Gawain* study, *Medieval Sign Theory and* Sir Gawain and the Green Knight (Toronto: University of Toronto Press, 1987, Ross G. Arthur attempts to unveil the poet's skillful employment of sign theory, an analytic tool elucidated in fourteenth-century schools and manifested in sermons, poetry, and heraldic treatises of the age. Zeroing in on important signs—the pentangle, the image of the Virgin, the green girdle, and the wound in Gawain's neck—Ross Arthur discloses the *Gawain*-Poet's role within the medieval literary tradition of ambiguity and multiple signification.

In addition to the numerous appraisals of *Gawain*, scholars of the 1980s have produced two books on *Pearl*: The first, Pearl: *Image of the Ineffable, A Study in Medieval Poetic Symbolism* (University Park, Pa: Pennsylvania State University Press, 1983), sheds light on the medieval penchant for symbolism, especially in artistic portrayals of the ineffable and the apocalyptic. Rooting his study in medieval aesthetics and symbolic theory, Bogdanos thus scrutinizes the Incarnation, the sacramental fusion of human and divine, as well as the incongruity developing between physical image and spiritual reality in *Pearl*. The final work under discussion, William Vantuono's *The* Pearl *Poems in*

Middle and Modern English (Lanham, Md: University Press of America, 1987), contains on facing pages the text of *Pearl* and a verse translation "as close to the original as possible" (p.ix); employing a Middle English text based upon Volume 1 of his Pearl *Poems: An Omnibus Edition* (1984), Vantuono generally retains the original orthography of the Cotton Nero manuscript. This edition-translation includes, likewise a short introduction (pp. xi-xxi), buttressed by references to scholars and their theories, devoted to the manuscript, the authorship controversy, the question of genre, and the theme and structure of *Pearl*; a brief commentary of rhyme, refrain and concatenation, rhythm and alliterative patterns, and diction; a set of lexical annotations; an appendix ("Poetic Mastery in *Pearl* "); and a bibliography ("Works Cited") cross-referenced to the introduction.

Retracing the 1980s, perhaps a *decas mirabilis* for students and scholars of the *Pearl* poems, we should note that the period began with the publication (1980) of W. R. J. Barron's *Trawthe and Treason : The Sin of Gawain Reconsidered*, an analysis of *Gawain* 's "chivalric idealism and human fallibility." Two years later, *Gawain* criticism was further enriched by Victor Yelverton Haines' book, *The Typology of* Sir Gawain and the Green Knight, an investigation of Gawain's link with Adam through the employment of the *felix culpa* motif. The most recent scholarly effort devoted to *Gawain,* in part, is Tadahiro Ikegami's *Gawain and the Arthurian Legend* (Tokyo: Shubun International, 1988), a collection of reprinted essays (in Japanese) originating in Japanese scholarly journals. Ikegami's *Gawain* topics include the poetic structure, the Green Knight and the Beheading Game, the temptation scenes, nature, courtesy, and *cortaysye* and *trawthe.* Between the appearance of the critical studies by Barron and Haines (1980, 1982) and the publication of the Ikegami anthology of essays (1988), then, twelve books—issued within a span of five years (1983-87)—focus on the Cotton Nero poems. With such a flurry of *Pearl*-Poet scholarship in mind, we are very pleased that this collection contains essays by three editors or authors of recent books on the Cotton poems—Jane Chance, Lynn Staley Johnson, and Ross G. Arthur.

Turning to the individual contributions to this volume, we trust that these essays provide a spectrum of current approaches to the *Pearl* poems, ranging from traditional questions of theology to more modern considerations of sign theory, of metalanguage, and of the problems of reading a text (Benson). Pervading this anthology, however, is a unity of critical concern, even in the midst of critical diversity, which prevents the collection from becoming a disunity set of mutually exclusive interpretations. Such "unity in diversity" is reflected, for instance, in the essays treating the problem of symbolism or "signification" in the *Pearl* poems. One analysis of *Pearl*, the essay by

Chance, employs the metaphors of patristic exegesis in order to uncover the poem's tripartite structure and meaning. Other interpretations, especially those by Schmidt and Reichardt, examine imagery and similes—traditional literary devices which illuminate the themes or the overall dramatic design of the *Pearl* poems. In particular, Reichardt explores animal similes (hawk,doe,quail) in *Pearl*, images which have been investigated by Bogdanos (p.73 and pp. 124-25) in his book-length analysis of *Pearl*. Still other studies, the Plummer, Ashley, and Arthur essays, trace the "semiotic" concerns of the poet. Complimenting R. A. Shoaf's reading (*The Poem as Green Girdle*) of the poem, Plummer, Ashley, and Arthur thus identify the important roles played by language, identity, signs, and multivalent imagery in *Gawain*.

Apart from the broad focus of these scholarly essays, the *Pearl*-Poet's concern with meaning and signification, this collection pinpoints the influence of the poet's cultural milieu—traditions, structures, entertainments, and themes. While Gross scrutinizes a conventional aspect of medieval linguistic practice, courtly diction (the courtly rhetoric of the maiden and dreamer in *Pearl*), Stock examines *acedia* (sloth) in *Patience* within the framework of medieval Vices and Virtues traditions. Two essays, those by Harwood and Weiss, explore the *Pearl* poems in the light of important fourteenth-century art forms or entertainments; whereas Harwood perceives a connection between diptych structure and the diction, imagery, and themes of *Pearl*, Weiss views *Gawain* within the context of courtly entertainments (interludes). Other essays—the Johnson essay on *Pearl* as well as the Wallace and Stanbury interpretations of Cleanness—are interconnected by their common concern with the themes of history and judgment and with the medieval conception of time, a recurrent strain in contemporary critical views of fourteenth-century poetry. Finally, Twomey employs patristic commentary and interpretations of canon, civil, and common law in order to unveil the theme of *untrawthe* in *Cleanness*.

In closing, it seems appropriate to make some mention of the genesis and production of this volume. Although we have long felt the need for a *Pearl*-Poet anthology of critical essays, one which would survey important approaches currently applied to the *Pearl* poems and which would suggest the unity of the works in the canon, the impetus for this collection may be traced to a convention. We are thus very grateful to Robert A. White and David G. Allen, co-organizers of the Fifth Citadel Conference on Literature: The poetry, Drama, and Prose of the Renaissance and Middle Ages (March 14-16, 1985, for allowing us (Blanch and Wasserman) to organize and chair two sessions on the *Pearl*-Poet.

The actual production of this volume, from a collection of manuscripts in disparate styles to its present (hopefully unified) form, involved a number of persons to whom we owe an enormous debt. They include Pamela Boan, for demonstrating patience as a "poynt" of virtue in dealing with the original manuscripts and our often illegible editorial marginalia, as well as the staff and director of Academic Computing Services at Loyola University, for their technical support—particularly James O'Meara who designed the runic characters employed in the text (and then figured out why they would not print)and Mike Klein whose unending patience and cheerfulness with translating "just one more disc" were much appreciated. We are also grateful our home institutions for the faith which they demonstrated in helping to underwrite costs of seeing this project to its completion. Specifically we would thank the Faculty Grants and Research Committee of Loyola University and Dennis R. McSeveny, Dean of Liberal Arts at The University of New Orleans, for their generous allocation of all too scarce funds. Finally, we should especially like to acknowledge the support provided by Marjorie A. Blanch, our editorial consultant, for assistance with stylistic matters.

Spring 1989

Robert J. Blanch
Miriam Youngerman Miller
Julian N. Wasserman

TEXT AND MATTER

THE *PEARL* DREAMER AND THE ELEVENTH HOUR

LYNN STALEY JOHNSON

In this essay I would like to examine the poet's handling of time in *Pearl*. His awareness, not only of various ways of considering time, but of the potential artistic uses of a temporal cycle or cycles, is apparent throughout his works. In *Sir Gawain*, he juxtaposes Camelot with Cyclic, Degenerative, and Regenerative schemes of time, in each case to the concept of motion.[1] His use of time in that poem points up Camelot's genuine instability; the city is not capable of withstanding motion but only of tracing its own cycle of declension. In addition, the poet's handling of the seasonal cycle at the beginning of the second section of *Sir Gawain* testifies to his awareness of the implications of judgment and warning inherent in medieval treatments of the period of time from spring to harvest. In *Patience* and *Purity* he dramatizes significant events of biblical history in such a way as to highlight those cycles of time that define and circumscribe human action and human choice. His handling of time in *Pearl* is equally purposeful, for, even as he specifies August as the month of the narrator's experience, he provides for this experience a setting that locates the dreamer within an entirely different temporal framework.

That much-discussed reference to August comes early in the poem, in section 1, lines 37-40:

> To þat spot þat I in speche expoun
> I entred in þat erber grene,
> In Auguste in a hyȝ seysoun,
> Quen corne is coruen wyth crokeȝ kene.[2]

There have been numerous suggestions about the exact date the poet intends us to associate with this "hyȝ seysoun." We can interpret the phrase as referring to Lammas (Gollancz, Gordon, and Andrew and Waldron), to the Feast of the Transfiguration (Madeleva, Knightley), or to the Feast of the Assumption (Hamilton, Osgood, Schofield). Or we can take Charles Moorman's ingenious suggestion that "hyȝ" is an unlisted alternative spelling of "hiȝ" or "heȝ" (hay), the phrase then referring simply to the "hay season."[3] Despite the fact that I incline toward the Feast of the Assumption, especially since *Pearl* seems to reflect many of the lessons, themes, and figures identified with this day, I would like to explore the poet's possible reasons for linking the dreamer's experience to a date in late summer, for that experience seems rather to belong to a genre of visionary narrative traditionally connected to late spring or early summer. By shifting the seasonal context of the dream, the poet offers an implied commentary upon the dreamer, the nature of his problem, and the Parable of the Vineyard, through which the maiden examines the proper use of time, a medium the dreamer seems initially to squander without regard for its limits. Ultimately, the reference to August early in the poem prepares us to apply the Parable of the Vineyard to the sorrowing dreamer as well as to the maiden, who describes herself as having begun vineyard labor at the eleventh hour.

The lines themselves describe two conventional but distinct scenes, whose separate elements the poet joins in a single sentence and a single pictorial frame. First, as several critics have pointed out, the description of August as the time when grain is scythed reflects the traditional occupation for August in both literary descriptions and pictorial sequences of the Labors of the Months.[4] As Trevisa describes the month in his translation of Bartholomaeus Anglicus' *De Proprietatibus Rerum*, "in þis moneþ corn is igadred into bernes and þerfore he is ypeynt wiþ a fleile þrossching corn … "[5] That the relatively uniform iconographic treatments of the month of August have their origin in the actual agricultural cycle is no doubt the case as Emile Mâle observed; when translated into art, however, man's labors also acquired meanings rooted in the medieval understanding of time. Put simply, time was conceived of as a medium for change or growth. Again I quote Trevisa:

> Tyme is mesure of chaungeable þingis, as Aristotel seiþ *de quinque substanciis* … Oþir as Rabanus seiþ, tyme is dymension of chaungeabil þingis, touchinge meovinge and abidinge, and duriþ in meovable þingis. As Austyn seiþ, noþing is more precious þan tyme … Tyme is schort, chaungeable, & vncurable … [6]

In each case, the attempt to define time depends upon a recognition of finitude, for—Aristotle, Rabanus Maurus, and St. Augustine agree—time is a medium for change, which can be measured just as a line that begins at one point and ends at another can be measured. However, medieval discussions of time are less abstract considerations of the nature of time than they are urgent preambles to exhortations regarding the use of time, since man can do little about time itself but can do much within his own time. As Rosemond Tuve noted, the urgency that informed references to the seasonal cycle and to the sequence of the Labors of the Months is characteristic of English verse, making "English seasons-descriptions from before Lydgate until after Spenser a contribution to that apology for poetry which sees in it the teaching of an active virtue."[7]

The reference to August notwithstanding, the first 180 lines of *Pearl*, up to the dreamer's first sight of the maiden, suggest the outlines of another convention, that of the love vision, linked not to late summer but to spring or early summer, the more timely season for dreams pertaining to or arising from frustrated desire.[8] The opening sections of *Pearl* could, in fact, be described as an especially focused and intelligent transformation of the traditions of the French love vision as handed on to later writers by Guillaume de Lorris. Moreover, the author of *Pearl* seems to be conscious of the ties between the *Romance of the Rose* and the biblical imagery of desire, since he adapts certain key elements of Amant's experience in ways that highlight the *Pearl* dreamer's state of mind. Guillaume de Lorris' account of the Garden of Deduit seems to provide the *Pearl*-Poet with the subtext for his description of the garden in which the dreamer goes to mourn the loss of his pearl:[9]

> On huyle þer perle hit trendeled doun
> Schadowed þis worteȝ ful schyre and schene,
> Gilofre, gyngure and gromylyoun,
> And pyonys powdered ay bytwene. (41-44)

These lines, together with the first two lines of the preceding quatrain ("To þat spot þat I in speche expoun / I entred in þat erber grene") distill an entire tradition, thereby suggesting a series of *topoi* linked to the literature of love, search, vision.

With only a few brushstrokes, the poet conjures up a garden inextricably joined to the visionary experiences of late spring or early summer. Like the innermost sanctum of the Garden of Deduit, the spot of the pearl's loss is doubly enclosed, first, in a garden, implied by the phrase "I entred in," and, second, by the plants that shade the spot, making of it a kind of bower.[10] The plants themselves evoke earlier spice gardens of desire. For example, the more elaborate garden Guillaume de Lorris describes, which boasts its own complicated literary and biblical pedigree, contains many exotic spices—cloves, licorice, fresh grains of paradise (or cardamom), zedoary (a ginger-like spice), anise, and cinnamon—a number of trees and animals, and an abundance of unnamed flowers—red, yellow, and white—in addition to violets and periwinkles. The Middle English translator of these lines, whom I will call Chaucer, is faithful to his original; following both the spirit and the letter of the French text, he ends his description of the garden's lushness by saying of the ground that it is "poudred, as men had it peynt."[11] Both verbs imply art rather than nature, design rather than accident, thereby conveying the garden's concealed artifice. The *Pearl*-Poet's description of the dreamer's garden focuses our attention upon those few details that establish the spot of loss as the setting for a certain type of experience. Like Chaucer, he translates Guillaume de Lorris' cloves as gillyflowers or clove pinks; he includes ginger but adds "gromylyoun," or gromwell, a commonly grown medicinal herb, which fits nicely into the line's alliterative pattern. On the other hand, as Gollancz also noticed, the word might reflect the poet's assumption that the gromwell's white seed and the "greyn de parys" mentioned in the Middle English *Romance of the Rose* were identical. Although I would not want to dismiss this possibility, I do not care to make too much of it. The poet may also have expected his audience to remember that the gromwell's white, pearl-like seeds are the source of the herb's medicinal benefits, perhaps hinting at an elaborate metaphoric pun whereby the lost pearl had indeed been transformed through the natural process of seasonal decay and growth and had borne fruit, the curative potential of which the self-absorbed dreamer is oblivious.[12] Finally, the *Pearl*-Poet up-roots the violet and the periwinkle from the garden, replacing them with peonies, which, like the gromwell, were grown for medicinal purposes. He, too, indicates the garden's artfulness by describing the peonies as "powdered" between the other plants.

These comments may seem to represent undue attention to an ostensibly random group of plants, but the tightly woven description functions as a trope, placing us, not in a real garden where pinks, peonies, ginger, and gromwell are all blooming simultaneously, but in a garden setting where both culinary and curative herbs form a bower for a lover's dream. The first of the manuscript illustrations to the poem suggests a similar contemporary awareness of the almost mannerist character of the poet's description of this spot. Its depiction of a male figure sleeping in a highly stylized pastoral setting could serve to introduce any number of works that recount moments of revelation or vision. For example, on the stalls of Carlyle Cathedral is placed a sequence of paintings depicting scenes from a life of St. Augustine. The panels portraying Augustine's experience of conver-sion in the garden are particularly striking, especially when we compare them to the manuscript illustrations for *Pearl*; both sequences are indebted to the iconographic conventions of the literature of love or vision, or, as Courcelle puts it, of conversion. Thus, the panel tracing that central moment in Augustine's spiritual life shows him reclining near an open book in a garden whose mounds are powdered with flowers while an angel leans toward him and carries a banner on which is inscribed *Tolle, lege*. If we erased the angel's wings and removed the banner, the picture, which looks remarkably like a reverse image of the first of the illustrations for *Pearl*, could be used in an edition of *The Legend of Good Women, The Romance of the Rose*, or *Pearl*.[13]

The poet's description of this garden would be less significant, or more conventional, did not the poem itself take place in August. By joining in one sentence in lines 37-40 a reference to an August field and to an enclosed garden, the poet seems to insist that we see the dreamer and his garden within a larger frame. In effect, he sketches for us a scene whose fundamental disunity underlines the spiritual conflict in the dreamer between himself and time. Thus the poet seems to mix metaphors on rather a large scale, dislocating the conventional protagonist of the literary dream vision and placing him and his garden of desire in the midst of a larger and equally significant frame—a calendar, open to August.[14] There are at least two other instances in the poem where the poet hints at an association between a calendrical sequence and the dreamer's experience, the first in the dreamer's initial reaction to the landscape of his vision and the second in the maiden's account of the Parable of the Vineyard.

When the dreamer first "awakens" in his vision, he finds himself in a realm whose characteristics identify it as a *locus amoenus*, an edenic landscape whose heightened clarity and sensual appeal serve as an *accessus* to the debate between the dreamer and his beloved guide. Here, the poet's awareness of the connections between literary convention and biblical imagery is particularly apparent, for he recasts materials that Guillaume de Lorris and others had drawn from the Song of Songs and the Book of Apocalypse in their attempts to describe other efforts to regain paradise. For example, in Apocalypse 22:2, St. John describes the River of Life as flowing from the throne of God. That river was thought to flow here on earth in baptismal water, thereby creating at once a rite of passage and a passageway for the man seeking entry to paradise. Guillaume de Lorris employs this detail in his depiction of Amant's gradual apprehension of another sort of paradise, for, when Amant first "awakens" in his dream landscape, he hears the sound of water. Drawn to the sound, he discovers a river whose cold water gushes from a nearby hill. While washing his face in the water—a social rite that ironically evokes the more fundamental cleansing of the baptismal fount—he notices the gravel that covers the stream-bed, a detail that adds to the richness and mystery of the landscape he inhabits. The *Pearl*-Poet restores this river to the landscape of the New Jerusalem; its force and majesty and the splendor of the stones along its bottom impel the dreamer towards revelation, not towards the outer reaches of fantasy. By drawing upon the details of such conventions, the poet not only indicates a relationship between his dreamer and other literary lovers and dreamers, but establishes his experience in a season appropriate for desire, when the year's fruit is yet nascent in the flowers dotting these landscapes.

But if the outlines of the narrator's visionary experience characterize him as a lover whose plaint is set in the beginnings of the annual cycle, the maiden insists that he recognize actual, not imaginary, time. She does so by recounting the Parable of the Vineyard (Matthew 20:1-

16), a parable in which human activity is circumscribed by the period of time from sunrise to sunset. Labor in the vineyard begins with first light and continues until the sun goes down, "þe date of day of euensonge, / On oure byfore þe sonne go doun" (529-30). Those who commence work at the "eleventh hour" begin, not at one hour before midnight, but in late afternoon, probably around four o'clock.[15]

In addition to recounting a parable whose message is bound up with the sun's daily motion, the poet describes a scriptural labor associated with the sun's annual movement through the zodiac, for the harvest of the grapes was linked to the month of September, or to the sign of Libra. As Trevisa describes September, "And þis moneþ is ende of somyr and biginny[n]g of haruest. In þis monthe grapis beþ ripe and þerfore he is ipeint in a vineʒerd as a gardeynere gadringe grapis in a basket."[16] Trevisa here evokes both the pictorial and the philosophical traditions, describing, first, September as a particular labor, and, second, the symbol for that labor. The description could be turned around so that we perceive, as the maiden seems to expect the dreamer to understand, that the gardener gathering grapes in a basket is a sign of the end of summer, a sign of harvest. When Virgo gives way to Libra, the season changes from one of growth to one of reckoning. It is Libra, or the Scales, that hangs low in the horizon over Chaucer's pilgrims as the Parson begins his tale of penance, a tale fittingly introduced by Harry Bailly with "Beeth fructuous, and that in little space." Here, as so often in *The Canterbury Tales,* Harry Bailly speaks more wisely than he may know, for the subject of fruitfulness was inevitably raised in considerations of Libra. If we extend Chaucer's allusion to Libra, with Libra in the sky, the Parson has but little space— or little daylight—left to urge spiritual fruitfulness upon the pilgrims, whose diverse loves the *Tales* recount, and who, in turn, have little time to repent.

The fact that September was frequently described as signifying the day of judgment makes the maiden's use of the Parable of the Vineyard even more pointed. As the first month of autumn, September is the month of the equinox, signalling days of shorter length and thus of diminished opportunity for human activity.[17] The maiden's handling of this parable captures the urgency associated with September and the sign of Libra, thus calling attention to the brevity of time available for human labor. Not only does she stress the passing of each hour, but she uses "date," connoting a specific period of time, as a link word in section IX, the section in which she describes the labor in the vineyard. Moreover, she uses "date" here in reference both to an annual and a diurnal measurement of time. First, she applies "date" to that time of year when the grapes are ready for harvest (lines 500-08); if we examine both the traditional associations between September and the gathering of grapes and the relationship between the parable and the theme of judgment, it seems likely that "date" in this case refers to September. However, she also uses the word to denote a time of day, as in "date of daye" (517), "welneȝ wyl day watȝ passed date" (528); and "At þe date of day of euensonge" (529). Her use of the word underscores the relationship between the two ways of telling time in the poem, implying that sundown and September are, in fact, the same date, particularly since she refers to evensong as one hour before sundown or as the eleventh hour, when she herself entered the vineyard. Indeed, the theme of judgment that informs her narration of the parable is most evident in her description of sundown,

> Ȝe sunne watȝ doun and hit wex late.
> To take her hyre he made sumoun;
> Ȝe day watȝ al apassed date. (538-40)

The end words for each line—"late," "sumoun," and "date" suggest that sundown, like that date when the sun moves into Libra, can be understood as the time of balance when the results of spring's planting and summer's growth are put to the scales. It is the note of finality struck by those words "late," "sumoun," and "date," that ought to alert the dreamer to the time of year in which he exists—August, one hour before sundown.

The maiden's account of the Parable of the Vineyard and the dreamer's account of the landscape of vision, are cast in strikingly visual language that evokes not only the language of the dream vision and of the Bible, but pictures of Spring or early summer, and of August and September. Such pictures can only be understood as individual elements of a larger sequence, the sequence of the year, the scheme by which man measures time. If we consider these pictures in relation to the early portrayal of the dreamer in his garden in the midst of August, we can detect the outlines of a calendrical sequence within *Pearl*, a sequence that underlies both the poem's patterns of language and imagery and its broader thematic concerns.

First, and most obviously, the references to time adumbrate a movement from spring to harvest that is directly relevant to the dreamer's efforts to come to terms with the fact or effect of mutability. Ultimately, the vision of the New Jerusalem, the Tree of Life with its twelve fruits for the twelve months at its heart, provides the dreamer, as it provides the poem's reader, with a visual token of permanence, offsetting the sense of time and transience that seems to dominate the poem. In the stanza describing the Tree of Life (1069-80), the narrator emphasizes the permanence and the clarity of the landscape of paradise. Those bodies by which we tell time here on earth, the moon, the planets, and the sun, are not only unnecessary in a realm without time, but pale in relationship to the refulgence of heaven. The splendor of that transcendent sphere is mirrored in the River of Life, which also reflects the trees growing by its bank:

> Aboute þat water arn tres ful schym,
> Þat twelue fryteȝ of lyf con bere ful sone;
> Twelue syþeȝ on ȝer þay beren ful frym,
> And renowleȝ nwe in vche a mone. (1077-80)

Whereas in the sun's movement through the sky and in the rotation of the months we on earth find our symbols for earth's impermanence, those twelve endlessly renewing fruits are visual symbols for eternity. The moon, our most persistent referent for change, not only has no power in heaven's sky ("The mone may þerof aproche no myȝte" [1069]), but is subsumed into a greater motion, the cycle of endless renewal played out by the banks of the River of Life.

Second, the implied movement from August to September adds one more strand to the poem's rich weave of allusions to cultivation and harvest. On the most basic level, "corn" is a generic term, referring to any grain. The dreamer's use of it echoes his allusion to John 12:24 only a few lines previously, "For vch gresse mot grow of grayneȝ dede; / No whete were elleȝ to woneȝ wonne" (31-32). From this early and rather arid reference to the natural cycle to his final description of the citizens of heaven as harvested pearls, his language sketches his growing recognition of a more fundamental process of cultivation and harvest. Thus his initial hopelessly literal reference to wheat is transformed—by a process as mysterious as transubstantiation itself—into the truly nourishing bread of the Mass mentioned in the poem's closing lines, grain that has not only been cut but ground, bolted, and baked. From the rotting body of the lost pearl to the risen body of Christ, the poem traces a pattern of resurrection and transformation, of spiritual harvest. If we interpret the dreamer's reference to corn in a more metaphoric sense, we should note that the word also was used to denote the end result of something, the desired product, associations that reverberate in the poem's many allusions to spiritual fruitfulness and cultivation. If the dreamer's early expressions of grief can be described as the barren harvest of his sorrow, then the poem that begins "Perle, plesaunte to prynces paye" surely can suggest true fruit, the bountiful harvest of love and labor.

Finally, and most importantly, the poet's emphasis upon time implies that the dreamer himself is in his eleventh hour. If we take the "hyȝ seysoun" as referring to the Feast of the Assumption, celebrated on August 15, the sun has indeed just entered the eleventh sign, Virgo, symbolized by a woman bearing sheaves of grain.[18] It is not improbable that the poet intends an annual cycle organized around the period from spring to harvest or around the sun's movement through the zodiac of human labor. First, medieval writers had many ways of organizing time, depending, in each case, upon the message they sought to illustrate. In his introductory remarks to *The Golden Legend*, Jacobus de Voragine uses a cycle that begins in winter with Advent and ends in fall; the poet's description of autumn in *Sir Gawain* directly contrasts seasonal change and the idea of harvest with natural fruitfulness, or implicitly, with human activity. Moreover, the Parable of the Vineyard at the center of *Pearl* focuses upon the sun's movement from dawn to evening or from first light to last. The poet's choice of August as the month for the dreamer's experience is particularly significant in relation to the picture outlined by the maiden's parable; a man gathering grapes is a sign for September, for Libra, when the equinox occurs, thus signalling days of shorter duration. If September corresponds to sundown, then August, like evensong, occurs in the last hour of light.

The August date of the poem marks the dreamer as sorely in need of an eleventh-hour work permit.[19] Whereas he is initially content to sleep (and, ironically enough, to inhabit a garden we associate with an earlier season of the year and other occupations) while all around him the fields are white with harvest, the maiden urges upon him timely labor, August's spiritual work that must precede the balance scales of September. The maiden's appearance is, however, timely in more ways than one, for, while the dreamer exists in a state of disharmony with the natural cycle, she verifies the essential orderliness of the natural cycle even as she bears witness to a realm whose cycles transcend our own. The dreamer's description of himself as a laborer in the closing lines of the poem, therefore, highlights his own awareness of time, a recognition of its use. By stepping away from the artificial spring he at first inhabits and by leaving the love-garden of his self-involved grief, he steps into his true place, a field whose ripe grain awaits the worker. Furthermore, if the dreamer's perception of the movement from August to September or his genuine comprehension of time serves as a catalyst for his spiritual transformation, the poem functions as such a reminder for its audience. Just as the maiden offers the dreamer the clemency figured in Virgo, the poem, like a true calendar, fulfills its end, rooting us in and reminding us of time and the uses of time, only to impel us beyond time to timeless harvests.

Notes

1.   See my study, *The Voice of the* Gawain-*Poet* (Madison: The University of Wisconsin Press, 1984), pp. 40-69.

2.   *Pearl*, ed. E. V. Gordon (Oxford: Clarendon Press, 1953, rpt., 1970). All quotations from *Pearl* refer to this edition and are cited by line number within the text.

3.   For a brief discussion of these suggestions, see William Vantuono's comments on lines 39-40 in *The* Pearl *Poems: An Omnibus Edition,Vol.1* : Pearl *and* Cleanness, ed. W. Vantuono, The Renaissance Imagination, No. 5 (New York: Garland Publishing, 1984), p. 220. For Moorman's more etymological remarks, see his comment on the line in *Pearl* in *The Works of the Gawain-Poet*, ed. Charles Moorman (Jackson: University of Mississippi Press, 1977).

4.   See particularly Ian Bishop, Pearl *in Its Setting* (Oxford: Basil Blackwell, 1968), p. 86; Theodore Bogdanos, Pearl: *Image of the Ineffable* (University Park: The Pennsylvania State University Press, 1983), p. 27.

5.   *On the Properties of Things, John Trevisa's translation of Bartholomaeus Anglicus' De Proprietatibus Rerum*, (Oxford: Clarendon Press, 1975), I, 532, hereafter cited as Trevisa. For discussions of the iconography of the Labors of the Months, see Emile Mâle, *The Gothic Image: Religious Art in France of the Thirteenth Century* trans. from 3rd ed. by Dora Nussey (1913; rpt. New York: Harper and Row, 1958), pp. 72-93; Rosemond Tuve, *Seasons and Months: Studies in a Tradition of Middle English Poetry* (Totowa, New Jersey: Rowman and Littlefield, 1976).

6.   Trevisa, I, 517-518.

7.   Tuve, *Seasons and Months*, p. 122.

8.   For this tradition, see the collection recently edited and translated by B. A. Windeatt, *Chaucer's Dream Poetry: Sources and Analogues* (Totowa, New Jersey: Rowman and Littlefield, 1982). Here I except Nicole de Margival's *Le Dit de la Panthere d'Amours*, c. 1300, which Windeatt also includes in this collection; this poem, like *Pearl*, is set at harvest time on the eve of the Feast of the Assumption. For discussions of the spring setting for poems recounting visions, love visions in particular, see Tuve's remarks in *Seasons and Months*, pp. 110-11; in addition, see A. B. Giamatti, *The Earthly Paradise and the Renaissance Epic* (Princeton: Princeton University Press, 1966, rpt. 1969), Chapter 1; Marc M. Pelen, "Form and Meaning of the Old French Love Vision: the *Fableau dou Dieu d'Amours* and Chaucer's *Parliament of Fowls*," *The Journal of Medieval and Renaissance Studies* 9 (1979): 277-305; J. I. Wimsatt, "Chaucer and French Poetry," in *Geoffrey Chaucer: Writers and Their Background*, ed. Derek Brewer (Athens: Ohio University Press, 1975).

9.   On literary influence, see Thomas M. Greene, *The Light in Troy* (New Haven: Yale University Press, 1982), particularly the remarks on pp. 48-53. For a differently directed study from my own concerning the relationship between

elements of the *Romance of the Rose* and *Pearl*, see Herbert Pilch, "The Middle English *Pearl*: Its Relation to the *Roman de la Rose*," in *The Middle English Pearl: Critical Essays*, ed. John Conley (Notre Dame: University of Notre Dame Press, 1970), pp. 163-84.

10.   On the characteristic details of medieval literary gardens, see D. W. Robertson, Jr., "The Doctrine of Charity in Mediaeval Literary Gardens: A Topical Approach through Symbolism and Allegory," *Speculum* 26 (1951): 24-49. On the garden in *The Romance of the Rose*, see John V. Fleming, *The Roman de la Rose: A Study in Allegory and Iconography* (Princeton: Princeton University Press, 1969), Chapter 2: "*The Hortus Deliciarum*." See also Charles Dahlberg's remarks in his edition, *The Romance of the Rose* (Princeton: Princeton University Press, 1971), Notes to Chapter 1, pp. 357-65.

11.   *The Romaunt of the Rose* in *The Riverside Chaucer*, ed. Larry D. Benson (Boston: Houghton Mifflin Co., 1987), 1436. The description of the garden is found in lines 1349-1438.

12.   For an understanding of the ways in which these plants appear in medieval writing, see the entries for each of them in the *Middle English Dictionary*, ed. Sherman M. Kuhn (Ann Arbor: The University of Michigan Press). Sir Israel Gollancz in his edition of *Pearl* (1891; rpt. New York: Cooper Square Publishers, 1966), p. 120, also makes this point about the gromwell. For a study of the details of this site, see C. A. Luttrell, "Pearl: Symbolism in a Garden Setting," in *The Middle English Pearl*, pp. 297-324. Luttrell (p. 311) also notes the harvest time opening in *Le Dit de la Panthere*. See also, Bogdanos, *Ineffable*, pp. 23-26.

13.   See Pierre Courcelle, *Les Confessions de Saint Augustin dans la tradition litteraire* (Paris, 1963). As Courcelle notes, the same cathedral has a life of Saint Cuthbert, for which (see B. Colgrave, "The Saint Cuthbert Paintings on the Carlisle Cathedral Stalls," *Burlington Magazine* 73 [1938]: 17) the artist copied the miniatures of a "Life" from the late twelfth century. It is, as Courcelle remarks, probable that the same is the case for the life of St. Augustine; the conception of scenes, iconography, and form seem to evoke the illustrations of the "epoque romane." For any analysis of *Pearl*, especially the link between that poem and the motif of the *Noli me tangere* that I have suggested in *The Voice of the Gawain Poet* (pp. 148-78), the inscriptions for two of the scenes in this "Life" are particularly tantalizing. The inscription for a scene depicting Augustine and Alypius in the garden includes the following details: "Her sore wepyng for hys gret syn / He went to morne a garth wythin." For the "Tolle, lege," the inscription is noted: "Her wepyng and walyng as he lay / Sodenly a voice thus herd he say: Tolle, lege, tolle lege." Both inscriptions emphasize the sorrow that precedes recognition and conversion, for Augustine is cast, like Mary Magdalene or the *Pearl* dreamer, as a mourner in a garden.

14.   Just how purposeful are these lines is even more apparent if we compare them, not only to the opening stanzas of French love visions, but to the opening of Boccaccio's "Olympia," a poem whose similarity to *Pearl* suggests *Pearl*'s elegiac form and purpose.

15.   For a discussion of the poet's use of the "eleventh hour" to describe the maiden's status in the vineyard, see D. W. Robertson, Jr., "The 'Heresy' of *The Pearl*," in *The Middle English Pearl*, pp. 291-96. As Roberson notes, the maiden seems to follow Bruno Astensis' lead in associating the "eleventh hour" with those individuals baptized only shortly before death rather than with those who become

Christians in old age. I concur with Robertson's reading of the passage, but would like to suggest that we apply the parable to the dreamer whose life, like any life, can be divided into twelve hours. For the "eleventh hour" as a time of day, see Chauncey Wood, *Chaucer and the Country of the Stars* (Princeton: Princeton University Press, 1970), p. 294; see also C. R. Cheney, *Handbook of Dates for Students of English History* (London: Office of the Royal Historical Society, 1945, rpt. 1970), p. 9.

16.   Trevisa, I, 533. In *The Pearl: An Interpretation* (New York: Barnes and Noble, 1967) p. 52, P. M. Kean associates the labor of the parable with March or early Spring, especially since the maiden describes the workers as cutting and tying up the vines: "Wryþen and worchen and don gret pyne, / Keruen and caggen and man hit clos" (*Pearl*, 511-12). There are, however, several reasons for linking the labor of the parable to fall, despite the fact that pruning was assigned to March in the schema of the Labors of the Months. (On March, see Trevisa, I, 530; Mâle, *The Gothic Image*, p. 71; Tuve, *Seasons and Months*, pp. 161-62.) First, the pruning ascribed to March could involve trees or vines whereas the more specific image of the vineyard was linked to September. Second, though it is unlikely the poet had any direct experience of viticulture, Virgil in the *Georgics* (Book II, 397ff.) recommends dressing the vines three or four times a year, contending that the soil should be broken up and the grove lightened of its foliage. He then notes that the vines should be cut and pruned into shape in the fall. On vinedressing and pruning in the fall, see also William Robert Prince, *Treatise on the Vine* (New York, 1830), pp. 276-281. Furthermore, as Fernande Braudel points out in *The Structure of Everyday Life* (vol. 1 of *Civilization and Capitalism*, trans. and revised by Sian Reynolds [New York: Harper and Row, 1979], p. 487), fall was the season in which landowners most frequently hired day laborers, the season, in fact, when the scene described in the parable was likely to have been a common one in the agricultural districts of Europe. However tempting it is to speculate about the reality that may underlie the poet's fiction, I think his account of the labors of the vineyard has more to do with commentaries on the Parable of the Vineyard than with medieval agricultural practices. Most obviously, his description of the labor is general enough to suggest how little he knew about such   matters, particularly if we juxtapose this section of *Pearl* with certain passages of *Sir Gawain*, wherein he demonstrates a more intimate knowledge of the customs of late four-teenth-century aristocratic life. More importantly, if we turn to the commentaries on the Parable of the Vineyard, we find the labor in the vineyard depicted in general terms, emphasizing its strenuousness and focusing on the broader issues of cultiva-tion and fruitfulness. By interpreting the vineyard as a figure for the Church or for the Kingdom of Heaven, the commentators stress the theme of harvest, directing our attention to our duties in the time left before the twelfth and final hour. Thus, the laborers' complaint in the parable that those who have borne the day's heat should receive the same wage as those who began work at the eleventh hour, together with the parable's inherent urgency, evokes a scene near the end of the yearly agricultural cycle. For comentaries on the parable, see St. Augustine, Sermo LXXXVII in *Sermones de Scripturis, PL* 38, cols, 530-39; Bede, *In Matthaei Evangelium Expositio, PL* 92, cols. 87-88; St. Gregory, Hom. XIX in *XL Homiliarum in Evangelia, PL* 76, cols. 1153-59; Rabanus Maurus, *Comment. in Matthaeum, PL* 107, cols. 1025-30. Finally, the poet may have taken a hint from St. Gregory in linking the parable to a particular month; near the end of his sermon, Gregory, in exhorting his hearers to penance, specifically relates his topic to his audience. He says: "Mense autem Julio nuper elapso, hujus quam nostis pestilentiae clade percussus est, qui, ad extremum veniens, urgeri coepit ut animam redderet" (col. 1158).

17.   See Wood, *Chaucer and the Country of the Stars*, pp. 272-97, for a discussion of Libra. In his massive encyclopedia, the *Reductorium Morale* (Colona, 1730), Petrus

Berchorius says of September, "Iste mensis significat diem judicii" V, p. 128). In discussing Libra (p. 108), Berchorius says: "Quando Sol est in libra, tunc facit noctes & dies aequos, & ideo dicitur libra, quia monstrat ponderum aequitatem. Sic vere quando Judex est in libra justitiae, tunc necessario facit aequinoctium, i.e. aequale judicium inter virum & proximum suum, alias non. Vel dic, quod quando Sol, i.e. Christus ascendet signum librae, i.e. thronum judicii, ubi facta omnium librabit & ponderabit ."

18.   See Trevisa's remarks about the appropriate signs for both August and September (I, 1, 532-33). For remarks linking the Feast of the Assumption to this same issue of fruitfulness, see Bruno Astensis, "De Humilitate," in *Sententiae,* Lib. II, v, *PL* 165, col. 198.

19.   The dreamer's idleness in the midst of an August harvest may also have been charged with more immediate ironies for the poem's first audience; as Georges Duby in *Rural Economy and Country Life in the Medieval West* (trans. Cynthia Postan, Columbia, South Carolina: University of South Carolina Press, Book IV, "Change and Upheaval in the XVth Century") points out, harvest time was a period of real activity throughout rural England, a time when each potential laborer was pressed into service.

ANIMAL SIMILES IN *PEARL*

PAUL F. REICHARDT

For the most part, studies of the imagery of *Pearl* have focused on details of the *erber* frame (i.e. the significance of the varieties of plants growing there) or those associated with the extra-terrestrial paradise and heavenly Jerusalem described in the *visio* portion of the poem (i.e. gem and precious metal symbolism). Yet, as I plan to show in this paper, *Pearl* contains another significant strain of imagery, one more related to bestiaries than to lapidaries or herbaria. In three similes which each link the poem's protagonist to qualities of particular animals, *Pearl* underscores the essential irony of its dreamer's relation to the marvelous vision he sees while also providing a key to his moral and spiritual progress during the course of this vision. Once understood, the animal similes in *Pearl* illustrate once more the tendency of this Middle English poem to generate its meaning through patterns of style, most notably the concatenation of structurally and semantically linked vocabulary and modes of expression.[1]

The three animal similes of *Pearl* span the central *visio* section of the poem, one being placed near the beginning of the vision, another near its middle, and the third at the end. Early on, as he gazes raptly at the Pearl-Maiden, the dreamer is described as "hende as hawk in halle."[2] Somewhat later, as he is being rebuked by the Pearl-Maiden, the dreamer is said to "daunce as any do" (345). Finally, near the poem's end, his wonder at the sight of the Lamb of God renders him "stylle as dased quayle" (1085). These three similes, though they represent a rather slender thread as concatenations go in *Pearl*, nonetheless depict a composite portrait of the dreamer's emotional and spiritual character, and this character in turn effectively determines the direction and ultimate outcome of the *visio* itself. To study these animal similes then is to learn more about the psychic forces at work in the poem's protagonist and, from the perspective of the traditional religious underpinnings of this fourteenth-century poem, to perceive as well certain accepted truths about human nature itself.

One measure of the importance of the three similes which are the focus of this paper is the extent to which each blends with its immediate poetic context. In the case of the initial hawk image, for example, the term used to describe the dreamer reinforces and extends implications already at work in the lines adjacent to this reference, and in particular the thematic and stylistic patterns of the poem's fourth stanza group:

> I stod ful stylle and dorste not calle
> Wyth y3en open and mouth ful clos
> I stod as hende as hawk in halle. (182-84)

Several details in this passage deserve comment. The dreamer, who is here conveying his intense interest in the Pearl-Maiden prior to addressing her and thereby initiating their dialogue, employs the term "hende" to describe his kinship with the hawk. "Hende" can mean many things in Middle English poetry, including "gracious" or "courteous," as a line from another Cotton Nero A.x. poem, *Gawain and the Green Knight,* reminds us.[3] In line 184 of *Pearl* ,however, the sense of the term would seem to be something like "attentive," thus suggesting a domesticated bird's habit of intently watching the movements of those around it. The fixity of such a gaze is in turn related to the link-word repeated throughout stanza-group four, *py3t,* the past tense of Middle English *pyche* This verb means to "pitch," "place," or "fix," and the majority of its occurrences in *Pearl* refer to the fixing of gems in their settings.[4] By extension, line 184 may be said to speak of the fixity of the dreamer, who is indeed transfixed by the sight of his beloved pearl.

Thus does the hawk simile aptly convey the rapt attention of the dreamer and the intensity of his gaze. But the fact that the figure of the hawk is the vehicle for these circumstances adds much to the complexity of the dreamer's characterization of himself, for the hawk, like all animals in the medieval bestiary, possessed particular traits which rendered it a moral sign as well as a zoological specimen. The key element in the hawk's status as sign is its reputation as a predatory bird, and the implications of this fact were conveyed to the medieval imagination as much by etymology as by experience and observation.

The typical Latin designation for the hawk is *accipiter,* which is derived from the verb *accipere,* "to take or seize." Thus Isidore of Seville treats the hawk's name as a description of its habits, and characterizes the hawk as a thieving and predatory bird ("Accipiter ... ab accipiendo, id est a capiendo, nomen sumpsit... hoc est raptor").[5] Hugh of St. Victor extends *accipiter's* aggressive and predatory instincts to the world of human motives, where such tendencies represent a form of pathological behavior ("accipiter... rapit et devorat, quia quilibet perversus actus... non cessat").[6] The appearance of similar sentiments under the entry for *accipiter* in the *Allegoriae in sacram scripturam* attributed to Rabanus Maurus indicates wide-spread acceptance of the darker implications of the hawk's Latin name. The *Allegoriae* entry cites a reference to the *accipiter* in the Book of Daniel ("Et ungues crescent quasi accipitres," "And his nails grew like birds' claws") and glosses the verse as referring to intellectual pride ("quod qui per superbiam in mente decipiuntur..."), thus linking the hawk to yet another human vice.[7] The hawk, regal in its bearing and accomplished in capturing and devouring its prey, thus serves to point to pride and rapacity in human nature as well. This attribution was, let it be noted, no negative reflection on the hawk; it was a noble beast much admired for its hunting skills and tractability for domestication. Humankind, however, was expected to rise above the instincts which dominated mere beasts like the hawk. Men and women who did not so rise were considered culpable for failing to realize the true potential of their nature when beasts like the hawk were able to realize the essence of their species.

The hawk simile of *Pearl* 184 ultimately points toward the dreamer's own temptation to seize the object of his desire (i.e. the pearl) just as a hawk would seize its prey. It goes without saying that such an attempt would be thoughtless and imprudent for the dreamer since he is separated from the pearl by spiritual boundaries, boundaries manifested in the *visio* in the form of the river which keeps the dreamer from joining the Pearl-Maiden in the realms of the terrestrial paradise and the Heavenly Jerusalem. Yet the dreamer will eventually attempt to cross this river in order to possess his lost pearl, and this attempt brings his vision to an abrupt ending. The hawk simile in a sense represents the first clue to the dreamer's faulty perception of his relation to the figures and scenes he sees in the vision. For him they are understood as objects capable of being possessed, and therefore, though he is attentive to every word and movement emanating from his dream, he mistakes the difference in character and the distance separating his mortal mind from the wisdom of the Pearl-Maiden. Through each of the subsequent two animal similes, the dreamer's misunderstanding of his relation to the figures and scenes in the vision is exemplified ever more pointedly and critically by the traits associated with the beasts to which he is compared.[8]

The simile of the doe, for example, which occurs next in order, is clearly meant to define the shortcomings of the dreamer since it occurs as part of the Pearl-Maiden's rebuke to her interlocutor:

> 'For þoȝ þou daunce as any do
> Braundysch and bray þy braþeȝ breme,
> When þou no fyrre may, to ne fro,
> Þou moste abyde þat he shall deme.' (345-48)

In many ways these lines contain the most ingenious of *Pearl*'s animal similes, for the moral implications of the figure of the doe are buried somewhat more deeply than those of the earlier reference to the hawk or the later allusion to the quail. The doe would seem to represent a fairly positive or at least neutral beast, and in a sense this is true. The key to the figure's significance lies once more in the characteristic behavior patterns of the animal named; that is, in the doe's propensity to *daunce*. *The Middle English Dictionary* glosses the phrase "dauncen as any do" as "to leap or run like a deer" (s.v. *do*), and this expression focuses our attention on the fleetness of the animal and its tendency to use its speed afoot rather than craft or strength to extricate itself from dangerous situations. In another Cotton Nero poem, *Gawain and the Green Knight*, the quarry of Bercilak's first hunt is "dos and oþer dere" (1322), and it is interesting to note that this rather timid animal is easily run to ground and dispatched by the burly hunter and his party:

> Þenne fersly þay flokked in folk at þe laste,
> And quickly of the quelled dere a querre þay maked.
> (1323-24)

Interpreters of this scene have noted the correspondence between the timidity and vulnerability of the deer Bercilak hunts and the conduct of Gawain and the lady in the boudoir on the same day of the hunt, with the implication that although a doe's retiring disposition may be an endearing trait, such behavior is not a totally successful means of dealing with serious threats to one's well-being.[9]

Similarly, the resemblance between the dreamer in *Pearl* and a doe would suggest the former's inadequacies when faced with adverse circumstances. This fact contrasts sharply with the previous identification of the dreamer with the rapacious hawk, but the difference in context helps explain why the ground of comparison shifts so abruptly. In the earlier hawk simile, the contextual issue is, I would maintain, the latent acquisitiveness of the dreamer, who eventually attempts to seize his pearl and the mode of existence that the figure of the pearl exemplifies. This mode of behavior reflects an aggressive side of his (and, in medieval eyes, "everyman's") disposition, a side generated by the desire to experience or possess whatever is perceived as profitable or pleasurable. In the doe simile, a contrary tendency is represented; that is, the tendency of the dreamer (and, once again, "everyman") to avoid what is unpleasant or painful. The Pearl-Maiden, in referring to the dreamer as a doe, has in mind his tendency to flee from adverse fortune, as the lines immediately preceding the doe simile make clear:

> For dyne of doel of lureȝ lesse
> Ofte mony mon forgos þe mo.
> Þe oȝte better þyselven blesse,
> And loue ay God, in wele and wo,
> For anger gayneȝ þe not a cresse. (339-43)

The virtue here espoused, of accepting circumstances of life meted out by fortune (and ultimately by providence) is emphasized by the link-word of stanza-group VI, *deme*, "judge, appoint, ordain." It is thus the very wisdom of divine providence which is questioned by the dreamer's aversion to the *wo* of losing his pearl. In the end, his attempted evasion of *doel* might even be characterized as a form of cowardice,[10] with the contrast between the rapacity of the hawk and the retiring nature of the doe pointing toward the contradictory and therefore unstable character of the dreamer in particular and human-kind in general.

From an intertextual perspective fully in keeping with the allu-sive nature of *Pearl*'s imagery, the phrase "daunce as any do" contains an echo of biblical references to the figure of the doe in Proverbs 6:5 (Deliver thyself as a doe [Latin *damula*] from the hand, and as a bird from the hand of the fowler)[11] and Isaiah 13:14 (they shall be as a doe fleeing away, and as a sheep: and there shall be none to gather them together ...).

The figure of the *damula fugiens* which appears in these verses is often understood as a figure for the attempt to evade the truth of Christian doctrine. The *Allegoria in Sacram Scripturam* speaks of the *damula* as an emblem of *diabolus* (probably too strongly pejorative for the image's appearance in line 345 of *Pearl*) and of the reprobate (*reprobus recedit ab Ecclesia*).[12] The *Glossa ordinaria* of Walafrid Strabo associates the *damula* of Isaiah with false religious teaching and those who promote it (*prava doctina, cujus magistri in damula significantur.*)[13]

The doe of *Pearl* 's second animal simile thus becomes a sign of the dreamer's misunderstanding of adverse fortune. Expressed in more modern terms, the issue of this particular simile may be the dreamer's maladjustment to the experience of loss. The dreamer, unable to accept the loss of his pearl (in whatever sense one chooses to take this image), is driven first to despair, then to desire, and finally to a form of delirium as he attempts to possess the object of affection once more. This degenerative progression is in fact registered in the succession of animals evoked in the three similes under investigation here. The boldness and aggression implied in the image of the hawk are re-vealed as a desperate attempt to avoid confronting misfortune by attempting to recapture, or more properly to force, the substitution of an earlier and more pleasant condition of life for a present less desirable situation. Through this revelation, the dreamer is also shown to be less and less noble, to the same extent that the skittishness of the doe is less noble than the regal demeanor of the hawk.

The descent through the ranks of "nobility" in the animal king-dom implied by the first two beast similes in *Pearl* suggests the dreamer's own retreat from the values exemplified by the spiritual vision he witnesses. The very choice of animals to convey a sense of his character at given points of the narrative associates the dreamer with the world of flesh and blood, a world which in turn stands as a foil to the "gostly" realm inhabited by the Pearl-Maiden. Indeed the final animal simile of *Pearl* sounds this same note of spiritual regression in most emphatic terms since the beast it invokes was proverbially linked to fleshliness and earth-bound existence:

> I stod as stylle as dased quayle
> For ferly of þat frelich fygure
> Þat felde I nawþer reste ne trauayle,
> So watȝ I rauyste wyth glymme pure. (1085-88)

The link-work of the stanza group in which these lines are found is *mone* (i.e. "moon"), a term connected to the image of the quail through reference to a subtext operative in this passage, the biblical account of the quails sent to feed the Israelites during their desert sojourn after fleeing Egypt (Exodus 16:4-15 and Numbers 11:31-34). The quail, both in the scriptural subtext and medieval commentaries on it, become emblems of a fleshly and carnal mind. This reading of the birds emerges quite naturally from their inability, due to weight and weak wing structure, to raise themselves much above the ground as they fly along. This trait of course makes them easy targets for hunters and perhaps accounts for the fact that these birds were sent to supply the Israelites with meat. In scripture, the quail appear each day at nightfall, which correlates with the rising of the moon ("So it came to pass in the evening, that quails coming up, covered the camp" [Exodus 16:13]).[14] The very appearance of these birds in the story of the Exodus is a sign of the carnality of the Israelites, for the quail are given in response to complaints about the quality of the food provided during the wilderness journey:

> And the children of Israel said to them: Would to God we had died by the hand of the Lord in the land of Egypt, when we sat over the flesh pots and ate bread to the full. Why have you brought us into this desert, that you might destroy all the multitude with famine? ... I have heard the murmuring of the children of Israel: say to them: In the evening you shall eat flesh, and in the morning you shall have your fill of bread: and you shall know that I am the Lord your God. (Exodus 16: 3, 12)
>
>   For a mixt multitude of people, that came up with them, burned   with desire, sitting and weeping, the children of Israel also being joined with them, and said: Who shall give us flesh to eat? ... We remember the fish that we ate in Egypt free of cost: the cucumbers come into our mind, and the melons, and the   leeks, and the onions, and the garlic. Our soul is dry, our eyes behold no thing else but manna. (Numbers 11: 4-6)

The quail thus becomes a scriptural sign of ingratitude and self-indulgence, and these themes are elaborated more than once by biblical exegetes who treat these passages.

The entry for quail (*coturnix*) in the *Allegoriae in sacram scripturam* for example links the bird directly to carnal pleasures ("Per coturnicem voluptas carnales, ut in Numeris: 'Ventus arreptas trans mare coturnices detulit in castra…").[15] Hugh of St. Victor offers a fairly extensive exegesis of the behavior of the quail described in Exodus and Numbers as a sign of moral predispositions observable among human beings. Hugh writes that the quail resembles humans in that it is naturally subject to frailty and disease ("Sola haec avis, sicut et homo, cadu cum patitur morbum"). As such, both human beings and the quail of Exodus 16 and Numbers 11 seem naturally drawn toward death and destruction. Driven by winds across the sea and into the Israelites' camp, these birds meet their destiny. In just such a way Hugh describes humanity as driven across the *mare mundi* by passion for pleasure ("calore dilectionis"), a flight which ever leads from *ardor charitatis* to *tentatio refrigeratae mentis*. The teminus of this same flight, as the terms of Hugh's commentary suggest, is death, a death that recalls the fate of the quail slaughtered by the hungry Israelites in Exodus 16 and Numbers 11.[16] In effect, the quail of scripture seem to have taken on the qualities of the humans in Exodus 16 and Numbers 11, with the carnal appetites of the Israelites being transferred in traditional commentary to the fleshy little birds on whom these people fed.

The precise terms of the quail simile in *Pearl* 1085 carry a latent signification that may be seen as appropriate to the dreamer in the poem. The use of the adjective "dased" in this passage, in addition to mirroring the quail's tendency to be easily frightened and therefore confused and erratic in movement and flight, may point once more to the Old Testament subtext in Exodus and Numbers that serves as the *locus classicus* for the quail's moral reputation in the Middle Ages. The quail who blunder into the Israelite camp seem panicked and disoriented ("And a wind going out from the Lord, taking quails up beyond the sea brought them, and cast them into the camp for the space of one day's journey, on every side of the camp round about, and they flew in the air two cubits high above the ground," Numbers 11:31), and this same sort of frantic, compulsive behavior is evident in the dreamer's attempt to cross the river to possess his pearl at the end of the poem. The dreamer, like the quail with which he has been compared, becomes an animated emblem of *voluptas carnales* as behavioral motive:

> Delyt me drof in yȝe and ere,
> My maneȝ mynde to maddying malte;
> Quen I seȝ my frely, I wolde be þere,
> Byȝonde þe water þaȝ ho were walt. (1153-56)

The thoughtlessness and impulsiveness of this act, an act which effectively shatters the dreamer's vision, is directly attributable to his "fleschly hert" (1072), which quality is referred to in the same stanza where the quail simile appears. The fleshly heart of the dreamer is in fact a central problem in *Pearl*, and it points to the kind of destructive self-indulgence that makes it nearly impossible for him to respond to spiritual realities except in physical and sensory ways.[17] It is the problem of the fleshly heart to which each of the animal similes points in its own fashion, since all the beasts named in these similes suggest dimensions of the physical and material preoccupations of human corporeal existence. Thus although it was a medieval commonplace to say that a human being is a soul which finds no peace until it rests in God, it must be recalled that this soul is joined to a body driven by its own needs, needs equivalent to the instincts that control the behavior of the beasts of the field.

By consistently correlating its protagonist with the realm of animals and the instincts which drive them, *Pearl* underscores the distance separating the spiritual realm of the *visio* from the dreamer's earth-bound consciousness. By choosing the specific animals mentioned in its text (the hawk, the doe, and the quail), *Pearl* illustrates the characteristic shortcomings of such a consciousness. The dreamer's blindness to spiritual truth is thereby attributable to the same pattern of proud rapacity, inability to deal with adverse fortune, and love of physical pleasure that colors the animals of the three similes.

That the rhetorical form of the simile is employed to convey this point is likewise significant to our understanding of these animal images. In contrast to the metaphor, which merges the tenor and vehicle of its figurative comparison, the simile insists on an essential difference between the terms of its analogy. Thus the dreamer of *Pearl* resembles the hawk, the doe, and the quail in certain aspects of behavior and attitude, aspects dramatized in the plot of the poem. Yet the dreamer is never totally or irrevocably identified with these creatures. The semantic distance between tenor and vehicle which characterizes the the rhetoric of the simile leaves room for the theological energies of grace, mercy, and free will to operate in the mind and heart of the dreamer. In effect, the distance between the tenor of dreamer and the vehicle of the three animals represents a spiritual space where the protagonist eventually recognizes the propensities of his fleshly heart and their consequences for his life. At the end of the poem, shocked into understanding by his own rashness in trying to cross the river and the disastrous effect of that attempt, the dreamer pointedly renounces the very attitudes which linked him to the moral emblematics of the animal world:

> To þat Prynceȝ paye hade I ay bente,
> And ȝerned no more þen watȝ me gyuen,

> And halden me þer in truwe entent,
> As þe perle me prayed þat watʒ so þryuen,
> As helde, drawen to Goddeʒ present,
> To mo of his mysterys I hade ben dryuen;
> Bot ay wolde man of happe more hente
> Þen moʒt by ryʒt vpon hem clyuen.
> Þerfore my ioye watʒ sone toriuen,
> And I kaste of kytheʒ þat lasteʒ aye.
> Lorde, mad hit arn þat agayn þe stryuen,
> Oþer proferen þe oʒt agayn þy paye. (1189-1200)

Note in these lines the implicit rejection of rapacity ("ʒerned no more þen watʒ me gyuen") and aversion to ill fortune ("Bot ay wolde man of happe more hente/Þen moʒt by ryʒt vpon hem clyuen"). Moreover, the poem's final lines show a double shift away from the dreamer's former self-indulgence and away from the rhetorical form of the simile as well: "He gef vus to be his homly hyne/ Ande precious perleʒ vnto his pay" (1211-12). The words "his pay" recall the opening line of the poem, in which the phrase "p rynces paye," that is, the pleasure or joy of Christ, is coined as the key concept of the entire text. No longer concerned about his own pleasure, the dreamer is now committed to pleasing God. With this change in attitude comes a significant alteration in figurative language, with the metaphor of the human self or soul as "perle" replacing the simile formula in which the particle "as" suggests the dreamer's resemblance to three specific animals (*"as* hawk in halle," *"as* any do," *"as* dased quayle").

This shift from the simile to the metaphor implies a profound truth concerning human nature and destiny as it is presented in *Pearl*, a truth which lies at the heart of the Christian vision of human identity: human nature, though tenuously linked to the animal world through the life of the body (hence the appropriateness of the mode of resemblance, the simile, in linking the dreamer to the animal world), is ultimately defined through a progressive manifestation of the spiritual values associated with an immaterial soul. The proper destiny of the soul is union with God and complete identification with the spiritual world (hence the appropriateness of metaphor, the rhetorical mode of complete identification, at the poem's end–"precious perlez"). The tension of these two dimensions of human nature, expressed rhetorically in the poem through the animal similes on the one hand and the persistent metaphor of the soul as pearl on the other, ultimately determines the dramatic character of the decision facing the dreamer in *Pearl*. In adopting the metaphor of the pearl at the end of the poem, he alignes himself with the more noble set of motives and impulses inherent in his nature. Laying aside the life of natural similitude, he now moves toward a life whose object is union with Christ and with his beloved pearl.

The use of an imagery pattern correlating a literary protagonist with a triad of beasts is by no means unique to *Pearl* in the canon of late medieval literature. Dante had employed such a strategy in the first canto of his *Inferno* when he described the path toward enlightenment for his Pilgrim as blocked by the figures of a leopard, a lion, and a wolf.[18] Closer to home, the *Pearl*-Poet himself had used the pattern of the three beasts to mirror qualities in the hero of *Gawain and the Green Knight*, where the prey on successive days of Bercilak's hunts (doe, boar, and fox) parallel the attitudes and behavior of the knight and Bercilak's lady in the boudoir of the castle.[19] The three animal similes of *Pearl* are less prominently displayed in its plot than the motif of the three beasts found in *Gawain* or the *Inferno*, but *Pearl*'s attention to the implications of phrasing and rhetorical style mark the development of its animal imagery as highly imaginative and fully appropriate to the poem's thematic intentions. Indeed *Pearl*'s penchant for assimilating its themes into patterns of verbal and rhetorical ornamentation is deftly demonstrated by the import and placement of the animal similes contained in its lines.

Notes

1.   One of the classic studies of *Pearl's* imagery, Wendell Stacy Johnson's "The Imagery and Diction of the *Pearl* : Toward an Interpretation, " *ELH* 20 (1953): 161-80, describes the subject in this fashion:

> ...the imagery of the poem can in the main be divided into two groups: on the one hand, images out of the world of growing things, images of the garden and the vineyard which are associated with the dust of the earth; on the other, images of light and of brilliant, light-reflecting, gems, free of any spot (dust) and associated with whiteness and with emblems of royalty. These two groups are directly and explicitly opposed to each other, sometimes in the manner of an obvious symbolism and sometimes only in implied contrasts. (165-66)

Most imagery studies simply ignore the three animal similes in *Pearl*, though one important study [Louis Blenkner, "The Theological Structure of *Pearl*," *Traditio*, 24 (1968): 63-64] comments that the hawk, doe, and quail similes are reminders of the soul joined to the flesh in its earthly existence and, more pointedly, that even though the dreamer's soul is temporarily released from its body by the dream, it is still subject to limitations of the earthly condition. With this basic observation my interpretation agrees, but I would also insist these similes possess both separate and conjugate significances not adequately defined by summary observational alone. These significances sharpen our understanding of the overall dramatic design of *Pearl* and its portrait subtle of the dreamer.

2.   *Pearl*, 184; the text of the poem cited in this study is that edited by E. V. Gordon (Oxford: Clarendon Press, 1953).

3.   The term is used in this sense, for example, of Gawain himself in *SGGK* 405 ("Quoþ þe gome in þe grene to Gawan þe hende") and of the Virgin Mary in *SGGK* 647 (Þat the hende heuen-quene had of hir chylde"); cf. *SGGK* 108, 827, 904, 946, 1633, 1731.

4.   E.g. *Pearl* , 117: "For vche a pobble in pole þer py3t / Wat3 emerad ..." Cf. lines 192, 193, 205, 216, *passim*.

5.   Isidore of Seville, *Etymologiarum sive originum* , XII, 7, 55. The edition of the *Etymologiarum* cited is that edited by W. M. Lindsay, in the *Scriptorum Classicorum Bibliotheca Oxoniensis* (Oxford: Oxford University Press, 1911).

6.   Hugh of St. Victor, *De bestiis et aliis rebus* (PL, 177, 21-22).

7.   *PL*, 112, 853. The reference to *accipiter* in Daniel 4:30 falls in the strange story of Nebuchadnezzar's degeneration to an almost bestial state of existence. This degeneration represents punishment for a king's pride. The Cotton Nero poem, *Purity*, relates this same story, and renders the *accipiter* line thus: "wyth ful grymme

clawres / Þat were croked and kene as Þe kyte paune" (1696-97). Though the word "kyte" is substituted for "hawk" in these lines for the purpose of alliteration, the resemblance between Nebuchadnezzar's plight and that of the dreamer in *Pearl* is not difficult to discern. Both exhibit symptoms of vainglory, and this vice offers the occasion for a fall from the life of pleasure each desires. The difference separating the tales of these two figures is also clear: Nebuchadnezzar's fall is drastic and shocking, while the dreamer in *Pearl* is shielded from a similar punishment through the agency of the Pearl-Maiden and the lessons of his dream.

8.   Another example of the hawk as negative moral emblem in Middle English literature may be found in John Gower's *Confessio Amantis* , Book One, lines 2670-80:

> Mi Sone, yit in other forme
> Ther is a vice of Prides lore,
> Which lich an hauk whan he wol sore,
> Fleith upon heihte in his delices
> After the likynge of his vices,
> And wol no mannes resoun knowe,
> Till he doun falle and overthrowe.
> This vice veine gloire is hote,
> Wherof, my Sone, I thee behote
> To trete and speke in such a wise,
> That thou thee myht the betre avise.

The edition cited is *The Complete Works of John Gower*, II, ed. G. C. Macaulay (Oxford: Clarendon Press, 1901), p. 108. On the background of moral interpretations of animals in the Middle Ages and the Renaissance, see Beryl Rowland, *Birds with Human Souls: A Guide to Bird Symbolism* (Knoxville: The University of Tennessee Press, 1978; for the figure of the hawk, see p. 60) and, by the same author, *Animals with Human Faces: A Guide to Animal Symbolism* (Knoxville: The University of Tennessee Press, 1973).

9.   On the relation of hunting and boudoir scenes in *SGGK* , see H. L. Savage, "The Significance of the Hunting Scenes in *Sir Gawain and the Green Knight*," *JEGP* 27 (1928), 1-15, John Speirs, *Medieval English Poetry: The Non-Chaucerian Tradition* (London: Faber and Faber, 1957), pp. 236-37, and Larry D. Benson, *Art and Tradition in Sir Gawain and the Green Knight* (New Brunswick, New Jersey: Rutgers University Press, 1965), pp. 160-161.

10.   This reading of the doe image's significance gives rise to another parallel between the thematics of *Pearl* and those of *Gawain and the Green Knight*. If indeed the first two animal similes of *Pearl* (hawk and doe) represent the vices of rapacity and cowardice respectively, then the overt moral shortcomings of Gawain, his admitted "cowarddyse and couetyse" (*SGGK*, 2374), are visible in the protagonist of *Pearl* as well.

11.   The version of the Bible cited throughout is the Douay-Rheims translation of the Latin vulgate.

12.   *PL*, 112, 906.

13.   *PL*, 113, 1089.

14.   The link between the moon and the figure of the quail in stanza group 18 is strengthened when it is recalled that the moon, a sign of mutability, can thus suggest the unreliability of the values associated with the pejorative reputation of this bird.

15.   *PL*, 112, 904.

16.   *De bestiis et aliis rebus, PL*, 177, 49.

17.   Cf. II Corinthians 3:3: "... you are the epistle of Christ, ministered by us, and written not with ink, but with the Spirit of the living God, not in tables of stone, but in the fleshly tables of the heart."

18.

> Edd ecco, quasi al cominciar de l'erta,
> una lonza leggiera e presta molto,
> che di pel macolato era coverta;
> e non mi si partia dinanzi al volto,
> anzi 'mpediva tanto il mio cammino,
> ch'i' fui per ritornar piò volte vòlto.
>
> * * *
>
> ma non sì che paura non mi desse
> la vista che m'apparve d'un leone.
> Questi parea che contra me venisse
> con la test 'alta e con rabbiosa fame,
> si che parea che l'aere ne tremesse.
> Ed una lupa, che di tutte brame
> sembiava carca ne la sua magrezza,
> e molte genti fè già viver grame,
> questa mi porse tanto di gravezza
> con la paura ch'uscia di sua vista,
> ch'io perdei la speranza de l'altezza.
> (*Inferno*, I, 31-36, 44-54)

The text of the *Inferno* cited is Charles S. Singleton, *The Divine Comedy: Inferno 1: Italian Text and Translation* , Bollingen Series LXXX (Princeton: Princeton University Press, 1970), pp. 4, 6.

19.   For a discussion of the significance of tripartite images of temptation and vice, see Donald R. Howard, *The Three Temptations: Medieval Man in Search of the World* (Princeton: Princeton University Press, 1966), pp. 43-75.

ALLEGORY AND STRUCTURE IN *PEARL* : THE FOUR SENSES OF THE *ARS PRAEDICANDI* AND FOURTEENTH-CENTURY HOMILETIC POETRY

JANE CHANCE

he structure of *Pearl*, relative to its other artistic aspects, has been little studied, although it has been generally accepted as tripartite. Explanations of its three major parts, however, have too often focused upon the literal meaning of the narrative or have made the poem appear incoherent, as if these parts did not relate to one another. For example, Dorothy Everett notes that the first part, comprising the initial four sections of the poem's twenty, describes the dreamer's state of mind, the dream-country, and the Pearl; the second part, comprising the next twelve sections, consists of argument and exposition; and the third part, comprising the last four sections, describes the New Jerusalem and the poet's reflections.[1] Greater coherence has been affirmed by Ian Bishop, who sees the Pearl-Maiden as a unifying figure. He sets off the first stanza group with its description of the pearl (including the description in Groups II-IV) and the last with the dreamer's return to reality (including the descriptions in Groups XVII-XIX), and divides the central portions of twelve stanza groups into eight (V-XII, on the maiden as Queen of Heaven) and four (XIII-XVI, on the maiden as Bride of the Lamb).[2]

A less cohesive but more figurative structure is reflected in Louis Blenkner's view: he sees the first and last stanza groups as the"frame" and the dream vision of eighteen groups as divided into three—earthly paradise (II-IV), theological dialogue (V-XVI), and heavenly city (XVII-XIX). He then relates the triple division to the three stages of the theologian's ascent of the soul to God, corresponding to the three sources of knowledge (sense, intellect, and inspiration).[3]

More recently, in a return to a literalistic and loosely connected structure justified by its arithmetic symmetry, William Vantuono remarks that the poem has a tripartite structure consisting of what he calls the Prologue (The Garden Setting), Body (Groups II-IX), and Epilogue (lines 1171-1212 of Group XX signalling a return to the garden).[4] Vantuono also sees the Prologue and Epilogue as set off from the Vision or "Body" (II-XIX), itself regarded as tripartite: terrestrial paradise and Pearl-Maiden, II-IV; Homiletic Center, V-XVI; and the New Jerusalem and the Procession, XVII-XIX, plus 1153-70. In addition he divides the Homiletic Center into three: the debate (V-VIII), the Parable of the Vineyard, with Explanation (IX-XII), and the Perle Mascelleʒ, the Lamb, and the 144,000 Virgins (XIII-XVI). He concludes by emphasizing the perfect symmetry of the poem, but without connecting its various parts:

> What may be considered the poet's greatest achievement from a structural standpoint is the nearly perfect symmetry of the divisions in *Pearl*. Within the twenty stanza-groups, not only is the Body (II-XIX) centered according to the proportions of the poem, and not only is the large middle of the Body (Part Two—V-XVI) centered in relation to passages that precede and follow, but the middle of the third triad (IX-XII) forms a neat center too. This structural heart, which presents the Parable of the Vineyard, is also the thematic heart of *Pearl*, a poem in which the perfect roundness of the three in one form corresponds to the pearl itself, the symbol of salvation in heaven with the Holy Trinity.[5]

While the above views of the poem's structure do not altogether convince, their emphasis on the number three is provocative.

I hope to present in this study a coherent and figurative justification for the tripartite divisions in the light of D. W. Robertson's gloss on the poem's central sign, the pearl, viewed through the filter of the multiple senses of scriptural interpretation. He applies the four senses to the different meanings of the pearl in "The Pearl as Symbol":

> The symbol of the Pearl may be thought of on four levels. Literally, the Pearl is a gem. Allegorically, as the maiden of the poem, it represents those members of the Church who will be among the 'hundred' in the celestial procession, the perfectly innocent. Tropologically, the Pearl is a symbol of the soul that attains innocence through true penance and all that such penance implies. Anagogically, it is the life of innocence in the Celestial City.[6]

Not only does the pearl manifest three significations on different levels, in addition all these significations cohere. Robertson continues,

> The allegorical value presents a clear picture of the type of innocence; the tropological value shows how such innocence may be obtained; and the anagogical value explains the reward for innocence. To these meanings the literal value serves as a unifying focal point in which the other values are implied to one who reads the book of God's Work on the level of the *sentence*.

While I do not wish to continue the general scholarly debate about whether medieval literature should be analyzed using patristic methods,[7] or even the specific debate about whether *Pearl* should be understood on the literal (or historical) level rather than on its allegorical (figurative) level,[8] it does seem to me that this approach links both theological and literary interpretations of *Pearl*[9] rather neatly with a convincing allegorical interpretation of its structure. Extending Robertson's hint, this essay will show how the three allegorical senses determine the structure and thus the meaning of the whole poem. Interestingly enough, the three senses provide demarcations within the poem that also correspond to evenly-spaced divisions of stanza groups. The moral or tropological sense would apply to the first part, stanzas 6-33 (Groups II-VII); the allegorical sense, to the second, stanzas 34-65 (Groups VII-XIII); and the anagogical sense, to the third, stanzas 66-96 (Groups XIV-XIX). Stanzas 1-5 (Group I) and 97-101 (Group XX) represent the garden frame, so that the poem relegates roughly a third to each of its three parts.

Such a poetic technique probably resulted from the use of the rhetorical arts of the preacher. That is, the rhetorical structuring of the poem derives from the medieval practice, not of *divisio*, rhetorical divisions, but of *amplificatio*, amplification, or *dilatio, dilatatio,* dilation. According to late medieval tracts on the art of preaching, the *ars praedicandi*, one means of amplifying a sermon occurred through the use of the three allegorical senses. Although these senses did not originate in preaching tracts, by the fourteenth century they had been assimilated into the preacher's art as a type of rhetorical ornament and would have been commonly understood and accepted by contemporary homilists and poets whose purpose was similar to that of the Church Fathers and early homilists, that is, to combat heresy at a time of weakening of the Church.[10] The figurative or theoretical sense of interpretation—often used from the earliest times in defense of Sacred Scripture—came to be applied to the art of sermon-making and then, by the fourteenth century, I would argue, to the art of poetry. In this list previous interpretations of certain aspects and backgrounds of the poem assume new luster—specifically that the well-known and popular treatises of Christianity held far more sway over the poem than "the esoteric and far less accessible corpus of scriptural exegesis,"[11] and that vernacular treatises of the fourteenth century influenced the depiction of both the Pearl-Maiden and the penny, according to Robert Ackerman. So perhaps the *Pearl*-Poet uses signs in his poem similar to the "riot" of figures—castle, ship, plow, etc.—used by the preacher.[12] Further, critics who have analyzed other poems by the *Pearl*-Poet have noted his knowledge and use of the *ars praedicandi* in at least *Patience* and *Cleanness*, if not in *Pearl* and *Sir Gawain and the Green Knight*.[13] In addition, the allegorical structure of *Pearl* appears in other fourteenth-century poems, chiefly *Piers Plowman*; poetic use of such a homiletic rhetorical device may explain the seemingly disjointed structure of other fourteenth-century non-homiletic poems such as Chaucer's *Book of the Duchess*.

The essay will first examine the preaching arts and their use of the definitions of the multiple senses, then apply them to *Pearl*, and conclude with a discussion of their context within fourteenth-century homiletic poetry.

I

The late medieval preacher, unlike his earlier brethren, was instructed to implement his moral aim through the use of the multiple senses of scriptural interpretation. While preaching was theoretically always significant, beginning with (presumably) the early defenders of the Old Testament, only in the third and most major phase of its history in the Middle Ages—following the early Church Fathers— might its influence be regarded as significant for fourteenth-century poets. Preaching was regarded in the fourteenth century as an imitation of the Highest Authority and was modeled apparently on the Act of Creation as a kind of communication between God and man: Robert of Basevorn in 1322 declared that when God preached to Adam, He preached through Moses and some prophets, through John the Baptist, and as Christ.[14] Most important in the history of preaching was the "thematic preaching" that developed in the third phase of its evolution, in the early thirteenth century following the few rather generalized contributions such as Gregory the Great's *Cura pastoralis* (591), Rabanus Maurus' *De institutione clericorum* (819), Guibert of Nogent's *Liber quo ordine sermo fieri debeat* (1084), and Alain de Lille's *De arte praedicatoria* (1199?).[15] Such "thematic preaching" depended heavily for implementation on various rhetorical strategies such as *amplificatio*. As exemplified by the tracts of Thomas of Salisbury, Richard of Thetford, Alexander of Ashby, and Robert of Basevorn, the rules for such thematic preaching offer the greatest applicability to the *Pearl* -Poet.

Indeed, even as early as the eleventh century, Guibert de Nogent, in *Liber quo ordine sermo fieri debeat*, forming his *Prohemium ad commentarios in Genesim* (a work to provide preachers with sermon materials), tells the preacher to enhance his moral aim by means of any or all of the four senses of scriptural interpretation.[16] *Amplificatio*, or amplification, frequently called *dilatio*, also depended upon the use of the multiple senses as one means of amplifying a theme. A late Dominican tractate indebted to St. Thomas Aquinas—a "more representative" manual than Guibert's, entitled "Tractatulus solemnis de arte et uero modo praedicandi"—lists nine ways to expand a sermon, the fourth of which is "multiplication of explanations,"[17] or a means of *dilatatio* in general. In addition, among the eight "modes of amplification"—

dilatio, or dilation—noted by one of the most prominent homilists of the early and middle thirteenth century, Richard of Thetford (fl. 1245?), in an "extremely popular" work on the *Art of Amplifying Sermons, Ars dilatandi sermones,* lists a seventh, "Exposing the theme through diverse modes, that is, literal, allegorical, tropological or moral, and anagogical senses."[18] Similarly, Robert of Basevorn, in his *Forma praedicandi* of 1322, writing on the "University-style" or thematic sermon associated with Paris and Oxford, defines the various ornaments, including division as the fifth ornament (applied to the way a statement is divided into parts for amplifying) and amplification as the eighth ornament. Among the eight ways of amplifying a theme, the seventh is through the four senses—"The seventh way is to expound the theme in various ways: historically, allegorically, morally, anagogically. For example, *Jerusalem which is built as a city* may be taken historically about the Church on earth; allegorically about the Church militant; morally about any faithful soul; anagogically, about the Church triumphant."[19]

To understand the *Pearl*-Poet's use of the four senses in constructing this homiletic poem it is necessary to define those senses and therefore also explain their origin, for their definitions vary depending on the source consulted. Developed to defend sacred texts from the charge of impropriety or heresy, the allegorical senses depended upon a figurative rather than a literal interpretation—the text meant other than it seemed to say literally. Of figurative senses, there were three, combining with the literal sense of historical interpretation to make four senses altogether—the moral or tropological, the allegorical, and the anagogical. That both interpretations of meaning could be, indeed were, true, has been demonstrated by Saint Bonaventure in discussing the fourth light, that which illuminates the mind for the understanding of truth: "Although in its *literal* sense it is *one*, still, in its spiritual and *mystical* sense, it is *threefold*, for in all the books of SacredScripture, in addition to the *literal* meaning which the words outwardly express, there is understood a threefold *spiritual* meaning."[20] The four senses might overlap, but there is no ambiguity or equivocation, according to St. Thomas: "These various readings do not set up ambiguity or any other kind of mixture of meanings, because, as we have explained, there are many, not because one term may signify many things, but because the things signified by the term can themselves be the signs of other things."[21]

The prevalence of the fourfold method of allegorical exegesis during the Middle Ages has been much attested in the works of the Greek Alexandrines, the Church Fathers, the Benedictine and Carolingian commentators, the Victorines and the Dominicans, among others, and even in little-known sermon writers of the fourteenth century like Robert of Basevorn and Master Robert Rypon who subscribe to the methods of the *artes praedicandi*.[22]

The four senses of scriptural interpretation used as *amplificatio* in the fourteenth century sermon were carefully distinguished to clarify individual relevance as well as to show coherence with one another. While individual treatments differed, there did exist a basic pattern. Basically these four senses, as we can see from a brief survey of those Fathers and rhetoricians writing on the *ars praedicandi*, include the literal or historical sense, the moral or tropological sense centering on the relation of the individual soul to the virtues and vices, the specifically allegorical sense dealing with the relation of humankind to Christ's life and his Apostles, and the anagogical sense involving the relation of the soul's salvation to the Church, whether Militant (on earth), or Triumphant (after life, apocalyptic). One example of a coherent scheme embracing all three senses is provided by Eucherius of Lyons (d. 449-55) in his Preface to *Formulae spiritualis intellegentiae*,[23] in which he relates the three senses to the body, the spirit, and the intellect. All three senses correspond to the microcosm man and his levels of understanding; Eucherius explains that these four kinds of knowledge veil the secrets of the future under a narrative of history: "Sunt etiam qui allegoriam in hoc scientiae genere quarto in loco adiciendam putent, quam gestorum narratione futurorum umbram praetulisse confirment." Thus the literal presses upon us the truth of deeds or the credibility of narration, "ueritatem nobis factorum ac fidem relationis inculcat"; the tropological, bearing the spirit, brings the intellect mysteries for the improvement of life, "ad uitae emendationem mysticos intellectus refert"; and the anagogical, holding the superior intellect, leads to more sacred secrets through celestial figures, "anagoge ad sacratiora caelestium figurarum secreta perducit." The three senses likened to the microcosm also can be linked with the macrocosm in terms of the threefold "wisdom of the world"—physical, ethical, and logical, or natural, moral, rational. According to this explanation, heaven could be understood literally as the sky, tropologically as heaven, anagogically as angels, and allegorically as baptism.[24]

A more explicit relationship between man the microcosm and the macrocosm of the world is perceived by Saint Bonaventure. He relates the three senses to the understanding of divinity (allegorical), the spiritual life of man (tropological), and the interrelationship between the two (anagogical). He declares that there is a threefold *spiritual* meaning:

> namely, the allegorical, by which we are taught what to believe concerning the Divinity and humanity; the *moral*, by which we are taught how to live; and the *anagogical*, by

which we are taught how to to be united to God. Hence all
Sacred Scripture teaches these three truths: namely, the
eternal generation and Incarnation of Christ, the pattern of
human life, and the union of the soul with God. The first
regards *faith* ; the second, *morals* ; and the third, the *ultimate
end of both*. The doctors should labor at the study of the first;
the preachers, at the study of the second; the contemplatives, at the study of the third. The first is taught chiefly by
Augustine; the second, by Gregory; the third, by Dionysius.
Anselm follows Augustine; Bernard follows Gregory;
Richard (of Saint Victor) follows Dionysius. For Anselm
excels in reasoning; Bernard in preaching; Richard, in
contemplating; but Hugh (of Saint Victor) in all three.[25]

A more practical and comprehensible explanation of the interrelationship is offered—not surprisingly, given his purpose—by Robert of
Basevorn, a sermon-writer of the fourteenth century who understands the senses to reflect the interrelationship of both microcosm
and macrocosm , in his *Forma praedicandi* of 1322. His allegorical sense,
like his tropological sense, focuses on man the microcosm: human
spiritual history (here represented by Old Testament figures and
thereby suggesting the older typological sense) concerns Christ: "An
allegorical exposition occurs when one part is understood by another.
For example, by the fact that David slew Goliath it is understood that
Christ overcame the devil." Robert explains that not all allegories are
about Christ—they can also concern the Church and her parts, whether
Gentiles, Jews, Apostles, the blessed Virgin, or the saints. The tropological sense focuses on our human and individual moral life: "A moral
exposition occurs when one deed that must be done by us is understood through another, as the fact that David conquered Goliath
signifies that every believer ought to overcome the devil." Finally, the
anagogical sense concerns the Church Triumphant and the relationship between earth and heaven:

An anagogical exposition is one in which by some deed on
earth is understood another that must be done in heaven or
in the Church triumphant. This is seen in many mysteries
concerning the temple, by which is meant the triumphant
Church as the Church militant is understood by the tabernacle. Anagoge is derived from *ana* and *goge,* the former
meaning 'up' and the latter, 'leading,' as if *leading up.*

The preacher's purpose in using the various senses differs in each
case. He continues, "Faith is built by allegory; morals are formed by
tropology; the contemplatives are raised by anagoge."[26]

How did the *Pearl* -Poet apply these senses to his homiletic poem?
We turn now to an examination of the way in which the senses in *Pearl*
reflect an interrelationship between man the microcosm and the
macrocosm, or between man and God, earth and heaven.

II

The pearl serves as a symbolic guide to each of the three parts (hence, allegorical senses) of the poem. All three senses refer back to the pearl—the literal pearl, the Pearl-Maiden, or Reason / Virtue, the Bride of Christ and Queen of Heaven signifying salvation, and the Heavenly Jerusalem itself. How each part relates specifically to the moral or tropological, allegorical, and anagogical senses must now be determined why there are three rather than four parts to the poem must also be answered before our analysis of *Pearl* begins. The tripartite division of *Pearl* most likely adheres to the idea that the literal sense within itself contains the three allegorical senses, as Saint Bonaventure suggested above. Such a thematic division may reflect the tripartite division favored by preachers: Basevorn notes that "in this method of preaching only three statements, or the equivalent of three, are used in the theme—either from respect to the Trinity, or because a threefold cord is not easily broken, or because this method is mostly followed by Bernard, or, as I think more likely, because it is more convenient for the set time of the sermon."[27] In line with this division one might note the three figurative settings succeeding the literal arbor—earthly paradise redolent of the biblical Eden (as in Genesis), parabolic vineyard described in the New Testament (the Gospel), and Heavenly Jerusalem (as in Revelation).

Note that these three parts do not exactly correspond to the divisions mentioned by Vantuono: that is, the moral or tropological sense dominates Groups II-VII, stanzas 6-33, on the relationship between the Pearl-Maiden (representing reason) and the Dreamer (representing the literalist, fallen will or passion). The allegorical sense dominates Groups VII-XIII, stanzas 34-65, or the Parable of the Vineyard, drawn from the life of Christ as represented in the Gospel and signifying the nature of salvation. The anagogical sense, or the understanding of things celestial, often related to the Otherworld, pertains then to the third section, Groups XIV-XIX, stanzas 66-96, or the Vision of the Heavenly Jerusalem. The first five stanzas, in Group I, provide a preface stressing the literal or historical sense of the poem, and the last six stanzas, in Group XX, provide a coda returning the reader to the literal or historical sense from which the poem began, but with the difference that the narrator has been educated, illumined, and convinced of a higher spiritual reality, one that will continue to guide and enrich his existence. Indeed, the divisions depend upon the narrator's confrontation with some problem relating back to the loss of the pearl and what it means, whether literally, morally, allegorically, or anagogically.

While the Pearl-Maiden remains generally responsible for teaching him a solution in each case, the narrator must also accept the solution in order to progress spiritually. In the prefatory group of stanzas, little doubt exists that the lost pearl mourned by the narrator is a literal (and valuable) pearl with a history, a past. Neatly set in gold (2),[28] round (5), small, with smooth sides (6), it has been lost in an arbor (9) in August (39) at the time of harvest. The literal swoon of the narrator that follows this recitation of its loss (59) leads to the Vision in lines 61 ff.

Why does the poet begin with the literal sense, why not plunge into the allegorical senses immediately? An answer suggested by Master Robert Rypon, sub-prior of Durham, in his tract on the art of preaching in 1400, argues that the historical or literal sense teaches faith, or what you believe, for the literal sense of Sacred Scripture opens the door to belief and supports faith. Therefore, just as faith is the foundation of intercourse with the sacred, so also the literal sense of scripture is the foundation of faith: "docet gesta seu facta, i.e. quid credas. Nam historias sacre scripture oportet credere et supponere tanquam fidem. Immo, sicut fides est fundamentum conversationis sacre, ita etiam historialis sensus scripture est ejus fundamentum."[29]

Indeed, in line with such an interpretation of the literal sense, the pearl imagistically represents a seed from which will grow "spryng ande spyceჳ" (35), a rich expression appropriate to the poem's time of harvest and the loss of the pearl amidst the shining "worteჳ" of gillyflower, ginger, and gromwell (42f). What will "grow" here and be harvested exists tropologically, the first of the three senses to be developed in the poem—the psychological maturation of the narrator provoked by the loss of the literal pearl. This maturation depends upon a movement away from an extraordinary literalism and preoccupation with passion, concupiscence, and things of this world. In dealing with his grief, his loss of a treasure of this world, the narrator will come not only to accept that loss, but also to move from that rational acceptance to faith in God. His own literal situation as well as his literalism contain the seeds, so to speak, of his own spiritual edification and faith, like the lost pearl that will grow "springing spices," with which the poem begins. The contrast between the narrator's heart and his head—his emotional response as distinguished from a more rational understanding of his loss, clearly missing at the poem's opening—suggests the spiritual direction he must now pursue, although he himself may not yet be capable of such a realization.

The figure of the narrator thus hinges the dream frame to the dream vision, in that he begins the poem as a dense literalist like Boethius's materialistic narrator at the beginning of the *Consolatio*, like Chaucer's *persona* in *The Book of the Duchess* who wants to offer a feather-bed to Morpheus as a bribe for sleep, and like the slothful and untutored Will at the beginning of *Piers Plowman* who must be instructed by his dreams. Accordingly, the literalism of our narrator emerges as the reason for his excessive pining: "I dewyne, fordolked of luf-daungere, / Of þat pryuy perle wythouten spot" (11-12). The pearl in times past relieved his sorrow (*wrange*, 15), and increased his happiness (*happe*, 16); its loss means his breast swells and burns (18). When he comes to the spot where he lost the pearl, "care ful colde" catches at him (50), with "dreary grief" ("deuely dele") lurking in his heart (51), even though reason "set my self at peace" (52).

The use of such a dense narrator illustrates dramatically and personally—for we identify with the narrator—exactly how the multiple senses of allegory educate: as one moves from one sense to the other, so one also improves and eventually ascends to God. Master Robert Rypon remarks on the spiritual progress of the student reflected in the three senses in terms of an ascent—the literal sense teaches history; allegory, faith; the moral, actions; and anagogy, to what end you are led, or the place to which you are directed—presumably Heaven ("Littera gesta docet; quid credas, allegoria; / Moralis, quid agas; quo tendas, anagogia").[30] The narrator must move from the literal to the moral or tropological sense—he must, that is, govern his emotions with reason.

The moral or tropological sense usually focuses on the virtues (or vices) of the individual soul. Indeed, Master Robert Rypon notes that the tropological sense derives from "tropos," virtue, or "virtus," and "logos," "sermo," or speech, that is, "speech of virtues." This occurs when the historical sense explicitly reveals the virtues. Such meaning is exemplified in the Epistles: "we brothers are not sons of slaves but of freed persons, by which freedom Christ has liberated us." Liberty is glossed above the line as "that by which we have been freed from sin...."[31]

The liberation of the narrator will occur through the Dream-maiden and the allegorical stages or parts of the dream-vision. Such help will "console" him in his grief in the manner of Boethius' Lady Philosophy and the *Consolatio Philosophiae* and educate him in the manner of Dante's Virgil and the *Commedia*. In this stage the Pearl-Maiden functions as Reason, or specifically *his* reason, his instructor, his higher soul. And the dream, by lifting his spirit away from the body (and earth), allows him to move from depression and darkness (the body) up to reason, the soul. Thus, while the "sleep" he succumbs to can be viewed initially *in malo* as a sleep of the soul, a spiritual sloth, eventually, because it allows him to be exercised spiritually, it should be viewed *in bono*. In #6 he suggests the eventual spiritual goal of his swoon:

Fro spot my spyryt þer sprang in space;
My body on balke þer bod in sweuen.

My goste is gon in Godeʒ grace
In auenture þer meruayleʒ meuen. (61-64)

Similarly, the paradise he enters in his dream signifies on one level the same arbor in which he lost the pearl, seen now tropologically. The moral or tropological sense operates as well as it does because of the iconography of the first part of the poem—the location of the poem, the arbor, suggests Eden, place of man's first loss, and the time of the poem, August, suggests harvesting, the after-effects or ripe fruits of planting rather than planting itself, seeds, new life. As such the arbor within the dream changes, fills with pearls and other gems within a gleaming forest—a middle place between the actual earthly garden and the Heavenly Jerusalem. Accordingly, the garden soothes the narrator's grief—the lovely forest "abated my baleʒ, / Fordidden my stresse, dystryed my payneʒ," he says (123-24). Thus the narrator typologically functions as a foil for postlapsarian Adam aspiring to regain paradise, another name for his own rational ease.

The literalist's sin from which the narrator must be freed in *Pearl* is pride, as reflected in the behavior of the dreamer in the first section of the poem, Groups II-VII (stanzas 6-33). This pride, a form of madness, the poet seems to be saying, involves a loss of reason and is expressed by selfishness. When the narrator first enters the dream garden, for example, his attraction to the garden's loveliness *as* loveliness and *only* loveliness suggests his preoccupation with himself and literal things of this world. He declares, in stanza 13,

More and more, and ʒet wel mare
Me lyste to se þe broke byʒonde,
For if hit watʒ fayr þer I con fare,
Wel loueloker watʒ þe fyrre londe. (145-48)

Too, when the dreamer sees the Pearl-maiden, he reacts by thinking of her physically and literally as his lost *pearl*—that is, selfishly rather than lovingly, charitably. For example, he uses the same language to describe her as he has the pearl earlier: she is "So smoþe, so smal, so seme slyʒt" (190). And of course she is completely adorned with pearls from head to foot. When he first speaks to her, he asks if she is the pearl he has lost and identifies himself as a "joylez juelere," but his address is filled with reiterations of first person pronouns and his longing for her—he does not realize she is not at all "lost" but indeed "found," home in a paradise setting. He also laments the fate (*wyrde*) that has brought his jewel here and distressed him so (in most un-Boethian fashion):

'O perle,' quod I, 'in perleʒ pyʒt,
Art þou my perle þat I haf playned,

> Regretted by myn one, on nyȝte?
> Much longeyng haf I for þe layned,
> Syþen into gresse þou me aglyȝte.
> Pensyf, payred, I am forpayned,
> And þou in a lyf of lykyng lyȝte,
> In Paradys erde, of stryf vnstrayned.
> What wyrde hatȝ hyder my juel vayned
> And don me in þys del and gret daunger?' (241-50)

Throughout their dialogue, the Joyless Jeweler emphasizes his misery and madness, while the Pearl-Maiden gently remonstrates with him over his pride, literalism, and selfishness. She claims (257-64) that he has misstated his tale when he declares the pearl is lost whereas she remains part of the gracious garden: "Sir, ȝe haf your tale mysetente, / To say your perle is al away / Þat is in cofer so comly clente / As in þis gardyn gracios gaye" (257-60). She also chastizes him for calling *wyrde* a thief, when in fact this "thief" has made something of nothing (largely because what the narrator lost was a rose, eventually intended for death, lines 269ff, and now that rose has become valuable). She says that he is mad—"Wy borde ȝe men? So madde ȝe be!" (290)—and accuses him of speaking "Vnavysed" words (292), "Þou ne woste in worlde quat on dotȝ mene," "You do not know at all what one means" (293). Most important, when he blames our Lord as a liar, she in turn blames him: "Þy worde byfore þy wytte con fle" (294) and

> 'I halde þat jueler lyttel to prayse,
> Þat loueȝ wel þat he seȝ wyth yȝe,
> And much to blame and vncortoyse,
> Þat leueȝ oure Lorde wolde make a lyȝe,
> Þat lelly hyȝte your lyf to rayse,
> Þaȝ fortune dyd your flesch to dyȝe.
> Ȝe setten hys wordeȝ ful west ernays,
> Þat louez noþynk bot ȝe hit syȝe;
> And þat is a poynt o sorquydryȝe.' (301-09)

Presumption is the dreamer's chief crime. Indeed, when the Maiden explains that the only way he can cross the stream separating them is to die, he presumptuously complains that he does not again want to lose what he has just found, which would cause him unbearable distress (336). She accuses him of speaking (or judging) of nothing but *dystresse* ("Thow demeȝ noȝt bot doel dystresse," 337); better far to bless himself and love God always (341-42).

Finally a stage is reached in which he becomes truly figurative rather than literal in his thinking, and truly charitable—considering her rather than his own selfish grief. In this stage we move from a focus on him to her—in Group VII, stanza #33. Even though he is "mournfully subdued," "mornyf mate," 386, he admits that he is happy, even joyful, that she has come to this state of "worschyp and wele" (394). He says, in this important speech:

'In blysse I se þe blyþely blent,
And I a man al mornyf mate.
Ʒe take þeron ful lyttel tente,
Þaʒ I hente ofte harmeʒ hate;
Bot now I am here in your presente,
I wolde bysech, wythouten debate,
Ʒe wolde me say, in sobre asente,
What lyf ʒe lede erly and late,
For I am ful fayn þat your astate
Is worrten to worschyp and wele, iwysse.
Of alle my joy, þe hyʒe gate,
Hit is in grounde of alle my blysse.' (385-96)

The Pearl-Maiden responds happily to his selflessness, seeing his charity as a movement *away* from his self and pernicious literalism, and indicating that he has learned from her instruction:

'Now blysse, burne, mot þe bytyde,'
Þen sayde þat lufsoum of lyth and lere,
"And welcum here to walk and byde,
For now þy speche is to me dere.
Maysterful mod and hyʒe pryde
I hete þe, arn heterly hated here.
My Lorde ne louez not for to chyde,
For meke arn alle þat woneʒ hym nere;
And when in hys place þou schal apere,
Be dep deuote in hol mekenesse.' (397-406)

Because the narrator has learned, has progressed, the poem shifts from the moral or tropological sense to the allegorical sense by focusing on a a new spiritual problem in stanza 40 (Group VIII). Initially and literally, the loss of the pearl comprised the first problem; morally the same problem can be understood as the narrator's lost rationality, his pride. But allegorically, the problem of the lost pearl involves the narrator's lack of belief in the Pearl-Maiden as a Queen, in that she died so young—at the age of two.

The narrator remains skeptical—and literalistic, doubting that the Pearl-Maiden could be made a queen of heaven so young, in lines 473-74 (just after a lacuna in the text): "Þyself in heuen ouer hyʒ þou heue, / To make þe quen, þat watʒ so ʒonge." He continues, in the lines following, by relating other reasons: she was not even two years old (literally, she lived only two years in this land, 483); she could not please God, or pray, or say either the Pater or the Creed—"and quen mad on þe fyrst day!" 486). The narrator's tainted, earthly understanding of rank interferes with his understanding of an allegorical rank:

'I may not traw, so God me spede,
Þat God wolde wryþe so wrange away.
Of countes, damysel, par ma fay,
Wer fayr in heuen to halde asstate,
Oþer elleʒ a lady of lasse aray;
Bot a quene—hit is to dere a date!' (487-92)

That the dreamer mistakenly wishes to distinguish his own lost pearl from this queen of heaven, the "Pearl of Price," becomes clear from line 745f ("O maskele3 perle in perle3 pure, / Þat bere3," quoÞ I, "Þe perle of prys"). What is this "Pearl of Price," and how does it differ from the dreamer's lost pearl or the pearl worn by the Maiden?

This "Pearl of Price" must be distinguished from the others because it can be interpreted according to a different sense—the allegorical, introduced here by the poet's new, symbolic phrasing. Within the narrative frame of the dream, the Jeweler was merely the narrator as pearl was only literal. In the first, narrative, part of the dream itself, the Jeweler represented tropologically the concupiscent self unguided by reason, and the pearl, now the Pearl-Maiden, with her crown of pearls, her ivory complexion, her pearl-adorned gown, and the great pearl at her breast, personified his forgotten or lost rational soul. Now, in this second part of the poem, the Jeweler is no longer the dreamer, but Christ, and the pearl is no longer the Pearl-Maiden, or the narrator's rational soul, so much as salvation itself, bought with Christ's life (or entry into the Heavenly Jerusalem), the "perle [Þat] wat3 mascelle3" (732):

> 'This makelle3 perle Þat bo3t is dere,
> Þe joueler gef fore alle hys god,
> Is lyke Þe reme of heuenesse clere.' (733-35)

The reason this pearl is like the "realm of heaven's brightness" is that it is spotless, pure, round, and fair (*wele3, clene, clere, rounde, blyÞe*), terms used from the beginning of the poem to suggest the literal pearl, but now resonating figuratively of heaven.

At this stage, the narrator has progressed to the second phase of his spiritual instruction, that of faith as taught by allegory. The allegorical sense of scriptural interpretation is carefully defined by Master Robert Rypon. "Allegory" derives from "alle," which is "other," and "gore," which is *sententia*, "meaning"—that is, "other meaning," for allegory is when one thing is said and another is understood. Master Robert uses a metaphor that fits *Pearl's* vineyard and pearl imagery in this second part of the poem to describe the allegorical sense, which in relation to Scripture exists as if a tree growing from a root from which two other senses blossom forth as if flowers and fruits. Master Robert points to the *exemplum* in the Apostle's letter which declares that Abraham had two sons, one by a free woman and one by a slave, that is, Ysaac from Sara, free wife of Abraham, and Ysmael from Agar, the concubine slave of Abraham. The two sons represent the two Testaments, Old and New, in that when they agree, *per allegoriam*, when one Testament prefigures and signifies the other.[32] Although other commentators would not necessarily include the ty-

pological under the allegorical sense, Master Robert's example agrees
with other versions in that it depends explicitly on Scripture.

To establish the allegorical sense of the Pearl in this part and
therefore counter the dreamer's doubts, the gloss on the Gospel
Parable of the Vineyard is related by the Maiden. The Parable of the
Vineyard indicates that "more or less" are one word in God's treasury
(# 51, or 601ff): salvation, like pregnancy, must be viewed as either /
or and not as a continuum or hierarchy. The vineyard, once again, like
the arbor we have seen at the beginning (and the distant fields being
harvested), has an allegorical rather than a tropological meaning
because it refers directly to the Gospel (a gloss within a gloss, so to
speak, like the dream within a dream of *Piers Plowman,* or even of
Dante in the *Commedia*) through the parable, "First shall be last, and
he who comes last shall be first in his turn" (# 48). Christ speaks:

> 'Þus schal I,' quoþ Kryste, 'hit skyfte.
> Þe laste schal be þe fyrst þat strykeȝ,
> And þe fyrst þe laste, be he neuer so swyft,
> For mony ben calle, þaȝ fewe be mykeȝ.' (569-72)

The real question is, how can a two-year old be saved—in what
way is it possible for good works to earn grace for her? If only payment
for works (pearls, treasure from "God's great treasury," 601) will
allow her to enter God's kingdom, then how can this non-worker earn
any treasure at all? The answer is that there are two ways to redeem
Adam's sin—baptism and grace (#53). The former, based on Christ's
crucifixion, washes away the sin of Adam even for children. Thus
Christ tells his disciples they cannot win any riches *unless* they are as
children, innocent and cleansed (saved, in short, like the Pearl of Price
on the Pearl-Maiden) (#61, 721-32):

> Ihecu con calle to hym hys mylde,
> And sayde hys ryche no wyȝ myȝt wynne,
> Bot he com þyder ryȝt as a chylde;
> Oþer elleȝ, neuermore com þerinne.
> Harmleȝ, trwe, and vndefylde,
> Wythouten mote oþer mascle of sulpande synne,
> Quen such þer cnoken on þe bylde,
> Tyt schal hem men þe ȝate vnpynne.
> Þer is þe blys þat con not blynne,
> Þat þe jueler soȝte þurȝ perré pres,
> And solde alle hys goud, boþe wolen and lynne,
> To bye hym a perle watȝ mascelleȝ.

In stanza 65—two-thirds of the way through—we come to the
third part, demonstrating the anagogical sense. To signal the change,
once again the narrator regresses to his problematic literalism; once
again the solution to his problem depends upon understanding figu-

ratively rather than literally. Here the narrator manifests his literalism by understanding the Maiden as the *only* bride of Christ, as his Queen, and by questioning the nature of the Lamb who would wed her, in that she climbed over so many others to "win" him:

> 'Ouer alle oþer so hyȝ þou clambe,
> To lede wyth hym so ladyly lyf.
> So mony a comly anvnnder cambe
> For Kryst han lyued in much stryf;
> And þou con alle þo dere out dryf,
> And fro þat maryag al oþer depres,
> Al-only þyself....' (773-79)

Similar literalistic obtuseness is revealed in #77ff when the narrator, having learned that this bride of Christ represents one of only 144,000 others, becomes curious about a dwelling place large enough for so many:

> 'Haf ȝe no woneȝ in castel-walle,
> Ne maner þer ȝe may mete and won?' (917-18)

He says that this spotless "meyny," this crowd, obliges the virgins to have a "great city"—again assuming their quantity should reflect their materialistic quality—although he does not see any building capable of holding so many:

> 'And by þyse bonkeȝ þer I con gele,
> And I se no bygyng nawhere aboute,
> I trowe alone ȝe lenge and loute,
> To loke on þe glory of þys gracous gote.
> If þou hatȝ oþer bygyngeȝ stoute,
> Now tech me to þat myry mote.' (931-36)

What he sees is what he thinks exists, a sign of his usual presumption. When he is told where the virgins live, he confesses, again materialistically, that he is eager to see the city of the New Jerusalem (#82). He is of course too literalistic and too skeptical to believe in the promise of salvation outlined by the Maiden, signified by the Lamb, and imaged forth by the City.

   In accord with this sign of literalistic regression in marking the last division of the poem, the Maiden once again corrects the dreamer. She introduces us to the anagogical sense, relating to the celestial kingdom (rather than to the life of Christ), by explaining how she and the 144,000 Holy Innocents can all be the Lamb's wives, as indicated by St. John in the Apocalypse. She admits that "Vnblemyst" (782) though she is, "Bot 'makeleȝ Quene' þenne sade I not" (784). She and they all constitute part of the Heavenly Jerusalem—understood anagogically. This answers the second problem.

This anagogical sense is also defined by Master Robert Rypon: "Anagogy" derives from "ana," because it is "sursum," "up high, above," and "goge," thus "leading upwards," said when the literal, allegorical, or tropological senses is transferred to the celestial. Master Robert exemplifies this sense by adapting the Epistle cited above, "I will not be a slave to sins or the letter but to the free," that is, the celestial Jerusalem, as written in the Epistle above, "Jerusalem, which is above [*sursum*], is our free mother." This figure makes famous the earthly city Jerusalem, but while "Jerusalem" signifies tropologically each good Christian, anagogically, it signifies heaven.[33]

The description of the city in *Pearl*, as well as the procession of the virgins and Christ, in #83-94 (from Revelation 21:10-22:7), uses the Pearl as soul, *anima*, bride of Christ to represent the life of innocence in the New Jerusalem, echoing the early commentaries on the city Jerusalem. To the city were applied the four senses: for example, Guibert de Nogent (1053-1174) notes that Jerusalem is a literal city; allegorically, Holy Church; tropologically, the faithful soul aspiring to vision of eternal peace; anagogically, the life of the dwellers in Heaven who see God revealed in Zion.[34] All of these meanings fit the heavenly Jerusalem of *Pearl*, although the third part of the poem understands the city primarily anagogically. That is, during this description the Maiden teaches the dreamer the location of the city in the land of Judea, the old Jerusalem, but also reveals a new Jerusalem "þat lyȝt of Godeȝ sonde," 943. In the old city, the Lamb suffered to give us salvation, in the new are eternal peace and glory and bliss:

> "Of moteȝ two to carpe clene,
> And Jerusalem hyȝt boþe, nawþeles,
> Þat nys to yow no more to mene
> Bot 'Ceté of God' oþer 'Syȝt of Pes'. " (949-52)

After the narrator begs her to bring him to that "bygly bylde" (963), she tells him that he cannot enter that heavenly tower although he can see it from the outside (970-2). Her point is that he still has difficulty understanding more than the literal sense—he can only see the old Jerusalem. And thus the pearls that reappear in lines 1036-38 to adorn the gates remind him of his loss of faith:

> 'Þe portaleȝ pyked of rych plateȝ
> And vch ȝate of a margyrye,
> A parfyt perle þat neuer fateȝ.'

Just as the poem begins with the mad grief of the narrator, so it ends with mad joy, the two extremes balancing one another. In Section XIX, just before the end, the vision suffuses the dreamer with delight and joy. This joy derives from faith, superseding and bolstering the understanding received earlier. Indeed, *delyt* is the concatenating word in stanzas 92-97: at the end of 92, the pearl is beyond delight; at the beginning of 93, the 144,000 virgins proceed over the golden roads in great delight. The virgins are also delighted, in 94, at his approach (1117), and even the narrator shares in the joy—"I wysse I laʒt a gret delyt," 1128. This delight comes from the narrator's observing of the Lamb (1129), but also the Lamb Himself is delighted (1141). Mostly, "Delyt me drof in yʒe and ere; / My manez mynde to maddyng malte" (1153). But even this joy must be qualified, must be refined of selfish and earthly pleasure.

At the very end, in Section XX (stanzas 97-101), the narrator reveals his earthly contamination by madly, ecstatically, attempting to swim the stream that separates him from the tower—again, he thinks it a literal stream. Note the words used by the *Pearl*-Poet to stress his madness, impulse, loss of reason:

> Hit payed hym not þat I so flonc
> Ouer meruelous mereʒ, so mad arayde.
> Of raas, paʒ I were rasch and ronk,
> ʒet, rapely þerinne I watʒ restayed,
> For ryʒt as I sparred vnto þe bonc,
> Þat brathe out of my drem me brayde. (1165-70)

His inability to separate himself from the blindness of earthly sight distinguishes him from Dante at the end of the *Purgatorio*—the narrator has no Beatrice to lead him into the tower. To do so, he would have to die and be washed in that cleansing Lethean stream, as does Dante to enter Paradise.

Recovery does come. When the narrator awakens from his dream, he resumes his journey through what might be termed the earthly purgatory. That is, the last "pearl" in the poem must of course be recognized as the communion wafer, itself a symbol of God's grace that allows us to be "precious pearls to his liking"—we as the saved, like the 144,000 virgins, like the Pearl-Maiden.

> He gef vus to be his homly hyne,
> And precious perleʒ vnto his pay. (1211-12)

The "vision" *has* educated the dreamer away from his literalism: he understands *figura,* a non-literal sign, in the communion wafer as pearl. The four senses of allegory have indeed served their didactic purpose—and the poem, in part an example of the preaching art, has served its homiletic purpose. At the end, although the narrator is dismayed at being driven out of paradise, he eventually replaces his own selfish joy and desire, without any help from the Pearl-Maiden, with a loving desire to please the Prince himself.

To pay þe Prince oþr sete saȝte,
Hit is ful eþe to þe god Krystyin,
For I haf founden hym, boþe day and naȝte,
A God, a Lorde, a Frende ful fyin.
Ouer þis hyul þis lote I laȝte,
For þyty of my perle enclyin,
And syþen to God I hit bytaȝte,
In Krysteȝ dere blessyng, and myn,
Þat, in þe forme of bred and wyn,
Þe preste vus scheweȝ vch a daye. (1201-10)

Ultimately, for the narrator, the "pearl" of the poem is not only the communion wafer, or the bepearled Maiden, but the poem itself—all of which, as 'pearls,' constitute a moral and didactic means of instructing others. In the third part of the vision, the anagogical, the Jeweler lives in an artful palace ornamented with pearls, that is, jewels adorning the structure and the virgins who represent the Saved—and all "inhabit" a jeweled creation entitled—*Pearl*.

Thus the poem moves from the first part, with its focus on the individual defined as the will (the narrator) and the rational soul (the Pearl-Maiden), to the second, with its focus on the integrated soul seeking the pearl of salvation from Christ the Jeweler, and finally to the third, with its vision of the city of Christ consisting of all saved individuals. The poem moves, that is, from darkness, madness, grief, and death, to light, joy, vision, and eternal life. The Augustinian movement ends with the vision of the City of God.

III

As we have seen, originally scriptural exegesis was used to defend sacred if not poetic texts from the charge of immorality or impropriety; early in the Middle Ages grammarians used it to facilitate the training of preachers; only later in the Middle Ages did preachers intent on blocking heresy among the faithful and poets in homiletic and religious poems like *Pearl* use it for rhetorical and homiletic purposes.

As early as the ninth to the tenth century the meaning in homiletic and religious poems like the Anglo-Saxon *Judith*, *Juliana*, and *Elene*, especially, came to unfold by means of what might be termed these same four senses;[35] such narrative structure was used in England as late as the fourteenth century in another important homiletic poem written during a time of concern over heresy and the need for reform[36]—William Langland's *Vision of Piers the Plowman*, a dream vision like *Pearl*. By indicating the relationship between the Visio, a vision of the literal "fair field of folk," and the tripartite structure of the more figurative Vitae, we also provide a way of understanding Dowel, Dobet, and Dobest, the three senses of allegory.[37]

The problem of distinguishing truth from falsehood provides a major concern for the Visio portion of *Piers Plowman* (*passus* 1-7), beginning with the vision of Lady Holicherche and Lady Meed on the fair field of folk and their allegorical genealogies—Holicherche as daughter of Truth and Lady Meed as daughter of Fals. Reason reveals her perfidy, causing her rejection when the King (in 2-4) adheres to the Counsel of Reason and Conscience. The point of these *passus* is that desire for *temporalia* can corrupt all orders of society; thus the process of purgation is complete when the Seven Deadly Sins confess.

Such concern with truth, literal and figurative, extends into the Vitae in relation to senses of truth, in particular, those of allegory. If the events that occur in the Visio can be seen as a literal and historical rendition of the search for truth in fourteenth-century England, then the "events" that occur in the Vitae can be understood, in the segments of the three Lives, as representing the allegorical equivalent thereof. Piers, like the pearl, can be understood by all four senses, but it is his relationship with the dreamer Will that makes the narrative structure embody those senses.

Dowel (8-14 of the B-Text) represents the moral or tropological sense, in that it focuses on the education of Will by personifications of the faculties of the soul such as Thought (8), Wit and Inwit (Intellect and Good Sense, 9), Wit's wife Study and her cousins Clergy (Learning) and Scripture (10), Reason, in the dream-within-a-dream (11), and Imaginatif (Memory and Imagination, 12). These all lead eventually to the active life: Haukyn the Active Man, as educated by Conscience and Patience, *passus* 13 and 14. Dobet (15-18) emphasizes the allegorical sense with its focus on Anima's lecture on charity (15), the vision-within-a-vision of the Tree of Charity and Abraham as a type of faith (16), Moses as a type of hope, the Samaritan as a type of charity (17), culminating in the Passion and Harrowing of Christ during which Jesus jousts in Piers's armor (18; the jouster looks like the Samaritan and Piers, but is actually Christ). Dobest (19-20) traces the anagogical sense through the vision of Grace, during which Grace makes Piers his reeve on earth, aided by the oxen of the gospels and the four bullocks of the Fathers; to defend against the coming of Antichrist, the Christians build Unite, Holy Church or the Church Militant (19). In *passus* 20 the battle with Antichrist is described as unending: even within the Church friars make penance so easy the people no longer fear sin and Conscience must once again depart on a pilgrimage to seek Piers, at which point Will awakens (presumably educated adequately by the figurative senses, like the narrator of *Pearl*, to conduct his own search for Piers).

It is possible to apply this same allegorical structure to homiletic poems by the author of *Pearl,* including *Patience* and *Purity* ; I would even go so far as to venture that Chaucer in early, non-homiletic, poems like *The Book of the Duchess* and *The Parlement of Foules* intended that their puzzling structures be unlocked by understanding the use of the four senses, and the unity of *The Canterbury Tales* depends in large part on the education of an obtuse narrator or character by *figurae* of various sorts.

A more familiar poetic model for the explicit use of the four senses applied to structure appears of course in Dante's *Commedia,* which in the context of our discussion of homiletic poetry warrants another look. In the now famous and much cited "Letter to Can Grande," Dante revealed his exegetical purpose in writing the tripartite work. Note that the allegorical meanings depend chiefly upon literal narrative meaning in interpreting the Psalm text (113:1-2, in the Douay version, 114:1-2 in the King James version): "When Israel came forth from Egypt, the house of Jacob from a people of alien tongue, Juda became his sanctuary, Israel his domain." Dante's interpretation of this passage in the light of the four senses basically supports the conventional hierarchy of senses, the salvation of the soul through Christ, the soul in relation to its virtues and vices, and the soul in the Afterlife:

> Now if we look at the letter alone, what is signified to us is the departure of the sons of Israel from Egypt during the time of Moses; if at the allegory, what is signified to us is our redemption through Christ; if at the moral sense, what is signified to us is the conversion of the soul from the sorrow and misery of sin to the state of grace; if at the anagogical, what is signified to us is the departure of the sanctified soul from bondage to the corruption of this world into the freedom of eternal glory.[38]

Dante does indicate to Can Grande that the third part of his work, the *Paradiso* presented to his patron along with the Letter of explanation, has its literal subject "restricted to the state of blessed souls after death." That is, he implies that this third part of the *Commedia* must be read with the promise of *anagoge* in mind:

> And if the subject of the whole work, considered allegorically [figuratively], is man, through exercise of free will, earning or becoming liable to the rewards or punishments of justice, then it is evident that the subject in this part is restricted to man's becoming eligible, to the extent he has earned them, for the rewards of justice. (p. 101.)

Did the *Pearl* -Poet know of Dante's letter to Can Grande and the four senses, as he apparently did know the *Commedia* ? Certainly the tripartite structure of *Pearl* resembles that of the *Commedia* , in that the setting of arbor at harvest leads to the underworld of the earthly paradise, the vineyard and the laborers suggest the *Purgatorio*, and the heavenly Jerusalem suggests the *Paradiso*—but in addition the structure depends on an allegorical system very like the one enunciated in Dante's Letter to Can Grande. And yet the *ars praedicandi* we have discussed herein also show convincing evidence of the use of the multiple senses of allegory.

Most probably there was some fourteenth-century connection among these essentially didactic poems and the arts of preaching, and that one means of amplifying a theme—whether literally or more figuratively homiletic, whether in sermons or in homiletic poems—depended upon the multiple allegorical senses. That structure mirrored allegory, as in the case of *Pearl* or the *Commedia* or even *Piers Plowman*, certainly seems plausible. Dante again declares in his Letter, now citing Aristotle, "'As a thing is with respect to being, so it is with respect to truth'; and the reason for this is that the truth concerning a thing, which consists in the truth as its subject, is the perfect image of the thing as it is" (p. 98). The form of *Pearl*, one might paraphrase, is the image of truth understood tropologically, allegorically, anagogically.

Notes

1.   "The Alliterative Revival," in *Essays on Middle English Literature,* ed. Patricia Kean (Oxford: Clarendon Press, 1955), p. 87.

2.   Pearl *in its Setting: A Critical Study of the Structure and Meaning of the Middle English Poem* (Oxford: Blackwell; New York: Barnes and Noble, 1968), pp. 32-34.

3.   "The Theological Structure of 'Pearl," *Traditio,* 24 (1968), 43-75, rpt. in John Conley, ed. *The Middle English Pearl: Critical Essays* (Notre Dame and London: Univ. of Notre Dame Press, 1970), pp. 220-71, passage cited here, pp. 266-67.

4.   *The* Pearl *Poems: An Omnibus Edition,* vol. 1: Pearl *and* Cleanness, ed. William Vantuono, vol 5. of The Renaissance Imagination (New York and London: Garland Publishing, Inc., 1984), p. xxxv. He also provides a summary of others' tripartite divisions.

5.   Pp. xxxv-xxxvii.

6.   "The Pearl as a Symbol," *MLN,* 65 (1950), 155-61; rpt. *Essays in Medieval Culture* by D.W. Robertson, Jr. (Princeton: Princeton University Press, 1980), pp. 209-14. In the headnote to the reprinted essay he suggests "Sign" would be more appropriate than "Symbol."

7.   See, for further information in this regard. Dorothy Bethurum's collection of seminal essays in *Critical Approaches to Medieval Literature: Selected Papers from the English Institute 1958-1959* (New York: Columbia University Press, 1960). In addition, Morton W. Bloomfield, in his essay, "Symbolism in Medieval Literature," *Modern Philology,* 56 (1958), 73-81, criticize the interpretation of medieval literature in terms of the exegetical method used in medieval biblical criticism (in the early Middle Ages) as an erroneous method of understanding a work historically, a statement with which no medieval exegete would have disagreed (p. 74). He proceeds then to suggest that all literature has a *nucleus,* or *cortex,* and conveys *sententia*—a singularly modern definition. He prefers symbolism to allegory, and his contribution may be seen itself historically as a rebuttal to Robertsonian exegesis.

8.   The debate can be followed more closely in Conley's collection, *The Middle English* ""Pearl": on the patristic side, see especially the articles by Robertson, Stern, Blenkner, Ackerman, Pilch; on the literal and "literary" side, with an eye to imagery in the poem, see the essays by Johnson, Conley, and Macrae-Gibson.

9.   Criticism on *Pearl* which applies other theological approaches or compares other works of literature to *Pearl* includes the following essays contained in Conley: Alfred L. Kellogg, *"Pearl* and the Augustinian Doctrine of Creation," pp. 335-37; Herbert Pilch, "The Middle English *Pearl* : Its Relation to the *Roman de la Rose,"* pp. 163-84; on lapidaries and *Pearl,* see Milton R. Stern, "An Approach to *The Pearl,"* pp. 73-85; on popular sermons and *Pearl,* see Robert W. Ackerman, "The Pearl-Maiden and the Penny," pp. 149-62.

Alternatively, essays that analyze the theme, diction, imagery, narrator, genre, and structure in a primarily literal way include Sister Mary Vincent Hillman, "Some Debatable Words in *Pearl* and its Theme," pp. 9-17; Wendell Stacy Johnson, "The Imagery and Diction of *The Pearl*: Toward an Interpretation," pp. 27-49; on the *consolatio* as genre, see John Conley, "*Pearl* and a Lost Tradition," pp. 50-72; on the elegiac nature of the poem, see Stanton Hoffman, "The *Pearl* : Notes for an Interpretation," pp. 86-102; on the narrator see, Charles Moorman, "The Role of the Narrator in *Pearl*," pp. 103-121; and also A.C. Spearing, "Symbolic and Dramatic Development in *Pearl*," pp. 122-48; O.D. Macrae-Gibson, "*Pearl*: The Link-Words and the Thematic Structure," pp. 203-19.

See also the recent trend, suggesting a *tertium quid* that links medieval symbolism with theology, in Theodore Bogdanos, "Pearl": *Image of the Ineffable. A Study in Medieval Poetic Symbolism* (University Park and London: Pennsylvania State University Press, 1983), in which he notes the aesthetic implications of the Incarnation for medieval poetic: "if the reality of the physical and spiritual, the human and the divine terms, is to be equally emphasized in any metaphor of the ineffable, the tension between these two terms, as they try to establish themselves in the perceiving mind, increases considerably. When the medieval poet manipulates and patterns this tension, the result can be a powerful spiritual and artistic experience," p. 10.

10.   Such usage of the four senses by preachers was intended to help in the attack on Lollard and Mendicant heresies, as evidenced in a sermon of ca. 1400 by Master Robert Rypon, sub-prior of Durham, to which we shall later return. G. R. Owst has concluded that "Biblical literalism, therefore, was clearly the mother of heresy. The Letter killed. It was only the Spirit that made alive." See G. R. Owst, in *Literature and Pulpit in Medieval England: A Neglected Chapter in the History of English Letters and of the English People* , 2nd ed. (1961; rpt. Oxford: Basil Blackwell, 1966), p. 61. For a discussion of the homilists' use of allegory and the four senses, see also Chapter Two, "Scripture and Allegory." Indeed, Owst states, "The homilist may prefer on other occasions to mingle natural and Biblical *figures* together to illustrate his point. We have now to examine the influence of current modes of expounding Scripture in a more formal and systematic fashion. For it is here that we find a source, not merely of the naturalistic type of *example*, but also of the animal satire and similitude, of marvellous narrations and devil stories, and certain lively allegoric features common alike to the later religious drama and to such famous allegories as *The Vision of Piers Plowman* and *The Pilgrim's Progress*" (pp. 56-57). For the history of allegorical exposition and the commentators thereupon, as well as the use of exposition in popular sermons, see Beryl Smalley, *The Study of the Bible in the Middle Ages* (1952; rpt. Notre Dame: University of Notre Dame Press, 1964), esp. Chapter Five, "Masters of the Sacred Page."

11.   Ackerman, Pearl-Maiden, p. 162, but see also pp. 149-62. Related and similarly ignored interpretations include the Pearl-Maiden as an allegorical teacher, like Boethius's Philosophy, or Grace Dieu in *Le Pèlerinage de vie humaine*.

12.   Owst, *Literature and Pulpit*, pp. 61ff.

13.   See Vantuono's preface to Vol. 2, *Patience and Sir Gawain and the Green Knight*, in which he claims that "*Patience* reveals the poet's knowledge of the *artes praedicandi* "(p. ii) in that it has a prologue (1-60) as a statement of theme, a body (61-257) in which the theme is dilated, and an epilogue (528-31) in which occurs the

peroration of the medieval sermon accompanied by a restatement of the theme. See also Vantuono, "The Structure and Sources of *Patience," Medieval Studies*, 34 (1972), 401-21; for comparable studies of *Cleanness*, see Michael H. Means, "The Homiletic Structure of *Cleanness," Studies in Medieval Culture*, 5 (1975), 165-72; and Doris E. Kittendorf, "*Cleanness* and the Fourteenth Century *Artes Praedicandi," Michigan Academician*, 11 (1979), 319-30.

14.   Robert of Basevorn, *The Form of Preaching* (*Forma praedicandi*), trans. Leopold Krul, in *Three Medieval Rhetorical Arts*, ed. James J. Murphy (Berkeley, Los Angeles, and London: University of California Press, 1971), pp. 126-27 (the entire tractate runs pp. 109-215). See also James J. Murphy, *Rhetoric in the Middle Ages: A History of Rhetorical Theory from Saint Augustine to the Renaissance* (Berkeley, Los Angeles, and London: University of California Press, 1974), p. 270, who notes that' "To the medieval mind, even Christ in his preaching was merely following a Creation-old pattern set by God the Father. Preaching was the second act of God following the creation of Man himself, and preaching formed for many ages the primary means of communication between God and man."

15.   Murphy, *Rhetoric in the Middle Ages*, p. 275. For the history of the art of preaching, see esp. Chapter VI.

16.   In *PL* 156, 25-6; see also Harry Caplan, "The Four Senses of Scriptural Interpretation and the Mediaeval Theory of Preaching," *Speculum*, 4 (1929), 282. Guibert has been translated: Joseph M. Miller, "Guibert de Nogent's *Liber quo ordine sermo fieri debeat* : A Translation of the Earliest Modern Speech Textbook," *Today's Speech* 17 (1969), p. 46.

17.   "Tractatulus," trans. H. Caplan, "A Late Mediaeval Tractate on Preaching," in *Studies in Rhetoric and Public Speaking in Honor of James Albert Winans* (1925; rpt. New York: Russell and Russell, 1962), pp. 70ff. The related principle of employing kinds of explication is a type of rhetorical *inuentio*.

18   Murphy, *Rhetoric in the Middle Ages*, p. 327. In 27 MSS. and echoed by Robert of Basevorn (see, e.g., Oxford Magdalen College MS. 168); it has been published (incompletely) as the third part of a work by St. Bonaventure, *Ars conciondani*, in *Doctoris seraphici S. Bonaventurae opera omnia* (Quarrachi: Ad claras aquas, 1901), IX, 16-21. Another translation appears in Harry C. Hazel, "A Translation, with Commentary, of the Bonaventuran 'Ars Concionandi' Diss. Washington State Univ., 1972). Murphy says, p. 328, "Richard's listings are remarkable only in that they demonstrate the continuing popularity of the 'four senses of interpretation,' the identification of metaphor as a separate form of support, and the relegation of reasoning to a place as merely one method among many."

19.   In Murphy, *Three Medieval Rhetorical Arts*, p. 183.

20.   See *De reductione artium ad theologiam* 5-7, trans. and ed. Sister Emma Thérése Healy, in *Works of St. Bonaventure* (Saint Bonaventure, New York: Franciscan Institute, 1955), pp. 26-29.

21.   St. Thomas Aquinas, *Summa Theologicae*, I, art. 10, reply obj. 3, ed. Thomas Gilby (Cambridge: Blackfriars, 1964), vol. 1, *Christian Theology*, p. 38 (trans. p. 39).

22.   The best—clearest, most concise—outline of the four senses of allegory and the varying definitions of each in the Middle Ages can be found in Caplan, who

relates them to the *ars praedicandi* in "The Four Senses," pp. 282-90; see also the fine discussion of the early history of the four senses in Chapter Nine, "The Bible and Allegory," in Robert E. McNally, S.J., *The Bible in the Early Middle Ages* (Westminster, Maryland: Newman Press, 1959), pp. 53-61) and also Charles Donahue, "[Patristic Exegesis in the Criticism of Medieval Literature:] Summation," in Bethurum, *Critical Approaches*, pp. 61-82. On the history of Greek allegorism see also J. Tate, "On the History of Allegorism," *The Classical Quarterly*, 28 (1934), 105-14. For classical origins of the various senses, see Jane Chance, "The Origins and Development of Medieval Mythography: From Homer to Dante," in *Mapping the Cosmos*, ed. Jane Chance and R.O. Wells (Houston: Rice University Press, 1985), pp. 35-64. The best study of allegory in the Middle Ages is Henri de Lubac, *Exégèse médiévale. Les quatre sens de l'Écriture*, vols. 41-42, 59; two vols. in 4 (Paris: Aubier, 1959-64). See the very recent discussion of the "Doctrine of the Four Meanings" in the chapter on Patristic Exegesis in Tzvetan Todorov, *Symbolism and Interpretation*, trans. Catherine Porter (Ithaca: Cornell University Press, 1982), esp. pp. 112-30. But see also an article distinguishing allegory from integument (used for pagan sources), in Hennig Brinkmann, "Verhüllung ('Integumentum') als literarische Darstellungsform im Mittelalter," *Der Begriff der Repraesentatio im Mittelalter: Stellvertretung, Symbol, Zeichen, Bild*, Miscellanea Mediaevalia, vol. 8 (Berlin and New York: Walter de Gruyter, 1971), 314-39.

For an example of a Greek Alexandrine who transmitted Stoic methods of mythographic exegesis in discussions of the four-fold method, see Origen, *De principiis* 4.11-16 (4.2.4-9), in *Origène: Traité 24 s principes*, trans. into French and Latin by Henri Couzel and Manlio Simonetti, vol. 3 (books 3-4), no. 268 of Sources Chrétiennes (Paris: Les éditions du Cerf, 1980), pp. 310-41.

For the Church Fathers and other early commentators, see St. Augustine, drawing upon Greek allegory in homiletic works like *Enarrationes in Psalmos*, who also used multiple explication, in *De utilitate credendi*, v ff, ed. Joseph Zycha, Corpus Scriptorum Ecclesiasticorum Latinorum, 25 (Prague, Vienna, and Leipzig, 1891), pp. 7ff. In *De doctrina Christiana* 3.5 he notes in the third book, Corinthians 3.6, that "Littera occidit," 5, in which the letter is linked with the flesh and the spirit with soul. The passage is also mentioned in *De spiritu et littera*, iv, in *PL* 44, 203. See also St. Augustine in *De Genesi ad litteram* 1, 1, ed. Joseph Zycha, Corpus Scriptorum Ecclesiasticorum Latinorum 28.1 (Prague, Vienna, and Leipzig, 1984), pp. 3ff. Ambrose (d. 397) offered the somatic (literal, grammatical), psychic (moral), and pneumatic (allegorical, mystical) interpretation of Scripture; note also Jerome, *Commentariorum in Ezechielem Prophetam*, 4, 16 (*PL* 25, 125). Also in *Epistola CXX ad Hedibiam*, *PL* 22, quaest. 12, as well as Ezech. 16 and Amos 4; John Cassian (360?-435?) declared that allegorical methods of exegesis opened up the deepest meaning of Scripture: see *Collatio* 14, 8, *De spirituali scientia*, *PL* 49, 962ff. Eucherius of Lyons, in the Preface to *Formulae spiritalis intellegentiae*, ed. Karl Wotke, Corpus Scriptorum Ecclesiasticorum Latinorum 31 (Prague, Vienna, and Leipzig, 1894), pp. 3-6, although he posits only three senses—literal, tropological, and anagogical; Gregory the Great (d. 604) in *Moralium libri, sive expositio in librum b. Job* (*PL* 75, 513), intended to interpret the book of Job according to the literal, allegorical, and moral senses, but after the fourth book concentrated on the moral and allegorical (valued as highly here as in his homilies on the Gospels and the Book of Ezechiel); Isidore of Seville (d. 636) wrote on the allegories of Scripture in a work entitled, *Allegoriae quaedam sacrae scripturae*, *PL* 83, 97-130, and also one on the exegesis of scriptural texts, *Mysticorum expositiones sacramentorum seu quaestiones in vetus testamentum*, *PL* 83, 207-424, which was important for the propagation of allegorical exegesis of the Bible. Thereafter every commentary on the Bible for three centuries shows Isidore's influence (McNally, *Bible*, pp. 55-56).

Merovingian and Carolingian commentators used multiple-sense allegorical exegesis: see Aldhelm in *De virginitate* 4, in *Aldhelmi opera*, ed. Rudolf Ehwald, Monumenta Germaniae Historica 15, p. 232; Rabanus Maurus, in *Expositio in Epistolam ad Galatas* 4, 24, *PL* 112, 330; Bede, who uses both a threefold (*Opp.* vii, 317; vii, 196, 197; viii, 22, 23) and a fourfold (*Opp.* vi, 96, 97; vii, 246, 247; viii, 100) system of classification, in Charles Plummer, ed. *Historia ecclesiastica gentis Anglorum* (Oxford, 1896), I, Intro., lvi ff. Bede identifies "typical" with "allegorical" (in *Opp.* vii, 246, 247, in Plummer, ed. *Historia ecclesiastica*, I, Intro., lvi ff. Incorporating Augustine's typological sense is Angelom of Luxeuil (9th c.) in *Enarrationes in libros Regum, praefatio apologetica, PL* 115, 243ff, cited by Caplan, "Four Senses," p. 287f.

Twelfth-century commentators include John of Salisbury, *Policraticus* vii, 12, ed. Clement C. J. Webb, II (Oxford: Clarendon Press, 1909), pp. 143, 144; Bonaventure, *De reductione artium ad theologiam*, in Healy, *Works of St. Bonaventure*, pp. 27, 29 and Hugh of St. Victor in *Didascalicon* urged three readings of Scripture, the historical, allegorical, and tropological: see *Didascalicon de studio legendi* 6.3, ed. Charles Henry Buttimer (Washington, D.C.: Catholic University Press, 1939), p. 116; and also *De Scripturis et scriptoribus sacris* III, in *PL* 175, 12: after Scripture is studied historically, then it can be studied allegorically and morally (tropologically).

St. Thomas Aquinas adheres to the four meanings of Scripture, literal or historical, allegorical, tropological or moral. These are divided into two classes, the historical and then the spiritual or mystical, in *Summa Theologica* Ia, I, art. 10, reply obj., ed. Plummer, pp. 36, 38, 40, and in *Summa Theologica* l, art. 10, reply obj. 3, part 2, ed. Plummer, p. 38.

In the thirteenth century, see Hugh of St. Cher, who compared the four senses to the four coverings of the tabernacle, the four winds, the fourfold cherubim, and the four rivers of Paradise. See Frederick William Farrar, *History of Interpretation* (London, 1886), p. 295. Hugh also said, "historia docet factum, tropologia quid faciendum, allegoria quid intellegendum, anagoge quid appetendum," in E. v. Dobschütz, "Vom vierfachen Schriftsinn," in *Harnack-Ehrung: Beiträg zur Kirchengeschichte ihrem Lehrer Adolf von Harnack zu seinem siebzigsten Geburtstage dargebracht von einer Reihe seiner Schüler* (Leipzig: Hinrichs, 1921), p. 12n.

In the fourteenth century, see Dante, "The Letter to Can Grande," in *The Literary Criticism of Dante Alighieri*, ed. and trans. Robert S. Haller (Lincoln: Univ. of Nebraska Press, 1973), p. 99; an excerpt from the *Convivio* (or *The Banquet*), 2.1.2-15, on the four senses is also included (pp. 112-14).

In a work acknowledging St. Thomas' influence, called "Tractatulus," it is declared that senses can be multiplied in four ways, in Caplan, "A Late Medieval Tractate," pp. 70 ff.

23.   Ed. Wothke, pp. 3-6.

24.   McNally, *Bible*, p. 55.

25.   *De reductione artium ad theologiam* 5-7, in Healy, *Works of St. Bonaventure*, pp. 27, 29.

26.   Robert of Basevorn, *The Form of Preaching (Forma praedicandi)*, trans. Leopold Krul, in *Three Medieval Rhetorical Arts*, ed. Murphy, p. 183 (the entire tractate runs pp. 109-215).

27.   Chapter Nineteen, in Murphy, *Three Medieval Rhetorical Arts*, p. 138.

28.   All references to the works of the *Pearl*-Poet derive from the Vantuono edition.

29.   Rypon defines the four senses in MS. Harl. 4994, fol. 114 and following (sermon for the 4th Sunday in Lent), in Owst, p. 58. By citing false etymologies he declares there are four senses.

30.   *Ibid.*, p. 59. These are also quoted by Nicolas of Lyra (p. 59*n*2); see also Harry Caplan, "Rhetorical Invention in Some Mediaeval Tractates on Preaching," *Speculum*, 2 (1927), 292. Owst notes that the verses are similar to those "used for summarizing the principles of sermon dilation," in *Preaching in Medieval England* (Cambridge: University Press, 1926), pp. 323-24.

31.   Owst, *Literature and Pulpit*, p. 60: "*Tropologia* dicitur a 'tropos', quod est 'virtus', et 'logos'—'sermo', i.e. 'sermo de virtutibus'; et hec est quando sensus historialis seu allegoricus secundum aliquam proprietatem ydiomatis littere refertur ad virtutes. Cuius sensus est exemplum in epistola antedicta ibi—'Itaque fratres non sumus ancille filii, sed libere, qua libertate Christus nos liberavit'. Super quo glosa—'Libertas est qua liberati sumus a peccato....' Note that he conflates the Greek moral/tropological sense with the Hebraic typological. In note 1, p. 59, from MS. Linc. Cath. Libr. A. 7.2. fol. 265b, the vernacular version of the above (also in MS. Harl. 2276, fol. 32b-33) indicates that the "sence tropologik" can be defined as "whan a man redith a story that spekith moche of myȝti dedis or of gode worchyng, and understondith that he shuld have stronge gostli dedis of holi lyving" (from Harley—Linc. replaces this with "that bitokneth wit of vertues").

32.   Owst, *Literature and Pulpit*, pp. 59-60: "*Allegoria* dicitur ab 'alle', quod est 'alienum', et 'gore'—'sententia', i.e.—aliena sententia; nam allegoria est quando aliud dicitur et aliud intelligitur. Et iste sensus secundus scripture est quasi lignum seu arbor procedens ex radice, de qua arbore crescunt et pullulant duo sensus alii quasi flores et fructus. De isto sensu est exemplum planum in epistola hodierna, ubi dicit Apostolus Abraham habuisse duos filios, unum de libera et alium de ancilla, viz. Ysaac de Sara uxore Abrahe libera, et Ysmael de Agar ancilla Abrahe concubina. Que omnia dicit Apostolus per allegoriam dictam, quia secundum ipsum duo signant testamenta, que, ut constat, sonant et notant longe alia quam historia resonat antedicta."

33.   Owst, *Literature and Pulpit*, p. 59: "*Anagogia* dicitur ab 'ana', quod est 'sursum', et 'goge'...; et notandum quod anagogia sive sensus anagogicus est quando sensus literalis, allegoricus seu tropologicus transfertur ad celestia, sicut in dicta epistola, ubi supra,—'Non sumus filii ancille, sed libere', etc. Glosa—'Non servi peccati seu legis, sed filii libere', i.e. celestis Ierusalem, de qua scribitur in eadem epistola—'Ierusalem, que sursum est, libera est mater nostra'. Cuius Ierusalem figura fuit ipsa famosa civitas terrena Ierusalem... .[Thus the name 'Jerusalem' comes to signify, tropologically—each good Christian man; anagogically—heaven.] Ex hiis premissis sequitur evidenter quod capiens sensum scripture sacre solum ad literam frequenter incidit in errorem, quia, viz., non intelligit dictos sensus."

34.   The passage by Guibert de Nogent has been translated by Murphy, *Rhetoric in the Middle Ages*, p. 302. But see also St. Jerome, in his *Commentary on Ezechiel*, who shows the meanings of Jerusalem as the earthly city, the Church, the

faithful soul, the heavenly city (literal, allegorical, moral or tropological, anagogical senses). See *Commentariorum in Ezechielem Prophetam* 4, 16 (*PL* 25, 125).

35.   See Jane Chance, *Woman as Hero in Old English Literature*, (New York: Syracuse University Press, 1986), Chapter Three: "Brave Judith, Juliana, and Elene: Figures of the Soul, Christ, and the Church."

36.   On *Piers Plowman* as a homiletic poem, see especially Owst, *Preaching in Medieval England*, p. 295; see also *Literature and Pulpit*, 1933, pp. 6, 40, 84, 228, 450, 597, 549. Owst declares, in *Preaching*, p. 295, "In reality, it [*Piers Plowman*] represents nothing more nor less than the quintessence of English mediaeval preaching gathered up into a single metrical piece of unusual charm and vivacity." For a discussion of other scholars viewing the poem as homily, see esp. pp. 96-99 and 117 of John Raymond McCully, Jr., "Conceptions of *Piers Plowman* : 1550's Through 1970's" (Diss. Rice 1976).

37.   Other scholars have discussed the use of allegory in *Piers*, but without relating the multiple senses to its narrative structure or the art of preaching. Howard William Troyer, "Who is Piers Plowman?" *PMLA*, 47 (1930), 368-84, analyzed the figure of Piers in terms of the allegorical, tropological, and anagogical senses; N[evill] K. Coghill first noted that the poem is a multi-sense work in "Langland, the 'Naket,' the 'Nauʒty,' and the Dole," *Review of English Studies*, 8 (1932), 305; he then perceived the three lives allegorically, tropologically, and anagogically, in "The Character of Piers Plowman considered from the B-Text," *Medium Aevum*, 2 (1933), 114; Henry W. Wells first explained the three lives mystically as active, contemplative, and mixed, then, in 1938, as anagogical, personal, and moral allegories, although he also declared that the three lives must be read literally, in "The Philosophy of Piers Plowman," *PMLA*, 53 (1938), 339-49; A.C. Hamilton, in "Spenser and Langland," *Studies in Philology*, 55 (1958), 545, in comparing *Piers* to the first book of *The Faerie Queene* , noted how the Dreamer can save his soul: allegorically, through the search for Piers; tropologically, through the search to know himself ("for Charity is within" p. 545); and anagogically, through Christ's jousting at Jerusalem (p. 545). See also Katherine Bache Trower, "The Plowman as Preacher: The Allegorical and Structural Significance of Piers the Plowman in *Piers Plowman*," *DAI*, 30 (1968), 712A (Illinois); and McCully's more general discussion of those scholars writing in the sixties and seventies whom he terms the "patristic allegorists," pp. 256-82.

In addition, Judson Allen argues that the only book owned by William Langland was a copy of Hugh of Saint Cher (see *The Chaucer Newsletter*, 6:1 [Fall, 1984], 1, 2). Such a statement is interesting to us, if true, because Hugh was most interested in the four senses (see note 22 above).

38.   See "The Letter to Can Grande" in Haller, *Literary Criticism*, p. 99.

PEARL AS DIPTYCH

BRITTON J. HARWOOD

he most powerful structure in *Pearl* may be chiastic. By that I
mean that stanza-groups X and XI are interlocked, IX and XII, VIII and
XIII, and so on.[1] When the poem is read back and forth in this way, it
divides into two halves of ten groups each. Even on a first reading,
Pearl appears to double back after the tenth group.[2] There, with the
dreamer's verdict against the Parable of the Vineyard, his conflict with
the maiden reaches its most intense point. Subsequently, it subsides.
When he asks in section XIII, for instance, what kind of person the
Lamb might be to marry her over everyone else, he seems genuinely
puzzled.[3]

While there is surely development, movement, plot in *Pearl*,[4] the
poem also has a simultaneous structure, most obviously the case,
perhaps, in the circle described when the last line leads back to the first
line, making the poem's own rhythm an "endeleȝ rounde"[5] metaphoric for the pearl. This structure less resembles a solid sphere, as Ian
Bishop points out, than a garland of linked units like a necklace or
rosary; and as a possible source in the material culture he suggests the
corona candelabrum, a gilded, jeweled circle that was taken to represent the heavenly Jerusalem.[6] That the structure of *Pearl*—the *disposi-
tio*, or the architectural aspect of form—is symmetrical as well as
circular has been recognized for a long while also. W. H. Schofield
found that a lengthy middle section, didactic in nature, was flanked by
two chiefly descriptive parts of some twenty stanzas each. Louis
Blenkner divides each of these descriptive sections into "erber" frame
(sections I and XX) and *visiones* (sections II-IV and XVII-XIX), and
Bishop separates two issues out of the debate: whether the maiden is
a queen in heaven, then whether she is a bride of the Lamb.[7]

Yet it would not be surprising in this "most structurally complex
of the great vernacular masterpieces of the later Middle Ages," this
"most elaborately and successfully wrought of the Middle English
poems which remain to us,"[8] if the symmetry was somewhat further
reaching and more detailed, or if the particularities of the chiasmus,[9]
inspired by a very common devotional object from the period, made
the poem in its simultaneity a devotional object too.[10]

I

Chiasmus in *Pearl* takes the particular form of subjecting a stanza-
group in the first half to critique by the correlated group in the second

half. To use very general terms already familiar in discussion of *Pearl*, the representations to the right (taking the text for the moment as an open book of two leaves) generally insist anagogically on the sense of things so far as they signify other things that lie ahead "in aeterna gloria."[11] Those to the left represent the historical. Further, the link-words of each group will be seen to have one meaning *in bono* and another *in malo*, as if they were objects that signified things of contrary value.[12] The *sensus bonus* of the link-words in sections IX and XII, for instance , will each signify something important in XII; the *sensus malus* of the same words will each signify something important in IX. Nevertheless, the experiences represented in the first ten groups do not become contemptible in light of the last ten just as Christian dogmatics does not evade time and history. The sides are related only as the inferior and the superior.

If there were an influence upon this structure, it may have come not from a verbal medium at all, but from diptychs. Since time out of mind, diptychs had been associated with the "boke with leue3 sware" that the enthroned Lamb is said by the "Apokalype3" to be reading (837).[13] A visual medium like an ivory diptych likely accounts for the *Pearl*-Poet's linking the mercy of the Virgin and St. John the Evangelist to Christ's own mercy once he had the Judging Christ in mind (405-06): "Bot Crystes mersy and Mary and Jon, / Þise arn þe grounde of alle my blisse" (383-84). In sculpture and then in carved ivory, the iconography of the Crucifixion had been transferred to the scene of the Last Judgment.[14]

Any "yuore" (178) that the poet had seen,[15] moreover, may well have been cut into diptychs. In the late thirteenth and the whole of the fourteenth centuries, these served as private devotional objects, typically with scenes from the Nativity, the Passion, and the life of the Virgin across their interior surfaces. When elephant tusks became available in good supply in western Europe in the middle of the thirteenth century for the first time since the fourth century, ivory carving became, in France at least, what one art historian has called "the most astounding and important example of trade work."[16] And diptychs and tabernacles were the pieces commissioned most frequently.[17] Raymond Koechlin catalogued five hundred eighty such Gothic tablets from France, many of them found in England. While at least one group of ivory diptychs of English provenance survives despite the "nearly total ruin" of English ivory in the Reformation,[18] it was the products of the Parisian workshops that dominated sales throughout Europe for a century.[19] Their iconography, choice of episodes, disposition of scenes, decor, and style of execution were decisively influential.

If the poet knew some of these carvings, there appear to have been two structural features that he may have borrowed. The most obvious feature, of course, he did not. From their beginning, Gothic diptychs were divided into horizontal registers extending across both leaves. Typically, such a diptych is two or three registers high, with scenes running from left to right. The episode coming first chronologically usually appears in the lower left-hand corner, but the arrangement thereafter is subject to much variation. The Soissons diptych,[20] for example, is read from the lower left all the way across to the lower right, then up to the middle register and across from right to left, and finally, in the upper register, from left to right again.

Although art historians seem not to point this out, the designers of at least a significant minority of diptychs made use of the opportunity for tension between the two leaves. For instance, in a diptych which has simply an Adoration of the Magi scene on the left panel and a Crucifixion on the right, a small crowned figure, kneeling, is added to the latter, as if to give the Adoration an ironic outcome.[21] In another carving with just the same two episodes, a king on the left panel points as usual towards the center, where the star is usually found. Here it has been omitted, however, and instead, Christ's right arm, running along the horizontal beam of the Cross, points back.[22] In a French diptych three registers high from the end of the thirteenth century, the designer disturbs chronological order evidently to bring the gift of spices in the Adoration scene (lower register on the left) into ironic relation with Joseph of Arimethea's anointment of the body in the Entombment (same register on the right).[23]

As against any notion, then, that the Gothic diptych is formed simply to lead the eye from one register to another in continuous fashion, the designers sometimes must have intended that the two panels be collated with each other. In a French piece from the later fourteenth century, in the Ascension scene in the upper band on the left leaf, the feet of the rising Christ occupy precisely the same position as the descending dove in the Pentecost on the right leaf. On the left, all the figures are looking up; on the right they all look down.[24] In another slightly later carving, in a Death of the Virgin at the extreme lower left, Mary's rising soul is perched, a miniature female figure, on the shoulder of Christ, who is present among the mourners; on the extreme lower right, in a scene of Gethsemane, Christ's own death is represented by the little cross that descends to him while he prays.[25] Another diptych plays off an Adoration against a Coronation of the Virgin. An identical treatment of Mary (carved in three-quarter face) on each side pulls earthly kings into tension with the King of Heaven.[26]

This tension seems sometimes to have been genuinely chiastic. The adoption of an unusual order of episodes in a fourteenth-century French carving[27] posits an opposition between the Crucifixion in the upper right (the upper register on the right leaf) with the Deposition from the Cross in the lower left. A *Noli me tangere* in the lower right, meanwhile, appears in ironic opposition to the Flagellation at the upper left. (This is not the only time in the diptychs these two scenes are opposed.) A French carving with four registers from the third quarter of the century, now in the Louvre, places the unction at the Entombment in the lower left and Christ's washing his apostles' feet in the upper right, the raising of Lazarus in the upper left, the Harrowing in the lower right.[28] An unusual *Maria lactans* appears at the upper right of one four-register diptych (following scenes of the Coronation and of the Trinity) to create a reference back to the Annunciation and the Nativity in the lower left.[29] A three-register carving from the third quarter of the century puts scenes with the Virgin (a Coronation and an Annunciation) in the upper right and lower left, scenes with Christ between two figures (a Resurrection and a Presentation) in the upper left and lower right.[30]

The chiasmus is sometimes relatively simple: the Death of the Virgin and the Death of Christ are upper left and lower right; in the lower left the three kings and in the upper right the Coronation.[31] Or Ecclesia and St. Peter will lie along one axis, Synagogia and St. Paul along the other.[32] Sometimes the chiasmus is more complex. A two-register French diptych of the later 1300s adopts an unusual narrative order so that the Virgin's offering the baby her breast in the lower left may play off against Stephaton's extending the gall-soaked sponge in a Crucifixion at the upper right. The election of the Virgin in the Annunciation at the lower right is recalled in her Coronation at the upper left.[33] Another French carving from the second half of the century places the Annunciation/Nativity and the Resurrection along one axis; along the other are Christ's entry first into the Old Jerusalem and then (with the Ascension) into the New Jerusalem.[34] Early in the fifteenth century, a French diptych with three registers puts the Death of the Virgin and the Crucifixion along one axis of the chiasmus and then—presumably because a message from the Father was delivered or sought in each case—an Annunciation and a Gethsemane scene along the other axis. Perhaps to achieve this effect, the narrator disturbs narrative order.[35]

Besides tension between the two leaves sometimes reaching to chiasmus, there is a second structural feature of the diptychs that seems to me paralleled in *Pearl*. While there are exceptions,[36] when there is a hierarchical distinction to be made between the subjects represented on a diptych, the superior of the two is depicted on the wing to the viewer's right. Even when the diptych was in liturgical use, the right wing appears to have been the privileged place: a Fulda diptych lists deceased kings on the left, deceased bishops on the right.[37] This is of course reversed in the case of triptychs, where the presence of Christ in the center panel makes his right, the viewer's left, the preferred position. The presence of Christ seems sometimes to have such a reorienting effect even when there are only two panels.

The beautiful Salting Diptych in the Victoria and Albert represents the convention: Virgin and Child are on the left wing, a standing Christ is to the right. In two other English diptychs, the designer disturbs chronological order so that scenes from the life of the Virgin might be grouped on the left, those from the life of Christ to the right.[38] The *Noli me tangere* episode, while coming later than the Crucifixion, typically appears on the left wing when the Crucifixion fills the right one.[39] Perhaps to situate weakness and dependency on the left, authority on the right, the designer of an ivory from the later fourteenth century places the Crucifixion and the Nativity in the upper and lower registers on the left panel, the Coronation and the Adoration in the comparable positions on the right.[40] In apparently every carved Madonna, the Christchild is to the viewer's right; in every Coronation of the Virgin, Christ is to the right.

In sum, what I wish to suggest, then, is that, if the *Pearl*-Poet actually had the opportunity to see ivory carvings like these, he would have found—in tension with the narrative order that usually moved with the register and tended to guide the eye in a continuous line over the whole surface of the diptych—a chiastic form emerging when the eye collated leaf with leaf. Moreover, such collation might have occurred with the expectation, also taught by the ivories, that the right-hand term of an opposition would stand in a superior relation to the left-hand one.

I would like to turn now to *Pearl* and briefly collate the two "panels" there, starting at what one might call the hinge.

II

Stanza-group X is part of the Parable of the Vineyard and includes the complaint by senior workers that late arrivals receive as much as they. In answering them in this section and the eleventh, the Lord of the Vineyard denies he has broken a covenant with anyone. Further, no one, the maiden goes on to say, *deserves* to be paid. Even in the unlikely event a person managed always to avoid mortal sin (579-80, 617-20), all were lost in Adam (637-44). Thus, the maiden does not suspend the notion of equity at this point but rather insists upon it. There is also, however, the fact of pardon, the gift that goes beyond what is due, infinitely costly in its purchase and inexhaustible. Our experience is only of finite quantities. When the complaining workers say, "Vus þynk vus oȝe to take more" (552), each of them means he has one such limit in mind and that it has not been reached. "Innoghe" *in malo* in the eleventh section also implies such quantifiability, but a quantity that has been produced: through baptism the newborn has "innoghe of grace" (625) to enter the living body of Christ immediately. Nevertheless, "innoghe" also means "abundant" in a way that ignores a limit. "Innoghe þer wax out of þat welle, / Blod and water of brode wounde" (649-50). "More" has such a meaning too: "Þe merci of God is much þe more," as that mercy overwhelms the humble efforts of those who arrive late (576). By how much, we do not know, but it is of course only through our experience of finite sums that the negative idea of limitlessness can be achieved.

Sections IX and XII are unified by the topic of degrees or stages. "Limit" is the *sensus malus* of "date," the link-work of IX, and anticipates one of the meanings of "more" and "innoghe." Limits can mark out a progression—over time, as in IX when the workers come into the vineyard at different hours, or through space, as in XII (literally, the stages of a journey up a hill [678, 692]). Section IX moves from old age backwards, with those entering the vineyard last being the youngest; XII is about two men moving up the holy hill, the "inoscente," who dies before he does "hondelyngeȝ harme" (681), and the "ryȝtwys man" (675) who lives to obey the Law at point after point. However, because no one may be able to keep himself within the limits established by the Law (687-88), the odds against righteousness mount with the stages.

Each such "date" is also a point, however, when grace is available through penance (661-62). Penance like every sacrament presupposes a specific historical moment: the "sely stounde" (659) of the Passion, which is nevertheless perpetually accessible. Hence, "date" *in bono* is any given moment—any date. The *sensus bonus* of "ryȝt," the link-word in XII, is this grace that is always at hand, the satisfaction of the Law available in the Atonement. *In malo,* it is the Law itself (708), the Old Covenant that becomes more straitening with every step of a person's life. Thus, the innocent is "saf by ryȝt" (720) and "not by ryȝte" (708): although the baptized infant has not lived long enough to be unrighteous, he is not for that reason saved without grace.[41]

Sections VIII and XIII both take up the question of whether the elevation of the maiden excludes or devalues anyone else. With position as one of the categories of what Kant called the *Verstand,* our experience is that only one substance can occupy any given position at one time. The revelation that a very large number of queens or brides somehow do not supplant each other (440, 785-86) can only frustrate the dreamer. Somehow, no queen or bride is "makeleȝ," this being the member *in malo* of the *maskelleȝ/makeleȝ* link-word in XIII. Where the notion of matchlessness bulks larger in VIII than in XIII, spotlessness is more prominent in XIII. Cleanness is anticipated in VIII, however, with the maiden's warning that members of Christ's body should take care not to affix any "hate" or "gawle" to "hys body" (460). While "cortaysye," the link-word in VIII, names the generosity[42] of all who enter the kingdom (450), finally it is God's love for the world that is the pearl of great price: the spotlessness of XIII is provided at God's own cost ("In hys blod he wesch my wede ..." [766]). The poor shadow of this—"cortaysye" *in malo*—is simply an absence of objection, as when an eldest son takes one of his father's titles during the latter's lifetime.[43] Hence, "kyng by cortayse" (480).

The link-word in VII comes as part of a phrase, "grounde of alle my blysse." Sections VII and XIV are both concerned with grounds, though of different kinds. Ground as metaphor has as its evil sense the maiden herself when the dreamer makes her earthly life the foundation of his happiness. Her death has made him voluble in grief (363, 374). In its good sense "grounde" figures the Lamb, on whom the maiden's happiness is built (407-08), whose injuries and crucifixion are displayed for a full stanza and a half on the right "panel" (799-816). In contrast to the rash "spelle" regretted in VII, the Lamb "closed ... hys mouth fro vch query, / Quen Jueӡ hym iugged ..." (803-04), dying without "playnt" (815). The link-word of the later section, "Jerusalem," names ground of another sort, the kind that is the vehicle of the metaphor. There are two Jerusalems also: the one "in Judy londe" (937), the other—the referent anagogically—where the author of the *Apocalypse*, whom the poet calls the "apostel John" (named in VII for the only time on the left "leaf"), saw the Lamb throned in glory (835-86). The historical Jerusalem, although far away "in Judee" (922), is continuous with the "grounde" that swallowed up the historical child (10). She was the wrong ground of the dreamer's happiness exactly because she could lose her place in this way. ("Blysse" *in malo* can alternate with "bale" [373]).[44] As geography, then, Jerusalem harks back to the left side of the poem.

In section VI, the dreamer blames the maiden for his grief ("My precios perle dotӡ me gret pyne" [330]). She responds that he is actually accusing God ("Deme Dryӡtyn, euer hym adyte" [349]), when it is not his place to argue: "Deme now þyself if þou con dayly / As man to God wordeӡ schulde heue" (313-14). She claims he is braying (346), chiding (353), making a "dyne" (339). To argue— promote a judgment—is one sense of "demen," the link-word in VI. Judgment in one sense cannot get beyond experience: you believe nothing, says the maiden, "bot ӡe hit syӡe" (308). The correlated stanza-group, XV,[45] returns to the dreamer's ability to "remen for rauþe wythouten reste" (858). In contrast to him, however, the 144,000 brides never think "of mote," 'dispute' (855), because they do not depend upon experience; they "þurӡoutly hauen cnawyng" (859), and consequently they sing. The left "leaf" insists on historical knowledge and the need to tame it, the right on anagogical. In XV, the "hue from heuen" (873), before it is followed by a "nwe songe" (882), recalls the dreamer's frenzied disapproval in VI. Such disagreement is captured by the link-word in XV, "neuerþeles," which in its *sensus malus* of "however" signals a retort. *In bono* it means the absence of diminution: "Lasse of blysse may non vus bryng ...," "neuer oneʒ honour [is] ʒet neuer þe les" (853, 864). Because in the flesh no one can experience this stability, knowledge of it comes only at God's initiative (893). God's ordaining in this fashion, which combines judgment and will and has, in the eternal present, no need of inference, is the second meaning of "deme" back in VII. In this *sensus bonus*, "Al lys in hym to dyʒt and deme" (360).[46]

Stanza-groups V and XVI are unified by the topos of enclosures. To the fatherly worry in the later section that the child should have to sleep out of doors (925-34), the maiden responds that the Lamb has brought her to the New Jerusalem. *In bono*, "mote," the link-word, names this city. The brides are not "moteleʒ" or "wythouten mote," then, in the sense of having no place to go. Home to "a pakke of joly juele" (929), this city is metaphorically a jewel box. In the earlier section, denying the dreamer's statement that she had simply vanished (his "out of daweʒ" [282] perhaps anticipating already the out-of-doors), the maiden refers repeatedly to jewel boxes. She tells him she is "in cofer ... comly clente," a proper "forser" for the dreamer himself. The "kynde" of this "kyste" is the body of Christ (259, 263, 271). (The Lamb, that is, is a coffer within a coffer.) She takes her metaphor here from the "perle" her father called her (241), confessing himself "a joyleʒ juelere" (252). *Sub specie aeternitatis*, the father had set his heart upon something bound to "flower and fail" (270), and the child's metaphor construes this as cupidity. "It is to be noted," Pamela Gradon has written, "that the refrain of this section with its play on the word 'jueler' underlines the theme, for the jeweller *possesses* his jewel" (p. 208). Cupidity, the stain that makes the "ioyfol jueler" inadmissible to the Kingdom (299), is "mote" *in malo*, the brides being "clene wythouten mote" (972).

"Jueler" has its *sensus bonus*, however. While the earthly jeweler is a collector, the good jeweler makes his gems to be what they are.[47] Through his own "kynde" Christ turns the failing rose into "a perle of prys" (272). In fact, he has made the jeweler himself (274). Where the earthly collector caters to his own satisfaction ("prynces paye" [1]), the Lamb suffers "for maneʒ sake" (940). The maiden became a pearl, matching in her spotlessness the New Jerusalem ("mote wythouten moote" [948]), because the Lamb chose to suffer in the earthly Jerusalem, making "oure pes ... at ene" (953).

Sections IV and XVII are both preoccupied with gems. In IV these are pearls, and, with the exception of the "wonder perle" (221) set in the middle of the maiden's breast, they do not beggar the imagination. Although the maiden no longer exists as an object of experience, the description of the glowing, richly adorned child does not subvert itself as a representation. (It will be the maiden who declares that the dreamer's senses are deceiving him.) By contrast, the New Jerusalem is derealized. To describe a single diamond as big enough to support a city, for instance, is simultaneously to deny that the stone or the city exists in time.

While the vast jewels on the right wing principally uplift and sustain, the pearls in section IV bind the maiden's linen (198-99, 203-04, 217) and enclose her hair.[48] They suggest confinement—the father's unwillingness to let the daughter go—in a section studded with the imagery of openings, openings that have been closed up, waistbands, and hems. ("Hemme" occurs in IV and XVII, and nowhere else in the poem.) Because the dreamer is happy that he has now found the maiden (283), it is the child herself, rather than simply her kirtle, that the dreamer would have "al vmbepy3te," a "precios pyece in perle3 py3t." (192). Setting something within boundaries is the *sensus malus* carried by "py3t." Yet when the dreamer, first spotting the maiden, says that "Perle3 py3te of ryal prys / Þere mo3t mon by grace haf sene" (193-94), "py3te" very likely means "chosen" (rather than "set" or "adorned"); and the *sensus bonus* that turns *py3t* into *pyked* (1036) means that the child, among the many who have been called, is one of the "fewe" who are "myke3" (572). "Apostel John," the link-word in XVII, has its opposing senses also. *In malo* it names the narrator himself,[49] whose "gostly drem" for the space of this section and the next coincides with John's; yet he will become again part of the church militant, still to struggle with his sins.

Sections III and XVIII are connected by rivers. For the first three stanzas of the earlier group, the dreamer follows the stream—in the direction of its source, as matters turn out. Although the bed of the stream is lit with jewels, the many-colored glow does not in itself confound human vision. The section ends with several lines reporting astonishment, but the paralysis comes with the dreamer's sight of the shining child. The source of this stream is given in XVIII, where the dreamer sees God enthroned: "A reuer of þe trone þer ran outry3te / Wat3 bry3ter þen boþe þe sunne and mone." (1055-56). The river—not only the source but the anagogical meaning of the finite stream—swirls through the streets and out of the city, where its incomparable light illumines its banks (1057-60, 1072-76). Now it is the light itself, bright enough to destroy the bodily senses, that ravishes the dreamer (1081-92).[50]

As section III began, pleasure was building in the dreamer as he followed the valley. He had the good "fortune" (129), he said, to be increasingly happy: "Þe wy3 to wham her [that is, Fortune's] wylle ho

wayneʒ / Hytteʒ to haue ay more and more." (131-32). Fortune—
change and chance ("Hytteʒ to haue")—is the extent of human experience; and by the end of the section, the link-word "more and more"
described increasing *pain* (brought on by the first sight of the child
[179-80]). *In malo*, then, "more and more" signifies increase, but
subject to time, space, history.[51] This changeableness of fortune is part
of the *sensus malus* of "mone," the link-word in the later group. "An-
vnder mone" (1068, 1081, 1092) are found decay and generation. The
"maynful mone" (1093), executrix of fortune, nonetheless loses its
power in eternity (1069-70).[52] There, "mone" in its good sense is
metaphoric for a kind of periodicity without birth or death: the twelve
trees of life on the brim of the glorious river "renowleʒ nwe in vche a
mone" (1080). In the New Jerusalem, change—articulation between
one thing and another—may amount to merely the logical condition
for meaning.

Section II represents the suspension of the will, section XIX the
satisfaction of it. The arrest of appetite occurs occasionally for perhaps
everyone, but the fulfillment of it is not a possibility in this life. The
sensus malus of "delyt" (the link-word in XIX) is the "wely wyse" (101)
in which the dreamer wanders through the landscape in the earlier
section. Contemplating any object with detachment from desire (if
this is possible) makes of it an art object, in one sense. And so section
II attributes an interruption of the dreamer's mourning ("The adub-
bemente of þo downeʒ dere / Garten my goste al greffe forʒete" [85-
86])[53] to an artificial landscape. He not only makes metaphors of
tapestry (71-72) and music (91-92); he puts blue trunks and silver
leaves on trees, pearls for gravel, crystal for granite. Thus, he represents the natural as reproduced.[54]

Section XIX, on the other hand, describes "delyt" *in bono*, the life
with which the company of the Lamb is fed: "How þay wyth lyf wern
laste and lade." (1146). This joy expresses itself in praise of the Lamb
(1117-26), for it has been bought at the his own cost: "Bot a wounde ful
wyde and weete con wyse / Anende hys hert, þurʒ hyde torente."
(1135-36). And I suggest that "adubbement," the link-word in II that
means *in malo* simply the spendor that distracts the dreamer, has as its
good sense this wounded side of the Lamb. The marks of slaughter,
drawn from Chapter 5 of the *Apocalypse*, have been attributed by the
poet to the Lamb in triumph, based on Chapter 14.[55] While readers of
Pearl have been warned against taking "adubbement" to mean *dub* or
dubbing,[56] "adubben" in Middle English clearly means "to confer
knighthood upon";[57] and Godefroy defines "adoubement" as "action
d'armer chevalier," "armure de chevalier." The poet's insistence on
adubbement as "splendor" or "adornment" in II can merely suppress,
not extinguish, its relevance to knighthood. It seems that he only

defers this. The knight's equipment in *Pearl* is the highly vulnerable hide of the Lamb, the human nature of Christ, as in *Piers Plowman* Jesus will joust in "pers armes, In his helm and in his haberion, *humana natura*."[58] On the other hand, all the hardness that would make such equipment conventionally serviceable seems to have been displaced backwards to the largely inorganic garden in section II.

Sections I and XX correlate, of course, as the entrance into the dream and the exit from it. The narrator enters by virtue of "a slepyng-slaȝte" (59). His own sudden movement (1169-70) terminates the vision. Where stanza-groups II and XIX focus on either the suspension of the will or the enjoyment in eternity of the object finally adequate to it, the groups at the extremities of the two "panels" take up a will that is not only active but limited in its objects to those of daily experience. The narrator's "wylle" is thus "wreched" (56). The first group lacks a moral context; the last, however, describes the essential question of whether the narrator will prefer another's good to his own. At the end it is enough for him that his child is "to þat Prynseȝ paye" (1188); and he tries, with less difficulty over the course of time, or so he reports (1201-04), to conform his own will to the divine will.

As his vision ends, the narrator's own "paye" is, for the moment at least, disappointed: "Me payed ful ille to be outfleme ..." (1177). This dissatisfaction metonymic for a human appetite unconformed to "þat Prynseȝ paye" is "paye" *in malo*. Such is the narrator's restlessness as the poem begins: hopeless brooding, he laments, "dotȝ bot þrych my hert þrange, / My breste in bale bot bolne and bele" (17-18). "Prynces paye" (1) is here metaphoric for his own. Through likening his daughter to a pearl and himself to a royal collector, he tries to diffuse the knowledge that this satisfaction has evaporated. He would like to make a virtue of necessity, understand the death of one lovely living thing as the condition for the birth of other ones (25-26); but behind the strategic metaphors there was a person, and he has a terribly hard time withdrawing his love. Moreover, to teach him of the comfort "of Kryst" (55), nature appears to be all he has. (By XX he will have had the divine assistance of his dream, no matter that he interrupted it.) In the earlier section, his precious pearl is now "wythouten spotte" only *in malo* : her "color" (22) *had* been flawless, and now it is nowhere.

Where the poem opens with the wheat harvest and the feast that celebrates the bodily assumption of the Virgin into heaven, it closes with bread and the consecration of it into the body of Christ. The dreamer's accusation of another ("O moul ... " [23]) comes to be balanced by self-accusation, criticism that he takes into himself when he identifies himself with the welfare of the pearl (1189-200). If his self-criticism does not clear itself of resentment altogether,[59] that is because he remains, as he must, the "homly hyne" (1210), not yet "wythouten spot" in the Church Triumphant. And the end for him may hardly be in sight (585-88). For the time being, be must make do with a knowledge far short of vision. Where the poem begins with a bauble from the East, it ends with a certain flatness, like the wafer itself, that appears "Oute of oryent" for the congregation in a much homelier sense, as the priest raises it above the altar.

The round wafer has long been recognized in *Pearl*'s own concatenated form. The poem in its simultaneity, that is, becomes something to be seen. This one sort of architecture may not exclude another—a form nearly as significant thematically, for it offers a sort of figure for the opposition between time and eternity. As diptych, *Pearl* uses form to reorganize its content and thus at points, perhaps, to reilluminate it. And in the tensions between its "panels," the poem may have served as something concrete in its own way, on which an uncertain faith might fix and that devotion might surround.

Notes

1.   Certain indications of a chiastic structure have already been noticed. James Milroy points out "the recurrence of certain imagery motifs at points roughly equidistant from beginning and end" ("*Pearl* : The Verbal Texture and the Linguistic Theme," *Neophilologus* 55 [1971]: 203). Cf. C. O. Chapman, "Numerical Symbolism in Dante and the *Pearl*," *Modern Language Notes* 54 (1939): 257.

2.   Cf. W. A. Davenport: "Reference backwards is made both by the recurrence of central ideas...and by the simpler echoing of earlier phrases and images...." [*The Art of the* Gawain-*Poet* (London: Athlone Press, 1978), p. 49].

3.   Cf. Davenport, *Art*, p. 21.

4.   For some description of the unfolding of the poem, see Lynn Staley Johnson, *The Voice of the* Gawain-*Poet* (Madison: University of Wisconsin Press, 1984), pp. 162-77; Piero Boitani, *English Medieval Narrative in the Thirteenth and Fourteenth Centuries*, tr. J. K. Hall (Cambridge: Cambridge University Press, 1982), p. 107; Pamela Gradon, *Form and Style in Early English Literature* (London: Methuen, 1971), pp. 207-11; Louis Blenkner, "The Theological Structure of *Pearl*," rpt. *The Middle English* Pearl: *Critical Essays*, ed. John Conley (Notre Dame: University of Notre Dame Press, 1970) esp. pp. 225, 229-30, 248; A. R. Heiserman, "The Plot of *Pearl*," *PMLA* 80 (1965): 164-71; and Chapman, Numerical Symbolism," pp. 257-58.

5.   *Pearl* will be quoted throughout from the edition of E. V. Gordon (Oxford: Clarendon Press, 1953).

6.   See Ian Bishop, Pearl *in its Setting* (Oxford: Blackwell, 1968), pp. 29-30.

7.   See W. H. Schofield, "The Nature and Fabric of *The Pearl*," *PMLA* 19 (1904): 162; Blenkner, "The Pattern of Traditional Images in *Pearl*," *Studies in Philology* 68 (1971): 26-27; Bishop, *Setting*, pp. 33-34.

8.   John V. Fleming, "The Centuple Structure of *The Pearl*," in *The Alliterative Tradition in the Fourteenth Century*, ed. Bernard S. Levy and Paul E. Szarmach (Kent, Ohio: Kent State University Press, 1981), p. 82; P. M. Kean, "Numerical Composition in *Pearl*," *Notes and Queries* ns 12 (1965): 51.

9.   Work on chiastic stucture (ring composition or *emboîtement*) in classical epic and medieval literature has been conveniently reviewed by Lee Patterson, "'For the Wyves love of Bathe': Feminine Rhetoric and Poetic Resolution in the *Roman de la Rose* and the *Canterbury Tales*," *Speculum* 58 (1983): 670-71.

10.   Cf. P. M. Kean: "In *Pearl*, with its wide theme of the meaning of mortality, its place in the divine scheme, and the moral problems it sets the individual who experiences its sorrows, [the author] comes nearest to qualifying as a devotional poet" [*The* Pearl: *An Interpretation* (New York: Barnes and Nobles, 1967), p. 242].

11.   Thomas Aquinas, *Summa theologiae* Ia.1.10 [ed. Thomas Gilby (London:

Eyre and Spottiswood, 1964), p. 38]. The anagogical sense raises the mind to invisible things, from the terrestrial to the heavenly Jerusalem, from history to that which limits it, teaching that part of Christian dogmatics which is called "eschatological" [Henri de Lubac, *Exégèse médiévale: les quatre sens de l'Écriture* (Paris: Aubier, 1959), pp. 1.621-33. For discussion of the poet's various means of achieving an anagogical sense, see, for example, H. V. Hendrix, "Reasonable Failure: *Pearl* Considered as Self-Consuming Artifact of 'Gostly Porpose'," *Neuphilologische Mitteilungen* 86 (1985): 462-65; Anne Schotter, "Vernacular Style and the Word of God: The Incarnational Art of *Pearl*," in *Ineffability: Naming the Unnamable from Dante to Beckett*, ed. Peter S. Hawkins and A. H. Schotter (New York: AMS, 1984), pp. 25-26, 29-30; Theodore Bogdanos, *Pearl: Image of the Ineffable* (University Park: Pennsylvania State University Press, 1983), pp. 11-12, 54-55; A. C. Spearing, *The Gawain-Poet: A Critical Study* (Cambridge: Cambridge University Press, 1970), p. 156; Bishop, *Setting*, pp. 51-61; W. S. Johnson, "The Imagery and Diction of *The Pearl* : Toward an Interpretation," *ELH* 20 (1953): 161-80; and D. W. Robertson, Jr., "The Pearl as a Symbol," *Modern Language Notes* 65 (1950): 160.

12.   The *locus classicus* within Christian tradition of the exegetical device of the two senses is Augustine, *De doctrina Christiana* 3.25 [ed. Joseph Martin, Corpus Christianorum Series Latina (Turnholt: Brepols, 1962), p. 98]. Readers of *Pearl* have noticed that at least some of the link-words embody sharply different senses. See, e.g., Edward Wilson, "Word Play and the Interpretation of *Pearl*," *Medium Ævum* 40 (1971): 126, 132; and J. C. McGalliard, "Links, Language, and Style in *The Pearl*," in *Studies in Language, Literature, and Culture of the Middle Ages and Later*, ed. E. Bagby Atwood and Archibald A. Hill (Austin: University of Texas Press, 1969), p. 283.

13.   Diptychs—hinged pieces of wood covered with wax on the inner surfaces—were familiar in the later Middle Ages as the piece of equipment on which authors often composed first drafts: See Wilhelm Wattenbach, *Das Schriftwesen im Mittelalter*, 3rd ed. (Leipzig: S. Hirzel, 1896), pp. 51-89. From at least the third century, an intercessory prayer, a form of litany, occupied part of the mass. Who precisely was included, where and how the prayer was spoken and by whom, differed from one rite to another and from the Western Church to the Eastern. The diptych, the material object widely connected with this prayer, lent itself to litany because of its earlier use as a notebook, perhaps, or because of the custom, in the case of consular diptychs, of listing on the inner surface in chronological order the names of all the consuls of Rome. Since it followed the recitation of names from diptychs, the prayer that survives to this day was called the *super nomina* or the *super diptichia*. And even after Charlemagne suppressed the Gallican practice of reading aloud from the diptychs the names of those living and dead in the faith, the diptychs survived in closely related, if not always liturgical, forms: as lists now referred to in memory by a priest, as altarpieces for the edification of the faithful (with the carvings, most frequently in ivory, that had decorated the exteriors now transferred to the inner surfaces of the panels), as devotional objects imitating such altarpieces for private use, or as monastic necrologies and obituaries. On the liturgical use of diptychs, see Fernand Cabrol, "Diptyques (Liturgie)," *Dictionnaire d'archaeologie chrétienne et liturgie* (Paris: Letourzey et Ané, 1907-), 4.1046-94. While liturgical use of the diptychs apparently ended ca. 1100 in the West, their connection with the *liber vitae* of the Apocalypse was remembered until at least the seventeenth century in England (see the *OED*, s.v.).

14.   See, e.g., Koechlin, *Les ivoires gothiques français* (Paris: Picard, 1924) for French diptychs from the end of the 13th century (Koechlin No. 37) and the first quarter of the 14th (Koechlin No. 234).

15. The dreamer describes the maiden's "vysayge" as "whyt as playn yuore." "Playn" here, as in *Cleanness* 1531, where the detached hand comes to write "vpon þe playn wowe" [ed. J. J. Anderson (Manchester: Manchester University Press, 1977)], evidently means "unembellished" [*Middle English Dictionary* s.v. , 3(a)]. In fact, carved ivory was usually painted rather than left plain.

16. Georg Swarzenski, "A Gothic Ivory Diptych," *Bulletin of the Fogg Museum of Art* 10 (1947): 183.

17. See *Transformations of the Court Style: Gothic Art in Europe, 1270 to 1330* (Providence: Department of Art, Brown University, 1977): 48.

18. Koechlin, *Les ivoires*, 1:162. On ivory diptychs, see also O. M. Dalton, *Catalogue of the Ivory Carvings of the Christian Era...in the Department of British and Medieval Antiquities and Ethnography in the British Museum* (London: British Museum and Longmans, 1909); Margaret H. Longhurst, *Catalogue of Carvings in Ivory*, 2 pts. (London: Victoria and Albert Museum, 1927-29); and J. O. Westwood, *A Descriptive Catalogue of the Fictile Ivories in the South Kensington Museum* (London, 1876).

19. Koechlin, *Les ivoires*, 1.309.

20. French, end of the 13th century [Victoria and Albert (V & A) 211-1865].

21. French, 14th century [British Library (BL) M&LA 56, 6-23, 86]. In a diptych from Cologne (1330-40), Mary holds a small cross in a Madonna scene on the left panel as if in anticipation of the Crucifixion on the right (V&A A.555-1910).

22. Cologne, ca. 1340 (V&A 235-1867). In a French diptych from the end of the 14th century (Koechlin No. 823), an Entry into Jerusalem occupies the lower register on the left panel. The usual gates of the city have been omitted. These seem to be supplied by the prominent hellgate in the Harrowing that fills the lower register on the right. As the eye moves from left to right, one entry by Christ is evidently to be understood retrospectively as the type of another one.

23. Koechlin No. 37. The sequence runs from the top down on the left panel, then from the top down on the right. But within this sequence, the Adoration is placed after the Flight into Egypt.

24. BL M&LA 55, 12-1, 34. Instances of mere balance are very numerous. For example, in this same diptych, the Virgin is made the center of both the Ascension on the left and the Pentecost on the right. In another carving, a kneeling Longinus in a Crucifixion balances the kneeling king in an Adoration (French 14th century; Dalton No. 298). In an English (?) carving from the first half of the 14th century, the pole used in the Flagellation on the left panel occupies the same position as the vertical beam of the Cross on the right (V&A, 300-1866). In a French piece from midcentury, two angels in the recesses of the arcading on the left panel bring a crown to the Madonna; two angels symmetrically placed on the right in a Crucifixion carry discs representing the sun and the moon (BL M&LA 56, 6-23, 67; cf. Dalton No. 269 and V&A 234-1867—both fourteenth century French). Elsewhere, a disc with the Agnus Dei held by John the Baptist is the mirror image of the wheel held on the opposite leaf by St. Catherine (French, 14th century, V&A A39-1923). In a Northern Italian ivory from late in the 14th or early in the 15th century (V&A A.566-1910), the great crush of people present in a Death of the Virgin scene on the left panel is

balanced on the right by no fewer than ten angels playing instruments crowded into the top of a Coronation of the Virgin.

25.   V&A A.553-1910. Similar tensions appear to run up and down all the registers of this carving. In the middle band, for example, an Escape into Egypt just to the left of center plays off against a Resurrection (Christ's stepping out of the tomb) carved just to the right of center.

26.   Cologne, about 1310-20 (V&A 6824-1858). In another diptych (French, first half of the 14th century, V&A 237 C-1867), the posture of the Christ child facing the three kings at the extreme lower left is symmetrical with his posture as he is turned towards Simeon in a Presentation on the right panel. This may bring secular power into tension with spiritual.

27.   BL 56 6-23 58. The upper register carries the Flagellation, Christ's carrying the cross, and the Crucifixion. The middle register, also from left to right, carries four scenes with Judas and then the Arrest. The lower register includes the Deposition, the Entombment, and the *Noli.*

28.   Koechlin No. 819

29.   The Cloisters 1970.324.8a,b.

30.   Koechlin No. 250.

31.   Second third of the 14th century (Koechlin No. 295).

32.   Fourteenth century (Koechlin No. 52).

33.   Koechlin No. 338. Cf. Koechlin No. 453.

34.   Koechlin No. 370.

35.   V&A A553-1910. From left to right, the upper register includes the Annunciation, Nativity, Christ's carrying his cross, and the Crucifixion. The middle register comprises the Presentation, Flight into Egypt, and the appearance to the Marys. The lower register includes the Death of the Virgin, Coronation, Flagellation, and Agony in the Garden.

36.   Among the exceptions are a mid14th-century French diptych with a Madonna and child on the left, St. Catherine trampling on the Emperor Maxentius on the right (V&A 4-1872), another from earlier in the century with a Coronation on the left and a scene of St. Lawrence being blessed by a bishop on the right (Koechlin No. 526), another of about the same period with a Crucifixion on the left, St. Margaret issuing from the back of a monster on the right (Dalton No. 279), and another with the Virgin, the Magdalene, and St. Catherine on the left, and St. Barbara (?), St. Agnes, and St. Margaret on the right (BL 56 6-23 83). Perhaps the chronological disparity between the subjects, drawn from different Christian ages, overwhelmed the convention of the superiority of the right-hand panel. However, in the Wilton Diptych (not ivory, of course), Madonna and Child are on the right panel, Richard II is on the left.

37.   See Cabrol, "Diptyques," col. 1090.

38.　See Margaret H. Longhurst, *English Ivories* (London: Putnam's, 1926),: Plates 49, 50. Longhurst assigns both to the middle of the 15th century. The latter carving does include an Adoration among the scenes on the left leaf and an Annunciation among the scenes on the right.

39.　See, e.g., BL 56, 6-23 84, and BL 56, 6-23 82.

40.　V&A A554-1910. On the other hand, leaving the question of the selection of episodes out of account, the order here is simply chronological.

41.　But see O.D. Macrae-Gibson, "*Pearl* : The Link-Words and the Thematic Structure," *Neophilologus* 52 (1968) : 59-60.

42.　Cf. Kean, The Pearl: *An Interpretation*, p. 189; and W. O. Evans, "'Cortaysye' in Middle English," *Mediaeval Studies* 29 (1967): 143, 154-55.

43.　See T. A. Reisner, "The 'Cortaysye' Sequence in *Pearl*: A Legal Interpretation," *Modern Philology* 72 (1978): 401.

44.　"Blysse" appears to be univocal. Its sense, good or evil, depends upon the object of happiness.

45.　Section XV, of course, includes one stanza more than the usual five. For recent discussion, see Fleming, "Centuple Structure," pp. 81-89, and D. M. Finkelstein, "The *Pearl*-Poet As Bezalel," *Mediaeval Studies* 35 (1973): 427-32.

46.　Gradon, *Form and Style*, describes the poet's use of *deme* as "a play on the ideas of man's judgement and God's ordaining"(p. 209).

47　Outside the correlated sections, there is another and probably closer *sensus bonus* for "jueler"—the merchant who is ready to sell everything to buy the Pearl of Great Price (729-32).

48.　Mabel Day, however, took line 210 to mean, 'Her hair floated loosely round her': "Two Notes on *Pearl*," *Medium Ævum* 3 (1934): 242. Schofield (p. 183) compared lines 210-14 with several lines in the *Roman de la Rose*. Yet there is evidently nothing comparable in the earlier description to the imagery of binding or confinement.

49.　"… Being merely human, … [the dreamer] cannot be anything but inadequate to the role he is called on to play. He is no John the Divine …": Spearing, *Gawain-Poet*, p. 105. An opposition between two Johns—John the Baptist announcing the historical Christ, John the Divine envisioning Christ in glory—is common in the diptychs: see, e.g., Dalton No. 246 (English, mid14th-century) and V&A A555-1910 (French, same period). Cf. *Pearl* 817-40.

50.　The dreamer's metaphor for this is his standing "as stylle as dased quayle" (1085). There is a comparable figure back on the left "panel," with the dreamer's stillness (182) making him "as hende as hawk in halle" (184). But this phrase occurs a few lines into section IV.

51.　*In bono* "more and more" names ever increasing fruition, an impossibility on earth. The maiden refers in XVI to bliss that "schal euer encres" (959).

52.   In the same lines the poet also makes the moon metaphoric for moral filth, perhaps the more important part of its *sensus malus*. For further discussion of the two senses of "mone," see Marie Borroff, *"Pearl* 's 'Maynful Mone': Crux, Simile, and Structure," in *Acts of Interpretation: The Text in Its Context 700-1600: Essays on Medieval and Renaissance Literature in Honor of E. Talbot Donaldson,* ed. Mary J. Carruthers and Elizabeth D. Kirk (Norman, Oklahoma: Pilgrim Books, 1982), p. 169. See also Macrae-Gibson, "Link Words," for a sensitive discussion of the poet's use of "mone" to hint that the vision is approaching its close (p. 62).

53.   Blenkner rightly remarks that it is only after this section that there is a "revival of will" ("Theological Structure," p. 245).

54.   "Human art supplants nature as comforter ...": Bogdanos, "Ineffable," p. 48. Cf. Elizabeth Petroff, "Landscape in *Pearl* : The Transformation of Nature," *Chaucer Review* 16 (1981): 187; and Nikki Stiller, "The Transformation of the Physical in the Middle English *Pearl,*" *English Studies* 63 (1982): 405. Gradon adduces earlier literature to make it clear that "the jeweled streams do not necessarily indicate the supernatural.... Nor is it necessarily a Christian paradise" (p. 204). Cf. R. J. Blanch, "Color Symbolism and Mystical Contemplation in *Pearl,*" *Nottingham Medieval Studies* 17 (1973): 62-63.

55.   See Rosalind Field, "The Heavenly Jerusalem in *Pearl,*" *Modern Language Review* 81 (1986): 13.

56.   McGalliard, "Links, Language," p. 283.

57.   *Middle English Dictionary,* s.v.

58.   C.20.21-22; ed. Derek Pearsall (Berkeley and Los Angeles: University of California Press, 1979), p. 320. The *Middle English Dictionary* records a figurative use of "dubben" from the *Northern Passion* that means Christ's clothing himself in human likeness.

59.   For some recent discussion of the narrator's state at the close of the poem, see A. C. Watt, *"Pearl,* Inexpressibility, and Poems of Human Loss," *PMLA* 99 (1984): 34; Bogdanos, "Ineffable," pp. 143-45; L. M. Sklute, "Expectation and Fulfillment in *Pearl,*" *Philological Quarterly* 52 (1973): 676-79; and J. P. Oakden, "The Liturgical Influence in *Pearl,*" in *Chaucer und seine Zeit: Symposion für Walter F. Schirmer,* ed. Arno Esch (Tübingen: Niemeyer, 1968), p. 337.

COURTLY LANGUAGE IN *PEARL*

CHARLOTTE GROSS

hen the bereaved narrator of *Pearl* at length encounters his lost daughter face to face in a spiritual vision, her first words to him are a stern and distant reproof: "Sir, ȝe haf your tale mysetente" (257).[1] The Pearl-Maiden of the Middle English dream-vision reproaches her earthly father for misconceiving her death as the loss of a precious pearl, and thus for willfully confounding the material and spiritual. But "ȝe haf your tale mysetente" may equally be read as an accurate comment on the narrator's use of language, for throughout the poem he consistently "tells his tale wrongly," employing a courtly rhetoric inappropriate to the "ghostly" matters that are or should be his concern. In the opening stanza of the poem, for example, he conveys his grief with the phrase "fordolked of luf-daungere" (11): like the speaker of some courtly lyric, he pines away, wounded by the power of his lady's love. At the beginning of the dream itself, he describes his spiritual *visio* as a journey "[i]n auenture þer meruayleȝ meuen" (64), as though he were embarking on a quest into a fabulous landscape of chivalric romance. The dream-vision abruptly ends when the narrator is so overcome by "luf-longyng in gret delyt" (1152) that he madly attempts to cross the barrier which separates him from the maiden, with unconscious irony vowing to swim the River of Life even if he dies in it. As these examples which frame the poem and the vision suggest, the *Pearl*-Poet uses the courtly language of lyric and romance to convey the dreamer-narrator's pitiable but often comic misapprehension of spiritual matters. The dreamer's courtly diction functions ironically, directing the attention of the audience to his over-attachment to the material world and above all to his inability to "deme" correctly—the Middle English word means both "to judge" and "to speak"—concerning things of the spirit.

If the *Pearl*-Poet uses courtly language to create a narrator who time and again reveals his spiritual ineptitude by "telling his tale wrongly," the poet also uses courtly language to convey the very religious concepts that the literal-minded dreamer has such difficulty grasping. When employed by the Pearl-Maiden, courtly diction becomes an effective vehicle for expressing spiritual truth. In her first interchange with the dreamer, for example, the maiden distinguishes between the earthly and the heavenly, explaining that what the narrator lost was "bot a rose / Þat flowred and fayled as kynde hyt gef" (269-70); that is, her body perished according to the laws of Nature, whereas the pearl, her immortal soul, dwells forever in

Paradise. The images of the rose and the pearl are used to differentiate the two distinct idyllic and courtly *loci amoeni* of the poem; the first, the pleasaunce surrounding the Pearl's grave, where flowers fade despite the dreamer's assertion to the contrary; the second, the otherworldly landscape of the vision, of which the jewelled and brilliant "adubbement" is equally courtly but everlasting.[2] This first example of courtly language pressed into the service of spiritual truth draws upon the French tradition of secular poetry, going back to the *Romance of the Rose* and the courtly lyric. Towards the end of the debate, the maiden describes her mystical marriage with Christ in courtly terms: she has been chosen as bride by "My Lombe, my Lorde, my dere juelle, / My ioy, my blys, my lemman fre" (795-96). This second use of courtly language continues the theological and exegetical tradition that imaged the individual soul as the bride of Christ, a tradition reaching back to St. Bernard's sermons *On the Song of Songs* and appearing in Middle English literature as early as the first third of the thirteenth century, with the courtly Christ-knight and lover of the *Ancrene Wisse*.[3] In using courtly diction to describe the ineffable, the *Pearl*-Poet also avails himself of the language of Scripture itself; the vision within a vision that forms the climax of the poem, for example, takes full advantage of the brilliance and majesty of Revelations 21.

The novelty of the *Pearl*-Poet's use of courtly language lies in his exploitation of an ambiguous rhetoric already associated with two opposing realities, the earthly and heavenly, to delineate and juxtapose ironically the spiritual states of his poetic *personae*.[4] Depending upon speaker and context, identical courtly diction conveys quite different significance and produces correspondingly different effects. Whereas the dreamer's inappropriate use of courtly language signals his attachment to the material world and his misapprehension of spiritual matters, the Pearl-Maiden's courtly rhetoric provides an accurate indication of her spiritual state and the most nearly adequate vehicle for the expression of the ineffable. At the same time, the similarity or even identity of courtly language and metaphor employed by the dreamer and maiden forces the audience to compare and connect earthly and heavenly loves. This latter impulse, to join rather than separate the human and divine, is characteristic of the achievement of the *Pearl*-Poet.

Pearl contains more than 500 words of French origin, a proportion comparable to that found in the works of Chaucer and Gower.[5] As such specifically religious terms as "innocens" and "bonerté" (beatitude) make clear, however, French origin is not synonymous with courtliness. If "courtly language" may be defined as a vocabulary often pertaining to love and reflecting the material conditions, social structure, and refined ideals of an aristocratic milieu, then the courtly language used by the *Pearl*-Poet derives from two discrete historical influences. The first wave of courtly language entering Middle English can in large part be attributed to the Franciscan friars, who (arriving in England in 1224) deliberately cultivated courtly and chivalric images from the Italian and Provençal in their efforts to use the vernacular English lyric as an effective missionary and devotional tool.[6] When in the Middle English lyric of the thirteenth and early fourteenth centuries Christ is represented as the "lemman" of mankind, "feir and gent," or when Mary is praised as the "heuene quene," "þat leuedy gent" or "fair" and "hende," courtly language appears in translation, in such words of Old English origin as "lemman," "quene," and "hende," or in words of French origin which entered Middle English through early Anglo-Norman influence, such as "gent."[7]

The second and later influx of courtly language into Middle English came directly from northern France and is more closely associated with an aristocratic high style. Such words of French origin as "adubbement," "dousour," "margyrye," "pensyf," and "reiateʒ" suggest the *Pearl*-Poet's familiarity with the French courtly tradition of the thirteenth and fourteenth centuries, or indeed a personal acquaintance with the international courtly culture of his age.[8] Although unambiguously secular, these French words were easily absorbed into the established Middle English courtly vocabulary, which from the first had been used in both secular and religious contexts. Judging from the Middle English lyric (which according to Ian Bishop "is indeed just the kind of poem that we might expect the author of *Pearl* to have known"), by the mid-fourteenth century the language of Christianity had been completely assimilated to the language of courtesy.[9] The courtly term "daungere," for instance, appears in a late fourteenth-century marian lyric in which the speaker says that unless he gives supreme love to the Virgin he will be guilty of "[d]aunger mad unskilfuly," unreasonable reluctance in love.[10] Indeed, even as uncourtly a poet as William Langland uses the expression "Crist of hus curtesye" to denote divine mercy and grace.[11] Thus the tradition of Middle English literature and contemporary usage made available to the *Pearl*-Poet a courtly language, containing words of both native and French origin, that might—depending upon context—signify with equal propriety either the secular or the religious.

In using courtly language as metaphor for the ineffable, the *Pearl*-Poet follows a well-established philosophical tradition. Medieval theories of linguistic symbolism begin with Augustine, whose thought on signification, according to Eugene Vance, "endured throughout the Middle Ages, even in polemical environments disposed against Augustinianism as a whole."[12] In *De doctrina Christiana*, Augustine defines a sign as "a thing which causes us to think of something beyond the impression the thing itself makes upon the senses."[13] Words are conventional signs agreed upon by men by common consent, used for the purpose of conveying emotion, sensation, or understanding (*De doc.* 2.2.3; 2.25.38). Augustine further distinguishes between the *signum proprium* or literal sign and the *signum translatum*, the figurative sign or metaphor (*De doc.* 2.10.15). For Augustine, the complexity or even obscurity of the *signum translatum* enhances rather than diminishes the expressive power of language; as he observes, "things are perceived more readily through similitudes and...[that which] is sought with difficulty is discovered with more pleasure" (*De doc.* 2.6.8). Since fallen man's knowledge of God is necessarily partial and based upon faith, perceived *per speculum in aenigmate*, metaphorical language provides the most suitable and nearly adequate signs for the ineffable. Since the confusion of Babel was redeemed in the Incarnation, figurative signs correspond accurately, if incompletely, to the realities they signify. Finally, since the signs we call words have no heuristic efficacy in themselves, signification ultimately depends upon the spiritual states of both speaker and auditor.[14] Thus while the Pearl-Maiden correctly employs courtly language as a metaphor for the ineffable, the dreamer's spiritual condition is such that he consistently misapprehends her teaching, mistaking the *signum translatum* for the *signum proprium*.

The dreamer-narrator's own inappropriate use of courtly language betrays his spiritual misorientation. In the opening stanza of *Pearl*, he superimposes a second metaphor, the pearl as courtly beloved, upon the initial conceit, the child as pearl. Ambiguous courtly overtones result:

> So rounde, so reken in vche araye,
> So smal, so smoþe her sydeȝ were,
> ....
> I dewyne, fordolked of luf-daungere
> Of þat pryuy perle wythouten spot (5-6; 11-12).

Noble in each setting—or is it dress?—the pearl has "sydeȝ smal," a conflation of the lyric and romance formula for a lovely and beloved woman, "sidis...long, ...myddyl small."[15] Suggested by this ambiguous description and reinforced by mention of the "erbere" (9), our impression of a courtly love-relation is confirmed by the key term "luf-daungere." Derived from the Old French *dangier*, itself from the Latin *dominiarium*, "luf-daungere" is glossed by Gordon as simply "the power of love," a power which wounds the narrator and causes him to pine away.[16] With greater precision, W.R.J. Barron translates "love-frustration." Arguing that the Middle English "daungere" here denotes not "dominion, power" but rather "reluctance, resistance" or "withholding," he concludes that the narrator is "grievously wounded by the frustration of [his] love for [his] own, flawless pearl."[17] This translation conveys the intensity and quality of the speaker's emotion but obscures the force of the courtly metaphor, for "luf-daungere" is grammatically an attribute of the pearl itself. More recently, Claude Luttrell has translated "luf-daungere" as "sweet thraldom." Comparing the Middle English word to the French courtly expressions "dous dangier" and "amoureus dangier," he argues that while alive the metaphorical lady exerted a sweet dominion, the *loss* of which wounds the narrator.[18] If we bear in mind that "luf-daungere" is a deliberately ambiguous courtly metaphor reflecting the narrator's spiritual state, both senses (i.e. dominion/resistance) are suggestive. As Luttrell's "sweet thraldom" the term functions ironically, suggesting that the narrator is not, as he would believe, in a state of deprivation, but rather continues under the dominion of the material. When he enters the jewelled landscape of the vision, for example, it is precisely its rich "adubbement" that assuages his ghostly grief (lines 85-86). Barron's thesis that "luf-daungere" refers to withheld love is even more provocative, for in this case the arbitrary "daungere" of a courtly lady acts as a singularly inappropriate metaphor for the experience of bereavement, revealing the dreamer's gross misconception of God's will.

According to this analysis, the *Pearl*-Poet uses courtly rhetoric implicitly to condemn the dreamer-narrator, whose rejection of the comfort of reason and religion is made clear by his inappropriate rhetoric and conceits. Nevertheless, the dreamer's courtly language has a more positive function in the larger context of the poem. First, the implied courtly relation prepares the audience for the central debate, in which the maiden possesses the authority of a Philosophia or a Holichurche. When the dreamer and maiden meet, the metaphor of his initial lament ironically becomes the reality of his ghostly vision: she is "a mayden of menske," he a self-proclaimed "blose" (162,911). Most importantly, the *Pearl*-Poet's courtly language evokes the invariable triad of the courtly love-lyric: a lady identified with ideal perfection, a lover who aspires to and is ennobled by this perfection, and the inviolable distance separating the two.[19] Thus the courtly relation introduced in the opening stanza of *Pearl* provides both a framework for juxtaposing the earthly and heavenly and a rationale for the impulse to bridge these two worlds.[20] The *Pearl*-Poet uses courtly language to create a tension between these opposing tendencies: whereas the ironic counterpoint of the dreamer's and maiden's rhetoric emphasizes the distinction between the material and spiritual, the maiden's use of courtly language as a vehicle for the ineffable connects the earthly and heavenly. In conclusion, I shall look more closely at examples of both uses of courtly language in *Pearl*.

Section V of *Pearl* opens with the maiden's explicit condemnation of the dreamer's rhetoric as "vncortayse" (303). To think to join her in Paradise, she explains, is to deny the fruit of the Fall, for each man must suffer death before God will judge if he may cross the stream, "Er ouer þys dam hym Dryȝtyn deme" (324). In an ironic counterpoint effected by *concatenatio*, the dreamer maintains his pose as courtly lover, attributing to the maiden (not God) sole power of "deming" and sole responsibility for his continuing existence: "Demeȝ þou me...my swete, / To dol agayn, þenne I dowyne" (325-26). The entire stanza (325-36) is a plaint in which the dreamer persists in viewing and addressing the maiden as the object of a metaphorical courtly love. Employing the lyric *topos* of the despairing and exiled lover, he concludes that men will speak of ("deme,"—336) his plight as "durande doel," enduring grief. The link-word "deme" is thus progressively debased, from "divine judgment" to "courtly sovereignty" to "human speech," and specifically to that mode of speech which would use the phrase "durande doel"—courtly rhetoric. The dreamer's rhetoric moreover provides ironic commentary on his spiritual condition: when, for example, he asks, "What serueȝ tresor, bot gareȝ men grete?" (331), the comparison of the lady to "tresor" is in the tradition of the Middle English love-lyric, but the question itself echoes the homiletic commonplace that the poor are without care. The courtly relation proposed in this stanza results from the dreamer's "misdeeming" in both senses of the word and stands in ironic contrast to the maiden's subsequent descripition of her spiritual marriage with Christ, the rhetorical propriety of which rests on the authority of Scripture and traditional exegisis: "He calde me to hys bonerté: / 'Cum hyder to me, my lemman swete, / For mote ne spot is non in þe'" (762-64).[21]

A second example of ironic counterpoint effected by *concatenatio* occurs in section XIII, immediately after the maiden has related the parable of the vineyard and directly enjoined the dreamer to forsake the world "[a]nd porchace þy perle maskelles" (744), the pearl of great price, here symbolizing the kingdom of heaven. "O maskeleȝ perle," he responds, reclaiming the epithet in courtly apostrophe, "what position do you hold in heaven?"[22] Both question and rhetoric are strikingly inappropriate, for in the lengthy vineyard parable the maiden had eschewed courtly language to teach·that all men are "homly hyne" and receive equal heavenly reward; coming from the elaborately-adorned maiden, the parable is a particularly stinging rebuke to the dreamer's misconception of heavenly hierarchy. The ironic effect of the *concatenatio* ("perle maskelles" / "maskeleȝ perle") is reinforced by a sudden efflorescence of courtly rhetoric in the rest of the stanza (745-56). Employing a common courtly trope, the dreamer declares that the maiden's beauty surpasses the creations of both nature and art and concludes with praise of her "angel-hauyng so clene corte3" (714).[23]

Nor does he recognize that his courtly hyperbole is in fact litotes: the maiden not only *has* an "angelic demeanor," but she *is* an angel. In sum, then, the dreamer's use of inappropriate courtly rhetoric to describe his plight, to pose questions about "ghostly" matters, and even to respond to a Christian imperative shows little progress in spiritual understanding. This paucity of progress is summed up by the narrator's last request in the dream-vision, "let me se þy blysful bor" (964). Joined with "bor," which inevitably recalls the alliterative formula "burde in bour" of the secular lyric, the epithet "blysful" remains ambiguous, suggesting both earthly and heavenly joy.[24] Thus the dreamer's final plea to the maiden recalls the original ironic juxtaposition that drew attention to the disparity of their spiritual states, his assertion that she "wat3 grounde of alle my blysse" and her stichomythic reply that "My Lorde þe Lamb.../...is þe grounde of alle my blysse" (372, 407-08).

Turning to the maiden's use of courtly language to convey the ineffable, we find that *concatenatio* again draws our attention to the issue of appropriate diction. She is "maskelles" or unblemished (781) but not "makele3" or matchless (784), an epithet reserved for the Virgin. In section VIII, the maiden uses the *signa translata* of courtly rhetoric to elucidate Mary's position in heaven:

> Þat emperise al heuen3 hat3
> And vrþe and helle, in her bayly;
> Of erytage 3et non wyl ho chace,
> For ho is Quen of cortaysye. (441-44)

Significantly, the maiden does not amplify the dreamer's title for Mary, "vyrgyn flour" (426) but, instead, represents the Virgin as a powerful feudal *domina*, empress of earth, heaven, and hell. While both speak of Mary in equally courtly language, then, the dreamer chooses an image of beauty from the natural world, while the maiden stresses the Virgin's nobility and power as preface to her metaphorical presentation of "[t]he court of þe kyndom of God alyue" (445). Although Marian piety had since 1215 been a strong part of the English devotional tradition, and although the title of "queen" had been attributed to Mary in patristic times to suggest her beauty, virtue, and dignity, the *Pearl*-Poet has relatively little precedent for his use of an extended feudal and courtly metaphor. According to Rosemary Woolf, "Up to the end of the fourteenth century there are no more than eight poems extant which praise the Virgin in semi-secular style, and...[these] are also very narrowly diffused"; it is not until the fifteenth century that Marian lyrics, often in aureate style, begin to

flourish in England.[25] In Brown's collections of Middle English religious verse, the title "quen[e]" is attributed to Mary in thirteen
thirteenth-century and five fourteenth-century lyrics, where she is
variously praised as "quen in parais," "heuene quene," and "quen of
blis"—never "Quen of cortaysye."[26] Moreover, in all but three of these
lyrics the title "quen[e]" is used in passing and without amplification,
as one of several conventional formulae of praise (e.g., "maiden
bricht," "flur of alle").[27] Thus, while supported by tradition and hardly
unprecedented, the *Pearl*-Poet's use of courtly language to present
Mary as "Quen of cortaysye" is more original than has generally been
recognized.

The *Pearl*-Poet's most significant use of courtly language to
convey the ineffable appears in the maiden's assertion that "cortaysye" is the essential condition of the Kingdom of Heaven. According to her account, in the court of God's kingdom not only is Mary
"Quen of cortaysye," but each Christian soul is either "kyng... [or]
quene by cortaysye" (468); and the term "cortaysye" itself expresses
the nature of divine mercy, grace, and charity. The rhetorical problem
presented by such striking courtly metaphors for the divine is summa-
rized by A.C. Spearing, who argues that the poet "really is presenting
the transcendent heavenly order in terms of material royalty, luxury
and grandeur; it really is the case that for him an earthly kingdom is
a valid 'image...of the Kingdom...of Heaven.' And in this he is following a powerful tradition in medieval religious writing...[and]in the
medieval visual arts...."[28] Still, Spearing's iterated "really" suggests a
certain uneasiness: can courtly language and metaphor indeed be
adequate vehicles for spiritual truth? He subsequently concludes that
such rhetoric results from the presence of the naive dreamer-narrator,
a literary device that allows the *Pearl*-Poet "to find a way of simultaneously using such material images for the divine and making us
aware of their inadequacy."[29] But while some of the maiden's courtly
language is clearly guided by a need to accommodate the dreamer, her
use of the term "cortaysye" to convey the nature of grace and beatitude is more complex and far-reaching and cannot be accounted for
solely with reference to the limiting consciousness of a naive narrator.

In *Patience*, the poet equates God's "cortaysye" with divine mercy;
in *Purity*, he speaks of Christ as "þat Cortayse."[30] When used by the
Pearl-Maiden, the term "cortaysye" is not simple metaphor but a
paradoxical *aenigma*, a sign mediated through the mirror of faith.[31] The
title "Quen of cortaysye," for example, signifies not so much the
hierarchy of courtly relations first suggested by "emperise" and
"bayly" as the equality of heavenly bliss made possible by the "cortaysye" which Mary and her Son supremely represent. Members of
Christ through "cortaysye," as the maiden explains in her paraphrase

of St. Paul, the blessed delight in each other's bliss, achieving what Derek Brewer aptly calls "unity in diversity."[32] Although the idea of equality within hierarchy is illogical and paradoxical, the notion that heavenly bliss is multipled and thus equalized by love is indeed a commonplace in medieval descriptions of heaven. In *Sawles Warde*, a thirteenth-century prose allegory, love among the blessed is such that "each one derives from the other's good as much joy as from his own...[so that] each has separately as much joy as they are many."[33] In *Pearl*, each heavenly "kyng" and "quene" is so glad of the other's bliss that—were increase possible—he or she would wish five crowns to the next. Thus in the maiden's version of 1 Corinthians 12 ("Of courtaysye, as sayt3 Saynt Poule, / Al arn we membre3 of Jesu Kryst,"—457-58), "courtaysye" signifies both divine grace and the community of love which, originating in love of God, prevails among the members and spouses of Christ.[34] The dreamer speaks accurately, for once, when he says that "[c]ortayse.../ And charyté grete" (469-70) must exist in heaven. In *Pearl*, "cortaysye" provides an adequate but aenigmatic metaphor for the ineffable precisely because the term itself denotes so elusive a concept. If for the *Pearl*-Poet "cortaysye" represents an ideal of perfection never fully realized by the imperfect beings who people his worlds, and if we glimpse true "cortaysye" in his works only when God Himself becomes manifest in *Patience* and *Purity*, then the word "cortaysye" itself suggests both the gap and the connection between the earthly and heavenly realms. In a like manner, the courtly language of the dreamer and the Pearl-Maiden teaches that all men are at once household servants and precious pearls.

Notes

1.   E. V. Gordon, ed., *Pearl* (Oxford: Oxford University Press, 1953), p. 10. All quotations are from this edition and are noted parenthetically. "Mysetente" ("not given proper attention to,"hence" told wrongly"[Gordon, p.143]) indicates the intimate relation between perception, cognition, and rhetoric which is crucial to the *Pearl*-Poet's use of courtly language.

2.   Following Gordon, I read "fede" as "faded"; for a dissenting view, see Edward Vasta, *"Pearl* : Immortal Flowers and the Pearl's Decay," *JEGP* 66 (1967): 519-31. "[M]ay not be fede" (29), however, does not signify that the flowers are immortal, but merely that the speaker desires them to be so. On the *locus amoenus* topos, see Ernst Robert Curtius, *European Literture and the Latin Middle Ages*, trans. Willard Trask (New York: Harper and Row, 1953), pp. 195-200; for a useful distinction between temporal and eternal or everlasting *loci amoeni*, see James J. Wilhelm, *The Cruelest Month* (New Haven: Yale University Press, 1965), pp. 49-50.

3.   St. Bernard writes, for example, that "every soul, if it is vigilant and careful in the practice of all virtues, can...enjoy the embraces of the Bridegroom" (Sermon 57:4, 11); see Bernard of Clairvaux, *On the Song of Songs, 2 vols.* (Kalamazoo, Michigan: Cistercian Publications, 1979). On Christ as courtly lover of the soul, see *Ancrene Wisse*, ed. J .R. R. TolkienEETS 249 (Oxford: Oxford University Press, 1962), pp. 198-200.

4.   For discussion of the *Pearl*-Poet's "carefully calculated ambiguity," dependent on his "exploitation of two semantic fields" (i.e. the secular and religious) and employed to mirror the dreamer's progress, see Pamela Gradon, *Form and Style in Early English Literature* (London: Methuen & Co., 1971), pp. 199-211.

5.   Gordon, ed., *Pearl*, pp. 101-02.

6.   On the Provençal origins of Franciscan verse, see David L. Jeffrey, *The Early English Lyric and Franciscan Spirituality* (Lincoln: University of Nebraska Press, 1975), pp. 22-27; on Franciscan verse in England, see pp. 169-214. Of course, a certain number of courtly words had already entered the English language during the reign of Henry III, when after the loss of Normandy in 1204 many nobles chose to live on their English lands. For an assessment of the influence of Provençal during the period, see H. J. Chaytor, *The Troubadors and England* (Cambridge: Cambridge University Press, 1923), pp. 23-25, *et passim*.

7.   Carleton Brown, ed., *English Lyrics of the XIIIth Century* (Oxford: Clarendon, 1932), pp. 35, 62, 87. Carleton Brown, ed., *Religious Lyrics of the XIVth Century* (Oxford: Clarendon, 1924), pp. 12, 31, 29. "Gent" is first recorded in Middle English in the *Owl and the Nightingale*, dated 1189-1216 by Eric G. Stanley, ed., *The Owl and the Nightingale* (New York: Manchester University Press, 1960), p. 19.

8.   According to Gordon, "Most of the French words in *Pearl* were probably of comparatively recent adoption, and some may well have been taken by the poet himself from his own knowledge of the language..." (p. 105). On the *Pearl*-Poet's

familiarity with French literature and courtly culture, see A. C. Spearing, *The Ga-wain-Poet: A Critical Study* (Cambridge: Cambridge University Press, 1970), pp. 5-6, 15-16.

9.   Ian Bishop, Pearl *in its Setting* (Oxford: Blackwell, 1968), p. 87. Bishop refers specifically to one of the lyrics of MS. Harley 2253, "A Wayle Whyte"; it should be remembered that the Harley collection includes both secular and religious lyrics.

10.   Brown, ed., *XIVth Century*, p. 178.

11.   W. W. Skeat, ed., *Piers the Plowman*, C.XX.207 (Oxford: Oxford University Press, 1886), II, 513. For similar uses of "curtesye" by Langland, see also C. II, 20, B.XII.79, and C.XV.215.

12.   Eugene Vance, "Mervelous Signals: Poetics, Sign Theory, and Politics in Chaucer's *Troilus*," *New Literary History* 10 (1979): 296. My account of Augustine's theory of signification is indebted to Marcia Colish, *The Mirror of Language*, Revised Edition (Lincoln: University of Nebraska Press, 1983), pp. 1-54.

13.   Augustine, *On Christian Doctrine*, 2.1.1., trans. D. W. Robertson (New York: Bobbs-Merrill, 1958), p. 34. All further references will be noted parenthetically.

14.   This epistemelogical theory is set forth in Augustine's *De magistro*, 10. 32-14.46. The student of this dialogue concludes that "in order to know the truth of what is spoken, I must be taught by [H]im who dwells within....I shall love [H]im the more ardently the more I advance in learning."

15.   Rossell Hope Robbins, ed., *Secular Lyrics of the XIVth and XVth Centuries*, 2nd ed. (Oxford: Oxford University Press, 1955), p. 21. For other examples of this formula, see Gordon, ed. *Pearl*, pp. 45-46. The Harley lyrics' "Alysoun" and "Fair Maid of Ribblesdale"both have a "middel smal" (G. L. Brook, ed., *The Harley Lyrics* [Manchester: Manchester University Press, 1956], pp. 33, 38)—difficult for a pearl.

16.   Gordon, ed., *Pearl*, pp. 46, 141.

17.   W. R. J. Barron, "Luf-Daungere," in *Medieval Miscellany Presented to Eugène Vinaver*, ed. F. Whitehead, A. H. Diverres, and F. E. Sutcliffe (New York: Manchester University Press, 1965), pp. 1-18.

18.   Claude Luttrell, "The Introduction to the Dream in *Pearl*," *Medium Ævum* 47 (1978): 275-77. The expression "dous dangier" is from Guillaume de Machaut, *Le Jugement dou Roy de Behaingne* (435), "amoureus dangier" from Machaut, *La Louange des Dames* (No. 40, 16).

19.   For critical commentary, see, for example, Peter Dronke, *Medieval Latin and the Rise of European Love-Lyric*, 2nd ed. (Oxford: Clarendon, 1968), I, 3-5 *et passim*.

20.   In the essentially Platonic paradigm of the courtly lyric, the gulf between perfection and imperfection is never crossed; in *Pearl*, as in all specifically Christian writing, the Incarnation provides a bridge between the eternal and temporal. For the *Pearl*-Poet, the Redemption makes possible the connection of the earthly and heavenly; but this connection is not apprehended by the narrative *persona* until the end of the poem, when, contemplating the Eucharist, he newly defines himself as

both a "homly hyne" and "precious perle" (1211-12).

21.   Cp. *Song of Songs* 4.7-8.

22.   The dreamer asks, "Breue me, bry3t, quat kyn offys / Bere3 þe perle so maskelle3?" (755-56). For textual and interpretative discussion, see Gordon, ed., *Pearl*, pp. 72-73.

23.   As Gordon notes (p. 72), the reference to Pygmalion and Aristotle is reminiscent of the *Romance of the Rose* (16013f); for an early variant of this courtly conceit (closer in sense to *Pearl* 949-52), see Bernart de Ventadorn, "Ai, bon' amors encobida /...cui Deus formet ab sas mas" ("Ah, good and desired love, whom God fashioned with his own hands"), in Stephen G. Nichols, ed., *The Songs of Bernart de Ventadorn* (Chapel Hill: University of North Carolina Press, 1962), p. 30.

24.   See, for example, "Ichot a burde in a bour" (Brook, ed., *Harley Lyrics*, p. 31) and "þe riche leuedies in hoere bour" (Brown, ed., *XIIIth Century*, p. 85).

25.   Rosemary Woolf, *The English Religious Lyric in the Middle Ages* (Oxford: Clarendon, 1968), pp. 114, 274.

26.   See Brown, ed., *XIIIth Century*, pp. 4, 24, 25, 27-29, 37, 67, 85, 87, 91, 112, 116, 118; and Brown, ed., *XIVth Century*, pp. 8, 19, 29-31, 47, 178, 236.

27.   Brown, ed., *XIIIth Century*, p. 118. For an example of amplification, see Brown, ed., *XIV th Century*, p. 47: "Þou art quene of paradys, / Of heuene, of erthe, of al þat hys; / Þou bere þane kynge of blye / Wyþ-oute senne and sore...."

28.   Spearing, *Gawain*-Poet, p. 155.

29.   Spearing, *Gawain*-Poet, p. 156.

30.   J. J. Anderson, ed., *Patience*, (New York: Manchester University Press, 1969), v. 417, p. 45. Robert J. Menner, ed., *Purity*, (1920; rpt. New Haven: Yale University Press, 1970), v. 1097, p. 42; see also *Purity*, 1089: "And 3if clanly he [Christ] þenne com, ful cortays þerafter."

31.   Augustine defines aenigma as "an obscure allegory"; the Pauline phrase "per speculum in aenigmate" denotes both an image ("speculum") and a likeness ("aenigma"), "yet a likeness that is obscure and diffcult to perceive...suited to lead to an understanding of God in the manner that is now possible." See Augustine, *The Trinity*, 15.9.15-16, trans. Stephen McKenna (Washington, D.C.: Catholic University of America, 1963), pp. 471-72.

32.   D. S. Brewer, "Courtesy and the *Gawain*-Poet," in John Lawlor, ed., *Patterns of Love and Courtesy* (London: Edward Arnold Ltd., 1966), p. 66.

33.   "[E]uchan haueþ of oþres god ase muche murhðe as of his ahne. ...euchan haueþ sunderlepes ase feole gleadschipes as ha beoþ monie alle," *Sawles Warde*, 11.343-46 (my translations), in J. A. W. Bennett and G. V. Smithers, eds., *Early Middle English Verse and Prose*, 2nd ed. (Oxford: Clarendon, 1968), p. 258. See also Colish, *Mirror*, p. 53. The "very obscurity" of *aenigmata* enhances their accuracy, for "metaphysical signification is far better suited to express realities that are themselves intrinsically obscure...."

34.   Gordon identifies this "courtaysye" with "divine grace" (p.61), as does Spearing, *Gawain*-Poet, (p. 11). On the other hand, Brewer, "Courtesy," argues that "there is, in fact, no word in the biblical text that corresponds with courtaysye, and Paul is discussing in this passage not divine grace but unity in diversity, which might indeed be an aspect of courtesy" (p. 66). Since "unity in diversity" results from the "manifestation of the Spirit" (1 Cor. 12:7) in all members of Christ, the two interpretations seem to me complementary rather than contradictory.

35.   An earlier version of this paper was read at a session of the International Courtly Literature Society, Twenty-First Congress on Medieval Studies, Kalamazoo, Michigan. I would like to express my gratitude to Professor Robert W. Hanning of Columbia University, for his kindness in reading and commenting on the essay.

CLEANNESS AND THE TERMS OF TERROR

DAVID WALLACE

osemary Woolf has observed that the religious author who wishes to write on death cannot concentrate upon the moment of death itself, since "this scarcely exists in time and may be imperceptible."[1] He must concentrate instead upon "some moment in the process of dying and burial: the appearance of the dying man, the poverty of the winding-sheet and the grave, or the repulsiveness of the decaying body."[2] Similar problems beset the author who wishes to construct a narrative centering on the moment which follows hard on the heels of death: the moment of judgment, in which God and the human subject come face to face.

The poem *Cleanness*, as its author tells us, is structured by a sequence of three Old Testament episodes: Noah's flood; the destruction of Sodom and Gomorrah; and Belshazzar's feast. Each of these episodes begins quietly before erupting into a terrifying panorama of mass destruction. The final episode features two such scenes: we witness the slaying of the most beautiful women of Jerusalem, the dashing-out of children's brains, the disemboweling of wives and daughters and the fettering of naked prisoners beneath horses; and later we witness a similarly violent vengeance visited upon Belshazzar's Babylon. At Sodom we see a rain of fire descending as five cities sink into a stinking pit. And as the waters of Noah's flood advance we see women, men, children and animals climbing to the high ground and then voicing a cry for mercy that their Creator will not hear:

> And alle cryed for care to þe Kyng of heuen,
> Recouerer of þe Creator þay cryed vchone,
> Þat amounted þe mase His mercy watz passed,
> And alle His pyte departed fro peple þat He hated.
> (393-96)[3]

Although each of these three Biblical scenes is terrifying enough without embellishment, the *Cleanness*-Poet takes pains to complicate and intensify our experience of terror. Most medieval accounts of Noah's flood, for example, situate us as readers within Noah's ark; and the medieval dramatists even undertake to entertain us with the marital problems of Mr and Mrs Noah. But the *Cleanness*-Poet locks us out of the ark, which is figured as a closed, water-tight casket, and leaves us to share the fate of drowning Creation:

> Luf lokez to luf and his leue takez,
> For to ende alle at onez and for euer twynne. (401-02)

This moment of imminent death is also a moment of imminent judgment: for all three of these Old Testament episodes were seen by medieval commentators as types of the Last Judgment.[4] This makes the terror of each scene complete, since the site of Judgment offers no hope of escape: the God that we would appeal to against such destruction is Himself the destroyer. The sequence of these narratives as types of the Last Judgment was doubtless suggested by 2 Peter 2, 4-13.[5] This passage discusses the fall of the rebellious angels, the righteousness of Noah, the condemnation of Sodom and Gomorrah and the saving of Lot before going on to condemn those who "walk after the flesh in the lust of uncleanness, and despise government.... Spots they are and blemishes, sporting themselves with their own deceiving while they feast with you."[6] Such a conjunction of uncleanliness and feasting is explored in the scene which prefaces the *Cleanness* Old Testament narratives, thereby framing them within the New Testament *lex Christi*. And this opening scene of courtly banqueting, developed from the parable of Matthew 22: 1-14,[7] is itself preceded by an earlier verse from the same gospel: 'Blessed are the pure in heart, for they shall see God'.[8] It is this verse which first activates the *Cleanness*-Poet, causing him to posit the question which consumes his entire narrative: "What must I do to be clean?" (169-70). This question, which is restated and reformulated with increasing urgency as the narrative advances, is a question which overlaps with *the* question that proved fundamental to those fourteenth-century theologians known as the *moderni*: "what must I do to be saved?"[9] These theologians, like the poet of *Cleanness*, could arrive at no final, unanimous or unqualified answer to their question: but like the poet they were fundamentally convinced of the urgent need to posit, reformulate and readdress such a question. In this essay I shall argue, albeit in drastically abbreviated form, that some understanding of the *moderni* enterprise proves essential to our comprehension of the peculiar strategies of the *Cleanness*-Poet, and specifically to his conceptualization of God's workings in human history and his masterful terrorizing of the reader.[10]

The *moderni* derive their name from Peter of Spain (d. 1277), who was hailed as the founder of modern logic. Thinkers such as Scotus, Ockham and Holcot were also referred to as nominalists or terminists, a designation which reflects their abiding interest in the technical properties and signifying functions of terms, or nouns. In the modernist project, all knowledge might be broken down to a series of propositions, which could then be analyzed by rational dialectic in their constituent parts. The *moderni* were, then, scientists of language: but they were also proponents of a new moral theology. For Ockham and his followers, logical and physical demonstration stopped short of God: the primacy and unity of God was considered indemonstrable. This meant that logical analysis was applied more to God's workings in this world than to God's nature *per se*. In short, the *moderni* concerned themselves more with the God down here than with the God up there. This concern generated an analysis of the covenant which binds man to God. This covenant evolved through three historical stages, each of which demanded obedience to a specific form of law: natural law; Old Testament law; and finally the *lex Christi*, the New Testament law which includes but goes beyond these earlier forms.[11] This evolution in man's understanding of his obligations to and contractual relationship with God is traced in the course of *Cleanness*, most notably in the dialogues between God and Abraham and God and Lot.

Not surprisingly, the *moderni* fell under the suspicion of more conservative theological minds. Their intense interest in logic and in the status of the signifier seemed to associate them with those philosophers condemned in 1277 for maintaining that all things happened by necessity; this view implied that God was not free. The *moderni*, however, protected themselves from the charge of necessitarianism by distinguishing two powers in God: the *potentia absoluta* and the *potentia ordinata*.[12] The *ordinata* is that power which establishes convenants between God and man in the way just described; salvation is promised to those who fulfill their part of the bargain. The *absoluta* is God's exclusion clause: it guaranteed God's absolute freedom in all things, no matter what might have been promised in any covenant. Much modernist thought was dedicated to exploring this complex dialectic of the two *potentiae*,[13] a dialectic which is evidently at play throughout *Cleanness*. Man is entirely confined by the terms of the *ordinata*; God is entirely or 'absolutely' free from such terms.

What, then, are the obligations of the human subject within the *ordinata*? He or she must strive to understand the terms of the *ordinata*; must strive to comply with these terms; and must believe through faith that it is possible for God to grant salvation, remembering that we cannot be owed beatitude: we can only prepare to receive God's grace. The human subject must remember that ethical status is determined by inner intentions rather than by overt acts; the overt act serves only as a possibly truthful sign of internal disposition. And finally it must be remembered that God is free, at any moment, to upset the applecart of the *ordinata*. This may make God seem arbitrary, barbaric, fickle and inhuman: the reader of *Cleanness* is often tempted to accuse God of all these shortcomings. But for the *moderni* and, I believe, for the poet of *Cleanness*, such accusations can only rebound upon the accuser: they mark the limits of human rationality and of human forms of representation.

Twentieth-century commentators have been puzzled, and sometimes scandalized, by the extent to which human passions and motivations are attributed to God in *Cleanness*. It is, indeed, remarkable to encounter a medieval God who thinks out loud, who is seized with sudden fits and longings, who is said to forget his own courteous manners and who waxes eloquent on the joys that flare up during sexual intercourse, creating an oblivion of erotic pleasure (697-708). Andrew and Waldron find this last detail "startlingly unusual" for "a medieval homiletic poem"; and they characterize the humanization of God throughout *Cleanness* as "a tendency [which] is very much at odds with the tradition of medieval Christian commentators, who took care to preserve the mysterious and unknowable quality of God's ways."[14] But this so-called "humanizing" of God in *Cleanness* does not, to my mind, make God seem any more "knowable": indeed, the very arbitrariness of God's excursions into human modes of feeling and expression makes this God seem less knowable and more enigmatic, dangerous and unpredictable. The *Cleanness*-Poet, I would suggest, shares the modernist enterprise of representing a God "down here," engaging with human subjects and evolving a covenant with mankind. At times the terms of this engagement seem clear; at other times God behaves in precipitate ways that no man-made rationality can make sense of. At times, that is, God acts within the limits of his own *ordinata*; at others he breaks free into the inscrutable realm of the absolute.

This complex interplay of God's two powers is realized most effectively throughout *Cleanness*. At line 581, for example, the poet takes pains to remind us of God's absolute power: he who created eyesight cannot be blind; he who created hearing cannot be deaf. (The comical consequences of human attempts to ignore these propositions are explored with great affection in *Patience*.[15]) But having reminded us that God is all-seeing and all-hearing, the *Cleanness*-Poet promptly proceeds to portray a God who (so he tells Abraham) must travel to Sodom in person to confirm with his eyes what he has heard with his ears.[16] And then having admitted to this unexpected split in his intelligence-gathering capacities, God delivers his celebrated speech on paramours and then decides not to go to Sodom after all: he will send in his spies instead. The spies chosen to reconnoiter the cultural practices of the Sodomites are described as being "noble men with beardless chins, with splendid, silk-like flowing hair and with skin that, wherever it was revealed, was briar-rose-like in complexion." Lot is naturally anxious to get such visitors off the streets of Sodom as soon as possible, arguing most forcibly against their plans for spending all night in the open. He attempts to save his visitors from being defiled by the townspeople by offering the Sodomites his own daughters, a practice which (as Rabanus Maurus observed) "nullo modo imitanda est."[17] Lot was later to commit incest with these daughters: he is certainly a curious choice as a champion of cleanness.

This narrative sequence is but one flamboyant instance of the wider problem of interpretation that the *Cleanness*-Poet embroils us in. The whole poem presents constant, seemingly random shifts in the relationship between outward appearance and inner truth; the meaning of any specific symbol of ascribed quality is rarely self-evident. Lot is "ryche," meaning wealthy. Jerusalem is "ryche"; Christ is born in "beþelen the riche." He is born poor in a cowshed, but this cowshed is more beautiful than any sacristy. No woman is as happy as Christ's mother, who groans with pain. Christ is "clene"; but so too are the battlements of Babylon. The Dead Sea stinks, suggesting the moral corruption that lies beneath its surface: but beautiful trees grow at its margin. These beautiful trees bear beautiful fruit; but once in the mouth, this fruit turns to ashes. This last image was, of course, often employed in representing the relationship of the gaudy surface of poetic narrative to its own inner substance. The *Cleanness*-Poet repeatedly represents and then interprets complex linguistic and symbolic figures. Each figure, it seems, must be investigated on its own terms, not in terms of what has gone before. We are therefore committed to a perpetual exercise of our interpretative faculties. The one option plainly not open to us is that which is similarly closed to *moderni* investigations of the *ordinata*: that interpretation itself should cease. If, like Belshazzar, we choose to go to sleep instead of acting on what God has made known, we may, like Belshazzar, be dragged out of bed by our heels to have our brains beaten out.

Belshazzar's death forms the conclusion of the third and final Old Testament episode in *Cleanness*, the episode in which the need for interpretation of God's self-inscribing within human history becomes overwhelmingly urgent.[18] As Belshazzar sits feasting, a fist without a wrist holding a stylus scrapes strange scripture into the rough plaster of the palace wall. The terrified Belshazzar embarks on a desperate search for a true interpreter. Following the failure of a bevy of sorcerers, wizards, exorcists, enchanters and dream-interpreters, Belshazzar beseeches Daniel to interpret for him. Daniel satisfies Belshazzar's request by working in the manner of a model medieval exegete, explaining first the literal and then the allegorical significance of God's text.[19] The truths of both text and interpreter are proved the very same evening. The inscribing of this text sees the language of Scripture cutting directly into human history: the motion of the stylus across the wall is explicitly compared with that of a plough through clay as it cuts the furrow (1547). But in writing such texts, does God not commit himself to following his own historical prescription, thereby losing his own absolute freedom? In describing the destruction of Sodom, the poet conjures up another extraordinary image to suggest that such is not the case:

And clouen alle in lyttel cloutes þe clyffez aywhere,
As lauce leuez of þe boke þat lepes in twynne. (965-66)

Elsewhere, the poet draws upon an image from homiletic tradition which figures God as the knife of fear which scrapes at the parchment of the individual conscience.[20] So if it is God's pleasure to write the text of collective or individual history with the pen, it is also his privilege to erase that history with the knife, or even to blow the entire book apart.

The function performed by Daniel as God's exegete within this final episode compares interestingly with the function performed by the exegete who brings the text to us: the *Cleanness*-Poet himself. How does this poet represent his own activity? Compared with Chaucer, who is always a solid mediating presence within or without his own narratives, this poet is virtually invisible. Such anonymity is, of course, sanctioned by homiletic tradition. The *Cleanness*-Poet takes full advantage of this privileged anonymity. In discussing the "humanizing of the motives and actions of God,"[21] Andrew and Waldron are led to compare the art of *Cleanness* with that of the Mystery Plays. This comparison is misleading. As spectators at a Mystery Play, we know that we are watching God the Father create the world; but we also know that we are watching Joe the butcher or Jack the saddle-maker. But in reading the Old Testament episodes of *Cleanness*, we detect no mediating body to point to. Through such artful anonymity, transparency, invisibility, the *Cleanness*-Poet abandons the reader to an unmediated narrative encounter with God himself. Such a strategy proves particularly appropriate in representing narrative moments which prefigure the unmediated encounter of the Last Judgment.

The *Cleanness*-Poet is not continuously absent from his own narrative. He sometimes comes forward to harangue us directly on the urgency of acting on his words. And on one occasion he does draw attention to his own person, or at least to a part of his own person. The false interpreters who can make no sense of the writing on the wall at Belshazzar's feast are, he tells us,

...as lewed...
As þay had loked in þe leþer of my lyft bote. (1580-81)

We do not see the poet's face or figure, but we do see his left (sinister) boot in a strange simile that somehow confirms our dependency on him as God's scribe and true interpreter. Within his own narrative, then, the *Cleanness*-Poet is sometimes a troublesome presence, but is mostly a troublesome absence, merging with the God he represents in some distant, absolute realm. What position, then, is offered to the reader of *Cleanness*? The reader, I would suggest, is repeatedly maneuvered towards the one position in the narrative that nobody wishes to hold, the seat that nobody wishes to occupy: that of the guest who incurs God's wrath at the New Testament wedding feast. How does the poet contrive to get us there? He begins by asking us a question: what earthly lord would not be enraged by a guest that comes to his table in clothes that are patched and torn? (35-38) Having made his readers accomplices in condemning such a guest, the poet runs the situation past us again: but this time within the narrative framework of Matthew's parable. A man holds a wedding feast for his son, but the invited guests will not come. Piqued, the lord fills his banqueting hall with strangers recruited from the street. Moving among these new guests at his banquet, this cheerful lord reminds us of the affable Arthur of *Sir Gawain*'s Camelot. But as his eye lights upon a man whose garment is "fyled with werkkez," his mood turns to furious indignation: the unfortunate is bound, fettered and consigned to a "doungoun þer doel euer dwellez." This change is shocking. Is it not to be expected that this man should be without a "festiual frok," since the banquet's guests (some bold, some timid, some lame, some half-blind) were recruited from countryside roads, scrublands and thickets? Andrew and Waldron attempt to meet this objection in a lengthy footnote which ends by suggesting that festival frocks may have been handed out to the new guests as they came in at the door.[22] This ingenious suggestion is indicative of a general determination on the part of modern commentators to discover an essential coherence or consistency in this poet's symbolism.[23] But it seems to me that this poet contrives to produce an opposite effect. He has already told us of priests who are dressed cleanly without but are filthy within: so it is already clear that outer garments are no secure guide to inward realities. And the unfortunate guest is described as being "fyled with werkkez": how, then, are we to assure ourselves of being clean? Your best clothes, the poet tells us, are the "werkkez" which you have performed (169-71). "Werkkez" defile our clothes; "werkkez" keep them clean. Our editors do, to their credit, admit that the term "cleanness'" the poem's most crucial term, is extremely difficult to pin down, something which they attribute to "an indeterminate metaphorical factor."[24]

What happens, it would seem, is that as the lord sights, condemns and damns the unhappy guest the poet is wrenching us from a literal to an allegorical and finally to an anagogical frame of reference. In so doing he exercises a form of power over us which might be described as a poetic *potentia absoluta*. Such shifts in *Cleanness* are always disorientating because the poet is such a master of the literal level: like the unfortunate guest at the banquet we become captivated by surface detail and oblivious to all else, until the literal is abruptly interrupted or discarded.

At intervals throughout his narrative, the *Cleanness*-Poet takes pains to point us back to this prefatory parable. How, then, are we to avoid being caught in the Judgment seat wearing the wrong clothes? Be clean, the poet tells us. How do we secure cleanness? The poet offers no answer to this question, but pours his formidable energies into three negative *exempla* which convince us more deeply of our need to be clean. For this poet, as for the *moderni,* our hope of salvation resides in this ceaseless forward movement, this continuous effort of interpreting. His final words offer no point of rest, only a reminder of God's absolute power: those who are well-dressed are those whom God deems to be well-dressed. This conforms with Holcot's understanding of righteousness: man must struggle to be righteous within the terms of the *ordinata.* But even he who achieves perfect righteousness within these terms cannot be sure of the reward of salvation: those are righteous whom God deems to be righteous.[25]

Like the other works of the *Gawain*-Poet (and the sequence of works as a whole) *Cleanness* is a circular text: the clothing imagery of its closing lines takes us back to the opening scene of the lord's wedding feast. This completed circle is appropriate for an interpretative enterprise which cannot hope to follow a simple linear progression and then stop. The quest for cleanness, like the modernist quest for salvation, cannot come to an end this side of death. To sit still is to risk seeing God before we are ready to face him. The ultimate terror of *Cleanness,* then, is the prospect of being caught in that seat of Judgment before our time.[26] Once in that seat, in the crucial moment of our individual salvation history, our powers of human reason will desert us and our power of human language will be of no use:

> Þat oþer burne watz abayst of his broþe wordez,
> And hurkelez doun with his hede, þe vrthe he biholdez;
> He watz so scoumfit of his scylle, lest he skaþe hent,
> Þat he ne wyst on worde what he warp schulde. (149-152)

Notes

1. This essay originally formed part of a session organized by James I. Wimsatt at the 1984 MLA Convention (Washington D. C.) entitled 'The *Pearl* Poet: Terror, Time and Grace'. In revising the piece I have learned much from discussions with Ernest R. Kaulbach (University of Texas). My interest in fourteenth-century philosophy was first stirred by Gordon Leff, particularly by his suggestive essay *The Dissolution of the Medieval Outlook* (New York: Harper Torchbooks, 1976). But in attempting to relate such philosophy to fourteenth-century imaginative literature I am most indebted to Janet Coleman (London School of Economics) for many conversations and two fine books: *English Literature in History 1350-1400 : Medieval Readers and Writers* (London: Hutchinson, 1981); Piers Plowman *and the "Moderni"* (Rome: Edizioni di Storia e Letteratura, 1981).

2. *The English Religious Lyric in the Middle Ages* (Oxford: Clarendon Press, 1968), p. 67.

3. Quotations from *Cleanness* follow *The Poems of the Pearl Manuscript*, edited by Malcolm Andrew and Ronald Waldron, York Medieval Texts, second series (London: Edward Arnold, 1978).

4. See Charlotte C. Morse, *The Pattern of Judgment in the* Queste *and* Cleanness (Columbia, Missouri: University of Missouri Press, 1978), pp. 131-33.

5. See Edward Wilson, *The* Gawain-*Poet* (Leiden: E.J. Brill, 1976), p. 94.

6. 2 Peter 2, 10-13 (A.V.).

7. This opening scene actually sees a fusion of two New Testament passages: Luke 14, 15-24; Matthew 22, 1-14. See Lynn Staley Johnson, *The Voice of the* Gawain-*Poet* (Madison: University of Wisconsin Press, 1984), pp. 98-103; and for the Vulgate passages, see Andrew and Waldron, pp. 371-72. Luke provides the sequence of excuses offered by the three guests who were originally invited to the feast. Matthew features the story of the man who is cast out of the banquet for wearing foul clothes. This moment from Matthew 22 was taken by Peter Lombard as a judgment to damnation: see *Sententiae in IV libris distinctae*, vol. I, Part II, third edition (Rome: Editiones Collegii S. Bonaventurae Ad Claras Aquas, 1971), II, xxxviii, 3, 13 (p. 549). The immense influence of Lombard's *Sentences* can hardly be exaggerated. F. Stegmuller provides entries for 1407 commentaries on this work: see his *Repertorium commentatorium in sententias Petri Lombardi*, 2 vols (Wurzburg: Wurzburg University Press, 1947). Scotus and Ockham both wrote commentaries on the *Sentences*. Scotus, in commenting upon II, xxxviii, discusses free will: see Ioannis Duns Scoti, *Commentaria Oxoniensia ad IV libros magistri sententiarium*, edited by P. M. F. Garcia, 2 vols (Florence: Typographia Collegii S. Bonaventurae, 1912-14), II, 849-51. It is not surprising that Matthew 22, 1-14 was associated with questions of predestination in the later Middle Ages: its final verse concludes that "many are called, but few are chosen." See also *Cleanness* 162, where the reader is given the first half of this verse (and is left to recall the second for himself).

8.   *Matthew* 5, 8. It is interesting to note that Peter Lombard, in the passage cited above, also moves from Matthew 22 to a verse from the Sermon on the Mount. He cites a passage from Augustine, *De sermone Domini in monte*: "Non debemus ideo evangelizare ut manducemus, set ideo manducare ut evangelizemus: ut cibus non sit bonum quod appetitur, sed necessarium quod adicitur; ut illud impleatur: *Quaerite primum regnum Dei, et haec omnia adicientur vobis*." Lombard quotes further from Augustine, emphasising that seeking the kingdom of God must be our first priority: all else will follow (20-34).

9.   See Coleman, Piers Plowman *and the "Moderni,"* p. 25.

10.   I am proposing that the *Cleanness*-Poet made the terrorization of his readers a matter of deliberate rhetorical strategy. It is interesting to note that a similar strategy was pursued by Felice Tancredi da Massa, an Augustinian who belonged to the *famiglia* of St. Catherine of Siena: see David Wallace, "Mystics and Followers in Siena and East Anglia," in *The Medieval Mystical Tradition in England* (Dartington 1984), edited by Martin Glasscoe (Cambridge: D.S. Brewer, 1984), 169-91 (p. 179). In his *ottava rima Fanciullezza di Gesù (Childhood of Jesus)*. Tancredi deliberately contrives to introduce moments of anxiety where, in his source text (the homely *Meditationes vitae Christi*), none exist. The most remarkable example comes during the Nativity scene. In the *Meditationes* this is joyful, intimate and straightforward: in the *Fanciullezza* Tancredi switches abruptly out of such a mood into a twenty-two stanza excursus on sodomy. At this moment, as Christ enters the world, all sodomites are struck down, buried and subjected to eternal torment. The dynamic here is obviously that of *Cleanness* : God's love of cleanness is exemplified by his hatred and intolerance of its opposite. But the sudden contrivance of such terror out of a scene of domestic harmony provides a more disturbing parallel between these two poets, who were exact contemporaries (Tancredi died in 1385).

11.   See Coleman, Piers Plowman *and the "Moderni,"* pp. 20-22, 28; Ernest A. Moody, "William of Ockham," in Moody, *Studies in Medieval Philosophy, Science and Logic. Collected Papers 1933-1969* (Berkeley: University of California Press, 1975), 409-439 (pp. 430-36).

12.   See Edward Grant, "The Effect of the Condemnation of 1277," in *The Cambridge History of Later Medieval Philosophy*, edited by N. Kretzmann, A. Kenney and J. Pinborg (Cambridge: Cambridge University Press, 1982), pp. 537-39.

13.   For a detailed and qualified account of the two *potentiae*, see Heiko A. Oberman, *The Harvest of Medieval Theology* (Cambridge, Mass.: Harvard University Press, 1963), pp. 30-56; Klaus Bannach, *Die Lehre Der Doppelten Macht Gottes bei William von Ockham* (Wiesbaden: Franz Steiner Verlag, 1975).

14.   *Poems of the* Pearl *Manuscript*, pp. 18-141.

15.   Ockham raises an interesting paradox, suggestive for *Patience*, by supposing that God might command a man to hate or disobey him. "To obey God is to love God, and to love God is to do his will; but if it is God's will that I do not do his will, I do his will if I don't, and don't do it if I do" (Moody, p. 435).

16.   Ockham opens Distinction xxxix of his *Ordinatio* or *Commentary on the Sentences of Peter Lombard (Book One)* by asking "whether God could know more than He knows": see William Ockham, *Predestination, God's Foreknowledge, and Future Contingents*, translated by M. M. Adams and N. Kretzmann (Indianapolis: Hackett

Publishing Company, 1983), p. 92. Ockham continues: "it seems that He could, for He can know something that He does not know; therefore He can know more then He knows. The antecedent is clear, for He does not now know that I am in Rome, and He can know that since it can be true" (p. 92). Ockham goes on to explore two differing ways in which 'know' (*scire*) may be applied. He explains that "it is not now known by God that I am in Rome, because it is not now true. Nevertheless, it can be known by God, because it can be true; and if it will be true, it will be known by God" (p. 93).

17.   *Commentary on Genesis*, cited by Andrew and Waldron, p. 147.

18.   The destruction of Babylon was interpreted as a type of divine justice and as a figure for the damned in the Last Judgment: see Morse, pp. 136-37.

19.   In the prologue to his commentary on Dante's *Inferno* Guido da Pisa maintains that the hand which writes upon Balthasar's wall "is our own poet Dante" ("est noster novus poeta Dantes"). Guido assumes the role of Daniel in leading us through the *Comedy*, which he sees as a *visio* , a type of dream "which is concealed beneath figures and made cloudy with ambiguities, and which is not to be understood or comprehended except through interpretation": see Vincenzo Cioffari, *Guido da Pisa's "Expositiones et glose super Comediam Dantis"* or *"Commentary on Dante's* Inferno" (Albany, New York: New York University Press, 1974), p. 18.

20.   See *Cleanness* 1133-8 and Andrew and Waldron, p. 159. It is interesting to note that Dante uses the word *coltello* (knife) seven times in his exegetical *Convivio* but just once in his entire *Comedy*. Dante clearly sees the knife as an instrument of exegesis: "my intellect scratches out (purga) the illicit and unreasonable in this way" [I, ii, 2 in the edition of Maria Simonelli (Bologna, 1966)]. Dante later exploits the dramatic and violent potential of this image in memorable fashion: "one would wish to reply to such bestial stupidity not with words but with the knife" (IV, xiv, 11). Matthew Paris of St. Albans (d. 1259) provides a fine illustration of a text being composed with both knife and pen in his frontispiece to *The Prognostics of Socrates the King*, a fortune-telling tract of the *sortes* genre (Bodleian Library, Oxford, MS. Ashmole 304, fol. 31ᵛ). Socrates is seated before a manuscript page; Plato stands behind him. Plato prods Socrates in the back with his right index finger and waves his left index finger above the page in admonitory fashion. Socrates scratches at the page with a knife held in his left hand; his right hand is dipping a pen into an inkwell.

21.   *Poems of the* Pearl *Manuscript*, p. 18.

22.   *Poems of the* Pearl *Manuscript*, p. 117.

23.   A. C. Spearing is exemplary in his openness to those aspects of *Cleanness* which resist tidy-minded schematizations: see *The* Gawain-*Poet. : A Critical Study* (Cambridge: Cambridge University Press, 1970), esp. pp. 50-55, 60.

24.   *Poems of the* Pearl *Manuscript*, p. 21. It might seem that these modern editors are suffering a loss of nerve in associating their interpretive difficulties with the indeterminacy of language itself, but their intelligent recognition of the inherent limitations of language was clearly shared by the *Cleanness*-Poet. We must work out our own salvation with fear and trembling (*Philippians* 2, 12). And this we can only work out in language; we have nothing else to work with. But human language is a woefully imperfect instrument within which to fix and frame divine truths. Language serves us; language fails us. Fear and trembling remain, so we can only

start again: *quaerite primum regnum Dei.*

Much modern criticism of *Cleanness* has set out to demonstrate the utter coherence and consistency of the poem's imagery and symbolism. To this end reference has often been made to the self-evident truths of thirteenth-century philosophy. But perhaps we should turn our attention to those fourteenth-century thinkers who, through rigorous and determined attention to the actual terms of language, demonstrated the untenability of many Scholastic assumptions. The *moderni* forced the world to recognize that there was much which could not, with certainty, be said. Perhaps, then, the indeterminacies of *Cleanness* should not be covered with philosophical fig-leaves borrowed from an out-moded system of thought; perhaps they should be considered as part of the poem's fourteenth-century meaning. And perhaps we might then go on to reconsider those mysterious signifiers which float through the other pages of this manuscript: the pearl of great price; the green girdle; patience.

25.   See Coleman, Piers Plowman *and the "Moderni,"* pp. 24-25; Leff, Dissolution, pp. 53-54; Moody, p. 435.

26.   For further consideration of the ways in which the *Cleanness*-Poet attempts to invest his narrative with "apocalyptic urgency" and to accentuate the imminence of death and judgment for each individual, see Morse, *Pattern of Judgment,* p. 137.

IN GOD'S SIGHT: VISION AND
SACRED HISTORY IN *PURITY*

SARAH STANBURY

In *Purity*, the reward for spiritual cleanness is to stand in the sight of God. The poet bases his series of *exempla* on the sixth beatitude, "Blessed are the pure of heart, for they shall see God." This promised vision of the sight of God appears not only at the beginning of the poem but throughout the work. The ending of the poem, for instance, represents a prayer for God to send us grace, "Þat we may serve in his syȝt þer solace never blynnez."[1] Following each of the major homilies, the poet traces the corrosive effects of sin on our attainment of the sight of God, reminding us after the Flood, "On spec of a spote may spede to mysse / Of þe syȝte of þe Soverayn þat syttez so hyȝe" (551-52), and after the destruction of Sodom that "To se þat Semly in sete and his swete face, / Clerrer counseyl con I non, bot þat þou clene worþe" (1055-66). In the homily on Christ that interrupts the series of parables, the poet also identifies the reward for cleanness with the sight of God, here explaining how the Christian may attain this vision of God on his throne through the sacrament of penance. The poet then turns the promise into a question, "How schulde we se, þen may we say, þat Syre upon throne?" (1112), which he answers with a depiction of the practice of shrift.

The promised vision of God on his throne in *Purity* is an iconographic detail with a special place in late medieval eschatological theory, for the sight of the enthroned deity suggests the beatific vision, the immediate, unveiled vision of God available to the purified soul after death. That *Purity* 's image of God on his throne refers to the beatific vision rather than to the mystical vision of God that can occur in this life, such as the viewing of God "spiritually in his glory" that Hilton describes in the *Scale of Perfection* (1.12),[2] is illustrated by *Purity*'s use of an iconographic motif, God enthroned, that often depicts the beatific vision in the visual arts. Further evidence of the link between *Purity* and the *visio pacis* may be found in the poem's employment of the sixth Beatitude, which medieval scriptural exegesis explains as a direct reference to the face-to-face vision of God. Augustine, for example, contends that the vision at the Resurrection will fulfill the promise of the Beatitude: "He does not say what we shall see; but what but God, that the promise of the Gospel may be fulfilled in us, 'Blessed are the pure in heart, for they shall see God'?"[3] Throughout his work, in fact, Augustine repeatedly asserts that the reward for the just after Purification will be the sight of God.[4] When this vision will be available, after death or on Judgment Day, was, however, a recurring topic of debate in the Middle Ages, particularly in the early fourteenth century.[5] In 1334, for example, Pope John XXII espoused St. Bernard's opinion that souls must wait for this vision until Judgment, thereby generating disputes between some Franciscans who supported Bernard and the Pope, and Dominicans who championed the popular traditional view, that the sight of God is immediately available after death. A conclusive answer to the question , however, was furnished in 1336 by Pope Benedict XII in his constitution "Benedictus Deus," in which he states, "By this edict which will prevail forever," that after death and purgation the vision can be beheld, before the resumption of our bodies and the general judgment: "the same vision and enjoyment without any interruption...exist continuously and will continue even up to the last judgment and from then even unto eternity."[6]

In *Purity*, the time when the vision of God on his throne will be manifest is never made clear; yet the poet implies that the sight of God will be directly available after death because of the immediacy of his promise, which intimates that the sight of God is the primary reward for the purified soul. Through his use of the sixth Beatitude with its intimate promise of salvation, the poet creates a personal eschatology that contrasts with the impersonal historical system outlined by the poem's Old Testament *exempla*. Direct, unmediated vision of God is the way of the End, the *summum bonum*. In *Purity* this direct vision contrasts with the means of seeing or knowing God in the time before Christ. Biblical history as outlined in the poem's progressive Old Testament narratives—stories of the Flood, of Abraham, of Lot and Sodom, and of Belshazzar—is useful to the Christian not only as a source book of sins and errors and as a series of moralizing *exempla* on the virtues of spiritual cleanness, but also as an explication of an historical process, the developing and unfolding knowledge of God that culminates in the beatific vision, the sight of God on his throne.

The arrangement of *Purity's* parables has been noted by critics, who have pointed out that the application of the historical tales to judgment in this life is illustrated by the movement of history through the ages of natural law and scriptural law as well as through the time of grace in which judgment is at hand.[7] The thematic implications of the beatific vision and the relationship of this image to the poem's historical and narrative structures, however, have not been explored.[8] The sight of God, a reiterated promise, stands in juxtaposition to other visual encounters or confrontations in the poem, including Abraham and Lot's greeting of the angels, the unclean guest's appearance before the lord at the wedding feast, or Belshazzar's presentation to his people. Each of the *exempla*, derived from both the Old and the New Testaments, in fact contains an important visual confrontation. Together these visual encounters form a system of oblique or analogous references to the promised vision of God and dramatize the developing relationship between man and God in Christian history.

One of the most indirect references to a personal encounter in which vision and recognition play a crucial part occurs in *Purity's* central homily on Christ. Describing Christ's purity of touch, the poet explains how Christ can miraculously break bread with his hands:

> So clene watz his hondelyng uche ordure hit schonied,
> And þe gropyng so goud of God and man boþe,
> Þat for fetys of his fyngers fonded he never
> Nauþer to cout ne to kerve wyth knyf ne wyth egge;
> Forþy brek he þe bred blades wythouten,
> For hit ferde freloker in fete in his fayre honde,
> Displayed more pryvyly when he hit part schulde,
> Þenne alle þe toles of Tolowse moȝt tyȝt hit to kerve.
> (1101-08)

It has long been recognized that this episode suggests the supper at Emmaus. On the day of the entombment two of Christ's disciples meet him on the way to the village of Emmaus. Only when Christ breaks bread with his hands do they recognize him: "When he was at table with them, he took the bread and blessed, and broke it, and gave it to them. And their eyes were opened and they recognized him; and he vanished out of their sight. They said to each other, "Did not our hearts burn within us while he talked to us on the road, while he opened to us the Scriptures?" (Luke 24:30-32).[9]

Most readers have suggested that the appearance of this episode in *Purity* is eucharistic, an allusion to the sacramental process of redemption.[10] Although the Emmaus episode may be, as Wilson says, "often in art and exegesis interpreted as a eucharistic feast,"[11] it is even more often understood in exegesis to illustrate the apprehension of divinity.[12] Gregory, whose commentary *In Evangelia* established an influential tradition for interpreting the Emmaus episode, claims that Christ is only outwardly visible to the disciples when they love and doubt:

> Behold, you have heard, beloved brothers, that to the two disciples walking in the way, not yet believing but still speaking about him, the Lord appeared. But he did not show them a figure which they might recognize. Thus he did outwardly, with the eyes of the body as was happening inwardly—with the eyes of the heart. For as the disciples within themselves were both loving and doubting, so the Lord was outwardly present, but he did not show them who he was. He exhibited his presence to those who were speaking about him, but he hid a recognition of him from those who were doubting.[13]

In a later commentary that follows Gregory's explanation of the Emmaus episode, a precise analogy is established between the disciples' love and miraculous recognition and the Christian's love that will lead him to the beatific vision: "We also, my brothers, are often enkindled when we hear Christ speaking in the scriptures. But if through contemplation or some revelation we taste his sweetness more openly, how much more ardent do we then become? And when, the cloud being removed, he will give himself to be seen by us forever face to face, then by how much more will we be ardent in his love?"[14] This analogy between the pilgrims to Emmaus and the individual contemplative delineates a series of incremental contingencies: the more we contemplate divinity, the more we love, until we attain the beatific vision when we can love God in unveiled apprehension.

In medieval English literature the Emmaus episode is also interpreted as an epistemological crux, an incident to illustrate the aporia between perception and recognition. In *Piers Plowman,* for instance, the breaking of bread reveals the difference between works and appearances; the disciples fail to recognize Christ by his clothes, yet do so by his "werkes" (B.230-31).[15] In the medieval cycle plays, the Emmaus story, known as the episode of the Pilgrim, is also dramatized occasionally; and in these plays the non-scriptural conceit that Christ broke bread more cleanly than if he had used a knife is used to dramatize the miraculous recognition.[16] In the Shewsbury play, for example, the second disciple explains to the apostles how he recognized Christ in the breaking of the bread: "Þat hit was Crist ful wel we knewe, / He cutt oure bred withouten knyfe."[17] In the Chester version of the Emmaus story, Luke and Cleophas, the two disciples, bemoan that they were unable to recognize Christ before he broke the bread; despite all his teaching on the road they do not know him until this visual and gestural sign: "By breaking of bread I knew his face/ But nothing ther before."[18]

In *Purity* the homiletic reference to Christ's ability to break bread would surely recall these common exegetical and dramatic traditions. That the breaking of bread refers at least in part to the miraculous recognition of Christ is also suggested by the description of the nativity, where both ox and ass instantly recognize the child:

> Þenne watz her blyþe barne burnyst so clene
> Þat boþe þe ox and þe asse hym hered at ones:
> Þay knewe hym by his clannes for Kyng of nature,
> For non so clene of such a clos com never er þenne.
> (1085-88)

Both the nativity and the Emmaus episode thus show how Christ exemplifies perfect cleanness in his birth and in the works of his hands; such incidents also show how Christ can be recognized in the instantaneous action of faith.

The reference to Emmaus in the homily in *Purity* thus offers a model of miraculous visual recognition which itself can lead to the highest vision, the sight of God on his throne which the homily promises will be the reward for cleanness obtained by penance. Both of these brief references to episodes when Christ was recognized instantly describe knowledge of God in the era of grace, the *tempus gratiae* when, according to medieval historians, Christ is revealed as directly perceived truth. Hugh of St. Victor, outlining the epochal divisions of time, explains repeatedly that the age of grace represents the age of direct revelation, a period that completes an historical process of growth in spiritual intuition.[19] Hugh shares with several medieval historiographers, in fact, the belief that not only is history linear, progressing relentlessly from the creation to the eschaton, but that human history mirrors the spiritual growth of the individual and that in each epoch man has increasing knowlege of God.[20] Similarly, a central thesis of Joachim of Fiore's *Liber Concordiae* and *Expositio in Apocalypsim* is the expansion of human understanding of the Scriptures through the passage of time.[21] St. Bonaventure expresses a similar view of linear time, though he alters Joachim's trinitarian view of the three *status* of history by dividing time into four ages: the time of nature, the time of law, the time of the prophets, and the time of the revelation of grace. The last age, the *tempus gratiae*, will be characterized by wisdom and mercy: "the redemption of man, the diffusion of gifts, and the opening of the Scriptures."[22] In Hugh of St. Victor's scheme, however, history falls into a similar epochal division, though Hugh makes a detailed analogy between human knowledge in history and the knowledge of the individual. From the Fall to Abraham man was ruled by the *lex naturalis,* an age which unveiled humanity's fundamental weakness his inability to rule himself. The second era, the time of Abraham, Moses, and the prophets, was the *lex scripta* or the age of written law when man became a reader of symbols that instructed him about Christ. In the final epoch, the *tempus gratiae* or time of grace, Christ is revealed as directly perceived truth.[23]

The developmental view of history that sketches within a progressive linear framework an epistemology, a theory of the growth of spiritual knowledge, can help us understand the structure of *Purity*, for the parables describe scenes of face-to-face encounters and ensuing acts of interpretation and of judgment that are juxtaposed with the direct perception of God illustrated in the Emmaus reference and promised as the reward for cleanness. In the Parable of the Wedding Feast the guest stands unfittingly dressed before the Lord, a visual encounter that the poet explicitly contrasts with the vision of God that we may have when our spiritual "limbs" are well attired (175):

> Wich are þenne þy wedez þou wrappez þe inne,
> Þat schal schewe hem so schene schrowde of þe best?
> Hit arn þy werkez, wyterly, þat þou wroȝt havez,
> . . . .

> And syþen alle þyn oþer lymez lapped ful clene;
> Þenne may þou se þy Savior and his sete ryche.
>   (169-76)

In the account of Lucifer's fall, the "falce fende" (205), like the unclean guest, also errs in the way he looks on his lord, performing an ocular act that inverts the iconographic system of the beatific vision. Whereas the purified soul turns his eyes up to God, Lucifer "hyȝe in þe heven" looks on himself, and he "seȝ noȝt bot hymself how semly he were" (209).

Within the long Old Testament parables that follow the *exempla* of Lucifer and Adam, the poet divides and interprets historical epochs according to familiar medieval schema, describing first the era of natural law and then the era of scriptural law, as Charlotte Morse has shown. I would also like to suggest that the episodes contained within these epochs serially illustrate an evolving, developmental relationship between man and God and describe scenes of direct visual encounters to represent this changing methodology. The poet makes it clear that the Flood occurred in the age of nature, for he describes the "law" of the time as the dictates of nature itself. The process of conformity to this law is even portrayed with a visual metaphor, a looking to nature: "Þer watz no law to hem layd bot loke to kynde" (263). In this era, God speaks to Noah directly by giving him a set of verbal commands and by making Noah a pawn of his power, an act graphically realized in the wonderful depiction of the storm as a force of nature. Knowledge of God in this era is realized as willing and blind obedience to a verbal command and natural precept. The enclosed ark, guided by God, tosses about on the wild flood, the culminating image in a long description that emphasizes the power of the hand of God, the willful misdirection of the doomed, and the blind obedience of Noah. One of the most dramatic moments in the delineation of the Flood is conveyed in a passage that suggests by analogy the beatific promise. People rush to high hills, creatures clamber on pillars, and the beasts "cryed for care to þe Kyng of heuen" (393). Creation looks upward to God, but here, of course, receives no vision or redemption.

In the poem's subsequent Old Testament parables, the poet gives instructions for reading and interpreting history. Unlike the incident of the Flood, the stories of Abraham, Lot, and Belshazzar occur in the *lex scripta* when, according to Hugh of St. Victor, man learns to read the signs of his salvation. Not only do the parables of *Purity* follow a scriptural chronology, but they emphasize a changing relationship between God and His people, one that is mirrored or dramatized in episodes of visual confrontation. In the explication following the description of the remains of the cities, the poet explains that such vestiges of human corruption are 'signs and tokens' of moral instruction' and evidence of wicked conduct. If we imitate clean behavior, we may come in God's court to see his face:

> Alle þyse ar teches and tokenes to trow upon ȝet,
> And wittnesse of þat wykked werk, and þe wrake after
> Þat oure Fader forferde for fylþe of þose ledes.
> Þenne uch wyȝe may wel wyt þat he þe wlonk lovies;
> And if he lovyes clene layk þat is oure Lorde ryche,
> And to be couþe in his corte þou coveytes þenne,
> To se þat Semly in sete and his swete face,
> Clerrer counseyl con I non, bot þat þou clene worþe.
> (1049–56)

The goal again is to stand in the sight of God, but with this biblical episode the poet explains the purpose of his parable and of Scripture itself. The Dead Sea, a real geological presence as well as a scriptural event, is also a visual and verbal sign of the hand of God; the ability to interpret that sign is necessary before we have access to direct vision of divinity.

The language and imagery of optics which define both the sin and the ideal of behavior also recur throughout the Abraham/Lot section of the poem as important structuring principles. Lynn Staley Johnson has pointed out that a common exegetical interpretation of Sodom's sin was visual cupidity, a sin of the eyes, and that the poet uses this episode to dramatize the second in a triad of sins—lust of the flesh, lust of the eyes, and pride of life.[24] Optical images and references to human encounters in this section are also consistent with the poem's structural and thematic employment of visual motifs in the poem as a whole. Clear-sightedness marks the just man, just as the gift of sight is given to those who can interpret divine signs. Abraham, who will be the father of his people, can "sende toward Sodomas þe syȝt of his yȝen" (1005); unlike Lot and Lot's wife, Abraham the chosen is allowed to gaze at the ruins of the cities. In contrast, the Sodomites who harass the angels are blinded "as blynde as Bayard" (886), and Lot's wife is turned to salt when she glances at the cities. Lot is also engaged in a visual drama when he encounters the angels:

> As he stared into þe strete þer stout men played,
> He syȝe þer swey in asent swete men tweyne;
> . . . .
> Ful clene watz þe countenaunce of her cler yȝen;
> Wlonk whit watz her wede and wel hit hem semed.
> (787–93)

Like Abraham who hastens to serve a supper to God at Mambre, Lot reacts properly to a visual sign, again a suggestion of disguised divinity. Lot stands face to face and eye to eye with God's angels, who are described as His spies, seeing the angels' clear eyes with his own.

In addition to his use of optical imagery to depict polar spiritual states, the poet also uses visual acuity to describe his characters' interpretive skills. Consistent with his fictional rendition of the epoch of scriptural and symbolic law, the poet shows how his characters are given or denied sight of God's signs in creation. In spite of the clarity of Lot's sight, the scope of his vision is limited. Indeed, Lot's salvation hinges on his refusal to look on the ruins of the city. Guided by angels and not by God himself, Lot is also not instructed in the interpretation of symbols. References to Lot's presence before and after the description of the destruction of Sodom emphasize that he has been denied vision. Lot not only refuses to look on the cities, he refuses to see his wife once she has turned; "Þay slypped bi and syȝe hir not Þat wern hir samen freres" (985). In contrast, when Abraham later sends "toward Sodomas Þe syȝt of his yȝen" to witness the destruction, he engages in an act of vision that has been denied Lot. Chosen by God to fill the world with his progeny, Abraham has also been selected to observe God's will, the sight of Sodom's ruins and a visual sign of God's act of judgment.

In *Purity's* final parable describing Belshazzar's idolatry, the poet also identifies a single reader of signs—in this case, Daniel—and again traces a complex series of visual encounters and acts of interpretation. Belshazzar, whose own palace recalls the perfect proportions of Jerusalem, appears before his God and his people in a posture suggestive of man before the face of God. Thus, Belshazzar kneels before his wooden gods set on high (1345). Later at his feast he himself is positioned above, the only figure on the dais, assuming the pose of sovereign before his people (1399).

The final section of the last parable, containing the episodes of the holy vessels and the writing on the wall, involves multiple levels of interpretation, however, for even as Belshazzar sets himself as a God on his throne, he is a flawed interpreter of visual ornament—the holy vessels—and of verbal signs, the writing on the wall. The poet makes a clear distinction between Belshazzar who is maddened by the writing on the wall and Daniel who reads and understands the meaning of the signs. Daniel later identifies Belshazzar's inability to comprehend the message with his blindness to visual signs:

> Bot Þou, Baltazar, his barne and his bolde ayre,
> Seȝ Þese syngnes wyth syȝt, and set hem at lyttel,
> Bot ay hatz hofen Þy hert agaynes Þe hyȝe Dryȝt[y]n,
> Wyth bobaunce and wyth blasfamye bost at hym kest,
> And now his vessayles avyled in vanyte unclene,
> Þat in his hows hym to honor were hevened of fyrst.
> (1709-14)

"Bot" in line 1709 contrasts Belshazzar with Nebuchadnezzar, who set himself as a God before his people even though he was given no signs from God. Belshazzar, on the other hand, has received not only the writing on the wall as a sign he cannot read, but also the vessels themselves that proclaim in their form the handiwork of God.

The interpretation of visual messages, dramatized in Daniel's act of prophetic reading, also occurs indirectly with the holy vessels.[25] Reversing the pattern of imagery used to portray the Dead Sea, the poet describes Solomon's vessels at length in a celebration of consecrated ornament. Like the Dead Sea, they also constitute a visual sign, brought before and abused by Belshazzar who is blind to their sacramental function. Through a protracted elaboration of visual ornament in this depiction of the vessels, the poet emphasizes their signatory value, although that value eludes the idolators at Babylon. The description is directed, instead, to the reader, as the poet suggests through the radical juxtaposition of an account of the vessels' form with a portrayal of their sacrilegious use at Babylon. The parishioner whom the group of parables literally addresses is finally the reader singled out to understand this elaborate visual sign; signifying the multiple meanings of baptism, the eucharist, man's body, and divine judgment, the vessels of the wrath of God—Solomon's cups and ewers—dramatize through visual ornament how the Christian interprets signs to effect his own salvation.

That this scriptural tale should, like his other parables, aid the audience in its own spiritual alignment is inherent in the poet's choice of a homiletic mode: these stories are intended explicitly to help us. Less obvious is the poet's use of a complex historical chronology that repeatedly juxtaposes the direct, unmediated, and non-symbolic vision available to man in the present time with knowledge of divine law in the past, the eras of nature and of Scripture. On the other hand, the parables have a simple and exemplary function, for their order suggests that Christian history is recapitulated on the level of a personal eschatology. As history moves through its linear epochs to the eschaton, so may we use scriptural history to understand sin and redemption as we prepare ourselves for our coming end. Yet the repeated epistemological concern of the parables, their dramatization of man's developing relationship with God and with God's law, as well as their thematic and imagistic use of vision as a sign of knowledge of God, suggest that they also describe the process by which the reader learns to use scriptural signs. In essence, the reader or the audience not only is instructed in a set of behaviors but in the reading of Scripture itself—the very parabolic process of the poem. The Dead Sea, the writing on the wall, and the holy vessels are visual signs given to Abraham, to Belshazzar and to Daniel. To the reader in the present era such signs are also direct scriptural figures in a visual poetic, and through the reader's exegesis they become agents of purgation that lead to the sight of God.

Notes

1.　All citations from *Purity* are derived from the edition by Robert J. Menner, *Purity, a Middle English Poem* (1920; rpt. Hamden, Connecticut: Archon Books, 1970).

2.　Walter Hilton, *The Scale of Perfection,* tr.　Dom Gerard Sitwell, O.S.B. (London: Burns Oates, 1953), p. 18.

3.　"Nec expressit quid videbimus; sed quid nisi Deum? Ut inpleatur in nobis promissum evangelicum: 'Beati mundicordes, quonian ipsi Deum videbunt...'." *De Civitate Dei,* ed. J. E. C. Welldon (London: Society for Promoting Christian Knowledge, 1924), 20.21.e.

4.　See esp. *De Videndo Deo,* Prol. 3, 15.37 (*PL,* 33.598, 612); and *Epist.*147, 8.20, 9.21, 22.51 (*PL,* 33.605, 606, 620). For a discussion of the vision of God in the writings of Augustine and St. Bernard, see Kenneth E. Kirk, *The Vision of God: The Christian Doctrine of the Summum Bonum* (New York: Longmans Green, 1932), pp. 319-358.

5.　See the *New Catholic Encyclopedia* (New York: McGraw-Hill, 1967), sv. Beatific Vision.

6　"Hac in perpetuum valitura constitutione auctoritate apostolica definimus....eadem visio et fruitio sine aliqua intercisione [*al. intermissione*] seu evacuatione praedictae visionis et fruitionis continuata exstitit et continuabitur usque ad finale uidicium et ex tunc usque in sempiternum." Henrico Denzinger, ed., *Enchiridion Symbolorum,* 32nd ed. (London: Herder, 1921), pp. 216-17; tr. Roy J. Deferrari, *The Sources of Catholic Dogma* (St. Louis: B. Herder Book Co., 1957), pp. 197-98.

7.　See especially Charlotte Morse, *The Pattern of Judgment in the Queste and Cleanness* (Columbia: University of Missouri Press, 1978), pp. 133-38.

8.　T. D. Kelly and John T. Irwin, "The Meaning of *Cleanness*: Parable as Effective Sign," *MS* 35 (1973): p. 233n, note that the image of the beatific vision in *Purity* is structurally important though they do not explore the uses of the motif in the poem.

9.　"Et factum est, dum recumberet cum eis, accepit panem, et benedixit, ac fregit, et porrigebat illis. Et aperti sunt oculi corum, et cognoverunt eum: et ipse evanuit ex oculis eorum. Et dixerunt ad invicem: Nonne cor nostrum ardens erat in nobis dum loqueretur in via, et aperiret nobis Scripturas?" *Biblia Sacra, iuxta Vulgatum Clementinam,* ed. A. Colunga and L. Turrado, 4th ed. (Madrid: Biblioteca de Autores Christianos, 1965).

10.　See, for example, Kelly and Irwin, "Parable", p. 250; and Edward Wilson, *The* Gawain-*Poet* (Leiden: Brill, 1976), pp. 74-75.

11. Wilson, *The* Gawain-*Poet*, p. 74.

12. For a detailed discussion of the patristic and vernacular treatments of Emmaus, with particular attention to the use of the image as a sign of spiritual pilgrimage, see F. C. Gardiner, *The Pilgrimage of Desire: A Study of Theme and Genre in Medieval Literature* (Leiden: E. J. Brill, 1971). For several exegetical discussions of Emmaus, see the *Glossa Ordinaria*, *PL*, 114.352; Ambrose, *In Lucam*, *PL*, 15.1847ff; and Augustine, *Sermon 234*, *PL*, 38.1115.

13. "Ecce audistis, fratres charissimi, quia duobus discipulis ambulantibus in via, non quidem credentibus, sed tamen de se loquentibus Dominus apparuit, sed eis speciem quam recognoscerent non ostendit. Hoc ergo egit foris Dominus in oculis corporis quod apud ipsos agebatur intus in oculis cordis. Ipsi namque apud semetipsos intus et amabant et dubitabant, eis autem Dominus foris et praesens aderat, et quis esset non ostendebat. De se ergo loquentibus praesentiam exhibuit, sed de se dubitantibus cognitionis suae speciem abscondit." Gregory, *Homiliae in Evengelia* 23, *PL*, 76.1182B; tr. Gardiner, *Pilgrimage* , p. 24.

14. "Nos quoque, fratres mei, cum audimus Christum in Scripturis loquentem, ardentes saepe sumus. Sed, si per contemplationem, vel per aliquam revelationem ejus dulcedinem apertius gustamus, quanto magis ardentiores efficimur? Sed quando ipse remota nube dabit se nobis facie ad faciem in aeternum videri, quanto magis, fratres, tunc erimus ardentissimi in amore ejus?" Radulphus Ardens, *PL*, 155.1861B; tr. Gardiner, *Pilgrimage* , p. 46.

15. See also the discussion of this episode in D. W. Robertson, Jr. and Bernard F. Huppé, Piers Plowman *and Scriptural Tradition* (Princeton: Princeton University Press, 1951), p. 141.

16. See Rosemary Woolf, *The English Mystery Plays* (Berkeley: University of California Press, 1972), pp. 329-330.

17. Cited in Woolf, *Mystery Plays* , p. 330.

18. *Christ Appears to the Disciples*, in *Medieval Drama*, ed. David Bevington (Boston: Houghton Mifflin, 1975), p. 632.

19. Hugh's vision of history is expounded chiefly in *De Sacramentis*; see Hugh of St. Victor, *On the Sacraments of the Christian Faith*, tr. Roy J. Deferrari (Cambridge, Masssachusetts: Mediaeval Academy, 1954).

20. For a general discussion of the ages of the world, see R. W. Southern, "Aspects of the European Tradition of Historical Writing," *Transactions of the Roly Historical Society*, 5th Series (London, 1971), pp. 159-79; see also Richard Kenneth Emmerson, *Antichrist in the Middle Ages* (Seattle: University of Washington Press, 1981), pp. 12-20. For a discussion of the motif of the world's decline, see James Dean, "The World Grown Old and Genesis in Middle English Historical Writings," *Speculum*, 57 (1982), 548-68.

21. *Liber Concordiae Novi et Veteris Testamenti* (Venice, 1591), 5.48, 5.118, and 5.1.11ff; and *Expositio in Apocalypsim* (Venice, 1524), fol. 5r. col. 2, and fol. 11, col. 2. See also Morton Bloomfield, "Joachim of Flora," *Traditio* 13(1957): 264-265.

22.   "Et sic tempora Scripturae distincte ad numerum duodecim consurgunt, quia in quolibet horum quatuor principalium temporum tria specilia tempora continentur tribus personis in Trinitate respondentia. Tempus naturae est tempus conditionis rerum, purgationis scelerum, vocationis patrum; Legis est tempus lationis legum, prostrationis hostium, promotionis iudicum; prophetiae est tempus unctionis regum, revelationis prophetarum, restaurationis principum; gratiae est tempus redemptionis hominum, diffusionis charismatum, reserationis Scripturarum." *Collationes in Hexaemeron* 3.2.3.12, ed. R. D. Delorme (Ad Claras Aquas, Florence: Collegium S. Bonaventurae, 1934), pp. 161-162.

23.   *De Sacramentis* 1.1.3, 1.3.3, 1.8.3.11, 1.10.4.6-7, 1.11.1-8, and 1.12.1.3.6.

24. Lynn Staley Johnson, *The Voice of the* Gawain-*Poet* (Madison: University of Wisconsin Press, 1984), pp. 117-30.

25.   The complex symbolism of these vessels is discussed by Charlotte Morse, "The Image of the Vessel in *Cleanness,*" *University of Toronto Quarterly* 40 (1971): 202-16.

THE SIN OF *UNTRAWÞE* IN *CLEANNESS*

MICHAEL W. TWOMEY

While sexual sin is certainly the focus of the Flood and Sodom episodes, the Baltassar episode illustrates that God is angry not only with the carnal filth of sexual sin but also with the spiritual filth of returning to sin after performing penance (1133 -56).[1] In the poem's conclusion, when he declares that he has shown in three "wyses" (1805) how uncleanness "entyses hym [God] to be tene, tel[des] up his wrake" (1808), the poet is clearly referring not only to the *exempla* of the Flood and of Sodom but also to Baltassar's Feast, under which he subsumes several minor *exempla*— an arrangement that has led to the ongoing critical debate over the connection among the kinds of uncleanness these *exempla* demonstrate.[2]

Almost seventy years ago Robert J. Menner noted that four of God's punishments in *Cleanness* fell on sinners against *trawþe*, particularly Lucifer (205 ff.), Adam (236), Lot's wife (996), and the Jews in Jerusalem (1161). Menner also pointed out that, in *Gawain*, Bercilak tests Gawain, the "tulk of tale most trwe" (638), for both *clannes* and *trawþe*.[3] Indeed, the association of *clannes* and *trawþe* is found also in Gawain's shield, "a syngne þat Salamon set sumquyle / In bytoknyng of trawþe" (625-26), whose fifth set of five points partly represents "his clannes and his cortaysye" (653). Conversely, the relationship between fleshly filth and *untrawþe* is indirectly suggested by Gawain when he describes the green girdle as a token of his fault and exchanges it for the pentangle as his emblem (2433-38), calling it "'þe token of vntrawþe þat I am tan inne'" (2509, cp. 2383). Though Gawain's fault is also a matter of cowardice and covetousness, as he says (2374, 2508), and may be regarded as an excessive, albeit forgivable, attachment to this world is the example of Gawain suggests the possibility of a like association of *clannes* and *trawþe* in *Cleanness*. In addition, *Gawain* demonstrates the poet's interest in the penitent who returns to sin after penance, for, after his first confession to the priest, Gawain continues to conceal the green girdle, then pulls his head away from Bercilak's blade.[4] The two poems treat sin differently, of course. *Gawain* is a poem of human mercy in which the sinner is released from the letter of his covenant. *Cleanness*, however, is a poem of divine justice in which sinners are judged according to the requirements of the covenant of faith and obedience—*trawþe*—and then destroyed by a Deity whose demand for purity is absolute and inflexible.

Covenants demanding faith and obedience from mankind play an important role in all the relations between man and God portrayed in *Cleanness*. Adam must not eat of the Tree of the Knowledge of Good and Evil (cp. Gen. 2.17),[5] and because he does so, the poet says he "fayled in trawþe" (236). After the Flood, God makes His covenant with Noah, pledging never to destroy the whole world on account of sin (513-20, 564-70), although this agreement does imply that God will continue to punish individual instances of uncleanness that merit chastisement. The homosexuality of the Sodomites, for example, shows man's disobedience to the commandment to procreate (521-22) that is, attached to this covenant as part of God's blessing on nature. God emphasizes this point when he tells Abraham, "I compast hem a kynde crafte and kende hit hem derne, / And amed hit in myn ordenaunce oddely dere.... / Now haf þay skyfted my skyl and scorned natwre" (697-98, 709).[6] Furthermore, Lot's wife disobeys her husband's command not to put salt in the bread she bakes for the angels (819-28) and is turned into a pillar of salt "For two fautes þat þe fol watz founde in mistrauþe: / On, ho served at þe soper salt bifore Dryȝtyn; / And syþen, ho blusched hir bihynde, paȝ hir forboden were. / For on ho standes a ston, and salt for þat oþer" (996-99). The covenantal quality of penance, from which, the poet warns, we must not return to sin, is expressed by the phrase *saȝtled and sakred* 'reconciled and consecrated' (1139), applied to the newly-shriven soul in the discourse on penance.[7] The Jews turn to idolatry, thereby breaking their covenant with God, and as a punishment He sends them the Babylonian Captivity "For þat folke in her fayth watz founden untrwe, / Þat haden hyȝt þe hyȝe God to halde of hym ever" (1161-62). When Jerusalem is "bet doun" and "brend ... in askes" (1292), the echo of *Gawain* 's opening lines reminds us of another city—Troy— that fell because of faithlessness. Baltassar, "funde ful fewe of hit fayth-dedes" (1735), breaks the implied covenant with God established by Nabuchodonosor (here, following Dan. 5.2 and 5.11, construed as Baltassar's father), whom Daniel holds up as an example of a sinner reconciled to God. For his idolatry and for his desecration of the temple vessels which represent the soul "reconciled and consecrated" to God through penance (1133-56), he suffers a fate recapitulating that of the faithless Jews in Jerusalem and thus corroborates his figural relationship to them. Finally, the poem's last lines define the heavenly reward for cleanness as the continuation of faithful obedience to God translated to an eternal plane: "Þat we gon gay in oure gere þat grace he uus sende, / þat we may serve in his syȝt þer solace never blynnez."

I

If the *trawþe* man owes to God may be compared to the loyalty a liege owes to his lord, the *Cleanness*-Poet, who frequently uses the terms "king" and "lord" for God, emphasizes the feudal, covenantal inature of man's relationship to God by employing a legal metaphor to describe it. The Sodom episode applies this metaphor through legal terminology as well as through the concept of *trawþe*. In the passage wherein He denounces the sin of the Sodomites, God articulates His scheme of natural sexual relations violated by the Sodomites—His *ordenaunce* (698), a term used in law to mean "destiny" or a sovereign's decree.[8] Other legal terms in this passage turn it nearly into a conceit construing natural sexual relations as a contractual obligation. The joys which God has *dyȝt* (699) in sexual intercourse are the "doole alþerswettest" of this ordinance. The couple must practice intercourse "honestly" (705), making the natural sexual bond so powerful that "alle þe *meschefez* on mold moȝt hit not sleke" (708; emphasis mine). But man has perverted God's *skyl* (709) through homosexuality.

By extension of its primary meaning, 'to compose, ordain' (*OED dight*, vb., I-II), the verb *dighten* can connote 'to make (a law, a prohibition)', as in *Cleanness* 243: "a defence þat watz dyȝt of Dryȝtyn selven."[9] Although *meschef* in *Cleanness* 708 certainly bears the general sense 'unhappiness, misfortune' attested in the *Middle English Dictionary* (*mischef*, 1a[a]), the word, which derives from Old French *meschief*, also bears a legal sense not recorded in the *MED*. In law, mischief is "the evil or danger which a statute is intended to cure or avoid."[10] Its use as such in the fourteenth century is substantiated by an axiomatic-sounding statement which John Mowbray, a member of the king's council, delivered in the course of a proceeding in 1341: "Lei deit acorder a resoun, et oster meschief" ['Law ought to accord with reason, and remove mischief']"[11] Mowbray's statement suggests the position of law with respect to the general condition of lawless chaos, mischief, which law places in order. Quite in keeping with Mowbray's legal platitude, God's sexual *ordenaunce* in the Sodom episode *meschefez on mold*. When God sums up the Sodomites' offense by saying, "Now haf þay skyfted my skyl and scorned natwre" (709), His *skyl* refers to the natural law. *Skyl* constitutes reason both as the discriminating or moral faculty, i.e., *ratio*, and as its products (see *OED skill*, sb., 1.a.b.c.; 2.a.b); this sense of *skyl* is emphasized in other poems in MS. Cotton Nero A.x.[12] As early as *The Owl and the Nightingale*, and in other places cited by the *OED* (*skill*, sb., 2.c "in prepositional phrases, denoting that something is in accordance with, or contrary to, what is reasonable or right. Obs."), *skyl* occurs in the legal formula "right and skill" (i.e., law and reason): for instance, the Nightingale urges the Owl that they "Mid riȝte segge & mid sckile" (186).[13] The formula expresses human law in its entirety: laws as codes conceived by man (positive law) and reason as the natural law which, according to medieval legal theory, underlies and directs them.[14]

Cleanness further reflects late medieval legal thinking on the relationship of human law to natural law by attributing civil disorder to sinners against nature. The giants living before the Flood, for instance, are the product of an unnatural union between human women and the devil (269-72), which, in turn, was inspired by the homosexuality of Adam's descendants living in a period of natural law (263-68). These giants are known for their mischief (273-76). This civil disorder, a macrocosmic reflection of the inner disruption produced by sin in an individual, is also found among the Sodomites, whose custom is to abuse strangers. When the Sodomites demand that Lot send them the two angels, they remind him that homosexual abuse is "þe asyse ['law of the land'] of Sodomas to seggez þat passen" (844).[15] In Sodom, lawlessness is the law. Knowing "þe costoum þat kyþed þose wrechez (851), Lot is fearful since he is a stranger in Sodom; indeed, the Sodomites threaten to kill him if he does not comply (875-78).

Sodom was especially known for inhospitality to strangers, a crime which violates the tacit covenant between host and guest, and this reputation is a key to its *untrawþe*. The *ius hospitii* represents an aspect of the *ius naturae,* as Nicholas of Lyra observes in his *postilla* on Gen. 19.8, where Lot attempts to mollify the Sodomites by offering them his two daughters: "He said this so that the greater evil might be avoided, namely, sin against nature and violence to his guests. Indeed, to protect one's guests falls under the natural law."[16] In *Cleanness,* Lot offers the Sodomites his two daughters not only to protect his guests but to teach the Sodomites natural sexuality:

> 'Oo, my frendez so fre, yor fare is to strange;
> Dotz away yor derf dyn, and derez never my gestes.
> Avoy! hit is yor vylaynye, ȝe vylen yorselven;
> And ȝe ar jolyf gentylmen, yor japez ar ille.
> Bot I schal kenne yow by kynde a crafte þat is better:
> I haf a tresor in my telde of tow my fayre deȝter,
> Þat ar maydenez unmard for alle men ȝette,
> In Sodomas, þaȝ I hit say, non semloker burdes;
> Hit arn ronk, hit arn rype, and redy to manne;
> To samen wyth þo semly þe solace is better.
> I schal biteche yow þo two þat tayt arn and quoynt,
> And laykez wyth hem as yow lyst, and letez my gestes one.'
> (861-72)

This strategy recalls the *Decretum*'s defense of what to modern sensibilities is a cruel violation of the family:

> *It is less serious to have intercourse according to nature than to transgress against nature.* Blessed Lot offered the chastity of his daughters. For although this uncleanness was also shameful, nevertheless it was less serious to have intercourse according to nature than to transgress against

nature. He considered the kindness due to his guests to be above the shame of his house, regarding it as inviolable even among barbarians (2.32.7.12).[17]

Although it is the Sodomites' sin against nature that sparks God's angry resolve to destroy them, when Abraham talks with God about it their sin emerges as a type of *untrawþe*:

'Now, fyfty fyn frendez wer founde in ʒonde toune,
In þe cety of Sodomas, and also Gomorre,
Þat never lakked þy laue, bot loved ay trauþe,
And reʒtful wern, and resounable, and redy þe to serue;
Schal þay falle in þe faute þat oþer frekez wroʒt,
And joyne to her juggement her juise to haue?' (721-26)

Abraham's words here are indebted to Gen. 18.23-25, where the patriarch contrasts the *iustus* 'law abiding', meaning particularly his kinsman Lot, with the *impius* ' disloyal, disobedient.' The *Cleanness* - Poet's use of *trawþe* to define the righteousness opposed to Sodom's disobedience is paralleled in *Cursor Mundi*, but his understanding of Sodom's impiety is rooted, perhaps, in a broader tradition which linked inhospitality and impiety as symptoms of pride, the sin alleged of Sodom in Ezech. 16.49, the chief scriptural passage on which the later image of Sodom is based.[18] The prophet says to Jerusalem: "Behold, this was the iniquity of Sodom, thy sister: pride, fulness of bread and abundance, and the idleness of her and of her daughters; and they did not put forth their hand to the needy and to the poor." Ezech. 16.49 exemplifies the nearly typological comparisons between Sodom and Jerusalem framed by the prophets, who saw the destruction of Sodom as an archetypal punishment and as a warning of the impending Babylonian Captivity (e.g., Isa. 1.9, 13.19; Ier. 23.14; Amos 4.11; Soph. 2.9). Sodom and Babylon are further linked by the genealogy of their founders: Sodom was built by the C(h)anaanites, descendants of Cham and ultimately of Cain, while in Gen. 10.6-20 Babylonians and Sodomites are both listed as descendants of Cham.[19]

II

In scriptural tradition, Sodom's unfaithfulness—its lack of *trawþe*— is expressed through the metaphor of spiritual sterility. Bede says the Sodomites lacked the *fructus pietatis* : "[The author] praises the fertility of the land, just as he notes the unfaith of its inhabitants, so that they may be understood to be the more deserving of damnation, because they converted the greatest gifts of God not to the *fruit of faith* but to the increase of lust" (emphasis added).[20] Although the land around the Pentapolis is fertile (cp. *Cleanness*,1006-07 and Gen. 13.10), the Sodomites are not: their homosexuality confutes natural law, and their impiety indicates their spiritual sterility. They do not cultivate the fruit of faith. "Bearing fruit" (cp. Ioh. 15.8)— a common metaphor for the valorization of the Christian life on earth through good works which achieve salvation for oneself and for others—is the result of "planting the seed" of spirituality, as in Gal. 6.8: "For what a man sows, that he will also reap. For he who sows in the flesh, from the flesh also will reap corruption; but he who sows in the spirit, from the spirit will reap life everlasting." The true faith of the Church, moreover, springs from the *verbum Christi* planted like a seed by the Apostles, who represent the "seed of the saving remnant" that replaces the "remnant" of Israel, according to the *Glossa ordinaria* on Rom. 9.29 [*ed. cit.*, 6:22E]; without the seed of faith "we had been made as Sodom" (Rom. 9.29, paraphrasing Isa. 1.9)].[21] In the Gospels, Christ appoints disciples to spread His word to an implicitly Sodomitical world, sending them forth in pairs, like the angels going into Sodom in Genesis (Luc. 10.1; cp. Matt. 10.1-5). Comparing those who reject His teachings to Sodomites, Christ charges his disciples to shake from their feet the dust of any town that spurns them: rejecting Christ is so grave an offense that "it will be more tolerable for the land of Sodom and Gomorrah in the day of judgment than for that town" that will not convert to the true faith (Matt. 10.15; cp. Matt. 11.24 and Luc. 10.12). In Jude and in 2 Peter 2 whose theme is faith, Sodom also becomes an emblem for the punishment of heresiarchs. As spiritual Sodomites, the heresiarchs bear no fruit (Iud. 12).

In *Cleanness*, Sodom's spiritual sterility is illustrated not only by its disobedience to God's scheme of natural sexual relations, but by the Dead Sea that represents the city after its destruction. In keeping with biblically-based popular traditions pervading the area around the Five Cities after the catastrophe, everything about the Dead Sea is sterile.[22] "Ded in hit kynde" (1016), this body of water is called the Dead Sea because its "dedez of deþe duren þere ȝet" (1021). Its waters do not sustain life; in fact, neither grass nor shrubs can grow where its waters overflow (1027-28). It confutes nature: lead floats in it, but feathers sink (1024-26); and someone thrust into it to drown will live in eternal torment in its waters (1029-32). Since faithlessness is Sodom's sin, the Dead Sea is the "terne of traytores" (1041) on whose shores grow trees bearing the so-called "apples of Sodom." Beautiful but seedless and filled only with ashes, this fruit is a figure for Sodom itself, for though the land around Sodom was fertile and the city wealthy, its inhabitants were spiritually sterile because of their sin. Since the Dead Sea, then, represents the typological fulfillment of

Sodom's "promise" in sin, the poet concludes his description of it with "Alle þyse ar teches and tokenes to trow upon ȝet, / And wittnesse of þat wykked werk and þe wrake after / Þat oure Fader forferde for fylþe of þose ledes" (1049-51). As a counterpoint to the apples of Sodom is the burgeoning Rose of the Nativity scene in 1069-88 (esp. 1079), in which the Virgin is celebrated for the fruit of her womb, Christ.

Just as the unnaturalness and sterility of Sodom and the Dead Sea signify spiritual fruitlessness, the paternity of Abraham, whose encounter with the three angels in the valley of Mambre is narrated in *Cleanness* as the first part of the Sodom episode, signifies fruitfulness in faith. In Ecclus. 44.20-23 Abraham is praised both for his seed and for his faith, and in the New Testament to be a "son of Abraham" is to be one of the faithful (e.g., Ioh. 8.39-44, Acta 3.25, Gal. 3.7-9). Abraham's faith and obedience to God are noted frequently in biblical commentary, but especially in exegesis of Gen. 22.1-18 and of Heb. 11.8-10, 17-19.[23] Abraham, moreover, acts as the spiritual father of the faithful through the line of Isaac, which flowers in the church of Christ. For example, the commentary on Ecclesiasticus by Rabanus Maurus emphasizes Abraham's position as a literal ancestor of Christ and as a figurative ancestor of the Church. Rabanus traces two genealogies for mankind through Abraham. One is the line of Ishmael, "sons of the flesh," later to become the "sterile Jews"; the other is the line of Isaac, "sons of faith," later to become all who believe in Christ. Only the faithful are Abraham's true "seed."[24]

The *Cleanness*-Poet places Abraham squarely in this spiritual role. As God sets out towards Sodom from Mambre, He determines to reveal His intentions to "Habraham þe trwe" (682) because he is "chef chyldryn fader, / Þat so folk schal falle fro to flete all þe worlde," and whose every descendant "blessed schal worþe" (684-86). Although this passage paraphrases Gen. 18.17-19, in order to suggest Abraham's paternity of the faithful it interpolates language from other biblical passages celebrating God's covenant with him. Whereas Genesis declares that Abraham will become a great people, *Cleanness* notes that Abraham will be the "chief father of children, from whom children will fall to flood the whole world," thereby applying the etymology of Abraham's name, *pater multitudinis gentium*, and the idea that his seed will inherit *a mari usque ad mare* from Gen. 17.4-7 and Ecclus. 44.20-23, which celebrate God's covenant with Abraham and the faithfulness with which Abraham kept it. Again unlike Genesis, *Cleanness* directly praises the faith of Abraham, calling him "Habraham þe trwe" (682), as he is described also in Hebrews 11.8-9.

III

Abraham's hospitality dramatizes his faithfulness and foreshadows Lot's reception of the two angels, for the poet has sharpened the implicit parallels between the two biblical visits. Abraham and Lot are both solitary men, Abraham dwelling alone in the valley of Mambre and Lot living as an outsider in Sodom, and each man is found seated outside a door when the angels approach. Each immediately notices the fair appearance of his visitors; each arises at once, greets the angels reverently and offers them hospitality (Gen. 18.10-12, 19.1-3; *Cleanness* 601-20; 784-812). In both instances, the visitors deliver a divine message; in Genesis, both Sara's and Lot's future sons-in-law do not believe the message (Gen. 18.10, 19.14), but in *Cleanness*, Sara laughs (653) and the young men refuse to get out of bed to flee Sodom (934-36). It is in light of these adaptations of the biblical narrative that we must view Sara's disbelief of the three angels' prophecy concerning the birth of Isaac (645-670).

Sara's obedience to her husband's command to prepare bread for the angels (623-44; cp. 1 Pet. 3.6) contrasts with the apocryphal detail of Lot's wife's disobedience of her husband's command to leave salt out of the bread she bakes (817-27) establishing Sara as both hospitable and faithful. The standard exegetical interpretation of Gen. 18.10-16, however, is that Sara's barrenness signifies a longstanding faithlessness embodied in her scornful laugh; when she conceives, it must be because she begins to believe the angels' prophecy.[25] Sara's unfaithful laugh is sometimes compared to Abraham's joyous laugh on hearing the same promise of Isaac's birth in Gen. 17.17.[26] But in his commentary on Heb. 11.11, where Sara is a model of faith, Hugh of St. Cher claims that Sara laughs out of fear of the angels, and in that moment her faith and her son are conceived.[27]

Thus converted, Sara exemplifies regeneration, in sharp contrast to Lot's wife, who is stubbornly attached to sin. In *Cleanness*, the angels' accusation, "'Se! so Sare laʒes, / Not trawande þe tale þat I to þe shewed'" (661-62), provokes Sara's presumably fearful assertion "by hir trawþe" (667) that she never laughed at the prophecy. Sara's denial is such an outrageous lie that perhaps we must view it through Hugh's gloss: converted from her faithless old self by her fear, Sara now declares her faith by dissociating herself from *untrawþe*. In the end Sara's momentary lack of *trawþe* goes unpunished—the angels dismiss it with "bot let we hit one" (670). Laughing, Sara is even "Sare þe madde" (654), as Lot's wife is "wod" (828); but the comparison—like the poet's comparison of Nabuchodonosor and Baltassar in the poem's third episode reveals differences through merely apparent similarities. Both Sara and Lot's wife are first seen inside a dwelling (623 ff., 811 ff.). From behind her door (653 ff.), Sara laughs at the angels' prophecy; while in her house (817-28), Lot's wife disobeys her husband's command. Both women then leave their dwellings; but leaving the house releases Sara from the prison of her doubt, while for Lot's wife there is no release—still tied to Sodom, she looks back at it and is transformed into a motionless figure of her sin. In Genesis, Sara does not step outside her dwelling: this detail added by the *Cleanness*-Poet distinguishes Sara from Lot's wife by serving as an objective correlative of her conversion.[28]

In Luke, Lot's wife is Christ's figure for reneging—returning to sin after repentance. After relating the Parable of the Wedding Feast in 14.16-24, Christ tells several parables representing the reward for repentance: the lost sheep (15.3-7), the lost coin (15.8-10), the prodigal son (15.11-32), and the unjust steward (16.1-13). These parables are followed by the story of Dives and Lazarus (16.19-31), which illustrates the punishment of the unrepentant. Then follow two similes on the efficacy of faith—the mustard seed (17.5-6) and the unprofitable servant (17.7-10)—and the narrative of Christ's healing the ten lepers, which concludes with the words, "Arise, go thy way, for thy faith has saved thee" (17.12-19). Having established the twin needs of faith and repentance, Christ then warns of the coming Judgment through the figures of the Flood and the destruction of Sodom, concluding with the admonition not to look back on this life at the time of Judgment:

> And as it came to pass in the days of Noe, even so will it be in the days of the Son of Man. They were eating and drinking, they were marrying and giving in marriage, until the day when Noe entered the ark, and the flood came and destroyed them all. Or as it came to pass in the days of Lot: they were eating and drinking, they were buying and selling, they were planting and building; but on the day that Lot went out from Sodom, it rained fire and brimstone from heaven, and destroyed them all. In the same wise will it be on the day that the Son of Man is revealed. In that hour let him who is on the housetop and his goods in the house, not go down to take them away; and likewise let him who is in the field not turn back. Remember Lot's wife (Luc. 17.26-32).

Christ ends this series of parables with a brief parable about the Last Judgment in which He likens God to a city ruler whom a widow has long been petitioning for revenge against an enemy; this parable concludes, "Yet, when the Son of Man comes, will he find, do you think, faith on the earth?" (Luc. 18.8). In scriptural tradition Lot's wife is understood chiefly through these parables, which offer eschatological warnings against faithlessness and urge the need for repentance

in a world headed for judgment.[29] In the *Book of Vices and Virtues* —
a work in which the third branch of *vntrawþe* is reneging—Lot's wife
represents those who break religious vows: "Lothes wif betokneþ
hem þat ben gon out of þis world in-to religion and after þat turnen
aȝen, as bi wille and bi desire þat þei haue; and ȝit neuer þe latter þe
bodies dwellen in þe clostre, but þe herte is in þe world."[30] The poet's
opening simile, about unclean priests who are "honest utwyth, and
inwith alle fylþez" (14), establishes the theme of reneging in *Cleanness*.
These priests are unfaithful to their appearance, for they "conterfete
crafte" (13).   Unfaithful to their office, they pollute the host, God's
own body (11-16), in much the same way Lot's wife disobediently
serves the angels with ritually impure bread.   Cleanness requires
"fayre formez" of speech in order to be adequately represented, says
the poet (1-3); the broken vows of the unclean priests distort the
relation between language and meaning in the same way Lot's wife,
turned into the pillar of salt, distorts the human form, which, like the
sacramental language of vows or of penance, is a sign pointing toward
a higher perfection, the eternal plane where bodies and words are not
signs but existence and meaning itself. In the *Book of Vices and Virtues*,
spiritual perfection is possible only to those who have faith. They are
the clean of heart who shall see God:

> After þe ensaumple of seynt Poule schulde þe goode reli-
> gious forȝete þe world and lete it bihynde hym, and alle þe
> goodes euere lastyng haue alwey tofore his eien, and
> euere-more go forþ fro vertue in-to vertue, al for-to he
> come to þe hil of þe endeles ioie, where he schal see God al
> clerliche, and he schal loue hym parfiȝtliche & þanke hym
> wiþ-out ende. Þis is þe blessyng whider þat þe ȝifte of
> cunnyng ledeþ hem þat kepeþ clennesse of herte and of
> body, as we haue schewed here-tofore; & þerfore seiþ oure
> lord þat blessed be þe clene of herte, for þei schulle see
> God.... and þerfore ben þe clene of herte blessed in þis
> world, for þei haue þe eien of þe herte and þe vnder-
> stondyng and þe wille so clere and so clene þat þei seen God
> and lyuen bi good fey and stedefast and certeyn, as we
> haue seid. (p. 269-70)[31]

If, typologically, Lot's wife offers a lesson to penitents, then
perhaps in *Cleanness* she anticipates both the poet's excursus on
penance in 1109-48 and the double stories of the Babylonian Captivity
and Baltassar's feast which illustrate God's anger with those who
"look back" to the world after their spiritual reformation. Insofar as
she embodies a warning not to covet the world after renouncing it
through penance, Lot's wife introduces the theme of reneging, the
theological term for which is "recidivism"—the spiritual sodomy of
untrawþe which informs the Baltassar episode. Lot's wife would thus
be a central figure linking the Baltassar episode to the Flood and
Sodom episodes in *Cleanness*.

IV

The poet's excursus on penance, which bridges the Sodom and Baltassar narratives, depends on the images of the pearl and the vessel. Like the vessel image, the pearl image is a motif in *Cleanness*. Besides its use in the excursus on penance, it concludes the Flood narrative and recurs in the Baltassar episode (545-56; 1467, 1472). In the excursus, the soul cleansed by penance is brighter than the pearl washed in wine (1115-32), an image which recalls the Christ-child in the preceding Nativity passage, for if the pearl is pure "by kynde" (1128), Christ is noted for his cleanness as the "Kyng of nature" (1087), and Christ is "burnyst" (1085), as if a jewel, at the moment of his birth.[32] Through penance we conform to Christ: "If þou wyl dele drwrye wyth Dryʒtyn, þenne, / And lelly lovy þy Lorde, and his leef worþe, / Þenne confourme þe to Kryst and þe clene make, / Þat ever is polyced als playn as þe perle selven" (1065-68). Although the poet insists on the need for penance, the image of the soul shifts from pearl to vessel when he considers God's anger at recidivism (1133-56). So when the purified soul returns to its sin, the spirit is metaphorically "robbed wyth þewes" ('robbed by thieves', or perhaps 'robbed of its virtues', 1142). The idea of robbery leads to the simile of the temple vessels which were stolen from Jerusalem and then defiled by Baltassar. Significantly, the vessels are decorated with pearls (1467, 1472). The image of the soul as a vessel is surely central here and throughout *Cleanness*, as Charlotte Morse has shown at length. The crime of *furta sacra* associates that image more closely with the sin of reneging which is at issue in this section of the poem.[33]

The minor *exemplum* which begins the final episode of *Cleanness* illustrates the sin of reneging. The unfaithful Jews under Sedecias revert to idolatry, for which God punishes them with the Babylonian Captivity: "For þat folke in her fayth watz founden untrwe, / Þat haden hyʒt þe hyʒe God to halde of hym ever" (1161-62; cp. 1163-68). As Morse points out, "This diction echoes the Christian betrothal promise: 'Here I take the ... to haue and to holde, ... tyll dethe us departe, and thereto I plyght the my trouthe'."[34] If the soul's union with God is like a marriage, then in this minor *exemplum* the Jews are to God what Lot's disobedient, *untrawþe*-ful wife is to Lot.

Nevertheless, at first glance the poet's imagery in this last episode seems incongruous, especially because the focus of unfaith shifts from the vessels in the excursus on penance, to the idolatrous Jews in the Sedecias narrative, and last to the sacrilegious Baltassar. The vessels might represent the sinner who renounces his penance and Baltassar in turn the fiend who tempts him away, but since God's punishment lights on Baltassar, not on the vessels, Baltassar himself must be considered the proper figure of reneging. Another problematic feature of the narrative lies in Nabuchodonosor's unusual role of reformed sinner. This role is untarnished, even though his duke Nabuzardan's men seize the temple vessels "as robbors wylde" (1269) and even though he receives the stolen temple vessels. The poet emphasizes Nabuchodonosor's reverential handling of the sacred objects as if to contrast Nabuchodonosor with the unclean priests in the poem's opening lines:

> He trussed hem [the vessels] in his tresorye in a tryed place,
> Rekenly, wyth reverens, as he ry3t hade. (1317-18)

> Thay teen unto his temmple and temen to hymselven;
> Reken wyth reverence þay r[ec]hen his auter. (9-10)

Nabuchodonosor is converted by Daniel's preaching and dies in humility (1326-32). Daniel later rebukes Baltassar with the example of Nabuchodonosor as a penitent who keeps his covenant with God. If Baltassar, not the vessels, is meant to serve as the chief example of reneging, then there is a clear parallel between Nabuchodonosor's conquest of the lapsed Sedecias and Darius's conquest of Baltassar, for in this episode, God does not punish sinners directly but through intermediaries. One must then explore how Baltassar can be considered a reneger.

Baltassar encompasses both pride and lechery, the first and last of the Seven Deadly Sins: "Þus in pryde and olipraunce his empyre he haldes, / In lust, and in lecherye, and loþelych werkkes" (1349-50). He is thoroughly sinful, guilty not just of one controlling vice but of the entire range of sin, capped by pride. His feast, an "avayment of his vayneg[l]orie" (1358), is set up "Prudly on a plat playn" (1379); generally, the description of it in 1405-19 recalls the description of pride of the table depicted both in the *Parson's Tale* (CT X.443-45); in its source, Peraldus's *Summ;*, and in *Winner and Waster*.[35] At this prideful feast, a parodic version of the wedding banquet of the parable, Baltassar drinks too much and loses his senses. Although *amentia* represents a well-known consequence of gluttonous imbibing, in the *Book of Vices and Virtues* madness is also a symptom of *vntrawþe*.[36] Further, the drunken folly of *mayster* Baltassar (1427) compares with the figurative drunkenness suffered by proud *maisters* in the *Book of Vices and Virtues*:

> For þan synne of pride is wel perilous, for it blyndeþ a man
> þat he ne knoweþ not hymself, ne seeþ not hymself. And
> þerfore it is cleped þe stronge wyn and my3ty þat þe deuel
> 3yueþ to men to maken hem dronke, and namely þe grete
> lordes and wise clerkes and riche men and worþi men and
> dou3ty men and generally alle men, but of alþermost þe

grete maistres, for þei ne knoweþ not ne seeþ not her euele
deedes ne her folies, ne þei haue no witt. (pp. 11-12)

The word *mayster* (1427) invites contrast with the lord in the Parable
of the Wedding Feast (125), with God (748, 771, 1113; cp.1328), and
with Darius the Mede (1793), and comparison to Nabuzardan (1237).
But Baltassar is also to be contrasted with Nabuchodonosor:

> So faste þay weȝed to him wyne, hit warmed his hert,
> And breyþed uppe into his brayn and blemyst his mynde,
> And al waykned his wyt, and wel neȝe he foles;
> For he waytez on wyde, his wenches he byholdes,
> And his bolde baronage aboute bi þe woȝes.
> Þenne a dotage ful depe drof to his hert,
> And a caytif counsayl he caȝt bi hymselven.
> Maynly his marschal þe mayster upon calles,
> And comaundes hym cofly coferes to lance,
> And fech forþe vessel þat his fader broȝt,
> Nabugodenozar, noble in his strenþe,
> In Jude, in Jerusalem, in gentyle wyse. (1420-32)

Whereas Nabuchodonosor was "noble in his strenþe," Baltassar is
"waykned [in] his wyt." Nabuchodonosor had received the vessels,
fashioned originally "in temple of þe trauþe trwly to stonde" (1490),
and left them undisturbed; but Baltassar will put them to unfaithful
use, "to serve Satanas þe blake, / Bifore þe bolde Baltazar, wyth bost
and wyth pryde" (1449-50). These lines suggest that reneging rededi-
cates the soul to Satan and indicate that Baltassar has returned to a
pattern abandoned by Nabuchodonosor.

As Sara is a foil for Lot's wife, Nabuchodonosor is a foil for
Baltassar. Daniel's interpretation of the handwriting on the wall
develops the image of Nabuchodonosor as a reformed penitent, an
example of *trawþe* from whom Baltassar has fallen away. Nabuchodonosor's sin is pride; like Satan earlier in the poem, he practices the
idolatry of self-worship:

> 'His myȝt mete to Goddes he made wyth his wordes:
> "I am god of þe grounde to gye as me lykes,
> As he þat hyȝe is in heven, his aungeles þat weldes.
> If he hatz formed þe folde and folk þerupone,
> I haf bigged Babiloyne, burȝ alþerrychest,
> Stabled þerinne uche a ston in strenkþe of myn armes;
> Moȝt never myȝt bot myn make such anoþer." (1662-68)

> For þe fyrste felonye þe falce fende wroȝt
> Whyl he watz hyȝe in þe heven, hoven upon lofte,
> Of alle þyse aþel aungelez attled þe fayrest;
> And he unkyndely as a karle kydde a reward.
> He seȝ noȝt bot hymself, how semly he were;
> Bot his Soverayn he forsoke, and sade þyse wordez:

'I schal telde up my trone in þe tramountayne,
And by lyke to þat Lorde þat þe lyft made.' (205-12)[37]

In turn, Baltassar worships gods made of "goods," not the God who grants all goods: "Alle þe goude golden goddes þe gaulez ȝet nevenen, ... / Bot hym þat alle goudes gives, þat God þay forȝeten" (1525, 1528; cp. 1326). Just as Sara's conversion is represented by stepping outside her dwelling, Nabuchodonosor's penitence is represented by his exile from Babylon: it is an exile from his former self. Unlike Lot's wife, who was permanently metamorphosed, the truly reformed king does not look back, In Dan. 4.32-34, from which the *Cleanness*-Poet adapted his description of Nabuchodonosor as a wildman in 1673-1700, he looks *up,* but by putting aside this detail and by interpolating instead the account of Nabuchodonosor's return to his senses from Dan. 5.21 before continuing with Dan. 4.36-37, the poet emphasizes not seeing but knowing: "Til he wyst ful wel who wroȝt alle myȝtes, / And cowþe uche kyndam tokerve and kever when hym lyked" (1699-1700). The poet treats Nabuchadonosor's pride as an error through which he confused his might with God's. Shown what he really is by comparison with his Creator, Nabuchodonosor eventually comes to his senses.

Baltassar resumes Nabuchodonosor's pride even though, as Daniel says, he "saw these signs with sight" (1710): he sees, but he chooses not to understand. Furthermore, Nabuchodonosor's grotesque bestial image itself, partly bovine and partly avian, suggests his redemption, whereas Baltassar's bestiality stands forth as a sign of his spiritual relapse and its punishment. If Nabuchodonosor resembles an ox, it is not without significance that the ox recognizes Christ for the king of nature in the Nativity scene (1086).If Nabuchodonosor is identified with an eagle, it should be noted that the eagle is Ezechiel's figure for Nabuchodonosor in the role of divine judge punishing the idolatrous Jews (Ezech. 17.2-10).[38] Baltassar's feast is adorned with animal figures and carried in on horseback (1409-12), while Baltassar himself is mainly like a dog. When he calls for the temple vessels, Baltassar says he wants to have his concubines "lap" from them (1434), which Edward Wilson terms "a verb notably associated with animals rather than human beings, and especially with dogs—an apt association in view of Belshazzar's corpse later lying like a dog in a ditch (1792)."[39]

The image cited by Wilson constitutes the poet's last word on Baltassar's sin: "The kyng in his cortyn watz kaȝt bi þe heles, / Feryed out bi þe fete, and fowle dispysed. / Þat watz so doȝty þat day and drank of þe vessayl / Now is a dogge also dere þat in a dych lygges" (1789-

92). This image may have been inspired by popular legends about Moslems, who were known by the epithet "dog" in the West and were often pictured as Cynocephali, a monstrous dog-headed race.[40] In the Old Testament, the dog is the most notorious of unclean animals forbidden to the Jews, a scavenger eating corpses and living at the edges of camps (3 Reg. 14.11, 16.4, 21.19, Ps. 21.17, etc.).[41] But chiefly, the poet may be alluding to the scriptural image of the faith-breaker who returns to his sin just as the dog "returns to his vomit." Such an image acts as the conclusion of the apocalyptic warning of 2 Pet. 2, a work often cited as an inspiration for *Cleanness* because so many of its details are echoed in *Cleanness*. 2 Pet. 2 refers to the fallen angels (verse 4) who figure in *Cleanness* 269-72; it also uses the Flood and Sodom as types of the coming Judgment and singles out Noe and Lot as righteous men (verses 5-8). Moreover, it specifically chastises "those who follow the flesh in unclean lust," who, like the antediluvians, the raven, and the Sodomites, hate authority and want only to please themselves (verse 10); it likens the unclean to beasts (verse 12) as is the case here with Baltassar; it points to their rioting, their feasting, and their worship of Balaam, again recalling Baltassar (verses 13-15); it refers to their punishment as "caligo tenebrarum" ['blackness of darkness' (verse 17)], which suggests the conclusion of Baltassar's last day (1760); and it ends with a warning against recidivism, the chief image of which is evoked by the dog returning to its vomit (verses 20-22), from Prov. 26.11.[42] Thus, if *Cleanness* is rooted in 2 Pet. 2, the image of Baltassar lying like a dog in the ditch—or, more precisely, having the *worth* of such a dog—may be one last image for his reneging.

The canine image emphasizes that Baltassar's sin is distinguished from Nabuchodonosor's in that, whereas Nabuchodonosor repented, Baltassar reverted to the old pattern. Baltassar worships gods made in Satan's image (1341; cp. 205), and, like Satan, he rebels, hurling challenges at the true God (1711-12; cp. 209-12). Indeed, Baltassar's conduct illustrates all three branches of *vntrewþe* from the *Book of Vices and Virtues*: as *vilenye*, his idolatry misuses goods and ungratefully scorns the Creator of all goods; in his drunkenness and wild feasting, he demonstrates *wodnesse*; by dedicating himself to Satan and by relapsing from the example of Nabuchodonosor, he demonstrates *reneiynge*.[43] Daniel's condemnation of Baltassar clearly links the Babylonian king with the minor *exemplum* of reneging, the fall of Jerusalem, which prefaced the Baltassar story, for just as the Jews "in her fayth watz founden untrwe" (1161), Baltassar's reign is "funde ful fewe of hit [i.e., wholly lacking with respect to its] fayth-dedes" (1735).

V

Although it represents the first major *exemplum* of sin in *Cleanness*, the Flood episode appears last in this essay because the theme of *untrawþe* pervading it is more easily demonstrated in connection with the other episodes. *Trawþe* is most obviously an issue, perhaps, in the narrative of the raven and the dove since the raven is openly rebellious against Noe. But Noe's faith makes him a key figure for focusing the poet's conception of sin, for his mastery over the natural order opposes the violations of nature practiced by mankind before the Flood and later by the Sodomites, while his great faith in God compares with Abraham's and contrasts with the idolatry of Sedecias and Baltassar.

As in the biblical story (Gen. 8.6-7), the raven is sent out of the ark first to search for dry land; but here the raven flies off to an apocryphal meal of soggy, decayed corpses (459-66). This raven is "ronk" and "untrwe" (455, 456). The Levitican and Deuteronomic codes considered the raven unclean (Lev. 11.15; Deut. 14.14). The raven's appetite for dead flesh is well-attested in medieval commentary on the Deluge and in popular tradition.[44] But the raven is also a common figure of faithlessness. To Richard of St. Victor, for instance, the raven is like "false Christians" who, attracted to temporal delights, leave the faith; the dove, in contrast, signifies those who cannot find rest in this world except through the Christian faith. In other allegories—Bruno of Asti's *Expositio in Genesim* and Rupert of Deutz's commentary on Gen. 8. 6-7, respectively—the raven acts as an emblem of heretics and schismatics or of unfaithful Jews.[45] Such allegories of faithlessness are the same as those derived from the excuses given by the guests who decline to attend the banquet in the Parable of the Wedding Feast; and in *Cleanness*. Noe waits fruitlessly for the raven, then curses it (467-68), just as the host waits fruitlessly for his invited guests, then curses them (61-76, 105-08). The *Glossa ordinaria* to Luc. 14.18, "And they all with one accord began to excuse themselves" (cp. *Cleanness* 62) reads, "For they excuse themselves who love earthly things more than heavenly things." For Luc. 14.20, "I have married a wife, and therefore I cannot come," the gloss is, "Three types of people are seen to be excluded from the great banquet: Gentiles, because of their immoderate love of earthly goods; Jews, who, spurning Christ, place the yoke of the law on their shoulders.... Heretics, who like Eve tempt the firmness of faith through feminine desire" (ed. cit., 5:163A,B).[46] *Cleanness* perhaps alludes to these allegorizations in 76:"'More to wyte is her wrange þen any wylle gentyl.'" In this way, the Parable of the Wedding Feast itself generates the theme of *untrawþe* and the figure of the raven directly reflects the sins illustrated by it.

The raven also reintroduces the sin of the antediluvians into the world, for like Baltassar's faults, the raven's sin is both *untrawþe* and *concupiscentia carnis* ['fleshly desire']. The physically perfect antediluvians (253-62), with no law to follow but the law of nature (263), take up homosexuality (265-68), whereupon their women find sexual gratification with demons (269-71), from which union springs the race of giants who flood the world with their violence (272-80). Hugh of St. Cher's gloss on Gen. 8.7 shows that the association between this sort of *concupiscentia carnis* and the raven's craving for flesh is more than just a bad pun:

> *The raven which went out, but did not return*, enticed by a floating corpse, that is, by wantonness. Osea 5.4: 'They will not set their thought to return to the Lord because the spirit of fornication is in the midst of them, and they have not known the Lord.' Behold how many evils wantonness performs. For as soon as the spirit of fornication occupies the heart, the knowledge of God immediately vanishes.[47]

The raven's carnality demonstrates the relationship of *luxuria* to unbelief in God, since with its onset "the knowledge of God immediately vanishes." Again, the *Glossa Ordinaria* makes this same connection in further glossing "uxorem duxi" from the Parable: "*I have married a wife*. Because many marry not for fruitfulness [i.e., to procreate] but on account of carnal desire. Thus, carnal desire is indicated by this act, by which the scornful one refuses to come to the banquet of God" (*ed. cit.*, 5:163B)].[48]

Although the antediluvians in *Cleanness* are not labeled *untrawþe*-ful, their contrast with Noe reveals the symptoms of *untrawþe*. The giants "'doten ['act madly'] on þis molde'" (286), their *wodnesse* representing a consequence of violating the covenant of natural law that prevailed during the Golden Age. Having abused the abundant gifts of God (259), their forebears have already committed *vilenye* and have quite literally joined themselves to the devil—a carnal type of *reneiynge*, although one need not force the application of all three branches of *vntrewþe* from the *Book of Vices and Virtues* in order to see this sin in the passage. Noe, on the other hand, counters the antediluvians' madness and ingratitude with his own right reason and righteousness: God thus favors him because he "'in reysoun hatz rengned and ry3twys ben ever" (328; cp. 294-96), a line echoed later when Abraham describes the just as "re3tful... and resounable" (724). He hastens to obey God's command to build the Ark (341-42) just as Abraham hastens to prepare a welcome for the three angels (610-44). When God asks him if he has followed His behest, Noe's answer uses diction reminiscent of the obedience formula employed by the ser-

vants of the host in the Parable: "'ȝe, Lorde, wyth þy leve,' sayde þe
lede þenne, / 'Al is wroȝt at þi worde, as þou me wyt lantez'" (347-48;
cp. 94: "'Lo! lorde, wyth yor leve, at yor lege heste'"). As Noe is
obedient, so is he faithful. Taking instructions on the building of the
Ark, Noe hears God only as a voice (360); once the earth dries after the
Flood, however, Noe waits patiently until "Godez glam" (499) sum-
mons him. On the Ark, Noe "ofte nevened þe name of oure Lorde"
(410)— an anachronism, since God revealed His name only to Moses
in Ex. 3.14.

   After the Flood in Genesis, Noe is placed in charge of the world
with the same command to "be fruitful and multiply" that was given
at Creation (Gen. 1.22, 1.28; 8.17, 9.1, 9.17). God's blessing on the
animals and mankind, which includes the commandment to be fruitful and multiply (*Cleanness*, 521-27), is crucial in *Cleanness*, since it
transforms Noe into a second Adam who does not fall and whose chief
function is to preserve seed for future regeneration. This role for Noe
is, of course, implicit in the Flood story, for the Ark itself resembles a
seed pod carried on the waters to a place where it will germinate.
Furthermore, the idea is emphasized in Christian tradition, first in the
Old Testament Book of Wisdom, and then by commentators and
vernacular authors; for instance, Isidore of Seville calls Noe the
"secundus pater orbis" ['second father of the earth'].[49] But God's
blessing is part of His covenant, a covenant which He renews with
Abraham. If, like Abraham, Noe is a patriarchal figure whose off-
spring ultimately are the "sons of faith," he embodies obedience,
righteousness, and faith as he does in the two central biblical *encomia*
about him and Abraham, (Ecclus. 44.17-23; Heb. 11.7-10). And if, like
Abraham, he is faithful, his obedience to natural law also contrasts
with the homosexuality of sinners destroyed by divine wrath.

   Such emphasis on faith in *Cleanness* is one way in which the poem
shares a concern for *trawþe* that is often found in late fourteenth-
century works such as *Gawain, Piers Plowman*, and Chaucer's *Fran-
klin's Tale*, and "Truth." In *Cleanness*, though, *trawþe* is characterized
as natural sexuality and as loyalty to the true God. Both are subsumed
by the metaphor of cleanness of heart; the Beatitude itself, which
emphasizes inner purity, establishes that the inner quality of faith is
the poem's true subject. Though they are indeed regarded as sinful in
themselves, the homosexuality and idolatry dramatized in the
poem's three main episodes are chiefly representative. "For *many*
faults [emphasis mine] may a man forfeit his bliss / So that he will not
see the Sovereign"—that is, so that he fails to attain the Beatific Vision

promised by the Beatitude (177-78). The three instances of sin narrated in *Cleanness* deserve special attention, says the poet, because in punishing them God was angrier that in any other cases (197-204, 1143-48). They are paradigms through which the poet anatomizes for his readers the way any sin destroys the covenantal relationship of man and God, a relationship defined through the concept of *trawþe.*

Notes

1.   All citations to *Cleanness* are to *Purity, A Middle English Poem*, ed. Robert J. Menner, Yale Studies in English, 61 (New Haven, 1920; rpt. Hamden, CT: Archon, 1970). Repunctuations and glosses are my own and are based on a consultation of other editions and of standard lexical tools.

2.   Since the Deluge and Sodom episodes of *Cleanness* demonstrate the Cleanness-Poet's contention that God's wrath is greater for "filth of the flesh" (202) than it is for pride of Satan and the disobedience of Adam, it would at first appear that in these first two *exempla* of uncleanness, sexual sin is the only concept expressed by the poet's image of "filth." A number of recent critics have maintained this view, which goes back as far as the earliest work on the poem. For example, see: Charlotte C. Morse, *The Pattern of Judgment in the* Queste *and* Cleanness (Columbia: University of Missouri Press, 1978), p. 151; Edward Wilson, *The* Gawain-*Poet, Medieval and Renaissance Authors* (Leiden: E. J. Brill, 1976), p. 87; A. Kent Hieatt, "Symbolic and Narrative Patterns in *Pearl, Cleanness, Patience*, and *Gawain*," *English Studies in Canada* 2 (1976), 128-30; T. D. Kelly and John T. Irwin, "The Meaning of *Cleanness* : Parable as Effective Sign," *Mediaeval Studies* 35 (1973): 235. Typical of earlier views is Sir Israel Gollancz's Introduction to his edition of *Cleanness* (London: Oxford University Press, 1921; rpt. Totowa, NJ: Rowman and Littlefield, 1974), pp. xv-xvi. Recently, Lynn Staley Johnson, *The Voice of the* Gawain-*Poet* (Madison: University of Wisconsin Press, 1984), pp. 97-143, has argued that the three episodes of *Cleanness* treat the sins of lust, avarice, and pride, respectively.

3.   Menner, Introduction to his edition of *Purity*, p. xlvii. Citation to *Sir Gawain and the Green Knight* is to the edition of J. R. R. Tolkien and E. V. Gordon, 2nd ed. by Norman Davis (Oxford: Clarendon Press, 1967; rpt. 1972). R. J. Spendal has observed that of the thirteen MS capitals in Cotton Nero A.x occurring in *Cleanness*, all of which indicate significant moments in the poem, two demarcate episodes in which *trawþe* is significant: "For example, section four (lines 249-344) ends at a point which illustrates Noah's obedience to God; section five (345-484) closes with the dove's obedience to Noah. The parallel endings of these adjacent sections draw attention to the poem's deep concern with loyalty or *trawþe*"; "The Manuscript Capitals in *Cleanness* " *Notes and Queries* 221 (1976): 340. Recently, Robert J. Blanch and Julian N. Wasserman have examined the legal overtones of *trawþe* in *Gawain* in their article, "Medieval Contracts and Covenants: The Legal Coloring of *Sir Gawain and the Green Knight*," *Neophilologus* 68 (1984): 598-610.

4.   Gawain is said to be "clean" after both these confessions: see John Burrow, "The Two Confession Scenes in *Sir Gawain and the Green Knight*," *Modern Philology* 57 (1959): 73-79, rpt. in *Sir Gawain and Pearl: Critical Essays*, ed. Robert J. Blanch (Bloomington: Indiana University Press, 1966), pp. 123-34; also see Burrow's *A Reading of* Sir Gawain and the Green Knight (London: Routledge and K. Paul, 1965), pp. 104-10, 127-33.

5.   All reference to Scripture is to Jerome's Vulgate and to the Douay translation; other translations into Modern English are my own. Text: *Biblia Sacra iuxta Vulgatam versionem*, ed Bonifatius Fischer *et. al.*, 2 vols. (Stuttgrt: Würtembergische

Bibelanstalt, 1975); punctuation is my own.

6.   On the homosexuality of the Sodomites as a sin specifically against the natural law, which mandates procreation of kind, see my dissertation, "The Anatomy of Sin: Violations of *Kynde* and *Trawþe* in *Cleanness*," Diss. Cornell Univ., 1979, Chapter One, esp. pp. 72-103; for a discussion of *immunditia* as a term for homosexuality in the later Middle Ages, especially in connection with *Cleanness*, see Barbara Florence Newman, "Sin, Judgment, and Grace in the Works of the *Gawain*-Poet," Diss. Cornell University, 1985, Chapter Two, esp. pp. 90-110.

7.   Though the *OED* (s.v. "settle", vb.) lists no legal senses of "settle" (here *saȝtle*) from before the Renaissance, its use here in a doublet with *sakred*, especially considering the penitential context, would suggest a formal relationship, perhaps a kind of peace after hostilities. The word seems to have this meaning also in 230, where it describes Satan's refusal to reconcile with God, and in 490, where the olive branch in the dove's mouth represents God's reconciliation with man after the Flood. In 1795 *saȝtlyng* refers to the peace Darius concludes with Babylon after conquering it.

8.   *OED ordinance*, sb., 5, 7. Cp. its use in *Handlyng Synne*, 1461-62: "Swyche ys goddys ordynaunce, / 'For veniaunce to take veniaunce'"; ed. Frederick J. Furnivall, EETS os 119 (London: K. Paul, Trench, Trübner, 1901). See also *ordinance*, sb., 6, and the example given there from Mandeville. William Stubbs offers a convenient discussion of the term in his standard study of English common law, *The Constitutional History of England*, abridged and with an introduction by James Cornford, Classics of British Historical Literature (Chicago: University of Chicago Press, 1979), pp. 426-28. One of the most famous sets of ordinances, which well illustrates the precise legal sense of the term in later medieval England, is the Ordinances of 1311, by which Edward II reformed the royal household. See further B. Wilkinson, *Studies in the Constitutional History of the Thirteenth and Fourteenth Centuries*, Publications of the University of Manchester, 253; Historical Series, 73 (Manchester: Manchester University Press,1937), pp. 227-46.

9.   *Middle English Dictionary, dighten*, 3a(c) and 4a. In the expression *dighten dom* it means 'to give someone the right to do something', as in *Gawain* 295 and Chaucer's *Troilus* IV.1188 (all citations of Chaucer will be from *The Riverside Chaucer*, ed. Larry D. Benson, et. al., 3rd ed. [Boston, 1987]). *Dighten* can also describe divine ordination (see *OED dight*, vb., I, 1-2), as in *The Pricke of Conscience* 7793-96, where the joys of heaven are *ordayned* and *dyght* to the righteous: "Eghe moght never se, ne ere here, / Ne in- tylle mans hert com þe ioyes sere / Þat God has ordaynd þare and dyght, / Tylle alle þat here lufes him ryght"; ed. Richard Morris (Berlin: A. Asher, 1863).

10.   Henry Campbell Black, *Black's Law Dictionary*, 5th rev. ed. (St. Paul, Mn: West Publishing Company, 1979); s.v. *mischief*.

11.   *Year Books of the Reign of King Edward the Third, Year XV*, ed. and trans. Luke Owen Pike, Rolls Series, 31 (London: Longman, 1891), p. 127. On Mowbray, see *The Dictionary of National Biography from the Earliest Times to 1900*, ed. Leslie Stephen and Sidney Lee, 22 vols. (London: Oxford University Press, 1921-22; rpt. 1949-1950), 13:1116-18.

12.   See *Pearl*, ed. E. V. Gordon (Oxford: Clarendon Press, 1953), 54, 312, 674; *Cleanness* 151, 569, 709, 823, 827, 1554; *Gawain* 1296, 1509. Note further *scylful*,

"reasonable," in *Cleanness* 1148, and the glosses *racio, racionabilis,* and *racionabilitas* for *skyle, skylful,* and *skylfulnesse* in the *Promptorium parvulorum,* ed. A. L. Mayhew, EETS ES 102 (London: K. Paul, Trench, Trübner, 1908), col. 413.

13.   *The Owl and the Nightingale,* ed. Eric Gerald Stanley, Old and Middle English Texts (1960; rpt. Manchester: Manchester University Press 1972). Legal elements in *The Owl and the Nightingale* are treated by Stanley, pp. 27-29; Kathryn Huganir, "The Owl and the Nightingale": *Sources, Date, and Author,* Diss. Univ. of Pennsylvania, 1931, pp. 81-96; Huganir, "Equine Quartering in *The Owl and the Nightingale," PMLA* 52 (1937): 935-45; and by J. W. H. Atkins, ed. *The Owl and the Nightingale* (Cambridge: Cambridge University Press, 1922), pp. lii-lv. For other instances of "right and skill" in distinctly legal contexts, see *The Seven Sages of Rome,* 4076, in the edition of Killis Campbell, Albion Series (Boston: Ginn, 1907); *Sancta Editha, sive Chronicon Vilodunense* 4010, in the edition of C. Horstmann (Heilbronn: Henninger, 1883); "Extraccio animarum ['The Deliverance of Souls']" 277, in *The Towneley Plays,* ed. George England and Alfred W. Pollard, EETS ES 71 (London: K. Paul, Trench, Trübner, 1897).

14.   For example, see Gratian's *Decretum* 1.1.1: "Omnes leges aut diuinae sunt, aut humanae. Diuinae natura, humanae moribus constant, ideoque he discrepant, quoniam aliae aliis gentibus placent. 1. Fas lex diuina est: ius lex humana.... Gratianus. Ex uerbis huius auctoritatis euidenter datur intelligi, in quo differant inter se lex diuina et humana, cum omne quod fas est, nomine diuinae uel naturalis legis accipiatur, nomine uero legis humanae mores iure conscripti et traditi intelligantur" ['All laws are either divine or human. Divine laws depend on nature, human laws on customs, and therefore they (i.e., human laws) disagree, because different laws suit different peoples. *Fas* is divine law; *ius* is human law....Gratian. From the words of this authority it is plainly given to understand the ways in which divine and human law differ between themselves, since all eternal law goes by the name of divine or natural law, while by the name of human law are understood customs written and handed down']; *Corpus iuris canonici,* ed. Aemilius Ludwig Richter, rev. Emil Friedberg, 2 vols. (Leipzig: Tauschnitz, 1879-1881; rpt. Graz: Akademische Druckund verlagsanstalt, 1959), 1:1; subsequent citations will be incorporated into my text. For a good introduction to this doctrine, see Charles Lefebvre and G. Simon, "Naturel (Droit)," in *Dictionnaire de droit canonique,* ed. R. Naz, *et. al.,* 7 vols. (Paris: Letouzey et Ané, 1935-1965), 6:966-79. For England in particular, see R. C. van Caenegem, *Royal Writs in England from the Conquest to Glanvill: Studies in the Early History of the Common Law ,* Selden Society, 77 (London: B. Quaritch, 1959), pp. 365-73.

15.   Augustine notes in *De civitate dei* 16.30 that in Sodom "stupra in masculos in tantam consuetudinem conualuerant, quantam leges solent aliorum factorum praebere licentiam" ['masculine bestiality was as allowable by custom as any other act is by the laws']; *De civitate dei,* ed. Bernard Dombart and Alphonse Kalb, CCSL 48 (Turnhout: Brepols, 1955), p. 535.

16.   "Hoc dixit vt euitaretur maius malum, scilicet vitium contra naturam, et violentiam hospitum suorum. De iure enim naturali est conseruare hospites"; 1:72F-G in the edition cited at the end of this note. In his *postilla* on Gen. 19.29, where Lot's wife is transformed into a pillar of salt, Nicholas explains that like the other Sodomites, Lot's wife was customarily inhospitable to visitors. The *Glossa ordinaria* to Gen. 19.1 (1:72B in the edition cited at the end of this note) holds up Lot as a model of hospitality: "Ex hoc autem loco scripture et multis alijs commendatur virtus hospitalitatis" ['For on account of this place and many others in scripture the goodness

of hospitality is commended']. All citations to Nicholas of Lyra and to the *Glossa* are to *Biblia sacra cum glossis, interlineari et ordinaria, Nicolai Lyrani postilla, ac moralitatibus, Burgensis additionibus, et Thoringi replicis* 6 vols. (Venice, 1588); subsequent citations will be incorporated into my text.

17.   *"Minus est secundum naturam coire, quam contra naturam delinquere.* Offerebat sanctus Loth filiarum pudorem. Nam etsi illa quoque flagiciosa inpuritas erat, tamen minus erat secundum naturam coire, quam aduersus naturam delinquere. Preferebat domus suae uerecundiae hospitalem gratiam, etiam apud barbaras gentes inuiolabilem."

18.   *Cursor Mundi*, 2757-62 (Trinity MS.) in the edition of Richard Morris, EETS, os. 57 (London: K. Paul, Trench, Trübner, 1874). In *"Cleanness* and *Cursor Mundi," ELN* 22 (1985): 6-11, Sarah M. Horrall argues that certain naturalistic details from the Flood episode in *Cleanness* derive from *Cursor Mundi.* On the image of Sodom in the Old and New Testaments, see Richard Kay, *Dante's Swift and Strong: Essay on Inferno XV* (Lawrence, KS: Regents Press of Kansas,1978), pp. 209-89; a concise discussion of the post-biblical reputation of Sodom is found in my article on Sodom and Gomorrah in the forthcoming *Dictionary of the Bible and Biblical Tradition in English Literature,* ed. David M. Jeffrey.

19.   On the association of Cain and the Chanaanites, see Oliver F. Emerson, "Legends of Cain, Especially in Old and Middle English," *PMLA* 21 (1906): 925-26.

20.   "[Gen. 13.10-11]. Fertilitatem terrae laudat, simul et incolarum notat impietatem, ut eo maiori damnatione digni esse intellegantur, quod maxima Dei munera non ad fructum pietatis sed ad incrementum uertere luxuriae"; *In Genesim,* 3.13.10; ed. Charles W. Jones, CCSL 118A (Turnhout: Brepolis, 1967), pp. 178-79; cp. 4.18.16: "Direxerunt autem oculos contra Sodomam, ut sicut fidem beati Abrahae laetis promissionibus remunerarent, ita perfidiam impiae ciuitatis flammis ultricibus perderent" ['They raised their eyes towards Sodom, for just as they might reward the faith of blessed Abraham with joyful promises, so might they destroy the faithlessness of the disobedient city with avenging flames'] (Ibid., 219).

21.   Cp. Jerome, *Commentarium in epistolam ad Galatas,* 3.6 (*Patrologiae Cursus Completus... Series Latina* [hereafter *PL*] 26.459-61); *Commentarium in Esaiam,* 1.1.9, ed. Marcus Adriaen, CCSL 73 (Turnhout: Brepolis, 1963), p. 14. A list of patristic *loci* for the image of bearing spiritual fruit may be found in Hieronymus Lauretus, *Silva allegoriarum totius sacrae scripturae* (10th ed. Cologne: Hermann Demen, 1681, rpt. Munich: Wilhelm Fink1971), p. 473.

22.   See Deut. 29.23, Sap. 10.6-7, Isa. 1.7-9, Ier. 49.17-18 and 50.40; Josephus, *Wars of the Jews* 4.18, in *Hegesippi qui dicitur Historiae libri V,* ed. Vincent Ussani, Corpus Scriptorum Ecclesiasticorum Latinorum [hereafter CSEL], 66 (Vienna: Hoelder-Pichler-Tempsky, 1932); *Mandeville's Travels* 12, ed. M. C. Seymour (Oxford: Oxford University Press,1967), pp. 73-74; also, *The Bodley Version of Mandeville's Travels,* ed. M. C. Seymour, EETS os 253 (London: Oxford University Press,1963), pp. 60-63, and *The Metrical Version of Mandeville's Travels 1241-79,* ed. M. C. Seymour, EETS os 269 (London: Oxford University Press, 1973). It is worth noting here that "Hegesippus" is the name given to an anonymous Latin translation of Josephus's *Wars* done ca. 367-374; Book 5 of this adaptation combines Books 5, 6, and 7 of the *Wars* into one book. "Hegesippus" circulated among the works of Ambrose during the Middle Ages. The other translation, *De bello judaico,* was falsely attributed to Rufinus. On both of these translations, see Heinz Schreckenberg, *Die Flavius-*

Josephus Tradition in Antike und Mittelalter, Arbeiten zur Literatur und Geschichte des Hellenistischen Judentums, 5 (Leiden: 1972), pp. 56-61.

23.   Augustine joins the Genesis and Hebrews passages in *De civitate dei* 16.32:"… temptatur Abraham de immolando dilectissimo filio ipso Isaac, ut pia eius oboedientia probaretur, saeculis in notitiam proferenda, non Deo…. 'Fide,' inquit, 'praecessit Abraham Isaac temptatus et unicum obtulit, qui promissiones suscepit, ad quem dictum est: in Isaac uocabitur tibi semen, cogitans quia et ex mortuis suscitare potest Deus'" ['Abraham was tested with the sacrifice of his most beloved son Isaac that his faithful obedience might be demonstrated, shown plainly to all the world, not to God…. "By faith," says [Scripture], "Abraham, who had received the promises (to whom it had been spoken, 'In Isaac shall thy seed be called'), taking into account that God was able to raise him even from the dead, brought forth Isaac when he was tested, and offered up his only son"]; ed. Dombart and Kalb, pp. 536-37. See also, on Gen. 22: Claudius of Turin (but attr. Eucherius of Lyon), *Commentarii in Genesim* 2 (*PL* 50.972); Alcuin, *Interrogationes et responsiones in Genesim* 205 (*PL* 100.545); Angelome of Luxeuil, *Commentarius in Genesin* 22 (*PL* 115.194-96); Remigius of Auxerre, *Commentarius in Genesim* 22 (*PL* 131.95); and Nicholas of Lyra, *ed. cit.*, 1:77C-D. On Heb. 11, see Hervé of Bourg-Dieux, *Commentaria in epistolas Pauli—ad Hebraeos* 11 (*PL* 181.1647-48); and the *Glossa ordinaria, ed. cit.*, 6:155A.

24.   " 'Abraham magnus pater multitudinis gentium. Et non est inventus similis illi in gloria. Qui conservavit legem Excelsi, et fuit in testamento cum illo, in carne ejus stare fecit testamentum, et in tentatione inventus est fidelis. Ideo jurejurando dedit illi gloriam in gente sua, crescere illum quasi terrae cumulum, et ut stellas exaltare semen ejus, et haereditari illos a mari usque ad mare, et a flumine usque ad terminos orbis terrae' [Ecclus. 44.20-23]. Abraham juxta nominis sui interpretationem pater est multarum, omnium videlicet gentium in Christo credentium; quia soli fideles aestimantur in semine, quoniam non qui filii carnis [i.e., the line of Ishmael] sed qui filii sunt fidei [i.e., the line of Isaac], ipsi semen sunt Abrahae…. Duplex ergo fit figura promissi seminis ejus, id est, in similitudinem arenae maris, in quo exprimuntur Judaei steriles; et in similitudinem stellarum coeli, in quo demonstrantur omnes gentes in Christo credentes, qui resurrectionis lumine in futuro coruscant sicut astra coeli…. Haereditavit ergo semen ejus a mari usque ad mare, et a flumine usque ad terminos orbis terrae, quia Christus ex semine Abraham ortus dominatur a mari usque ad mare, et a flumine usque ad terminos orbis terrae, quia Christus ex semine Abraham ortus dominatur a mari usque ad mare, et a flumine usque ad terminos orbis terrae, et Ecclesia ejus, hoc est, corpus ipsius universos terminos occupat mundi."

" 'Abraham was the great father of a multitude of nations. And there was not found the like to him in glory, who kept the law of the Most High, and was in covenant with Him. In his flesh he established the covenant, and in temptation he was found faithful.   Therefore by swearing an oath he gave him glory in his posterity, that he should increase as the dust of the earth, and that he would exalt his seed as the stars, and they should inherit from sea to sea, and from the river to the ends of the earth" (Ecclus. 44.20-23). According to the interpretation of his name Abraham is father of many—namely, all—nations believing in Christ, because only the faithful are numbered in his seed; for not those who are sons of the flesh [i.e., the line of Ishmael], but those who are sons of faith [i.e., the line of Isaac], these are the seed of Abraham…. Therefore the figure of the promise of his seed is twofold: that is, in the likeness of the sands of the sea, in which are expressed the sterile Jews; and in the likeness of the stars of heaven, in which are shown all peoples believing in Christ, who glitter as the stars of heaven through the light of the future resurrection…. Therefore his seed inherited "from sea to sea, and from the river to the ends of the earth," because Christ risen out of the seed of Abraham reigns from sea to sea, and from the river to the ends of the earth; and His church, that is, His body, fills all the ends of the earth."

Commentarium in Ecclesiasticum 10.5 (*PL* 109.1084-85); similarly Rupert of Deutz, *Dialogus inter Christianum et Judaeum* 2 (*PL* 170.580-81) and the *Glossa ordinaria*, the interlinear gloss, and Nicholas of Lyra's *postilla* on Ecclus. 44. 20-23; *ed. cit.*, 3:432F-433D. The distinction between "sons of the flesh" and "sons of the faith" is a commonplace in commentary on Gen. 21.12 and Rom. 9.6-7; for example, see Ambrose, *Commentaria in epistolam ad Romanos* 9 (*PL* 17.132-33).

25.   See Heb. 11.11-13 and Rupert of Deutz, *Dialogus inter Christianum et Judaeum* 2 (*PL* 170.580-81); Herve' of Bourg-Dieux, *Commentaria in epistolas Pauli—ad Hebraeos* 11 (*PL* 181.1648-52); Peter Lombard, *Collectanea in epistolas sancti Pauli—in Hebraeos*, 11 (*PL* 192.492).

26.   Alcuin, *Interrogationes et responsiones in Genesim* 176 (*PL* 100.540); Remigius of Auxerre, *Commentarius in Genesim* 17 (*PL* 131.89); Nicholas of Lyra, *postilla* on Gen. 17.17, *ed. cit.*, 1:68H.

27.   "Credidit esse eum, qui repromiserat. Primum quidem risit, etsi ex gaudio, non tamen plena [fide], sed post verba Angeli in fide solidata est. Sic enim dicitur Genes. 18.b [10-15]. Quod risit dicens, postquam consenui et Dominus meus vetulus est, voluptati operam dabo? Dixit autem Dominus ad Abraham, id est, Angelus in persona Domini: Quare risit Sara, dicens: nunquid paritura sum anus? Nunquid Deo quicquam est difficile. Iuxta condictum reuertar ad te vita comite, et habebit Sara filium. Negauit Sara dicens, non risi, timore perterrita. Et sicut dicit Chrysostomus, risus fuit ab infidelitate; timor autem a fide. Item in prima ergo promissione quando primo dictum est ei de filio concipiendo, infidelis fuit. In secunda autem promissione credidit, et timuit."

"She believed that he who had given the promise was faithful. Indeed, although at first she laughed out of joy, she was not filled with faith, but after the angel's words she was made firm in her faith. For thus it is said in Gen. 18.12-15 that she laughed, saying, "After I am grown old and my lord is an old man, shall I give myself to pleasure? And the Lord said to Abraham (that is, the angel in the person of the Lord): Why did Sara laugh, saying: Shall I who am an old woman bear a child indeed? Is there anything hard to God? According to appointment I will return to thee at this time, life accompanying, and Sara shall have a son. Sara denied it, saying: I did not laugh, for she was afraid." And according to Chrysostom, her laugh was out of unfaithfulness, while her fear was out of faith. Likewise, by her first avowal, therefore, when it was first told her about conceiving a son, she was unfaithful. But by her second avowal she believed and she was afraid."

Opera omnia in universum Vetus et Novum Testamentum (Lyon: Joannes Antonius Huguetan and Guillielmus Barbier, 1669), 7:267[r]. The passage in Chrysostom's works to which Hugh seems to be alluding is in the ancient Latin translation of *In epistolam ad Hebraeos* 11, *Homilia* 23: "Quomodo fidelis quae risit? Risus quidem certe est ex incredulitate, metus autem a fide; dicere enim, Non risi (Gen. 18.15), factum est a fide. Propterea ergo, exinanita incredulitate, ingressa est fides" (*Patrologia Graeca* 63.162-63).['In what way is she who laughed faithful? Most assuredly, her laugh was out of unbelief, while her fear was out of faith; for to say I did not laugh (Gen. 18.15), was said out of faith. On that account, therefore, when unbelief departed, faith entered in']. In *De Abraham* 1.5.43, Ambrose maintains that Sara laughed unconsciously in prophetic confirmation of Isaac's conception: *Sancti Ambrosii opera*, ed. Karl Schenkl, CSEL 32.1 (Vienna: F. Tempsky, , 1906), pp. 533-34.

28.   Although they do not treat the contrast between Sara and Lot's wife, S. L. Clark and Julian N. Wasserman, "The Significance of Thresholds in the *Pearl*-Poet's *Purity*," *Interpretations* 12 (1980): 114-27, do suggest that in *Cleanness* doors are important symbolic boundaries between inner and outer experience; hence Lot's house is a like a person assaulted on one level by homosexual rapists and on another by sin (pp. 120-21). As the structuralist anthropologist Mary Douglas points out in *Implicit Meanings: Essays in Anthropology* (London: Routledge and K. Paul, 1975), p. 56, "... all margins, the edges of all boundaries which are used in ordering the social experience, are treated as dangerous and polluting."

29.   For example, Augustine, *De civitate dei* 16.30: "Nam quo pertinet quod prohibiti sunt qui liberabantur ab angelis retro respicere, nisi quia non est animo redeundum ad ueterem uitam, qua per gratiam regeneratus exuitur, si ultimum euadere iudicium cogitamus? Denique uxor Loth, ubi respexit, remansit et in salem conuersa hominibus fidelibus quoddam praestitit condimentum, quo sapiant aliquid, unde illud caueatur *exemplum*" ['For what does it mean that those who were freed were forbidden by the angels to look behind them, but that the soul must not return to its former life—which, regenerated by grace, it has put aside—if we think to escape the final judgment? In the end Lot's wife remained where she looked back, and turned into salt. She remains as a condiment to faithful men to take heed by the example']; ed. Dombart and Kalb, p. 535; also Isidore, *Quaestiones in Vetus Testamentum—in Genesin* 15.5-6 (*PL* 83.245-46); Rabanus Maurus, *Commentarium in Genesim* 2.23 (*PL* 107.558); *Glossa ordinaria* on Gen. 19.26, *ed. cit.*, 1:73D.

30.   The *Book of Vices and Virtues*, ed. W. Nelson Francis, EETS, os 217 (London: Oxford University Press, 1942), p. 268. Subsequent citations will be incorporated into my text.

31.   The passages on understanding referred to here ("as we haue schewed here-tofore") occur in the discussion of the petitions of the *Pater Noster*, pp. 106-07, where "thy kingdom come" (a distinctly eschatological petition) is interpreted as a request for the spirit of understanding to cleanse the heart so that the kingdom of God may lodge within it, "And þis doþ he wiþ þe scholue of verray schrift."

32.   For a discussion of the poet's use of lapidary lore on the pearl and of the Eucharistic overtones of washing the pearl in wine, see Kelly and Irwin, pp. 251-54. Menner, note to 1131 (p. 104), cites the image of burnishing the heart in Rolle's *Twelve Profits of Tribulation*, in which it is linked with the Beatitude from Matt. 5.8. In *The Gawain-Poet: A Critical Study* (Cambridge: Cambridge University Press, 1970), pp. 33-36, A. C. Spearing argues for the coherence of the poet's pearl image of the soul purified by penance in *Pearl*, *Cleanness*, and *Gawain*.

33.   On the pervasive vessel imagery of *Cleanness*,, see Charlotte C. Morse, *The Pattern of Judgment in the* Queste *and* Cleanness (Columbia: University of Missouri Press, 1978), pp. 12-55 and 129-207, passim.

34.   Quoted by Morse, *Judgment*, pp. 186-87.

35.   Guilelmus Peraldus, *Tractatus de viciis* 2.6.3.21 in *Summa virtutum et vitiorum*, printed in parallel to the *Parson's Tale* in Kate Oelzner Petersen, *The Sources of the Parson's Tale* , Radcliffe College Monographs, 12; (Boston: Ginn, 1901), p. 41.

A Good Short Debate Between Winner and Waster 332-57, ed. Israel Gollancz (London: Oxford University Press, 1921; rpt. Cambridge/Totowa: D. S. Brewer/Rowman and Littlefield, 1974). King Edward III passed sumptuary laws regulating just such pomp: see the comments about King Arthur's love of feasting and fine clothing in the Alliterative *Morte Arthure* in Karl Heinz Göller, in cooperation with R. Gleissner and M. Mennicken, "Reality versus Romance: A Reassessment of the Alliterative *Morte Arthure*," in *The Alliterative Morte Arthure: A Reassessment of the Poem*, ed. Karl Heinz Göller, Arthurian Studies, 2 (Cambridge: D> S> Brewer, 1981), pp. 20-21.

36.   "Þe secounde braunche of vntrewþe þat comeþ of pride is wodnesse. Men holdeþ a man wod þat is out of his witt, in whom resoun is turned vp-so-doun. Þan is he a gret fool, and turned vpsodoun & out of his witt, þat, witynge hardeliche, euele dispendeþ þe goodes þat beþ nouȝt his; for þei beþ his lordes goodes, wher-of he mote streitliche ȝelde acountes & resoune. Þat is to wyte þe precious tyme and þe worldely goodes þat he haþ in kepynge. Þe vertues of his body, þe þenkynges and assentynges and þe wylles of his soule, wasteþ and spendeþ in folies and outrages riȝt to-fore his lordes eiȝen, ne ordeyneþ hym not to ȝelde his acountes, and wel wot þat he mot acounte, and ne wot whanne, ne in what stide, ne what day; such folie is wel cleped wodnesse. Of þis vice ben ful þese grete proude men þat vsen wikkidly þe grete good þat God haþ lente hem." (p. 14)

37.   In much medieval commentary, Nabuchodonosor is antitypally the devil as king of the Earthly City. Pierre Bersuire, for example, notes: "Rex iste est Diabolus, qui in Babylonia, quae interpretatur confusio, id est, in mundo regnat, ubi perpetua confusio dominatur" ['This king is the devil, who reigns in Babylon, which means "disorder"—that is, he rules in the world, where perpetual disorder rules']: *Moralitates* 24.1, in *Opera omnia*, 6 vols. in 3 (Cologne: J. W. Huisch, 1730-32), 1:168. Cp. Isidore, *Allegoriae quaedam sacrae scripturae* 127 (*PL* 83.116).

38.   On this image see William A. Stephany, "Pier della Vigna's Self-Fulfilling Prophecies: The 'Eulogy' of Frederick II and 'Inferno' 13," *Traditio* 38 (1982):198-202.

39.   Wilson, Gawain-*Poet*, p. 111.

40.   See John Block Friedman, *The Monstrous Races in Medieval Art and Thought* (Cambridge: Harvard University Press, 1981), pp. 67-69 and fig. 27 on p. 68; on the use of animal epithets for unbelievers in biblical tradition, see Harald Dickerhof, "*Canum nomine gentiles designantur* : Zum Heidenbild aus mittelalterlichen Bibellexika," in *Secundum regulam vivere: Festschrift für P. Norbert Backmund O. Praem.*, ed. Gert Melville (Windberg: Poppe, 1978), pp. 41-71; on dogs, see pp. 55, 58, 61, 68. The association of dogs and heathens with *immunditia* and *idolatria* was prominent.

41.   D. Winton Thomas, "*Kelebh* 'Dog': Its Origin and Some Usages of it in the Old Testament," *Vetus Testamentum* 10 (1960): 410-27, also discusses the use of "dog" to mean "male temple prostitute" in Deut. 23.18 and Apoc. 22.15; thus, the dog image may figuratively associate homosexuality and idolatry here in the Baltassar episode.

42.   Most recently, parallels between *Cleanness* and 2 Pet. 2 have been drawn by Lynn Staley Johnson, pp. 106-07 and by Edward Wilson, Gawain-*Poet*, pp. 96-98.

43.   Þe first braunche of pride, þat is vntrewþe, is departed in þre braunches, wher-of þe first is eule, þat oþer is wors, þe þridde is alþerworst. Þe first is vilenye; þat

þat men þanken not God oure lord as men schulde.... þe secounde braunche of vntrewþe þat comeþ of pride is wodnesse. Men holdeþ a man wod þat is out of his witt, in whom resoun is turned vp-so-doun. Þan is he a gret fool, and turned vpsodoun & out of his witt, þat, witynge hardeliche, euele dispendeþ þe goodes þat beþ nouȝt his; for πei beþ his lordes goodes, wher-of he mote streitliche ȝelde acountes & resoune .... þe þridde braunche of vntrewþe þat comeþ of pride is reeiynge .... þis synne doþ euery man and woman þat synneþ dedly; for in as moche as in hym is, he makeþ omage to þe deuel and bicomeþ his cherl .... But specially in þre dyuerse wises is a man cleped a renegatt and false cristene: or for he leueþ not as he scholde, as doþ bougres & heretikes and apostatas þat reneyen her feiþ. Or for he is out of þe feiþ, as men forsworn and brekeres of her trwþes. Or elles for he leueþ more þan he schulde, as doþ þes diuinours and wicches and seche .... (pp. 13, 14, 15)

44.   See Menner's note to 459 on p. 85.

45.   Richard of St. Victor, *Liber exceptionum* 2.1.16, ed. Jean Chatillon, Textes Philosophiques du Moyen Age, 5 (Paris: J. Vrin, 1958); Rupert of Deutz, *De sancta trinitate et operibus ejus—in Genesim* 4.22, ed. Hrabanus Haacke, CCSL, Continuatio Mediaevalis, 21 (Turnhout: Brepols, 1971), p. 307; Bruno of Asti, *Expositio in Genesim* 8 (*PL* 164.181-82).

46.   *"Et coeperunt simul omnes excusare"* "Excusat autem se omnis, qui plus terrena quam celestis diligit" *"Uxorem duxi, et ideo non possum venire"* Tria genera hominum a magna cena videntur excludi. Gentiles propter immoderatum affectum temporalium. Iudaei, qui Christum respuentes iugum legis ceruicibus suis imponunt.... Haeretici, qui velut Eua femineo affectu tentant rigorem fidei."

As *untrawþe*, the raven's disobedience is a sin of pride, for which in Scripture the raven's descendants do penance by serving Elias in the desert (3 Reg. 17.4-6); see the Old English *Adrian and Ritheus* 22, in *The Prose Solomon and Saturn and Adrian and Ritheus*, ed. James E. Cross and Thomas D. Hill, McMaster Old English Studies and Texts, 1 (Toronto: University of Toronto Press, 1982), p. 37 and commentary at p. 146.

47.   *"Qui coruus [sic] egrediebatur, et non reuertebatur.* cadauere natante illectus, id est, luxuria. Osea 5.b [i.e., 5.4] Non dabunt cogitationem, vt reuertantur ad Dominum, quia spiritus fornicationis in medio eorum est, et Dominum non cognouerunt. Ecce quot mala facit luxuria. Ex quo enim spiritus fornicationis possedit cor, statim recedit cognitio Dei" (Hugh of St. Cher, 1.11^v-12^r).

48.   *"Uxorem du[xi].* Quia multi non propter foecunditatem, sed propter desideria carnis vxores ducunt. ideo per rem istam carnis voluptas designatur, propter quam ad coenam Dei fastidiosus uenire recusat"

49.   Sap. 14:6: "Sed et ab initio cum perirent superbi gigantes, spes orbis terrarum ad ratem confugiens, remisit saeculo semen nativitatis quae manu tua erat gubernata" ['But from the beginning when the proud giants perished, the hope of the world fleeing to a vessel which was governed by hand, it [i.e., wood, the subject of this passage] left to the world seed of generation']; Isidore of Seville, *De ortu et obitu patrum* 4 (*PL* 83.132). See further the OE *Genesis* 1310b-13a, and *Exodus* 366-76, in *The Junius Manuscript*, ed. George Philip Krapp, ASPR 1 (New York: Columbia University Press, 1931); *The Middle English Genesis and Exodus* 630; *Cursor Mundi*, rubric ante 1627 (Göttingen and Trinity MSS).

*This article was completed in February, 1987 and revised in September, 1989. Issues raised in it will be explored more fully in the book-length study of *Cleanness* which I am now preparing. I am grateful to T. D. Hill and the late R. E .Kaske for their suggestions on earlier drafts of this essay.

THE IMPATIENT READER OF *PATIENCE*

C. DAVID BENSON

Although it is good to be reminded, as we have been during the last generation or so, that medieval writers are Christians, we must not forget that some are great poets. The chief English Ricardian authors—Chaucer, Langland, Gower, and the *Gawain*-Poet—are deeply involved with spiritual questions, but each is also a complex and difficult artist. The achievement of these writers is not to restate, but to revivify, Christian beliefs—to put old wine into strikingly new bottles. Rather than merely repeating a traditional lesson, they use all their literary craft to make it immediately and powerfully alive for a contemporary audience. The Ricardians reach orthodox destinations by unusual, risky, and memorable routes. The seriousness of their accomplishment is a direct result of their extraordinary poetic skill.

An often overlooked example of such poetry is *Patience*, a brief work usually attributed to the *Gawain*-Poet, which lacks even a provocative editorial title like *Cleanness*. In contrast to the impressively original plots of *Pearl* and *Sir Gawain and the Green Knight*, *Patience* is the only poem by a great Middle English poet that is primarily the retelling of a single Biblical story: in this case the adventures of Jonah—his flight from a divine command, ingestion and conveyance by a whale, and reluctant preaching to the Ninevites, who, much to his disgust, repent and are pardoned by God. One obvious reason why biblical narrative was often avoided by the best medieval writers is that its pre-eminent authority restricted artistic freedom. Yet the poet of *Patience,* while closely following the original story, manages to add narrative energy and moral complexity to his source.

The story of Jonah is an unusual biblical episode to illustrate patience—Job is the standard example—but the poet knows what he is doing. His Jonah is a wonderfully comic character, but one whose final significance is by no means simple. On the allegorical level, the reluctant prophet is a figural type of Christ (identified as such by Jesus himself), while, on the literal level, he is a clear illustration of human rebelliousness from the divine will. Thus the poet uses Jonah to signify both God's patient redemption of mankind and the impatient sinfulness that made such redemption necessary. Readers have long recognized such examples of exegetical wit in *Patience*, but the central moral teaching of the poem has usually seemed straightforward enough. Whatever his figural significance or our human sympathy, the story of Jonah is a negative *exemplum* of one who lacks patience in both tribulation and prosperity.[1] Jonah is angry when the order to preach God's wrath seems to put him at risk from the Ninevites, and angrier still, though now from indignation rather than fear, when the Ninevites are spared and his woodbine bower destroyed.

I want to suggest that the lesson of *Patience* is even more subtle and more personal than has yet been recognized. The poet not only uses Jonah to illustrate impatience, he also forces his readers to understand the same sin in themselves. In this short, comic work, with its deceptively casual style, the reader is led into a moral trap. The poet does all he can to make us scorn the reluctant prophet. We are encouraged to laugh at Jonah's undeniable foolishness, vanity, and rebelliousness and made to feel superior to his many faults. But in our self-righteousness, we, too, become guilty of Jonah's sin, for we conspicuously lack patience toward him. *Patience* is thus much more than a theoretical discussion of a virtue; it also directly involves the the experience of the reader with that virtue. In his introduction to the story, the poet says that he will "play" with the themes of both patience and poverty (35-36); equally significant are the ways in which he plays with us as readers.[2]

Critics have long debated the degree to which *Patience* is homiletic.[3] Obviously *Patience* is not a literal sermon (for one thing, the *exemplum* of Jonah is too long), but it is designed to remind us of one, and it contains many homiletic elements, as the poet suggests by his opening citation of the Beatitudes, which, he insists, "I herde on a halyday, at a hyȝe masse" (9). *Patience* has the function of a sermon, if not its exact form. The purpose of any homily is not so much to explore the abstract questions of Christian doctrine as to involve its audience so that they learn a lesson that can be put to practical spiritual use. A preacher intends to move his listeners' hearts as well as their minds and to show the relevance of Christian doctrine to daily life. Just before he begins to tell of Jonah himself, the poet speaks directly to the audience: "Wyl ȝe tary a lyttel tyme and tent me a whyle, / I schal wysse yow þer-wyth as holy wryt telles" (59-60). This adaptation of a common minstrel formula is our first direct indication that the poet is very much aware of his audience in adapting the story of Jonah.

Although Jonah was regarded both positively and negatively in the Middle Ages (for despite his rebelliousness, he is a prefiguration of Christ), the negative view is almost inevitable when the story is told literally, which is the dominant mode in *Patience*.[4] The Middle English poet describes Jonah as the silliest and most inept of prophets. His rebellion against God reminds us not so much of a tragically ruined Lucifer, as the petulance of a spoiled child. Jonah gets no respect from us because he seems to deserve none. He is foolish and ineffectual from the start. Whereas God is awesomely powerful, the deity of wind, waves, and whales, Jonah is always presented as puny and helpless.[5]   We continually see him in small enclosures where he has vainly sought protection—the hold of the ship, the whale's belly, and the woodbine bower—and he is usually asleep. Jonah is an extreme example of the Ricardian anti-hero described by John Burrow: ignorant, weak, vain, and vulnerable.[6] The pervasive comedy of the poem lies in the contrast between Jonah's self-assertion and our knowledge of its futility.

From the beginning, the poet does all he can to make the reader feel superior to Jonah. His way of retelling the story, especially the additions to the bare Bible narrative, stresses the foolishness of Jonah and ensures that our view of him is always condescending. In the first reference to Jonah, the poet refers slightingly to his actions as a "jape" (57), and when we initially see our hero, he is already "vnglad" at God's speech (63)–a characterization of mood not in the biblical account. The long opening scene describing Jonah's instant and unreasonable anger against God's command (73-96), which notes that the prophet "wrathed in his wyt" (74) and went "ay janglande for tene" (90) is almost wholly original, deriving from the less than half a verse in the Vulgate: "And Jonas rose up to flee into Tarsis from the face of the Lord" (1:3). Jonah's second burst of impatience, after the Ninevites are spared, has some biblical support, but the Middle English poet again stresses the extremity of the response. Immediately after the event, Jonah waxes wroth toward the Lord, "so hat3 anger onhit his hert" (410-11; see also 433), and then later, when he awakens to find his bower destroyed, he calls on God "with hatel anger and hot" (481).

Jonah's initial attempt to run away from God's command is made to seem as childish as his anger, and the poet clearly underlines the paradox of Jonah's actions: "To sette hym to sewrte, vnsounde he hym feches" (58). Here, as always, Jonah's own attempts to achieve safety simply put him at a greater risk. The reader knows that Jonah is not embarking for Tarshish, as he fondly imagines, but for the stinking belly of the whale and then the dangers of Nineveh. When the whale finally disgorges Jonah, the poet stresses the ironic appropriateness of his destination: "Þe bonk þat he blosched to and bode hym bisyde, / Wat3 of þe regiounes ry3t þat he renayed hade" (343-44). He has found the very place from which he was fleeing. Because Jonah insists on being in control of his own destiny in defiance of God, he always lacks control.

In contrast to Jonah's blind ignorance, the reader of *Patience* is given an almost God-like perspective on events, from which we clearly see the futility of Jonah's efforts to escape the divine will. If we are moved by sympathy for the prophet's human faults and failures, as some have argued, our response always remains condescending in the extreme, similar to that for a character like Bottom in A *Midsummer*

Night's Dream. At the most terrifying moment in the story of Jonah , when he is thrown from the ship into the maw of the whale, the reader is kept from any close emotional identification. Although the poet often attributes thoughts and motives to Jonah not found in the Bible, this episode is narrated entirely from the outside. Moreover, distance from the event is increased by seeing it twice: first in a brief, almost contemptuous description of the sailors' disposal of their troublesome passenger ("Tyd by top and bi to þay token hym synne; / In-to þat lodlych loȝe þay luche hym sone" [229-30]), and then, several lines later, in a second, more comic account, with the addition of the whale: "Þe folk ȝet haldande his fete, þe fysch hym tyd hentes; / With-outen towche of any tothe he tult in his þrote" (251-52). In neither description are we allowed to share or sympathize with Jonah's feelings. Indeed, throughout Jonah's harrowing stay in the whale, the poet takes care to block our natural pity with moral condemnation. The disgusting slime of the whale's belly is explicitly associated with the Devil and Hell (274-75), suggesting that Jonah is being punished for his rebellion, and the mention of his filthy clothes when he finally arrives on land seems a clear suggestion of his sinful condition (342).[7] Although the prophet himself frequently feels put-upon and ill-used, as the poet emphasizes, the reader is never encouraged to agree; rather, Jonah is continually presented as selfishly petulant, a more extreme version of the dreamer in *Pearl*.

Speeches expanded or added to his biblical source are an important way in which the author of *Patience* encourages a negative view of Jonah. Again and again, the poet exposes Jonah's self-regarding foolishness through the prophet's own words.[8] When Jonah is first ordered by God to go to Nineveh, the Bible is silent about what he thought or said. The Middle English poet, however, supplies an original fourteen-line utterance that fully defines Jonah's intense, if comic, selfishness (75-88). In the first six lines, Jonah uses some form of the first-person pronoun or adjective no less than ten times. The prophet never once considers God's command seriously or wonders if his duty might be to obey; instead he indulges in a vivid fantasy of the horrors he imagines are in store for him from such "typped schrewes"(77). Jonah's emphasis is all on the physical, with no thought at all for the spiritual. When he finally does mention God, Jonah's expression is sharply sarcastic: he refers to the Lord's "meruayl message" (81) and to "my gaynlych God" (83). Of course, as throughout *Patience*, the sarcasm rebounds squarely on Jonah. God is indeed gracious and his message a marvelous one not only for the people of Nineveh but for all mankind.

The extent of Jonah's error is underlined by his next speech, in which he bitterly justifies his attempt to flee the divine command:

'Our syre syttes,' he says, 'on sege so hyȝe,
In his glowande glorye and gloumbes ful lyttel
Þaȝ I be nimmen in Nunniue and naked dispoyled,
On rode rwly to-rent with rybaudes mony.' (93-96)

The reader, of course, cannot miss the reference to the Crucifixion. While complaining that God is too high and mighty to care about individuals, Jonah unwittingly defines the measure of the Creator's love—he descended from heaven to become man and was obedient even unto the cross. What Jonah will not do for the Lord, the Lord will do for everyone, even Jonah.[9]

Other speeches further illustrate Jonah's vain petulance. In the belly of the whale, Jonah calls out to God with amazing cheekiness in an original passage: "Now, prynce, of þy prophete pite þou haue" (282). Jonah, who had done all he could to avoid the office of prophet, now claims its privileges. One is reminded of the popular definition of *chutzpah*: the man who kills his mother and father and then asks the court for leniency because he is an orphan. After the Ninevites have been spared, Jonah addresses God in a speech much developed from its biblical source, in which he notes the harm done to *him* by God's mercy, specifically to his reputation as a prophet (413-28). He compounds this absurdly by blaming God for being too courteous and merciful (417-20), the same virtues that had rescued Jonah himself from the whale. In a later speech with only the briefest source in the Bible, Jonah once again upbraids God, this time for taking away his woodbine bower, and again liberally uses the first-person (482-88). When God asks why he is so angry about so little, Jonah haughtily claims that he is defending principle: "'Hit is not lyttel,' quoþ þe lede, 'bot lykker to ryȝt'" (493). It is the last time we hear Jonah in the poem and perfectly defines his ridiculous self-regard.

The poet of *Patience* encourages the reader to scorn Jonah, not only by the way in which he tells the story, but also directly though the voice of the narrator. Critics have often noted the prominence of the narrator in *Patience*.[10] For example, Williams mentions the "narrator's ferocious scorn," Spearing argues that the "narrator takes sides in the poem, enters into it as a partisan, and thus makes the case against Jonah more forcefully than a neutral narrator could," and even Davenport, who thinks that we are meant to feel sympathy for Jonah, concludes that the "reader's sense of Jonah's wrongness is increased by the narrator's distancing ironies and that he is laid open both to condemnation and to scornful, dismissive laughter."[11]

The most striking example of this narrative contempt is particularly important because of its length, because it has no warrant in the biblical source, and because it occurs so early in the poem. After Jonah sails from Jaffa, the narrator interrupts the story to ridicule Jonah in twenty lines of direct abuse. The first quatrain notes that "watȝ neuer so joyful a jue as Jonas watȝ þenne" because he believes he has escaped God's power (109-10). But the narrator quickly shows the absurdity of such a conclusion: "He wende wel þat þat wyȝ þat al þe world planted / Hade no maȝt in þat mere no man for to greue" (111-12). The narrator then becomes explicitly insulting, calling Jonah "þe wytles wrechche" and sarcastically noting that because Jonah would not suffer God's command "Now hatȝ he put hym in plyt of peril wel more" (113-14). The narrator once again points out Jonah's folly ("hit watȝ a wenyng vn-war") in believing that he can escape God's sight (115-16). In addition to treating the belief with superior contempt ("ȝise, he blusched ful brode, þat burde hym by sure"), the narrator quotes a harsh passage from a psalm of "dyngne David," the poet's only admitted addition to the *Book of Jonah*, in which those like Jonah are excoriated as "foleȝ" and "stape fole" for assuming that he who made every ear and eye is incapable of hearing and seeing (117-24).[12] The digression ends with further ridicule—comparing Jonah to one "þat dotes for elde"—and with the narrator's smug gloating over the failure of Jonah's flight: "Bot I trow ful tyd ouer-tan þat he were, / So þat schomely to schort he schote of his ame" (127-28).

The reader of *Patience* has good reason to feel self-righteously superior toward Jonah after this explicit condemnation, for everything we later learn supports the narrator's opening scorn. Jonah is vain and foolish, concerned only with himself and absurdly ignorant of God's power as well as his love. During the rest of the story, events themselves and Jonah's own words are generally sufficient to condemn the prophet, as we have already seen, but the narrator occasionally reappears with brief, direct comments to reinforce his initial ridicule. For example, Jonah's sleeping during the storm at sea may itself suggest his sinful state, but the narrator's words further increase our censure—he explicitly notes that Jonah has taken refuge out of fear (183) and describes him like a skid-row bum: "Slypped vpon a sloumbe-selepe, and sloberande he routes" (186).[13] The narrator's contempt is echoed by the sailors. The cleverest among them declares that the storm results from the divine punishment for sin of "sum losynger, sum lawles wrech" (170), and when Jonah's guilt is known, the others insult him as a "doted wrech" and "syn-ful schrewe" (196-97), judgments with which almost every reader of *Patience* has concurred. Jonah is not only foolish, but vainly foolish; not only blasphemous, but self-righteous in his blasphemy. He is as ridiculous in happiness as in anger, and the narrator's description of his delight with the woodbine bower again emphasizes his silliness. The biblical source says only that "Jonas was exceeding glad of the ivy" (4:6), an account that is expanded into eight lines that detail Jonah's lounging in the bower ("lotrande") and capering about ("balteres") so happily that he forgets about food ("þe deuel haf!"), as he wishes he could take the bower home with him (457-64).

II

If *Patience* were a less subtle poem, there would be nothing remarkable about the negative *exemplum* just outlined. Jonah is certainly guilty of impatience in both adversity and prosperity, and he deserves censure. But to condemn Jonah alone is to understand only part of the lesson of *Patience*. Although the telling of the poem (and especially the censorious narrator) consistently encourages the reader to take a strict view of Jonah, the result is not Christian insight, but the very sin of which Jonah is guilty. In judging Jonah as harshly as the poem seems to demand, we ourselves lack patience. Although the poet deliberately encourages us to look down on Jonah and self-righteously blame him for his faults, our sense of superiority is empty. We may be given a God-like perspective of events in the story, but we manifestly lack God's love and mercy. For who are we to demand justice? We smugly judge Jonah by standards that would condemn us. In so doing, we have made the same mistake as the reluctant prophet, with somewhat less justification.

The real point of *Patience* is the need mankind has for mercy instead of justice, which the poet demonstrates through a double irony. When Nineveh is spared, Jonah indignantly calls for justice, and upbraids God for his softness: "Wel knew I þi cortaysye, þy quoynt soffraunce, / Þy bounte of debonerte and þy bene grace" (417-18). He scornfully attacks God for being too generous with his mercy ("and ay þy mercy is mete, be mysse neuer so huge" [420]), and falsely claims that the reason he fled God's original command to preach retribution is that he knew how easily the Ninevites could escape their proper punishment: "Wyth a prayer and a pyne þay myȝt her pese gete" (423). Later, when his woodbine bower is taken away, Jonah again stands on strict justice, as we have already noted (493). The first level of irony in the poem, as previous critics have well pointed out, is that Jonah's pompous demands for justice would long since have destroyed him. In the belly of the whale, Jonah sounds a very different note. He fervently seeks God's peace with the same sort of "prayer" and "pyne" that he subsequently derides: he begs "pite," while admitting to being a fool "and fykel and falce of my hert" (282-83). During his own tribulation, Jonah prays not for justice but for "rauthe" (284), and in a devout prayer closely modeled on the Bible, though these lines are original, he makes his petition explicit: "Þou schal releue me, renk, whil þy ryȝt slepez, / Þurȝ myȝt of þy mercy þat mukel is to tryste" (323-24). But later Jonah forgets all about the divine forgiveness he has received. He seems not to recognize any similarity to his own recent ordeal when he warns the Ninevites that they will be plunged "depe to þe abyme" and "swolȝed swyftly" by the earth (362-63). Jonah wants justice for others, but mercy for himself. The second level of irony in the poem, which has not been previously recognized, is that the self-righteous reader of *Patience* is similarly inconsistent. We apply a standard of justice to Jonah that would damn us all.

As we have seen, *Patience* is so constructed that the reader must inevitably scorn Jonah. At the end of the poem, especially, when the reluctant prophet is furious because Nineveh has been spared and his bower taken away, we can hardly avoid being disgusted by such hypocritical selfishness. In our rejection of Jonah, however, we are exactly imitating his error, as a final divine utterance shows. For if we are impatient with Jonah, God is not. Despite Jonah's outrageous and rebellious behavior, God speaks to him sweetly and seriously, even respectfully, carefully explaining the love he has for his creation and his reluctance to destroy any of it (494-523). This is not, I think, the reaction the reader expects. All along, the poem has encouraged us to judge Jonah harshly, and the gentleness of God comes as a great surprise. God has patience with Jonah long after ours has run out. At the end of *Patience* the self-righteous reader is forced to realize that he lacks patience as surely as Jonah. Jonah withholds his mercy from the Ninevites, just as we withhold ours from him, although, being human, we both are desperately in need of it.

Even though *Patience* often encourages us to feel superior to Jonah, close examination of the story reveals that he is not all bad. As some critics have pointed out (though the self-righteous reader may overlook), Jonah's faults, especially his inflated self-regard, are very human. Far from being a monster, Jonah at times displays moral courage and spiritual insight. He admits his sin to the sailors and asks them to throw him overboard to save themselves (205-12), and, during his second prayer in the whale's belly, which is closely modeled on the Bible, he clearly recognizes God's sovereignty (305-36). Moreover, Jonah has some excuse for his impatience that is not available to the reader of *Patience*. An Old Testament character can be expected to uphold the principle of strict justice, whereas the Christian reader, to whom a New Law of love has been revealed, should know better. Even though Jonah is a major prefiguration of Christ, he himself is completely ignorant of the Incarnation; as a result, the reference to the Crucifixion explicitly evoked in lines 95-96 condemns us more than Jonah. The reader of *Patience* has been given the good news of Christianity and should therefore act differently, with more patience and mercy, than "Jonas þe jwe" (182).

The difficult lesson of *Patience* is to recognize Jonah's situation as ours. In the famous words of Walt Kelly's cartoon character Pogo, we have met the enemy, and he is us. At first, the self-righteous reader is

likely to approve of the obedience of the other humans in the story—
the sailors and the Ninevites. In contrast to our reluctant prophet, they
listen to God and do his will. The sailors' reaction to their ordeal is
conversion and belief, and the Ninevites' swift and complete submis-
sion to the divine seems equally ideal. The problem is that their
responses are much too perfect and do not address the human condition. The account of the Ninevites' instant and total repentance is
more than a little comic. The alliterative verse emphasizes their
maniacal, not to say mechanical, response, as they all instantly strap
on hair-shirts ("Heter hayreʒ þay hent þat asperly bited"), which are
luckily at hand, and cover themselves with dust (373-76). Not to be
outdone, the king races from his throne, tears off his "ryche robe," and
dives precisely into a pile of ashes: "And of a heþ of askes he hitte in
þe myddeʒ" (377-80). In the more sedate Vulgate, he merely sits in the
ashes (3:6). Although the *Book of Jonah* says that the king orders that
"neither men nor beasts, oxen nor sheep" shall eat or drink (3:7), the
royal decree of fasting in *Patience,* including the order that babes be
ripped from the breast ("Seseʒ childer of her sok, soghe hem so
neuer"), is greatly expanded (385-404).[14] Although undoubtedly
admirable, this response to the divine will is so extreme as to be
unbelievable; Ninevites act more like brute nature—like the obedient
winds, waves, and whale earlier in the poem—than like real human
beings. Their exemplary behavior has little relevance to the fear, self-
regard, and sloth that is Jonah's condition and ours.

Luckily for Jonah (and for the reader), the strict justice both
demand for others is not the final message of *Patience.* Although God
is portrayed as harsh and vengeful at the beginning of the poem, by the
end we are able to see his love and mercy. God first speaks with a
roughness added to the biblical account ("With a roghlych rurd
rowned in his ere" [64]), and his words contain a direct threat not in
the original: "Bot venge me in her vilanye and venym bilyue" (71).
Jonah himself, we will remember, sees his Lord as a "syre" who
"syttes...on sege so hyʒe" with no regard for the evil that may happen
to his prophet on earth (93). The narrator's direct address to the reader
early in the poem, whose main effect is to encourage our scorn of
Jonah, similarly stresses only God's power and might: as the creator
of the world, he is able "for-to greue" man, and he sees and hears all
things (109-24). The watchful control and angry ruthlessness of the
divine will is then further emphasized, in lines added to the biblical
source, as God calls on the winds to create the tempest:

> For þe welder of wyt þat wot alle þynges,
> Þat ay wakes and waytes, at wylle hatʒ he slyʒtes.
> He calde on þat ilk crafte he carf with his hondes;
> Þay wakened wel þe wroþ eloker, for wroþ ely he cleped.
> (129-32)

If God were no more than the vengeful seeker of strict justice that he seems at the beginning of *Patience,* both Jonah and the reader would be doomed. As the poem progresses, however, we are gradually shown a more merciful God.[15] When Jonah has been swallowed by the whale, the poet notes that divine power can protect, as well as threaten, the sinful. In lines added to the biblical original, the narrator asks what human would be able to live in such a place as the whale's belly had not "þe hyȝe heuen-kyng, þurȝ his honde myȝt, / Warded þis wrech man in warlowes gutteȝ" (257-60). God's "honde myȝt" has "warded" Jonah, and, in the next line, the poet recalls the prophet's own sarcastic alliterative formula to stress that the high God does care for his servants on earth, whether or not they recognize it: "Bot he watȝ sokored by þat syre þat syttes so hiȝe, / Þaȝ were wanleȝ of wele in wombe of þat fissche" (261-62).

None of the early hints of God's vengeance, which Jonah fully believes, turns out to be true. The Ninevites, the first object of divine wrath, are spared without great difficulty, and even the violent storm finally harms no one. For all its apparent danger, the tempest is actually providential, bringing all it affects closer to God: it forces Jonah to call for heavenly mercy, a request that is soon granted, and converts the sailors, who praise "oure mercyable God" at the end of their ordeal (238)—in contrast to the fearful sacrifices and vows in the Vulgate (1:16). As the poet observes with apparent inappropriateness while hapless Jonah is desperately looking for safety in the belly of the whale: "bot euer is God swete" (280). After he has been "ay þenkande on dryȝtyn" for three days and nights (294), Jonah himself is capable of accepting this more positive view of the Almighty, for he acknowledges both" his myȝt" and "his merci" (295). A few lines later the prophet best expresses the final relationship of these two aspects of the divine when he suggests that God's might is best exercised through his mercy: "Þurȝ myȝt of þy mercy þat mukel is to tryste" (324). The extent of his mercy for his entire creation is, of course, precisely the argument God makes to Jonah at the end of the poem, when he tries to explain his reluctance to destroy even the sinful: "I may not be so malicious and mylde be halden, / For malyse is noȝ to mayntyne boute mercy with-inne" (522-23). Despite its grim beginning, *Patience* is a Christian comedy in which all ends happily.[16]

Even before God's final declaration to Jonah of his love for all humankind, we have come to understand that the definition of patience in this poem in much wider than it had seemed at first. As presented by the Middle English poet, patience is more than simple endurance in tribulation; instead, it becomes nothing less than the fundamental Christian virtue that permits a relationship between man and God, which is how it was seen by many others in the Middle

Ages.[17] Before the story of Jonah itself, the narrator seems to define patience as no more than a limited, practical virtue. He states that because he is poor, he is constrained to practice patience (35-36) and thus make a virtue of necessity: "Syþen I am sette with hem samen, suffer me by-houes" (46). In order to reinforce the lesson that it is useless to resist the inevitable, he cites the example of his "lege lorde" bidding him to go to Rome on an errand (49-52). Why complain, he argues, when the result will only be more trouble, for his master can always force him to carry out the order (53-56). Once the story of Jonah begins however, we gradually see patience as much broader and more positive quality: not merely stoic endurance but something quite close to *caritas* itself. In the course of the poem, patience grows from a practical to a spiritual virtue, just as the demanding secular lord of the prologue is replaced by the merciful divine Lord, whose concern for all , even sinners like the Ninevites and Jonah, the reader must strive to imitate. Although the poem at first encourages us to scorn Jonah, we have not understood its real message until we accept that we must love him.

Patience is a negative *exemplum,* but the reader, just as much as Jonah, is the poet's example. If an obtuse protagonist/dreamer is a central device of *Pearl*, its fellow poem in the Cotton manuscript, *Patience,* may be said to feature an obtuse reader. Both the dreamer of *Pearl* and the reader of *Patience* come to learn how different, and how unreasonably generous, are God's ways from man's. An extensive critical debate has occurred over the exact point at which God stops speaking to Jonah during his last speech and the narrator's voice takes over to address the reader. The distinction may be quite irrelevant, for the purpose of this last section is to demonstrate that Jonah's particular situation is capable of a more general application. When God (or the narrator) says, "Be noȝt so gryndel, god-man, bot go forth þy wayes / Be preue and be pacient in payne and in joye" (524-25), the words could apply to Jonah, but it is much more important that we see that they also apply to us. We have been "gryndel" toward Jonah throughout the poem, with a self-righteousness that is far from the humility recommended in the opening Beatitudes.

Patience is a sophisticated moral work that teaches its message with great skill. The poet's method is exactly that used by God with Jonah: instruction by experience, not authority. When Jonah becomes insanely indignant over the destruction of his woodbine, we might have expected God to preach a reproving sermon on the evils of worldly covetousness, but his actual words are very different. He tells Jonah to look into his own heart ("þenne by-þenk þe, mon" [495]) and recognize that if he loves the woodbine, then God must also love his handiwork. Jonah is not asked to accept a lesson imposed from outside, not even a divine lesson, but only one that conforms to his own experience. Similarly, the Middle English poet forces each one of his readers to experience impatience, so that we can understand the same sin in Jonah and forgive it. The first line of the poem warns us that patience is a difficult virtue, and the rest of the work demonstrates this to be true, for the reader has as much trouble practicing it as Jonah. But just as Jonah must learn to give up his self-regarding impatience and learn to love, so must the reader. Jonah must come to love the Ninevites as much as he loves his woodbine, and we must come to love him. God's love for Jonah at the end of the poem—despite all the prophet's failures, hypocrisy, and arrogance—is so presented as to astonish us, but it is also our only hope for salvation. The poem teaches us that we need patience to receive patience; we must forgive others, even silly Jonah, so that we shall be forgiven.[19]

Notes

1.   For example, Malcolm Andrew and Ronald Waldron, eds., *The Poems of the* Pearl *Manuscript* (1978; rpt., Berkeley: University of California Press, 1982), p. 20, assert: "The story of Jonah is conceived primarily as a negative *exemplum* ; he is an example of angry rebellion to be avoided, and, at the same time, in the cosmic scale of the poem, of the folly of all sin." Ordelle G. Hill, "The Audience of *Patience*," *Modern Philosophy* 66 (1968): 106, discusses the long medieval tradition of seeing Jonah in the wrong; and St. John Fisher, at the end of the English medieval tradition, sees Jonah as both a positive and negative symbol, sometimes signifying Christ, sometimes the sinner ("Treatise Concerning the Seven Penitential Psalms," in *The English Works of John Fisher*, ed. J. E. B. Mayor, EETS es 27 (London: 1876), p. 201. But see also Jay Schleusener, "History and Action in *Patience*," *PMLA* 86 (1971): 964, who argues that the poem is more than simply a negative *exemplum,* and W. A. Davenport, *The Art of the* Gawain-*Poet* (London: Athlone Press, 1978), pp. 103-35, who stresses our sympathy for Jonah's human failings.

2.   All citations of *Patience* are to the edition of J. J. Anderson (Manchester: Manchester University Press, 1969).

3.   For example, J. J. Anderson, "The Prologue of *Patience*," *Modern Philology* 63 (1966): 285, calls the poem essentially "a verse sermon"; Andrew and Waldron, *Poems*, pp. 17 ff. classify it, with *Cleanness*, as a "literary homily"; and Hill, "Audience," thinks it was probably addressed to an audience principally concerned with preaching, perhaps even to preachers themselves. See also William Vantuono, "The Structure and Sources of *Patience*," *Mediaeval Studies*, 34 (1972): 401-21, who argues that the poem is a formal homily. Even Morton W. Bloomfield, "*Patience* and the *Mashal*," *Medieval Studies in Honor of Lillian Herlands Hornstein*, ed. Jess B. Bessinger, Jr., and Robert R. Raymo (New York: New York University Press, 1976), p. 41, who denies that the poem is a homily, admits that it has "sermonic elements."

4.   F. N. M. Diekstra, "Jonah and *Patience* : The Psychology of a Prophet," *English Studies* 55 (1974), esp. 211-17, discusses medieval works that treat Jonah negatively.

5.   See Laurence Eldredge, "Sheltering Space and Cosmic Space in the Middle English *Patience*," *Annuale Mediaevale* 21 (1981): 126.

6.   J. A. Burrow, *Ricardian Poetry* (London: Routledge & Kegan Paul, 1971), esp. Chapter Three.

7.   See the notes to these lines in *The* Pearl *Poems: An Omnibus Edition*, ed. William Vantuono (New York: Garland, 1984), 2:222, 225. See also Diekstra, "Jonah and *Patience*," pp. 214-17

8.   See Edward Wilson, *The* Gawain-*Poet* (Leiden: Brill, 1976), p. 57.

9.   Throughout *Patience*, the poet creates many other such ironic moments to make the reader disdain Jonah. In the storm, the sailors angrily question Jonah,

asking him, among other things, if he has no God on whom to call and demanding to know his errand (199-202). But we have just seen that it is Jonah's refusal to carry out his God's message that has caused him and the sailors their trouble. Later in the poem, Jonah is furious that the Ninevites have been spared the punishment he had preached to them, and he is described as "wroth as þe wynde" (410). The formula is a common one in alliterative poetry, but the reader cannot fail to remember the four winds who had earlier been decribed as instantly carrying out the divine will, in contrast to Jonah's unceasing reluctance.

10.   See, for example, Bloomfield, "*Patience* and the *Mashal*," p. 43; Charles Moorman, "The Role of the Narrator in *Patience*," *Modern Philology* 61 (1963): 90-95, notes the narrator's constant intrusions.

11.   David Williams, "The Point of *Patience*," *Modern Philology* 68 (1970): 133; A. C. Spearing, *The Gawain-Poet* (Cambridge: Cambridge University Press, 1970), p. 75; and Davenport, *Art of the Gawain-Poet*, p. 132.

12.   See Lynn Staley Johnson, "*Patience* and the Poet's Use of Psalm 93," *Modern Philology* 74 (1976): 67-71.

13.   Diekstra, "Jonah and *Patience*," p. 215, notes the narrator's contempt at line 186 and then when Jonah sleeps again at line 466.

14.   Davenport, *Art of the Gawain-Poet*, p. 123, notes that the king's rhetoric is exaggerated to the point that it seems false.

15.   Schleusener in his excellent "History and Action," esp. p. 964, argues convincingly that the relationship of God's power, justice, and mercy is the most fundamental theme in the poem.

16.   For Jonah as a "high comedy," see Elizabeth D. Kirk, "'Who Suffreth More than God?': Narrative Redefinition of Patience in *Patience* and *Piers Plowman*," in *The Triumph of Patience: Medieval and Renaissance Studies*, ed. Gerald J. Schiffhorst (Orlando: University of Florida Press, 1978), pp. 88-104. Of course, the greatest example of God's mercy is his becoming a man to redeem the world, of which Jonah is a major prefiguration. When Jonah himself unwittingly refers to this typology, he mentions only the shame and destruction of cruxifixion (95-96), but the end of the episode, the Resurrection, is more optimistic. And so, in addition to Jonah's swallowing by the whale, *Patience* also tells of his safe rescue. During the poem we may be reminded of the agony of Holy Week (during which the Book of Jonah was read as a part of the liturgy), but by the end we experience the unexpected joy of Easter. R. H. Bowers, *The Legend of Jonah* (The Hague: Martinus Nijhoff, 1971), pp. 21-17, notes the long tradition in which Jonah is seen as primarily a symbol of resurrection.

17.   See Diekstra, "Jonah and *Patience*, pp. 206-07; Bloomfield, "*Patience* and the *Mashal*," p. 44; and Laurence Eldredge, "Late Medieval Discussions of the Continuum and the Point of the Middle English *Patience*," *Vivarium* 17 (1979): 90-115. Chaucer's Parson says of patience that "This vertu maketh a man lyk to God, and maketh hym Goddes owene deere child, as seith Crist" (*The Riverside Chaucer*, ed. Larry D. Benson [Boston: Houghton Mifflin, 1987], X.660).

18.   The association of patience with mercy and love, which is found elsewhere in medieval thought, is perhaps expressed most memorably in *Piers Plowman* (see Kirk, "Who Suffreth," pp. 97-102). See also Ralph Hanna III, "Some Com-

manplaces of Late Medieval Patience Discussions: An Introduction," in *The Triumph of Patience,* pp. 77-78; and Vantuono, "Structure and Sources," p. 421.

19. A shorter version of this paper was read at a conference on the Bible at the Center for Medieval and Early Renaissance Studies at the State University of New York at Binghamton on October 19, 1985. My thanks to all, especially Professors Bernard Levy and Paul Szarmach.

THE "POYNT" OF *PATIENCE*

LORRAINE KOCHANSKE STOCK

atience, the shortest poem contained in BL MS. Cotton Nero A.x, has been the subject of much critical speculation about such issues as: its genre—whether a sermon, negative *exemplum, consolatio,* parable, or *Mashal;*[1] its use of typology;[2] the poet's truly puzzling choice of the Old Testament story of Jonah instead of Job to exemplify, even if negatively, the virtue of patience for the poem's fourteenth-century audience;[3] and, given that questionable choice of Jonah over Job, the ways in which the poet has translated as well as expanded the Book of Jonah into the poem, *Patience.* To address this last issue, most critics have explored how the poet invented various psychological motivations for the behavior exhibited by Jonah, which is left bafflingly unexplained in the presumed main source for the poem, the Vulgate Book of Jonah.[4] This essay shall contribute to that exploration of Jonah's "psychology" in *Patience* by examining it in the context of the medieval Vices and Virtues traditions about the Deadly Sin of *acedia* or sloth, the nature of which was fully described by the early Church Fathers and the later Scholastic theologians in their exegeses of biblical texts and in the late medieval works of popular vernacular penitential instruction.

After presenting a brief summary of the range of medieval analyses of *acedia* and its opposing remedies or virtues, I shall examine how the *Patience*-Poet shaped his characterization of Jonah as an example of the vice of *acedia,* so that his experiences in the poem constitute a negative *exemplum* proffering the antidote virtue for the vice of *acedia*: patience. This reading will account for most of the poetic innovations which make *Patience* such a unique rendering of the biblical story of Jonah and thus will reveal a major "poynt" of the poem.

I

From the fourth through the twelfth centuries, *acedia* was considered primarily a monastic vice which deterred monks and religious from the performance of their spiritual and manual duties. The vice was associated with the Noonday Demon of Psalm 90:6, which caused the midday sun to beat down so relentlessly that it made the religious disinclined to work and inclined to slumber, and drove him to flee his responsibilities and physically wander from his cell or monastery.[5] In the *Benedictine Rule, acedia* was synonymous with disobedience.[6] Under the leadership of Bernard of Clairvaux, the Cistercian reformists

reemphasized the original definition of the vice presented by Evagrius, Nilus, and especially, John Cassian:

> Acediae genera duo sunt.   Unum quod ad opus Dei
> pigritare monachum ac dormitare compellit. Aliud, quod
> vagari huc illucque facit, ac fugere cohortatur de fratrum,
> cum quibus vivit, societate.
>
> There are two kinds of *acedia*. One drives the monk to be
> lazy in the service of God and to fall asleep; the other makes
> him roam about and encourages him to flee from the
> society of his brethren.[7]

The earliest remedy or virtue corresponding to the vice of *acedia*
was patience. Both Evagrius[8] and Nilus had countered *acedia* with
patience.[9] Cassian, on the other hand, designated manual labor and
fortitudo as the remedies for *acedia*,[10] and subdivided the vice into such
progeny as: idleness, somnolence, rudeness, restlessness, wandering
about, and mental and physical instability,[11] all of which are exhibited
by Jonah in *Patience*. In the popular "Septenaries" systems of related
or opposed groups of sevens (i.e., the Gifts of the Holy Ghost, the
petitions of the Pater Noster, the Sacraments, the Deadly Sins, the
Virtues, the Beatitudes, etc.), which formed the basis for much of the
popular penitential literature of the later Middle Ages, the remedy for
sloth was fortitude, one of the Gifts of the Holy Spirit. For example,
in the Middle English *Book of Vices and Virtues*, fortitude or "prowesse"
was associated with the patience of Job and was subdivided into seven
degrees, the fourth of which was patience.[12] Thus, in both the early
Patristic and the later popular vice systems, patience was opposed to
the vice of *acedia*.

Several important modifications of both the nature of the vice as
well as the corresponding virtue which opposed it occurred in the
twelfth and thirteenth centuries when the Scholastic theologians
discussed the vice of *acedia*, sometimes called *tristitia*. Whereas early
Patristic discussions of *acedia* concentrated on how it afflicted a
narrowly defined social group and even physical area—cenobites
isolated in either the desert or monastery—the Scholastic analyses
broadened the nature of the sin and thus correspondingly expanded
the size of the group susceptible to it. For example, Thomas Aquinas
redefined *acedia* as "tristitia de spirituali bono"—that is, sorrow about
or aversion to man's spiritual good, the "bonum divinum," or God
Himself. In that *acedia* is opposed to the joy one should experience in
fulfilling the divine will, it negates the spiritual "gaudium" which is an
aspect of the virtue of *caritas*.[13] Thus, as Wenzel puts it, for Thomas
"*Tristitia* is the very fundamental reaction… to draw back from anything that presents itself as evil, whether the object is present or
anticipated, real or imagined, easy to flee or hard to overcome."[14] The

Scholastic definition of the vice encompasses cheerlessness in activities that relate to God,[15] confusion of the mind, weariness, and
despair, most of which are exhibited by Jonah in *Patience*. Albertus
Magnus added another symptom to the profile of the sin—a weak or
feeble voice—by drawing upon an old, spurious etymology of the
Latin noun *acedia* derived from the Greek αχοσ (achos), a species of
sorrow or depression which produces speechlessness.[16] As I shall
show later in this essay, this aspect of *acedia* is important to the
Patience-Poet's characterization of Jonah. Although certain of the
most influential Scholastics like Aquinas and Albert the Great emphasized the ways in which this vice negated charity, nevertheless, other
Scholastics continued to use the earlier monastic definitions. Thus,
Hugh Ripelin of Strassburg, in his *Compendium theologicae veritatis*,
distinguishes between two branches of *acedia*: *tristitia*, which is opposed to spiritual joy in spiritual exercise, and *acedia*, which is opposed
to fortitude.[17] Moreover, Hugh of St. Victor, in his treatises on the
Septenaries, related *acedia* to the Pater Noster's fourth petiton for daily
bread, which would provide inner nourishment for the soul through
fortitude.[18]

As a logical extension of the expansion that *acedia* underwent at
the hands of the Scholastics, the popularization of the vice as the sin
of sloth in vernacular penitential treatises and manuals of preaching
of the thirteenth through fifteenth centuries further secularized and
universalized the concept of *acedia*. This "popular image," as Siegfried
Wenzel calls it, emphasized the aspects which are usually associated
with sloth: idleness, somnolence, instability, weariness in God's service, falling asleep in church services or at prayer, omission of prayers,
neglect of penance, and idle speech, referred to in Middle English as
"janglynge."[19] Many of these symptoms also inform Jonah's characterization in *Patience*.

Finally, as Siegfried Wenzel summarizes:

> In looking over the whole medieval period, one can there-
> fore distinguish three types of *acedia*: monastic, Scholastic,
> and popular, which can be localized with some accuracy in
> time ... and in literary genres. But never did a later one
> completely replace an earlier one. The laicization or de-
> monasticization of the vice in the twelfth and thirteenth
> centuries did not entail the total loss of monastic ele-
> ments... .[P]oets like Dante, Petrarch, and Langland were
> much closer to the total tradition of the vice as it was
> reflected in popular literature than has been understood by
> critics who, in commenting upon their works, usually rely
> on a few exclusively Scholastic treatises.[20]

This last statement about the three named writers applies equally well
to the poet who created the Middle English poem, *Patience*.[21] In the
remainder of this essay, I shall argue that the *Patience*-Poet recognized

and exploited the potential in The Book of Jonah for the depiction of *acedia*, the vice which historically had been opposed to patience, the subject of his poem. Moreover, the changes and additions he made were designed to emphasize and further develop what is perhaps his most important "poynt"—the ways in which his audience might avoid committing the various permutations of *acedia* by practicing that vice's opposing virtue, patience. Those branches of *acedia* which the Jonah of *Patience* manifests comprise five major aspects of his characterization in the poem, either as derived from the biblical source, or invented and emphasized for this fourteenth-century version of the Jonah story. They include: Jonah's literal wandering from his duty to preach to the Ninevites; his general idleness or lack of activity; his sleeping; his feeble voice; and of course his frequent lapses into a state of such despair as to desire the end of his life—all of which are classic symptoms of a case of *acedia*.

II

At the very start of the narrator's account of the career of Jonah, the hapless prophet manifests half of the earliest definition of the vice of *acedia*—the notion that *acedia* makes a religious flee from his spiritual duties by wandering. Indeed, to God's command to "Rys radly," "Nym þe way to Nynyue wyth-outen oþer speche" (65-66) and prophesy his vengeance on the sinful Ninevites, Jonah responds, "I wyl me sum oþer waye" (86).[22] Foolishly assuming that God will not notice where he is going, "he ryses radly" (89), not to go to Nineveh but to flee toward Tarshish on a ship. Though Jonah's physical flight from his duty is biblically canonical, the reasons he gives for his disobedience are invented by the poet, as critics of the poem have acknowledged, to provide the psychological motivation for the disobedience which the Vulgate version omits.[23] Jonah's justification for his flight from duty and wandering to Tarshish is a wildly imaginative and hysterically conceived list of anticipated physical tortures which the Ninevites will inflict on him for his prophecy: prison, the stocks, the gouging of his eyes, naked despoilment, crucifixion, and death (79-96). While this addition substantiates, as critics have noted, a typological relationship between Christ and Jonah because of Christ's real and Jonah's anticipated sufferings, it also illustrates Aquinas' view of *acedia / tristitia* as the tendency to "draw back from anything that presents itelf as evil, whether the object is present or anticipated, real or imagined, easy to flee or hard to overcome."[24] Jonah's disobedience also fulfills the definition of *acedia* in the *Benedictine Rule*, as mentioned earlier.

Since idleness is the aspect of the vice most commonly associated with *acedia*, the poet of *Patience* features Jonah's exhibition of this symptom of sloth not only by presenting Jonah's inactivity, but by heightening the comparatively greater activity of other characters in some of the most vivid and original passages of the poem. It is difficult to imagine a more inert character than the Jonah in *Patience*.   He neither completes the errand which God imposes on him (until he is literally punished into compliance by his three-day sojourn in the whale's belly), nor does he succeed in converting the sailors on the ship. If they sacrifice in thanks for being saved, it is not because of the efforts or influence of their cursed passenger, but because they have witnessed evidence of God's merciful nature (237-40).   In fact, his failure to do God's errand is underscored in a departure from the Vulgate; when the sailors question their passenger, they ask him, "what is þyn arnde?" (202), reminding him and the audience of Jonah's reluctance to act.   And when Jonah erupts into petulant anger and despair at the loss of his woodbine, he is reproached pointedly by God because he "trauaylede3 neuer to tent hit þe tyme of an howre" (498), and thus should not complain of losing something to which he contributed nothing.   As physically sluggish as Jonah is, he is made to seem even more inactive by contrast with the veritable frenzy of activity by which the poet characterizes the other human and divine characters in the poem.   Expanding upon one Vulgate reference to God in his capacity as creator (Jonas 1:9, "... Dominum Deum caeli ego timeo qui fecit mare et aridum"), the poet takes every possible opportunity to capitalize on this aspect of the Old Testament God in a series of epithets that, in stressing God's creativity, emphasize His activity.[25] For example, God is called: "þe fader þat hym *formed*" (92); "þat wy3 þat al þe world *planted*" (111); he who "eres alle *made*" and "*bigged* vche y3 e" (123-24); "*Welder* of wyt" (129); the "wy3 e... þat *wro3t* alle þynges / Alle þe worlde with þe welkyn, þe wynde and þe sternes, / And alle þat wone3 þer with-inne, at a worde one." (206-208); and "*maker of man*" (482, emphasis included throughout). Moreover, the references to God's "honde my3t" (257), "honde-werk" (496), "werk" (501), and "trauayl" (505) subtly reinforce the poet's revelation that it was God who "carf with his hondes" (131) the ship on which Jonah buys passage, grew "of his grace" the woodbine, and finally "con sende" the dawn by which Jonah first discovers his beloved "lefsel" (443-45). Juxtaposed with the busyness of such an active God, Jonah's feeble efforts at activity seem especially pathetic.   But it is not only God who keeps busy in this poem; in a lengthy addition to the Vulgate source, the poet invents a vivid description of the sailors' preparations of the ship, a passage containing at least ten verbs of vigorous action, contrasting emphatically with Jonah's passivity:

> Then he tron on þo tres, and þay her tramme ruchen,
> Cachen vp þe crossayl, cables þay fasten;

Wi3t at þe wyndas we3en her ankres,
Spynde spak to þe sprete þe spare bawe-lyne,

Gederen to þe gyde-ropes, þe grete cloþ falles,
Þay layden in on ladde-borde and þe lofe wynnes.
Þe blyþe breþe at her bak þe bosum he fyndes,
He swenges me þys swete schip swefte fro þe hauen.
                                                    (101-08)

Another invented passage which produces a similar effect presents the personified winds so immediately submissive to God's command that they allow no time "bytwene his tale and her dede" (135), in their eagerness "his bone for-to wyrk" (136). Presumably, the poet's personification of the winds is meant to juxtapose them against the human protagonist and thus exacerbate the impression of Jonah's disobedience in comparison with the immediacy of their compliance. And even the poet's handling of the whale sets up this beast as a positive foil for Jonah's spiritual lassitude and physical laziness. Indeed, the whale "wende3 at [God's] wylle" (339), spits out the man "as bede hym oure lorde" (340), and "walteres...þur3 mony a regioun ful ro3e" (297-98) for three days despite the fact that the "mote in his mawe mad hym...to wamel at his hert" (299-300). Thus, God, the sailors, the winds, the whale—through significant alterations of the poem's source—are active agents who underscore Jonah's idleness in *Patience.*

Probably the aspect of the poet's depiction of Jonah which is most emblematic of slothfulness is Jonah's tendency to sleep.[26] Expanding upon one verse in the Vulgate Book of Jonah 1:5: "...et Jonas descendit ad interiora navis, et dormiebat sopore gravi" ("and Jonas went down into the inner part of the ship, and fell into a deep sleep"),[27] the poet creates three separate occasions during which Jonah falls asleep, and reminds the audience of these occasions whenever possible. Jonah's two-word-long biblical sleep is translated and expanded in the poem thus: "[he] jowked in derne... Slypped vpon a sloumbe-selepe, and sloberande he routes." (182, 186). He is then "arayned" by a sailor who asks why "In such sla3tes of sor3e [he] slepe[s] so faste" (192) and later why he "slydes on slepe when þou slayn worþes /" (200). Moreover, the poet will not let the audience forget Jonah's shipboard sleep. When Jonah tucks himself into another "hyrne" in the whale, the narrator compares this place of refuge to "þe bulk of þe bot þer he byfore sleped" (292). From the mere hint that Jonah might be fatigued after building his booth outside of Nineveh, (the Vulgate Jonah 4:5 merely explains, "laboraverat enim"), the poet invents for the first night in the booth a non-canonical second occasion for sleep: "And þer he swowed and slept sadly al nyght" (442). Ironically and significantly, this invented bout of torpor occurs while God is busy planting and growing the "bynde." In a single inspired modification, the poet manages to emphasize mutually both Jonah's slumbering inactivity and God's wakeful "busyness." Finally, having awakened to discover his delightful "lefsel," Jonah "Lys loltrande þer-inne" (458) for the rest of that day. At nightfall of the second day, it behooves him to "nappe" again and the poet repeats the line about his shipboard sleep: "He slydeʒ on a sloumbe-slep sloghe vnder leues" (466), which allows the worm to ruin the woodbine. Not only has the poet created three sleeps out of one, which of itself would reinforce the impression that Jonah is exhibiting one of the classic signs of *acedia*, but he has employed vocabulary such as "swowed," "sloghe," and "sloberande" (applied by Langland to the personification of Sloth in *Piers Plowman*),[28] that particularly connote sloth.

In his portrayal of Jonah's feeble voice as another indication of the *acedia* which Albertus Magnus believed derived etymologically from αχοσ, the sadness that produces the loss of the voice, the poet employs the same methods of negative characterization by contrast that he used to develop Jonah's idleness. Indeed, one of the most provocative aspects of the poem on an initial reading is how noisy its characters are—all, of course, except Jonah. This is pointedly ironic because one would expect that a prophet would be gifted with an especially strong voice. Throughout the poem, excepting his sojourn in Nineveh, Jonah's voice and the sounds he produces are characterized as follows: "ay janglande for tene" (90), an "vn-cler steuen" (307), a "sloberande" snore (186), and "ronk noyse" (490), all of which sounds are specifically associated with *acedia*. God, the personified winds, the sailors, and the Ninevites, on the other hand, are strikingly characterized by the intensity of the noise they produce. The God of *Patience* is a God of sound and fury whose "glam" has a "roghlych rurd" (63-64), whose "steuen... stowned [Jonah's] mynde" (73), whose command to the winds is "wroþely... cleped" (132), whose "bidd" to the whale is issued "ferslych" (337), and whose "soun" to the despairing Jonah "swey in his ere" (429). In his elaboration of one verse of the Vulgate version, the poet defines the role of the personified winds in the storm as "þe noys bigynes" (137), and it is ironically the "loud... lot of þe wyndes" (161) that frightens Jonah into the hold of the ship where he sleeps sloth-fully. As even "þe see souʒed ful sore, gret selly to here" (140), the sailors' response is "þe cry ryses" (152). Moreover, the sailors' inter-rogation of Jonah is conducted "ful loude" (195). Appropriately, it is when the Ninevites are in a state of initial despair that "þe peple pitosly pleyned ful stylle" (371), for in this poem weakness of the voice is symptomatic of *acedia*. When the king advises that they "al schal crye...with alle oure clere strenþe; / Þe rurd schal ryse to hym þat rawþe schal haue; /...þat in his mylde amesyng he mercy may fynde"

(395-96, 400), he is delivering a clear warning against and repudiation of the most dangerous aspect of *acedia*, the despair which sins against the Holy Ghost by denying God's mercy and grace. The clear strength of their cry is emblematic of that repudiation, just as the "cler" cry (357) with which Jonah, newly chastened by his experience in the whale, preaches and prophesies to the Ninevites, is the only sound he makes in the poem which is not symptomatic of sloth. When the narrator describes how Jonah's clear, prophesying "speche sprang in þat space and spradde alle aboute" (365), the poet has effectively rendered speech and action synonymous; it is as though Jonah's speech is so active and vigorous that it takes on a life of its own.[29]

Unfortunately, Jonah's voice fails to sustain this level of active, unslothful assertiveness. Indeed, upon the conversion of the Ninevites and their preservation by a merciful, patient God, Jonah again reverts to the whining "janglande" (433) which had characterized his speech prior to this one episode. Also unfortunately, Jonah does not take the king's warning about despair to heart, for his most dangerous and characteristic manifestation of *acedia* in the poem is his tendency to lapse into despair so deep that he wishes to die. Here again, the poet's method is negative characterization by contrast. Like the Ninevites, the sailors in the dire situation of the storm "dispayred wel nere" (169), but not quite, because they have hope in "oure mercyable God" (238). Rather than wanting to die, as Jonah does, the sailors affirm that "þe lyf is ay swete" (156). Jonah, on the other hand, is consistently described in imagery that indicates Aquinas' "tristitia de spirituali bono," which negates the "gaudium" or joy one should experience in fulfilling the divine will. He is "vnglad" (63), full of "muche sorȝe" (409), "al joyles and janglande" (433), "ay janglande for tene" (90), weeping "for sorȝe" (480) and insistent that "I dure to longe" (488). Ironically, the scornful narrator—who calls him a "wytles wrechche" (113)—describes Jonah as a "joyful... jue" (109) precisely as he attempts to avoid doing God's will by fleeing to Tarshish. His later delight in the woodbine evaporates in the blast of heat which God sends with the dawn. These failures to "stere" his "hert" (27) toward a joyful acceptance of God's will all indicate the severity of Jonah's case of *acedia*, for the final stage of this vice is desire for death or else the actual commission of suicide.[30] It is ironically appropriate that, even in Jonah's despairing desire for death, he persists in his utter passivity. Notice that he makes no attempt to take his own life. Instead, he places responsibility for his death on God, demanding, "Why ne dyȝtteȝ þou me to diȝe? I dure to longe" (488) and "I wolde I were of þis worlde, wrapped in moldeȝ" (494). This last use of the subjunctive "were" perfectly captures the spirit (or rather lack of spirit) of the *Patience*-Poet's characterization of Jonah.

Thus, the poet incorporates many classic symptoms of the vice of *acedia,* in both its Patristic/Scholastic and popular definitions, within his unorthodox characterization of the Old Testament prophet: Jonah's wandering from his responsibility to God; his idleness; the several incidences, both canonical and invented, of his sleeping; his "uncler" voice; and his ultimate despair.   The complementary/antithetical relationship between *acedia* and patience accounts for the unusual emphasis on Jonah's commission of the vice of *acedia* in the poem as it intersects with the poem's simultaneous presentation of the equally prominent, also canonically quirky recommendation of the virtue of patience.   Indeed, although editors entitle the poem with the name of that virtue, rather than with some reference to the prominent biblical figure who is its main character, there has been little, if any, scholarly acknowledgment that the important relationship between *acedia* and patience might be "a" or "the" structuring principle for the poem.[31] To be fair, while the inevitable critical discussions of the blatant images of sleep and despair in Patience have occasionally suggested *acedia* or sloth as keys to Jonah's psychology, these analyses bear out Wenzel's accurate observation about Langland and Dante scholars, for their authors rely on a few Scholastic treatises and fail to show how *Patience* encompasses the total tradition of the vice as it was reflected in popular literature.[32] Other critics inadvertently have offered this virtue/vice opposition in the course of exploring their own approaches to the poem.   Three studies of *Patience* have cited a passage from Julian of Norwich's *Revelations of Divine Love* to support very different alternative interpretations of the poem.   One uses it to illustrate how the poem is a parable about the contemplative life.[33] Another cites it to illustrate how Jonah's lack of understanding of God's "cortasye" exemplifies the temporal fragmentation of language which is a major concern of the poem.[34] A third quotes it to illustrate how "instead of offering *fortitudo* as the virtue opposing sloth, ... mystical commentators turned for safety to patience and the allied virtue of humility."[35] In the passage cited in the three articles, Julian explains that God has revealed to her two sorts of sickness that prevent mankind from sharing fully in Christ's Passion:

> God shewid ii manner of sekenes that we have: that on is onpatience or slaith, for we bere our trevell and our pey[n]es hevily; that other is despeir or doubtfull drede.... And full helpe of this ful mekely our lord shewid, the patience that he had in his herd passion, and also the ioyeing and the lykyng that he hath of that passion for love.[36]

The real significance of this coincidental proffering of the identical passage to support three very different scholarly agendas is the classic nature of Dame Julian's assertion.   That she should so casually, yet authoritatively, equate impatience with sloth and supply the patience of Christ as the corrective for this failing is hardly remarkable in light of the long history of the relationship between patience and *acedia* presented earlier in this essay.   By the time the *Patience*-Poet availed himself of it in his unusual depiction of the story of Jonah, the relationship between this vice and virtue was a commonplace derived from Patristic, Scholastic, and popular assumptions about how to avoid the commission of *acedia*.   The relationship between patience and *acedia* accounts for the unorthodox narrative, thematic, and doctrinal strategies that have traditionally puzzled the critics of this Middle English "interpretation" of a well-known biblical figure, and indeed may be considered the "poynt" of *Patience*.

Notes

1.   Charles Moorman, "The Role of the Narrator in *Patience,*" *Modern Philology* 61 (1963): 90-95; Sylvia Tomasch, "*Patience* and the Sermon Tradition," *Centerpoint* 4 (1981): 83-93; David Williams, "The Point of *Patience,*" *Modern Philology* 68 (1970): 128; John T. Irwin and T. D. Kelly, "The Way And The End Are One: *Patience* As A Parable Of The Contemplative Life," *American Benedictine Review* 25 (1974): 37; Morton W. Bloomfield, "*Patience* and the *Mashal,*" in *Medieval Studies in Honor of Lillian Herlands Hornstein,* ed. Jess B. Bessinger and Robert R. Raymo (New York: New York University Press, 1976), pp. 41-49.

2.   Jay Schleusener, "History and Action in *Patience,*" *PMLA* 86 (1971): 959-65; John B. Friedman, "Figural Typology in the Middle English *Patience,*" in *The Alliterative Tradition in the Fourteenth Century,* ed. Bernard S. Levy and Paul S. Szarmach (Kent, Ohio: Kent State University Press, 1981), pp. 99-129; R. A. Shoaf, "God's Malayse: Metaphor and Conversion in *Patience,*" *Journal of Medieval and Renaissance Studies* 11 (1981): 273; Malcolm Andrew, "Jonah and Christ in *Patience,*" *Modern Philology* 70 (1973): 230-33.

3.   For surveys of typical medieval treatments of Jonah and Job respectively see R. H. Bowers, *The Legend of Jonah* (The Hague: Martinus Nijhoff, 1971); Lawrence L. Besserman, *The Legend of Job in the Middle Ages* (Cambridge, Mass.: Harvard University Press, 1979). Chaucer's references to these Old Testament figures are standard: the patience of Griselda is compared to that of Job in the *Clerk's Tale* vv. 932-38; Jonah's release from the whale's belly is an example of God's merciful intervention to which His preservation of Custance on the rudderless boat is compared in the *Man of Law's Tale* vv. 484-90 in *The Works of Geoffrey Chaucer,* ed. F. N. Robinson, 2nd ed. (Boston: Houghton Mifflin, 1957). Most critics of *Patience* have commented on the surprising choice of Jonah as the protagonist of a poem about that virtue.

4.   F. N. M. Diekstra, "Jonah and Patience: The Psychology of a Prophet," *English Studies* 55 (1974): 205-17.

5.   Siegfried Wenzel, *The Sin of Sloth: Acedia in Medieval Thought and Literature* (Chapel Hill: University of North Carolina Press, 1967), pp. 3-10. Wenzel's history of medieval attitudes toward *acedia* remains the classic study of this vice in medieval literature; my discussion of the history of the opposition between sloth and patience depends heavily upon and often summarizes from Wenzel's book.

6.   Benidict, *Regula,* 1, ed. Rudolph Hanslik (Vienna: CSEL, 1960), vol. 75, pp. 17-19.

7.   Bernard of Clairvaux, *Tractatus de ordine vitae* 10:30 (PL 184:579).

8.   Evagrius, *Tractatus ad eulogium* 4 (PG 79:1144).

9.   Nilus, *De octo spiritibus malitiae* 13-14 (PG 79:1158-59).

10.   John Cassian, *De institutis coenobiorum* 10:14, ed. Michael Petschenig (Vienna: CSEL, 1886; rpt. New York: Johnson Reprint Corp., 1966), vol. 17, pp. 185-86; *Conlationes*, 5:23, ed. Michael Petschenig (Vienna: CSEL, 1888), vol. 13, p. 148.

11.   Cassian, *Conlationes*, 5:16, op. cit., p. 141.

12.   *The Book of Vices and Virtues: A Fourteenth-Century English Translation of the Somme le roi of Lorens d'Orleans*, ed. W. Nelson Francis (London: Early English Text Society, 1942), os 217, pp.161, 164-69.

13.   Thomas Aquinas, *Summa Theologiae: Latin Text and English Translation* II-II, qu. 35, a.1 reply (New York: McGraw-Hill, 1972), vol. 75, pp. 22-25.

14.   Wenzel, *Sloth*, p. 55.

15.   Thomas Aquinas, *De malo*, qu. 11, a.2 reply.

16.   Wenzel, *Sloth*, pp. 53-54, traces this idea through the works of John of Damascus, Burgundio of Pisa, and Albertus Magnus.

17.   Hugh Ripelin of Strassburg, *Compendium theologicae veritatis*, III, 18 in *Alberti Magni opera omnia*, ed. A. Borgnet, vol. 34 (Paris: 1895), p. 110.

18.   Hugh of St. Victor, *De quinque septenis*, (PL 175:409).

19.   Wenzel, *Sloth*, pp. 78-96.

20.   Wenzel, *Sloth*, pp. 179-80.

21.   Several critics have suggested the centrality of sloth to the meaning of *Patience* while neither adequately following up the implications of the use of the vice in the poem, nor acknowledging how thoroughly the poem depicts the various forms *acedia* could take. Davenport, *The Art of the* Gawain *Poet* (London: Athlone Press, 1978), for example, merely mentions Jonah's shipboard sleep as an "image of sloth" (118) and his "proneness to accidie" (125) and lists sloth among several other sins of which Jonah is guilty (132). Citing a few Scholastic treatises, Diekstra examines Jonah's psychology as a case of "*tristitia* turned into *acedia*" ("Psychology," 208) but fails to show that the poem contains "the total tradition of the vice" as remarked by Wenzel. Elizabeth D. Kirk, "'Who Suffreth More Than God?': Narrative Redefinition of Patience in *Patience* and *Piers Plowman*," in *The Triumph of Patience: Medieval and Renaissance Studies*, ed. Gerald J. Schiffhorst (Orlando: University Presses of Florida, 1978), 88-104, esp. 90-91 uses one citation of Aquinas to point out that suffering leads to "depression, sloth, despair, and anger hardening into hatred."

22.   Quotations from the poem are from the following edition: *Patience*, ed. J. J. Anderson (New York: Barnes and Noble, 1969).

23.   See Diekstra, "Psychology," 207; Davenport, *Art*, p. 117; Lynn Staley Johnson, *The Voice of the* Gawain-Poet (Madison: University of Wisconsin Press, 1984), p. 7.

24.   Wenzel, *Sloth*, p. 55.

25.   For the *topos* of God as "maker" see Ernst Robert Curtius, *European*

Literature And The Latin Middle Ages, ed. Willard R. Trask (New York: Harper and Row, 1963), pp. 544-46. On God's creativity see A. C. Spearing, *The* Gawain-*Poet* (Cambridge: Cambridge University Press, 1970), pp. 91-95.

26.   Critics' explanations of Jonah's sleep vary. Johnson, *Voice,* p. 9, says it shows "man at his most bathetic." Spearing, Gawain-*Poet,* p. 82, says, "This sleep was commonly interpreted in the Middle Ages as standing for the obliviousness of the sinner.... But for the *Gawain*-poet it was in the first place a literal sleep in which Jonah... was slavering and snoring...." Schleusener, "History and Action," 962, calls it "the sleep of error." Laurence Eldredge, "Sheltering Space And Cosmic Space In The Middle English *Patience," Annuale Mediaevale* 21 (1981): 122 says, "On the one hand to sleep is to give expression to the trust he has in his shelter: only when one feels secure can one relax enough to sleep. On the other hand his sleeping represents an effort to dream his security into place around him." S. L. Clark and J. N. Wasserman, "Jonah and the Whale: Narrative Perspective in *Patience," Orbis Littera-rum* 35 (1980): 16 say, "Jonah's obliviousness to the infinite is consistently portrayed through the metaphor of sleep." Notwithstanding these interpretations, sleep was one of the most common iconographic representations of a state of sloth.

27.   See Appendix I in Anderson's edition, p. 70.

28.   See Anderson's note to line 186, p. 59.

29.   On the transformation from Jonah's "uncler" to "cler" voice see Johnson, *Voice,* p. 14; Davenport, *Art,* 106-07.

30.   The despair of God's mercy culminating in suicide is best illustrated in the morality play *Mankind* in which the Vice characters attempt to drive the protagonist to suicide. See *Mankind* in *The Macro Plays,* ed. Mark Eccles (London: Early English Text Society 262, 1969). For an interpretation of that play as an illustration of the same relationship between patience and sloth which is operative in *Patience,* see my article, "The Thematic and Structural Unity of *Mankind," Studies in Philology,* 72 (1975), 386-407.

31.   John M. Bowers, "*Patience* and the Ideal of the Mixed Life," *Texas Studies in Literature and Language* 28 (1986): 1-23, an article which appeared while my essay was in press, establishes the importance of the theme of patience and *acedia* in order to examine "the poet's concerns with the mystic apprehension of God's will as it was understood to lead toward some worldly endeavor, ideally expressed by sharing this personal revelation through the voluntary act of preaching," 1.

32.   This is particularly true of Diekstra and Kirk.

33.   Irwin and Kelly, "Parable," p. 42.

34.   Shoaf, "Malayse," p. 276.

35.   Bowers, "Mixed Life," p. 8.

36.   Julian of Norwich, *A Revelation of Love,* ed. Marion Glasscoe (Exeter: Exeter Medieval English Texts, 1976), Chapter 73, p. 88.

"ÞIS WRECH MAN IN WARLOWES GUTTEZ": IMAGERY AND UNITY OF FRAME AND TALE IN *PATIENCE*

GARY D. SCHMIDT

ong neglected in favor of its sister poems in the *Gawain* manuscript, the Middle English *Patience* has received increased critical attention in the last twenty years. Most of this attention has focused on the re-telling of the Jonah story, particularly emphasizing recurring motifs and analogues in the other poems of the manuscript. This trend has led to a growing awareness of the artistry of the work as well as an appreciation of its structural soundness. One aspect of this artistry is the poet's use of imagery to support and enhance traditional meanings of the story of Jonah. At the same time, the imagery works out the concerns of poverty and patience established in the frame of the poem.

The process whereby imagery is employed to lend support to traditional commentary is most evident in the encounter between Jonah and Warlow, the whale. The poet draws upon conventional identifications of the meaning of Jonah's experience within Warlow, but he uses imagery of death and Hell to strengthen typological connections. Much of this imagery represents an expansion of scriptural detail; where the biblical book of Jonah is sparse in its description, the poet inserts his own imaginative details for the sake of the artistry and of the typological meaning of the work.

In addition, the imagery associated with the swallowing and expulsion of Jonah mirrors the prophet's spiritual state and supports the religious concerns suggested within the frame of the poem. Such concerns are not typological, for the poet is not especially intent on proving the relationship between Christ and Jonah. He is interested, however, in focusing on the story of Jonah as an *exemplum* illustrating the relationship between poverty and patience. The poet promises to "wysse yow þerwyth" (60),[1] to instruct the reader by using this story, and his instruction centers on both the narrator's and the reader's need to endure a present woe patiently. Jonah thus stands as an example of one who refused such endurance and who consequently suffered an even greater state of poverty, here defined as physical hardship.

The first sixty lines of the poem represent a commentary on the relationship between poverty and patience. The poem opens, for example, with advice to accept a given evil patiently, "For quoso suffer cowþe syt, sele wolde folȝe" (5). It is then better to endure than to rage about ill usage, the poet argues, since the suffering will only get worse, advice which the narrator will apply to himself though critics have disagreed on the nature of the poverty which the narrator experiences. But whether the poverty is monetary or spiritual, the lesson is the same: under the constraints of necessity, one must endure and accept.[2] To do less is to encourage an even worse state.

The poet's commentary on the virtues of patience and poverty is intertwined with his discussion of the Beatitudes. He begins his list with an explanation of poverty, which the Vulgate defines as spiritual poverty: "Beati pauperes spiritu" (Matt. 5.3). The poet then indicates the spiritual nature of the quality by connecting it to the heart: "Thay arn happen þat han in hert pouerte" (13). Nearly half of the Beatitudes in *Patience*, moreover, are linked to the heart; only one appears in the scriptural version. The artistry of the poet thus suggests that this linking is not due to mere alliterative necessity, but comes about because of the poet's stress on the relationship between the spiritual and physical world, wherein spiritual poverty and physical hardship might well go hand in hand. In addition, each of the beatitudes connected to the heart deals directly with Jonah and the nature of patience. Jonah will experience poverty in the form of difficult circumstances, mercy in the form of expulsion from the whale, purification through the symbolic need to cleanse his soiled garment, and the essential lesson of learning to steer his own heart.

The poet concludes the enumeration of the Beatitudes with an apparent departure from the Vulgate text: "Þay ar happen also þat con her hert stere, / For hores is þe heuen-ryche, as I er sayde" (27-28). The promised reward is the same as that for patience; however, the Beatitude in the scriptural version promises the reward to those "persectionem patiuntur propter iustitiam" (Matt. 5.10). Malcolm Andrew and Ronald Waldron suggest that this difference represents a "radical departure from the Vulgate text."[3] While this is true in terms of the literal text, it is not a radical departure from the meaning of the passage, particularly since the need for self-control and endurance in the face of difficult circumstances has been stressed from the poem's outset. Indeed the poet identifies this virtue of steering one's heart as the province of Dame Patience, and thus the meaning underlying this line is the same as that suggested by the scriptural line: patiently accept hardship and persecution. It should be noted that the story of Jonah is closely linked to this line in *Patience*, for the story hinges on the question of whether Jonah will learn to guide his heart—a lesson learned in the midst of justified persecution.

The poet expressly links poverty and patience in the stanzas following his recitation of the Beatitudes, noting that

> Thus pouerte and pacyence arn nedes playferes.
> Syþen I am sette with hem samen, suffer me byhoues;
> Þenne is me lyȝtloker hit lyke and her lotes prayse,
> Þenne wyþer wyth and be wroth and þe wers haue. (45-49)

The poet then attempts to limit his definition of the fusion of the two virtues by placing them in the context of feudal ties of obedience:

> Oþer ȝif my lege lorde lyst on lyue me to bidde
> Oþer to ryde oþer to renne to Rome in his ernde,
> What grayþed me þe grychchyng bot grame more seche?
> (51-53)

Thus having identified poverty with difficult and unavoidable circumstances and patience with endurance of poverty and obedience to the commands of a liege lord, the poet concludes that it is useless to struggle against necessity. The story of Jonah follows naturally as an *exemplum* for this commentary.

But this exemplum mirrors imperfectly the connection between poverty and patience. Jonah's example bears negative connotations for he illustrates the poet's warning rather than the beatitudes' reward. Because Jonah refuses to accept the command to go to Nineveh—because he does not show patience in the midst of poverty—he is forced to undergo extreme hardship in the form of the "swallowing." He never receives the Kingdom of God, at least not in the context of the poem. Nor does he fully learn the lessons of patience and poverty, as demonstrated by the woodbine episode, an incident which in many ways echoes his experience within Warlow.

With his depiction of the whale episode, the poet draws most extensively upon traditional interpretations of the experience of Jonah.[4] At the same time, he uses imagery derived from these interpretations to develop the personal story of the character of Jonah and the frame of the tale. In the poem, the typological and exegetical levels, for instance, are subordinate to the personal and developmental levels. Although the poet employs traditional commentaries, he is more interested in depicting the character of Jonah, the renegade prophet, in the context of poverty and patience than in merely presenting a sermon-like recounting of the prophet's experience.

This subordination takes place even before Jonah is swallowed by the whale. When Jonah first receives the command to go to Nineveh, the poet writes that Jonah's mind was "stowned" (73), and he then determines to escape. The prophet flees, moreover, because he believes that God is remote to care "þaȝ I be nummen in Nunniue and naked dispoyled, / On rode rwly torent with rybaudes mony" (95-96). The reference to the Crucifixion suggests the traditional typological link between Christ and Jonah, and here, of course, Jonah is meant to be an anti-type of Christ, one who refuses death where Christ accepts. However, this typological link is not as significant as the delineation of personal motivation: Jonah flees because of his fear and his refusal to accept the commands of his Lord. And such behavior is the poet's main concern as expressed in the opening lines.

The same subordination of the exegetical to the personal continues once the prophet is swallowed by the whale. Jonah has his most introspective moments within the belly of Warlow; such insights represent his first accurate assessments of his own nature and of the meaning of his actions. Both these self-evaluations and the imagery of the physical setting reflect movements in the prophet's spiritual journey toward obedience and patience.

Jonah's descent into the whale, however, represents the most important typological connection between Christ and Jonah since this incident is mentioned by Christ, Himself, in two of the Gospels. In Matthew 12. 39-41 and Luke 11. 29-30, 32, Christ identifies the sign of Jonah—three days in the belly of the whale—with his own imprisonment in the tomb.[5] In *Patience*, the "wylde walterande whale" is driven from the bottom of the abyss "as Wyrde þen schaped" (247). The creature swallows the prophet even as the sailors hold his feet and dives to the bottom, returning to the abyss from which it issued. In terms of Jonah's spiritual journey, the swallowing represents his descent into hell.

Although the Warlow of *Patience* does not express a particularly malevolent nature, it cannot help but be painted with the strokes of a long tradition which connects the whale to death, to Satan, and to Hell. In Christian commentaries and bestiaries, the whale was conventionally described as either an image of Hell itself or as an agent which led souls to the underworld.

Most of the exegetical works preceding *Patience* which dealt with the story of Jonah envisioned the swallowing as a type of death resulting from Jonah's disobedience. He thus represents not only Christ, but the damned soul who refuses to obey God. This use of the prophet's experience occurs as early as the fourth century. In a series of anonymous verses on Jonah once attributed to Tertullian, the prophet is roused from his slumber and found to be the cause of the storm. The sailors then reluctantly toss Jonah to the "mortis hiatum," and he finds himself surrounded by images of death, such as wrecks of fleets and putrid carcasses. The poet makes the linkage between the swallowing and death explicit when he writes that Jonah is "in life / Learning the process of his death"[6]

Origen, likewise, tied Jonah's experience to death in his discussion of prayers in *De oratione*. Origen refers to Jonah implicitly when he notes that "in many cases men who had fled from the laws of God and had been given over to the death which was strengthening its grip on them, were saved from such a terrible fate through repentance: They did not despair that they could be saved even when subdued in death's belly."[7] Origen's commentary underscores the occasionally ambiguous nature of the whale, for although Jonah is in one sense dying, he is also purged and saved so that the whale is for him an instrument of both damnation and redemption.

In his *In Jonam Prophetam*, Jerome is principally concerned with exploring the typological connections of Jonah to Christ; consequently, Jerome emphasizes the tie between the whale and death so as to link Jonah's three days in the whale to Christ's three days in the tomb. Furthermore, in Jerome's commentary, Jonah orders the sailors to throw him into the sea not because they need to save themselves but because death wishes to devour him. At this point, Jonah is not aware of his impending extraordinary experience, but it is significant that that experience is specifically associated with death by devouring. Later, God commands death and Hell, not the whale, to receive the prophet.

According to Jerome's commentary, once Jonah is plunged into the sea, it is the terrible sight of the gaping mouth of the whale that turns the prophet's mind to God. Thus the potential of being swallowed by something already identified with death and Hell recalls Jonah to obedience, in much the same way that in later visionary lore those granted visions of Hell are recalled to their Christian duty.[8]

In terms of its artistic representations, the whale's evil and death-like nature is often emphasized by connecting it to Leviathan, the diabolic associations of which pervade Jewish and Christian tradition. Most Christian writers agreed with Caesarius of Heisterbach, who wrote that "Leviathan iste signficat diabolum, serpentum antiquuum, qui ad similitudinem draconis volat in aere superbie, graditur in terra avaricie, natat in aquis luxurie."[9] Caesarius, moreover, quotes extensively from St. Gregory, the most influential disseminator of Leviathan material, who identified Leviathan with the ever-present deceiver, who, with his open mouth, is always ready to swallow the sinful soul.[10]

When early Christian and medieval artists sought to represent Jonah's whale, they used images of Leviathan as models. Leviathan is traditionally depicted as a coiled monster, a description derived from the prophetic book of Isaiah, 27.1: "In that day, the Lord will punish with his sword, his fierce, great, and powerful sword, Leviathan the gliding serpent, Leviathan the coiling serpent; he will slay the monster of the deep." Thus Leviathan is generally delineated as a dragon-like sea monster, whose body coils around itself several times. Often he is part reptile, part fish, and sometimes part lion, with taloned legs, fin-like wings, or an elongated snout perched on the end of a winding neck.

The close identification of a dragon-like Leviathan and Jonah's whale appears in a set of eleven fourth-century tomb sculptures now housed in the Cleveland Museum. Four of these early Christian sculptures depict the life of Jonah; two include the episode of the swallowing. In both representations of the swallowing, the whale is clearly pictured as Leviathan, with a dragon-like mouth, ears arched forward, and tail coiled high overhead.[11]

Literary evidence of the tradition of the malevolent whale appears in the OE *Physiologus*, rooted in the Greek *Physiologus*, which couches its description in very Anglo-Saxon terms. The whale is thus the "miclan hwale" (13), "frecne ond fer3grim" (5) to all sea-faring men, 'fyrnstreama geflotan' (7).[12] The poet records the traditional island encounter story where sailors, thinking the whale's back is an island, build a fire on it and are drowned when it submerges. The OE *Physiologus*, however, slightly alters the original version of the tale so as to emphasize the malicious nature of the beast. Here, the whale, instead of plunging into the sea to escape the fire, is "facnes craeftig" (24) and waits until men are firmly settled upon its back before it descends into the sea, thereby bringing them to drown in the hall of death. This account is moralized so that the whale is associated with demons, who, unseen, betray men through a sense of false security. Eventually the false and malicious foe seeks to bring the men to a locale identified as "grundleasne wylm under mistglome" (46-47) and a place appropriate for both the whale and damned souls.

The poet also notes the whale's habit of emitting a pleasant smell to draw fish into its mouth. This narrative detail is allegorized into a striking image of the mouth of hell, for those who are led away by false desires will find the cursed one opening hell for them: "Þonne he þa grimman goman bihlemme3 / Aefter feorcwale faeste togaedre, / Helle hlindura" (76-78). The doors of hell are thus equated with Satan's jaws, and, as the poet goes on to note, there is no return or escape or passage through these.

The poet of *Patience* does not explicitly connect the whale to Leviathan, and, because of his interest in the character of Jonah and the prophet's relationship to poverty and patience, he spends very little time on the whale itself. Instead, he emphasizes the personal predicaments of Jonah, who is miraculously preserved inside the whale.

> For nade þe hy3e Heuen-Kyng, þur3 His honde my3t,
> Warded þis wrech man in warlowes guttez,
> What lede mo3t leue bi lawe of any kynde,
> Þat any lyf my3t be lent so longe hym withinne? (257-60)

The narrator here makes explicit a number of elements. Jonah, having refused to endure the hardship of the earlier command by God, finds himself in an even worse situation, as the poet foretold in the frame. Poverty always increases when an individual is impatient. At the same time, Jonah is miraculously preserved because of God's will, a recognition which comes later when the poet notes that God is sweet.

The poet implies that if God could preserve Jonah in the belly of the whale, could he not also preserve him in the city of Nineveh? God is not too remote and indifferent to ignore the prophet's fate, as Jonah earlier complained. The folly of not yielding to necessity is thus made evident.

Though the character of the whale is not developed, the poet of *Patience* does highlight the act of swallowing, focusing in particular upon the image of the mouth of the whale. As we have already seen, the swallowing was often envisioned as a type of death or damnation. In *Patience*, the jaws and throat of the whale reflect this understanding in that they are associated with Hell.

One of the most striking images associated with the jaws of Jonah's whale is the Hell-mouth. By the fourteenth century the mouth of Hell was the standard iconographic representation of the infernal realm. The genesis of this image lies in the middle of the tenth century when the Benedictine monastic reform movement which had spread through Europe, crossed the Channel and established itself in southern England. The reform movement used its keen interest in art to create new images aimed at the lay audience. Such images were designed to express theological principles in vital and accessible ways, thus extending the church's teaching and influence beyond the monastery walls. In searching for new ways to visualize dramatically the notion of damnation, monastic artists used the bestial Hell-mouth to symbolize the entrance to Hell. Its most vivid appearance occurred on church walls and *tympana*, where the gaping mouth opened to swallow lines of chained souls from all three estates. The oral form of the image emphasized the physical nature of damnation, for the mouth served not only as an entrance to the torments of the underworld, but as a torment in itself.

The Hell-mouth, then, was an appropriate metaphor to attach to Jonah's whale, especially because of the linkage between the whale and Hell. By the eleventh century a number of manuscript illustrations use the Hell-mouth to evoke typological meaning: Jonah's descent into and ascent from the whale prefigured not only Christ's experience in the tomb, but also man's resurrection from death. An early fourteenth-century *Biblia pauperum*, Vienna MS. 1198, fol.7v, for instance, makes the connection between Jonah's whale and the mouth of Hell explicit by portraying the jaws of the whale as the jaws of Hell.[13] The folio depicting the burial of Christ also contains the descent of Joseph into the pit and the descent of Jonah into the whale, both of which are typologically associated with Christ's death and burial. The later folio, fol. 8r, which provides the corresponding resurrection motifs, continues to represent Jonah's whale as the mouth of hell, thus emphasizing the spiritual meaning of the prophet's experience.

In *Patience,* Jonah's descent into the whale follows a period of inactivity in which he has slept in the ship's hold. But the storm precipitates Jonah's first clear self-evaluation, for instead of taking refuge behind rationalization and self-deceit, he admits his identity and guilt. "Alle þis meschef for me is made at þys tyme" (209), he moans, and allows himself to be tossed sacrificially into the sea. The poet then notes that the whale "swyftely swenged hym to swepe, and his swolȝ opened" (250). Such a concentration on the open mouth recalls the traditional Hell-mouth and represents an imaginative expansion of the scriptural text which both fits conventional typology and underscores the horror of Jonah's personal experience.

Jonah's "swallowing" mirrors, in a very real sense, his confused identity and his rejection of the natural order of obedience to a lord, as shown by his reluctance—his refusal—to endure patiently the command given to him. In describing the act of Jonah being swallowed, the poet concentrates on the intense physical movement of the prophet. Having left Jonah in order to focus on the activities of the sailors, the narrator returns to find him being swallowed and swiftly borne to the sea bottom. Jonah, the poet writes, is "malskred in dred" (255), for no man, by any law of nature, would be able to live in Warlow's guts.

But the whale is not only an instrument of purgation; Jonah's "drede" will contribute to his salvation and resurrection. The whale is thus the setting for Jonah's repentance, something the poet emphasizes by developing Jonah's first contact with Warlow's jaws:

> For he knew vche a cace and kark þat hym lymped,
> How fro þe bot into þe blober watz with a best lachched,
> And þrwe in at hit þrote withouten þret more,
> As mote in at a munster dor, so mukel wern his chawlez.
> (265-68)

The action of the stanza moves in a descending line as Jonah is tossed from the safety of the enclosing boat to the peril of the enclosing beast which is itself enclosed by the stormy sea. But the simile in the final line of the stanza suggests more than the possibility of death. Instead, Jonah seems to enter into a minster, a place to work out his broken ties of obligation to his liege lord.

Malcolm Andrew has argued that line 268 contains more meaning than the association with hell.[14] Noting the improbable perspective, he argues that the simile stresses Jonah's weakness and God's power, thereby corroborating what Andrew sees as the principal point of *Patience*: that resistance to God's will is futile. Furthermore, S.L. Clark and J.N. Wasserman note that the perspective of the simile emphasizes the size of the whale's jaws, thus making it possible for Jonah to be swallowed without touching any of the teeth.[15] The phrase, they later note, is also used as a synonym for the city of Nineveh, an epithet which formulates a comparison between the prophet and the city. "Thus the 'mote' comes to represent the smallness of the sinful man (299), the city-like largeness of the penitent man (422), and, finally, the righteous man who cannot be cast into Hell, as opposed to Jonah, who is locked inside his own dark bowe" (456).

The simile's emphasis on proportional size is significant, for it not only stresses the relative weakness of Jonah, but it recalls again the frame's comments on necessity. Here again, Jonah is faced with poverty which might be perceived as physical hardship—the same way the prophet understood the command to go to Nineveh. But here, however, the necessity of the thing is immediately apparent and overwhelming: Jonah cannot help but be swallowed by the whale. Once inside the whale, Jonah will perceive that the command to go to Nineveh, at first circumvented, must be obeyed, particularly when a rather exasperated God gives him the command the second time.

In addition, the simile is used only after Jonah has evaluated his actions and acknowledged his guilt. He tells the sailors:

> Alle þis meschef for me is made at þys tyme,
> For I haf greued my God and gulty am founden;
> Forþy berez me to þe borde and baþes me þeroute,
> Er gete ȝe no happe, I hope forsoþe. (209-12)

Here Jonah speaks as a prophet; his assessment is correct, unlike his prediction of what would happen if he went to Nineveh. Though he is not aware of the whale's presence when he is tossed overboard, Jonah enters the sea as a willing sacrifice, recognizing his own sin. In so doing, he embraces a form of poverty far beyond that which he had anticipated at Nineveh. The comparison of the jaws to a minster door thus emphasizes this spiritual transformation: it is here, as in a church, that Jonah is saved, where he will move to penitence and obedience.

The union of salvation and damnation is emphasized in the next few stanzas. As he is swallowed, the prophet glides though the "glaym ande glette" (269) of the whale's guts as though they were the road to hell and then finds himself in a cold, dark hall, a place where there is no rest, but only reeking mire. The poet himself makes this identification:

> And þer he festnes þe fete and fathmez aboute,
> And stod vp in his stomak þat stank as þe deuel.
> Þer in saym and in sorȝe þat sauoured as helle,
> Þer watz bylded his bour þat wyl no bale suffer. (273-76)

Jonah will later make the connection with Hell even more explicit when he prays from "hellen wombe" (306), a phrase which appears also in the scriptural version. The irony of the last line of the stanza recalls the warning of the frame, that failure to endure patiently will trigger a worse sorrow. Jonah's enclosed bower is no longer in a ship but in the womb of Hell.

This description of the disobedient prophet is reminiscent of another motif popular during the Middle Ages: that of the damned soul swallowed by Satan or his demons. Although the most well-known illustration of this theme is Dante's representation of Satan gnawing upon the souls of the three traitors, for several centuries before the appearance of the *Inferno*, Satan had been portrayed as a greedy and hungry creature who opened his jaws to swallow souls. Once inside Satan, the souls are tormented within his belly until they are vomited or defecated out, only to become whole again and swallowed anew.

The motif of the devouring Satan was particularly popular in wall paintings, where he functions as a type of Moloch. A fresco in the Collegiate Church of San Gimignano from 1230, for instance, draws Satan as an ancient yet fierce demon whose three mouths eternally chew Brutus, Cassius, and Judas. He holds two other souls by the neck and excretes another which he had previously swallowed.[16] Similarly, a late thirteenth-century mosaic in the cupola of the Baptistry in Florence depicts a Bosch-like scene with Satan sitting on a fiery throne and gnawing on the torso of a soul. Snakes from his buttocks have swallowed the heads of two souls; snakes from his ears clutch two other souls.[17]

This same motif occurs in a literary form in visionary literature, particularly in the twelfth-century *Vision of Tundale*. The Latin original, *Visio Tundali*, was composed by Brother Mark at the St. James Irish Monastery in Ratisbon, Bavaria. He notes that he heard of the vision from Tundale himself and translated it from Irish into Latin at the request of the abbess Gisela. But despite the ostensibly primary source, it is clear that Tundale's vision draws extensively upon the infernal journey tradition, including material from Old and New Testament Apocrypha, the *Visio Pauli*, the *Aeneid*, Irish mythology and romance, and Bede's version of the vision of Drythelm in his *Historia ecclesiastica*.

During his voyage through hell Tundale encounters two creatures who function in ways similar to Jonah's Warlow: both swallow damned souls in order to torment them. The first creature is remarkable for the size of his mouth: "in all his mowthe that was so wyde / Nyne thowsand armyd in myght ryde / Betwene his toskys that were so longe."[18] Hanging from the top of the mouth are two giants, later identified by Tundale's guardian angel as Forcusus and Conallus, or Fergus and Conall—individuals who refused to follow God's decrees.

Next to the giants stand two pillars, positioned so as to hold the mouth open and to form three gates. From these pillars issue long flames, a foul smell, and the groans of thousands of souls suffering within; thousands of demons stand in front of the mouth, clutching the wretched souls. An angel then explains that the beast is named Acheron—thus transforming the river of Hades into a monster—and that it swallows all covetous men: "So muche thurst hathe that best," explains the guide, "That all the water most and lest / That ever ran est or west / Myght not stanche the bestys thurst." Tundale is thrown in and endures the fiery torment for a time.

The second creature is encased in a field of ice, thus recalling Dante's Satan. Tundale depicts this monster with black wings, iron-nailed feet, and a great head: "His mowthe was wyd and syde lyppud / Hys snowt was with yron typpud." Out of his mouth burns a fire, never-ending because of an inexhaustible supply of fuel. The beast then swallows nearby souls which burn in his stomach until they are almost wasted away. Finally, such souls are spewn out and inhabited by adders and vermin until they are ready to be swallowed again.

A number of striking parallels between the experience of the visionary and that of Jonah in *Patience* can be delineated. Both individuals represent disobedient souls who are doomed to experience in advance of death some of the torments of Hell and who enter into that experience by being swallowed by a creature designated as the emissary of Hell. In both cases the swallowing—the means of entering the infernal realm—is emphasized. And particularly important, the experiences are purgatorial rather than damning; both Tundale and Jonah emerge as chastened and penitent souls. Jonah's experience, if one is aware of this background, stands forth as a voyage to and from Hell; his resurrection thus becomes an especially dramatic event.

The poet of *Patience* veers sharply from the images of Hell after noting that Jonah has found no place of rest, only reeking guts in the belly of the whale. Next to this olfactory and tactile image, the poet includes a half-line of striking contrast: "bot euer is God swete" (280). The distinction between the stinking womb of hell and the nature of God is drawn by the poet, but the same image seems to be in the mind of the prophet, for such a figure leads to another introspective moment. Jonah thus recognizes that he is the "gaule of prophetes" (285), an image which evokes the filth of the whale's throat. Praying for mercy, Jonah asks God to prove that He is Lord on both land and water; almost immediately he finds a place of refuge from the mire.

Early exegesis of the Book of Jonah used the prophet's prayer as an example of proper petition, penitence, and obedience. Origen, for example, discusses Jonah in a chapter from his *De oratione* which lists a series of heeded prayers. After citing a number of examples of Christ's prayers, Origen notes that "Jonah also, having not despaired of being heard out of the belly of the whale that had swallowed him, escaped from the whale's belly and so fulfilled the rest of his prophetical mission to the men of Nineveh."[19] This explanation and similar commentaries underscored Jonah's repentance as demonstrated by his proper prayer.

In *Patience,* however, Jonah finds a place free from defilement only after his short confessional prayer:

> With þat he hitte to a hyrne and held hym þerinne,
> Þer no defoule of no fylþe watz fest hym abute;
> Þer he sete also sounde, saf for merk one,
> As in þe bulk of þe bote þer he byfore sleped. (289-92)

Having confessed, Jonah is able to find a place of relative safety. He thus enters into a period of inactivity, which follows his frantic movement down the throat of the whale and the fumbling within the hall-like interior. The poet connects this incident to the prophet's time in the ship's bower, thus emphasizing the sense of safety.

Here, as before, the poet uses the physical world to reflect the spiritual. Jonah's escape from the entanglement of Hell—though he has not yet been resurrected—suggests that he has begun to learn the lessons of poverty and patience; he has no choice but to endure the present hardship. But he has been prepared for these lessons by his hellish experience. Accordingly, his proper prayer and penitential attitude spring from his poverty.

Jonah's ejection from the whale—iconographically envisioned by medieval writers as a type of resurrection—comes after a thirty-two line prayer, thereby representing another introspective moment which occurs during a period of inactivity. In essence this prayer amplifies the meaning of his earlier short prayer; Jonah yields to necessity and submits his will. He gradually becomes spiritually poor after undergoing physical poverty, but the prayer's movement from despair to hope mirrors, both on the physical and the spiritual plane, the experience of the prophet.

He begins the prayer with twenty lines describing his present bleak position—emphasizing his burial under the sea rather than his entombment in the whale: "Þe grete flem of þy flod folded me vmbe" (309)—he cries:

> I am wrapped in water to my wo stoundez
> Þe abyme byndes þe body þat I byde inne;
> Þe pure poplande hourle playes on my heued;
> To laste mere of vche a mount, Man, am I fallen ... (317-20)

This version of Jonah's prayer closely follows that of the Vulgate though the poet is not a slavish imitator. Images of binding and entrapment, such as the reference to the abyss holding the prophet's body, do not appear in the Vulgate; such images are derived from traditional interpretations of Jonah's expulsion as a type of the soul's resurrection. And, fittingly, the lines of the prayer both in *Patience* and in the Vulgate suggest Jonah's hope that he will be saved.

Recognizing the justice of his situation, Jonah acknowledges the judgment of God yet prays for mercy. "ʒet surely I hope / Efte to trede on þy temple and teme to þyseluen" (315-16), he cries. This aspiration is somewhat different from the sentiment expressed in the Vulgate version, where Jonah hopes to look again at God's temple; he alludes here to the promised reward of heaven's kingdom to those who endure poverty and can guide their own hearts. In addition, the poet calls attention to the re-establishment of the ties of obedience. Similarly, the last line of the prayer emphasizes Jonah's desire to unite himself with God, for he promises to "halde goud þat þou me hetes: haf here my trauthe" (336). This line, also absent from the scriptural version, recalls Jonah's spiritual regeneration through patient obedience. His position at the beginning of *Patience* has, by the force of circumstances, been dramatically reversed.

Having pledged to do God's bidding, Jonah seems assured of divine mercy. For the first time in the poem, then, God speaks directly to the whale, "ferslych" commanding it to spit the prophet up onto dry land (337). Moreover, in the space of four lines, the poet claims three times that the expulsion derives from God's command (337, 339, 340), thus fulfilling Jonah's earlier request that God show himself lord on both land and water. Such a focus on God's will recalls again the necessity of obedience. Jonah is thus expelled onto dry land, finding his garment soiled with the filth of the whale. His personal cleansing, then, represents both a literal and symbolic need, for with cleanness his previous disobedient attitude peels away. He is now summoned to the same task which he had earlier refused.

When Jonah is ejected, the command of God sounds again, only this time set in the form of a question: "Nylt þou neuer to Nuniue bi no kynnes wayeʒ?" (346). And Jonah, in obedience and patient endurance, replies to the more gentle, though slightly irritated, command, "lene my þy grace / For to go at þy gre: me gaynez no oþer" (347-48). He then "radly ros as he myʒt" (351), and that same day reaches Nineveh, a city so large that it takes three days to traverse it, perhaps an oblique allusion to the length of the prophet's stay in the whale. He now may be viewed as a type of Christ, rather than an anti-type, because he accepts the command of God. At the same time Jonah fulfills the concerns of the frame, for he patiently endures an expected hardship. His humble reply to the command is also evidence of his spiritual poverty, a remarkable change for a man who once dreaded "no dynt" (125).

When Jonah preaches to the Ninevites, his exhortations are colored by his own experience. He warns, for example, that the city "Schal tylte to grounde; / Vp-so-doun schal þe dumpe depe to þe abyme,? / To be swolӡed swyftly wyth þe swart erþe" (361-63), a fate not particularly different from his own. He also threatens that the Ninevites will lose their sweet lives, thereby evoking the earlier comparison of his own situation in the belly of the whale with God's sweetness (364). They, like Jonah, turn to God and repent, and God forgives them, much to Jonah's chagrin. His fit of pique then leads him to rationalize his prior disobedience. God, Himself, must upbraid him— this time more gently—by advising Jonah to "be preue and be pacient in payne and in joye" (525). The poet's repetition of the poem's first line flows naturally from this exhortation.

Jonah thus functions as both a negative and positive example for the poet. The prophet's linear movement from one spiritual state to another allows the poet to expand the relationship between poverty and patience which he had established in the frame. And though the poet's tale of Jonah focuses on the rather disturbing aspects of that relationship, his version of the beatitudes emphasizes the rewards of patient endurance. Still, the poet remains one step back from the meaning of the poem, for though he counsels patience in the midst of poverty, he notes that such patience is not always pleasant. Indeed, the tone of the frame indicates that the poet himself would not function as a proper type. And it is this relationship between types and personal spiritual life that the poet uses to structure his work and develop his tale.

Notes

1.   All citations from *Patience* are from Malcolm Andrew and Ronald Waldron, eds., *The Poems of the* Pearl *Manuscript* (Berkeley: University of California Press, 1979).

2.   See the discussion of the nature of poverty in *Patience* in John T. Irwin and T. D. Kelly, "The Way and the End are One: *Patience* as a Parable of the Contemplative Life," *American Benedictine Review* 25 (1974): 33-55. They argue that "poverty of heart comprehends more than simply patient suffering of physical deprivation ... for what the narrator means by poverty of heart is poverty of will." This definition is central to Jonah's conversion, but the prophet moves to spiritual poverty only because of the circumstances of physical poverty in which he finds himself. For Jonah, at least, the physical world is more immediate than the spiritual, and its demands seem more pressing. See also John M. Bowers, "*Patience* and the Ideal of the Mixed Life," *Texas Studies in Language and Literature* 28 (1968): 1-23; Sandra Prior, "*Patience*–Beyond Apocalypse," *Modern Philology* 83 (1986): 337-48.

3.   Andrew and Waldron, *Pearl Manuscript*, 27.

4.   For a summation of early commentators on the book of Jonah, see Jean Allenbach, "La Figure de Jonas dans les textes preconstantiniens," in *La Bible et les Peres: Colloque de Strasbourg (1-3 Octobre 1969)* (Strasbourg: Centre D'Etudes Superieures Specalise d'Histoire des Religions, 1969), pp. 97-112.

5.   Matthew 12. 39-41: "Qui respondens ait illis: Generatio mala et adultera signum quaerit: et signum no dabitur ei nisi signum Ionae prophetae. Sicut enim fuit Ionas in ventre ceti tribus diebus, et tribus noctibus, sic erit Filius hominis in corde terrae tribus diebus et tribus noctibus. Viri Ninivitae surgent in iudicio cum generatione ista, et condemnabunt eam: quia poenitentiam egerunt in praedicatione Ionae. Et ecce plus quam ionas hic." This connection was a commonplace during the Middle Ages. It is found, for example, in a sermon once attributed to St. Augustine, "Sermo ad catechumenos" (*PL* 40: 666): "In ventre bestiae marinae positus Jonas sanctus oravit: in inferno Christus descendens mortuous suscitavit." See the discussion of Jonah's typological associations in Malcolm Andrew, "Jonah and Christ in *Patience*," *Modern Philology* 70 (1973): 230-33, and John Block Friedman, "Figural Typology in the Middle English *Patience*," in Bernard S. Levy and Paul E. Szarmach, eds., *The Alliterative Tradition in the Fourteenth Century* (Kent, Ohio: Kent State University Press, 1981), pp. 99-129.

6.   Latin text in *PL* 2: 1107-14. English text in Alexander Roberts and James Donaldson, eds., *Ante-Nicene Fathers* 4 (Grand Rapids: William B. Eerdman's Publishing Co., 1968), pp. 127-29.

7.   Origen, *De Oratione*, 13.4 (*PG* 11: 455).

8.   Jerome, *In Jonam Prophetam*, 2 (*PL* 25: 1131-32). R. H. Bowers, in *The Legend*

of Jonah (The Hague: Matinue Nijhoff, 1971), p. 26, refers to this argument as Jerome's fussiness about verb tense, but in reality Jerome is basing his argument on a strict, literal interpretation of the text.

9.   Quoted and discussed in R. B Huygens, "Deux commentaires sur la sequence 'Ave praeclara maris stella,'" *Citeaux commentarii Cistercienses* (Abbatia, Westmalle, Belgica) 20 (1970): 108-69.

10.   Gregory, *Moralia in Job*, XXIII, c. 37 (*PL* 76: 713-14). For complete discussions of the iconography of Leviathan, see Jessie Poesch, "The Beasts from Job in the 'Liber Floridus' Manuscripts," *Journal of the Warburg and Courtland Institutes* 33 (1970): 41-51, and John Block Friedman, "Antichrist and the Iconography of Dante's Geryon," *Journal of the Warburg and Courtlauld Institutes* 35 (1972): 108-22.

11.   Pictured in "Cleveland Museum of Art: Golden Anniversary," *Archeology* 19 (1966): 277-83. Cf. an ivory casket held in the Civic Museum of Brescia dating to 312 A.D. Devoting two of its front panels to the story of Jonah, it shows a toothy, elongated whale with two sets of coils in its body. Pictured in J. Kollwitz, *Die Lipsanothek von Brescia* (Berlin and Leipzig, 1933), frontispiece.

12.   Citations from this work are from "The Whale," ed. George Philip Krapp, in *The Exeter Book, Anglo-Saxon Poetic Records*, 3 (New York: Columbia University Press, 1936), pp. 171-74. See the discussion of this poem in Stanley Greenfield, *A Critical History of Old English Literature* (New York: New York University Press, 1965), pp. 182-83.

13.   Pictured in Franz Unterkircher, ed., *Die Wiener Biblia Pauperum: Codex Vindibonensis* 1198, 3 vols., (Vienna: Verlag Styria, 1962). See the discussion of this manuscript in Andre Blum, "Un Manuscript Inedit de XIIIᵉ siecle de la 'Bible des Pauvres,'" *Academie des inscription et belles- lettres: Monuments et memoires* 23 (1925-26): 95-111.

14.   Malcolm Andrew, "*Patience* : The 'Munster Dor,'" *English Language Notes* 14 (1977): 164-67.

15.   S. L. Clark and J. N. Wasserman, "Jonah and the Whale: Narrative Perspective in *Patience*," *Orbis Litterarum* 35 (1980): 1-19. A very similar image is applied in rabbinical exegesis, in which the whale is generally depicted as a rather benign creature. The early eighth-century *Pirke de Rabbi Eliezer*, for example, notes that when the great fish swallowed Jonah, the prophet "entered its mouth just as a man enters the great synagogue, and he stood [therein]." This simile, like that of the minster, hints at spiritual renewal. Gerald Friedlander, trans., *Pirke de-Rabbi Eliezer* (rpt. New York: 1965, c. 10, pp. 68-73). See also Louis Ginzberg, *The Legends of the Jews*, (Philadelphia: Jewish Publication Society of America, rpt. 1968), pp. 249-50.

16.   Portrayed in Robert Hughes, *Heaven and Hell in Western Art* (New York, 1968), p. 33.

17.   Pictured in John Block Friedman, "Medieval Cartography and Inferno XXXIV: Lucifer's Three Faces Reconsidered," *Traditio* 39 (1983): fig. 1. A similar image occurs in Giotto's "Last Judgment" at Scrovegni Chapel, Padua, from the early fourteenth century, depicted in Hughes, *Heaven and Hell*, p. 21. See the discussion of this image in Michael Thomas, "Der Decensus ad inferos in theologischen Programm der Giottofresken in der Arenakapelle zu Padua."

18.   All citations from this work are from Thomas G. Stevenson, ed., *The Visions of Tundale* (Edinburgh, 1843). See the discussion of some of these devouring beasts in Robert L. McGrath, "Satan and Bosch: The *Visio Tundali* and the Monastic Vices," *Gazette des beaux-arts* Series 6, 71 (1968): 45-50.

19.   Origen, *De oratione*, 13.2 (*PG* 11: 455).

SIGNIFYING THE SELF:
LANGUAGE AND IDENTITY IN *SIR GAWAIN AND THE GREEN KNIGHT*[1]

JOHN PLUMMER

The subject of *Sir Gawain and the Green Knight* is not deeds but words. Love and battle, sex and violence, the traditional matter of romance, hover over the story as potentials but are realized only in symbolic, displaced forms. Neither the battle Arthur expects on seeing the Green Knight at Camelot nor the battering Gawain anticipates at the Green Chapel materializes, and martial prowess is reduced to two blows, both harmless, falling twelve months apart, leading one reader to remark on "the sense of physical activity and of masculine prowess in which Sir Gawain is, in comparison to most romances, ... so conspicuously lacking."[2] The sexual energies gathered into the three temptation scenes are likewise sublimated into a few kisses. Language, on the other hand, is central to all of Gawain's important tasks: he answers the initial challenge of the Green Knight at Camelot with a careful, order-asserting speech; he gives his word to the Green Knight to exchange blows and to Bertilak to exchange winnings; he spends a week in "luf talkynge"; and he makes three separate confessions. Though each of these instances of Gawain's use of language has received individual critical attention, the implications of the poem's evident concern for language and its intimate relationship with identity might be more thoroughly explored. As the poem illustrates, identity—Camelot's corporate and Gawain's individual— is essentially a social construct. We are the "person" (as opposed to the purely biological object) that, simultaneously, we claim to be and our contemporaries accept us as being. The arena for the negotiation of this identity is a linguistic one. The creation, destruction, and modification of identities is a game played according to linguistic rules, and, as both Gawain and Arthur discover, not only words but also actions and objects take on the function of signs in this negotiation.

The knight of the Arthurian romance identifies himself by revealing his name and/or by bearing his coat of arms and other personal signs; the widespread motifs of mistaken identity, of knights who refuse to give their name, or who ride deliberately or haphazardly bearing unknown arms and are not recognized, suggest not only a certain thematic interest among romance writers in the attestation of identity, but also an interest in the problematics of identity. The *Gawain*-Poet in particular seems aware that language and other signs may not only denote an extant identity, but may also modify it, bring it into being, or even destroy it.

That a "person" can be created or destroyed by symbolic action is, on reflection, an unsurprising notion. While no physical transformation takes place during the wedding ceremony when two people are pronounced "man and wife," we admit that a "wife" now exists who did not before. So too, as writers like J. L. Austin and John Searle[3] have recently reminded us, "hero," "priest," and "lawyer" are created by acts of language and are certainly no less real for being intangible. The "Gawain" about whom there is so much discussion in this romance is such a social entity: he comes into being as his interlocutors accept him at his nominal value. It is Gawain's right to assert, to lay claim to, an identity, and it is the right of others, as Lady Bertilak and the Green Knight demonstrate, to accept or reject his claim, just as one represents a "hero" only insofar as one's group accepts one as such. It may also be important, the poem suggests, to disclaim an identity.

The language most clearly connected to identity is nouns, especially personal names, the public use of which carries implications which go well beyond distinguishing among Tom, Dick, and Harry. Much of the dramatic tension in *Sir Gawain and the Green Knight* involves Gawain's reputation, the connotations of his name. Medieval writers divided words according to their modes of signifying, *modi significandi* (or *proprietates significationum*); hence the parts of speech differ not in their referents but in their manners of signifying the referent. As is well known, the *modi significandi* assumed greater and greater importance for language theory from the twelfth century on. For the name, or nouns in general, the *modus significandi* was dependent upon the qualities of the referent, thus Priscian's formula for the noun of *substantium cum qualitate*.[4] It was held that the noun signified the substance (*substantium*) by virtue of its quality (*cum qualitate*). Logicians added the parallel terms of *suppositum* and *significatum* and the notion that the noun signifies *quod est* and *quo est*, the former denoting 'that which is,' and the later its manner of being 'that which it is.' In order for a noun to signify an object, that object must therefore have those qualities denoted by that noun. The absence of the qualities leads directly to a failure of meaning. When, near the poem's end, the Green Knight says scornfully to Gawain that he is not Gawain, he is not referring to his physical self, but neither is he being metaphorical. The issue is whether Gawain the physical or biological entity retains (or ever possessed) those qualities whereby he might lay claim to the name "Gawain." Obviously, Gawain is not going to disappear physically if the Green Knight persists in denying him his name, but the character he hoped to be will. The claim to the name rests in turn upon his words and deeds, and the deeds themselves function in this regard as signs.

In addition to words, we readily accept the sign value of acts in creating identity: "Big boys don't cry," and "real men don't eat quiche" are two negative injunctions illustrating this proposition. Medieval people were aware, probably more so than we, of the sign value of objects as well. In part because late medieval culture was organized by estates, patterns of dress and virtually every other form of personal physical sign were very highly codified. Two examples of such codification are the English sumptuary legislation of Edward III, Richard II, and Edward IV, and the heraldic codes. But in fact the codification of the physical personal environment was more complete, and more subtle, than those few laws. Zygmunt Bauman's remarks on the "propensity of estate- and caste-type societies, either slave or feudal, to subject unequivocally all kinds of cultural elements—including attire, houses, furniture, arms, transport, and etiquette—to ascribed statuses"[5] applies perfectly to late medieval England.

Late medieval Europe as a whole was a culture in which signs like a tonsure, a crown, and a tabard unambiguously informed the world at large that their wearers had the status of cleric, monarch, and laborer, respectively. Even objects not specifically addressed by such codes as sumptuary laws and heraldic rolls might act as signs under the influence of Paul's statement in Romans 1:20 that "Invisibilia enim ipsius, a creatura mundi, per ea quae facta sunt, intellecta, conspiciuntur." Both sacred and secular impulses, then, worked together to make objects significant, especially and most interestingly in relation to their bearers. That is, heraldic and other sanctioned signs of social identity (e.g., sword, miter) allowed their bearers to make themselves known as members of this or that status, and in some cases (heraldic cognizances for example) as this or that particular member of the status. To bear a coat of arms is a complex act of signification, because it both announces and claims an identity. When Edward III claimed France in 1340, he "quartered the arms of France, had the fleur de lys engraved on his seal, and furnished himself with a red and blue surcoat sewn with [both the] leopards [of England] and [the] lilies [of France]."[6] To do so was not merely a colorful way of making a claim on the territory of France; what mattered was not so much what Edward claimed to own, but rather who he claimed to be, viz., both England and France. The claim was not, of course, allowed to go unchallenged. Similarly, the identity Arthur claims through his signs of regal splendor is challenged by the Green Knight.

Heraldic signs specified identity, not merely distinguishing one knight from another, as numbers might do equally well, but in the fuller sense of outlining the qualities—parentage, deeds, and possessions—of the identity in question, as did Edward's surcoat. Gerard Brault's thorough study of heraldic terminology in French Arthurian romance[7] has demonstrated that their authors were keenly conscious of the relationship between the name, coat armor, and identity (in the fullest sense of the term) of their heroes,[8] a consciousness singularly appropriate in a genre so concerned with the personal growth, testing, and change of its hero. A similar consciousness, as I hope to show, is exhibited by the *Gawain*-Poet. The challenge of the poem is not for Gawain to accomplish something but to become something, and to become aware of what, or who, he is. The same may be said of Camelot corporately, though the corporate is largely embodied in Arthur. A final prefatory remark is that such self awareness may, in part, be gained from a careful scrutiny of the signs of someone else. We model our actions after those of people we admire, people we would like to "be like," and we avoid the actions and objects closely associated with those we dislike. Put simply, a striking character makes us aware of ourselves, and the Green Knight is nothing if not striking.

The Green Knight's appearance (in both senses of the word) at Camelot presents the court with a challenge in beheading and in the correct use of signs, the latter being the more difficult.[9] The Green Knight would ask who Camelot is, check the fit between its reputation ("los") and its actions, between signifier and signified; and he would also have them discover who he is, interpret his complex cognizance. He is "half etayn," but also a man, "and þat þe myriest in his muckel þat myȝt ride" (140-42).[10] He is huge but well proportioned, bushy but also embroidered. He carries the "unmete ax" in one hand, but a holly bob in the other. He is ferocious of demeanor and yet bears no arms save the axe. It is worth noting that the challenge to the beheading game does not require this kind of ambiguity. The axe and a few pointed words from a knight of ordinary color suffice to initiate the contest and challenge where bravery is the only issue, as analogue versions show.[11]

The Green Knight is in sum a lexical knot, combining terms normally opposed to one another: the wild on the one hand and the civil on the other. In so doing, the Green Knight echoes the opening stanzas of the poem, which displayed multiple instances of similar opposed pairs: the splendor of Troy reduced to ashes; bliss and blunder characterizing equally the history of Britain; the image of Camelot, in its first free, green age, set against a background of winter; indeed that youth itself combining positive energy and a probably dangerous, unstructured "childgeredness." The court's response to the Green Knight is, of course, wonder; the poet emphasizes the court's silence, but we should note that during this silence the court is busy "reading" the knight: "Ther watz lokyng on lenþe þe lude to beholde, / For vch mon had meruayle quat hit mene myȝt" (232-33), and "Al studied þat þer stod, and stalked hym nerre / Wyth al þe wonder of þe worlde" (237-38). Arthur's challenge is not merely to be courageous but to read the Green Knight's complex signs, yet for all the study and wonder, in this last task he fails and is rebuked: "Sir cortays knyȝt, / If þou craue batayl bare, / Here faylez þou not to fyȝt" says Arthur, looking at the axe. But, "Nay, frayst I no fyȝt, in fayth I þe telle" (280), replies the knight, who has only a moment before said "ȝ may be siker by þis braunch þat I bere here / þat I passe as in pes, and no plyȝt seche" (265-66). Further, he has drawn the court's attention to his lack of armor, shield, spear, and armor, adding that "for I wolde no were, my wedez ar softer" (271). That the Green Knight carries no shield, whereon one might find the customary cognizance of a knight, makes it even more incumbent upon Arthur and the court to interpret the remainder of the objects he bears. The number of such scenes of recognition in the romance tradition, thematizing the establishment and adjustment of identity based on the display and interpretation of personal signs, is quite large. One thinks for instance of Chrétien's Perceval, who first comes to court on his hunter, with his javelins and rude skin clothes, an instance particularly instructive in that it shows us the possibility of variant interpretations of the stranger's signs. Other examples would include Lancelot in his cart, the maiden who wears a sword in Malory's story of Balan and Balin, and Tristan before King Mark. It is indeed not unusual for a knight issuing a challenge in Arthur's court to have something mysterious about his appearance. Successful interpretation of such mystery leads typically to a recognition of the knight's identity and an appreciation of his qualities, as in the cases of Yvain, the Knight of the Lion, and Perceval, in Chrétien. What is remarkable in *Sir Gawain*, however, is the dramatization given the (ultimately unsuccessful) attempt to read the knight. There has been a good deal of modern critical argument over the symbolic value of the Green Knight, interpretations ranging over a spectrum which includes vegetation deity, death, and Satan; I would argue that the essential point of the Green Knight's ambiguous appearance is the ambiguity itself.

In addition to baffling Arthur and Camelot with his complex self-identification, the Green Knight makes a great show of reading theirs: He has ridden his horse up to the high table, and now looks them over, and says "Wher is ... þe gouernour of þis gyng?" (224-25) blythely ignoring such chivalric signs as Arthur's crown and central placement at the chessboard-like high table between queen and bishop; in fact, he moves up and down the table, stopping, and "studying who might be of most renown" (229-31). Once the Knight has "recognized" Arthur and issued his challenge, he accuses the court of using false signs. Their reputation of bravery, and the splendor of Camelot, is contradicted by their failure to respond to his challenge:

"What, is þis Arþures hous? ...
þat al þe rous rennes of þurȝ ryalmes so mony?
Where is now your sourquydrye and your conquestes,

> Your gryndellayk and your greme, and your grete wordes?
> Now is þe reuel and þe renoun of the Rounde Table
> Ouerwalt wyth a worde of on wyȝes speche." (309-14)

"Ouerwalt wyth a worde" is both an accurate characterization of the power of language and the fragility of reputation and at the same time an effective taunt. Arthur responds only to the taunt, misreading the entire text of the knight's appearance and words, and waxing "as wroth as þe wind."

The Green Knight comes to Camelot as a tester, but not only of courage. If the moral question of the poem were simply whether Arthur and Gawain deserved their reputations, whether their actions would conform to their words, then correct action would consist in an angry Arthur himself chopping off the Green Knight's head and Gawain acting upon his apparent reputation and sleeping with Lady Bertilak. Both these actions would clearly be wrong. What in fact is required is restraint from action. Indeed, the Green Knight tests whether Arthur and Gawain can refrain from acting on their reputations, can sublimate action into symbol. Put another way, the Green Knight tests Camelot's ability to qualify, modify, or complicate its identity, and to signify such subtleties. To be brave does not mean to chop off any given head, and to be courteous does not mean to sleep with any given woman.

The social fabric in Troy, Rome, or Camelot depends for its integrity upon the human capacity for complex symbolic action, centered in language. John of Salisbury wrote, in Book I of his *Metalogicon,* that "deprived of their gift of speech, men would degenerate to the condition of brute animals, and cities would seem like corrals for livestock, rather than communities composed of human beings united by a common bond for the purpose of living in society, serving one another, and cooperating as friends."[12] Indeed, in *De vulgari eloquentia* Dante, following Aquinas, shows that language defines man, holding that neither animals, who are without reason and thus have nothing to share with one another, nor angels, who communicate with one another without mediation, use language.[13] Man, the rational animal, needs language to share his ideas: "Oportuit ergo genus humanum ad communicandas inter se conceptiones suas aliquod rationale signum et sensuale habere."[14]

The (half) brutish Green Knight forces an awareness of these considerations upon Camelot, forces Arthur's knights to recognize that what makes them men and not livestock is their ability to speak, to create and act upon a social identity through symbol rather than symptom. I would argue that the task of Camelot is not entirely to bring its actions into line with its reputation, but also the converse: to align its reputation with its deeds, to signify itself with precision. In the term the poet uses, "trawþe" means not only keeping one's word, doing what one says, but also saying what one does, and has done.

It is for Gawain, in a speech, to sublimate, modify, and complicate the identity of Camelot, to answer the question "Is this Arthur's house?" and all that implies with "Well, yes, but ...." Gawain's speech before the court (341-61) often strikes modern students, and some critics, as overly elegant, near paralyzed by etiquette, if not absolutely sissified. But in it Gawain accomplishes two important tasks. First, he "rereads" the text of the court for the Green Knight: rather than beardless boys, Arthur is surrounded by "mony ... bolde, / þat vnder heuen I hope non haȝerer of wylle" (351-52); Arthur's taking the challenge himself signifies that he is "talenttyf," rather than out of control; that no one responded to the challenge signifies, Gawain argues *a fortiori*, that the challenge is beneath everyone in the court but himself, the weakest. Second, and more importantly, in asking permission to leave the side of the Queen, in alluding to the rules governing the assignment of adventures ("I have frayned hit at yow fyrst"), begging leave to give counsel, and denigrating both the challenge and himself, Gawain reasserts the signs of the other side of Camelot's reputation: courtesy, rule-bound behavior, restraint. Those signs of elegance and decorum had dominated the opening stanzas of the poem, from the hierarchical placement of the knights, bishop, king, and queen right down to the tableware (107-29), but had been obscured or ignored by the Green Knight's emphasis upon signs of martial valor—or their absence. Gawain's essential task here is the reassertion of the place of symbolic behavior in the definition of Camelot. The idea then emerges that, like the Green Knight, Camelot is a complex entity, requiring a complex sign for full self-identification, an idea reiterated at the poem's end.

In Bertilak's court Gawain is faced, as was Arthur, with problems of signifying clearly who he is and in interpreting the signs used by others. As with Arthur at Camelot, Gawain's identity is first established, but as the complete stanza which the poet devotes to this issue immediately following Gawain's meal makes clear, the knight's reputation is centered in his linguistic and cultural, not his martial, facility: he identifies himself first as of Arthur's court (903-05) and then as "Wawan hymself" (906). At this information, the as-yet-unidentified lord of the manor laughs aloud, and "alle þe men in þat mote maden much ioye / To apere in his presense ... / þat alle prys and prowes and pured þewes / Apendes to hys persoun, and praysed is euer" (910-13) so that,

> Vch segge ful softly sayde to his fere:
> 'Now schal we semlych se sleȝtez of þewez
> And þe teccheles termes of talkyng noble,

> Wich spede is in speche vnspurd may we lerne,
> Syn we haf fonged þat fyne fader of nurture.
> ... ...
> I hope þat may hym here
> Schal lerne of luf-talkyng.' (915-27)

Whatever identities have been associated with the name of Gawain in other romances, our poet has gone to some trouble here to identify his hero with refined behavior and speech. This stanza is for our benefit; the poet does not show Gawain as aware of the public perception of him as the "father of nurture," but he is soon to face equally daunting expressions of his self in the bedroom scenes.

As Arthur had been confronted by the complex Green Knight, so is Gawain confronted by the Lady, who appears hand in hand with the old dame Morgan. The menace and caress of the Green Knight's signs (axe and holly, bushiness and embroidery) are echoed in the ʒep and ʒolʒe, red and wrinkled, bare breast and kerchiefed breast, snowy white and black, of the double lady. W.A. Davenport sees in the two women

> the moralist's emblems of transience and mutability ...
> Youth and Age, the fair and ugly faces of Fortune, as am-
> biguous as the holly branch and the axe, as reassuring and
> threatening.... The poet's most ingenious effect is to weld
> the two of them together, not only by the antithetical de-
> scription, but also by presenting the younger as an append-
> age of the older .... I think the poet may well have expected
> his audience to suspect an allusion to the tale of the Loathly
> Lady and to have a flashing idea that the two women are
> really one, present both in her young and old guises.[15]

And as Arthur had been able to focus only on the axe, sign of battle, so Gawain mistakenly splits off and attends to only half of this sign, simplifying it into the young lady, sign of sensuality. As Arthur had missed that part of the Green Knight that signified culture and game, so Gawain misses that part of the lady that signifies perhaps death, perhaps age. The point is in fact not what either half of the sign might mean alone, but that the two belong together, signifying as a unit the complexity both attractive and repellent of the late medieval notion "woman." While the brute that shows in one half of the Green Knight is a reminder of the consequences of unbridled martial ener-gies, the repellent "olde auncian wyf" of Bertilak's court is similarly a reminder, Like la Vielle in the *Roman de la Rose,* of the consequences of unbridled venereal energies. More importantly, these double figures (in a poem rife with doubleness) are like a Saussurian coin; the two sides are inseparable, mutually define one another, and signify Camelot's humanity. Together, male and female, the Green Knight and the double lady are sign of Gawain's and Camelot's aspirations, its sought-for identity of splendid military power and stylish courtesy. The multi-facetedness of the sign externalizes the implications of those aspirations, but as Gawain's and Arthur's inadequate readings suggest, neither is yet ready to inspect those implications, to consider what *qualitates* may be implied in the names they so casually use. And, like Arthur, Gawain must face the taunt that he enjoys false fame, that he does not show evidence of those qualities his name supposedly denotes. As the Green Knight had found Camelot deficient in signs of martial prowess, the lady finds Gawain weak in signs of the venereal. He cannot be Gawain, she insists on day one of the temptations, or he would have craved a kiss, by his courtesy. On the second day, too, she argues that if he were Gawain, he would not have forgotten the lesson of kissing from the day before.

If we wonder what connection there might be between the definition of Gawain as user of language and the temptation scenes, the lady herself provides it, for throughout her temptations she quite consistently associates speech and sex, complaining of being slighted equally of kisses and speeches. Though she had publicly received "derne wordez, / Wyth clene cortays carp closed fro fylþe" (1012-13) on Christmas day, in private she desires more "daynté wordez" (1253), and she moves rapidly back and forth on the first day of temptation between expressions of desire for linguistic ("karp") and physical ("cors") intercourse: she refuses Gawain leave to rise from his bed so that she may "karp wyth my knyȝt þat I kaȝt haue; / For I wene wel, iwysse, Sir Wowen ȝe are" (1225-26), a Gawain whom she defines as "hendelayk" (1228). She adds immediately that they are all alone in the castle (1230), the door locked (1233), and so she will spend her time well, while it lasts, not—as one expects from her allusions to their safe seclusion—in lovemaking, but "with tale," that is, in talk (1236); she then immediately adds, "ȝe are welcom to my cors" (1237). She is quite consistent in this linkage, complaining on day two of having sat by him twice and having heard "no wordez / Þat longed to luf" (1523-24), concluding with another linkage which is only superficially a non-sequitur, "Dos, techez me of your wytte, / Whil my lorde is fro hame" (1533-34).

As at Camelot, Gawain answers the question "are you not Gawain?" with "Yes, but ...."[16] As one example among many, he does kiss, he explains, but "on command," a qualification he states twice.[17] As the Green Knight had tempted Arthur to act upon his reputation, and as Gawain had responded with a speech which qualified, attenuated that martial reputation, so Gawain in the bedroom replies with speeches which qualify his "courteous" reputation. The lady, however, would like some further sign, some "tokenez of trweluf craftes" (1527), and she refers to lovemaking as "token and text" (1515) of chivalry.

Indeed, the least ambiguous sign Gawain could give in satisfaction of the lady's demands for some proof of his purported identity as lover would be lovemaking. But the least ambiguous sign is often not the best to use in establishing one's identity. Though lovemaking and head-chopping, for example, are unambiguous actantial signs of venereal and martial ability respectively, both are normally engaged in for purposes other than signifying, often as ends in themselves, and in any case have potential consequences apart from their value as signs (birth and death, respectively). In this respect such acts or objects differ from such signs as words, which (as Augustine noted[18]) are primarily signs, and only technically things. To use another example, the deer and the boar which Bertilak brings home on days one and two are signs of his hunting prowess, but they are also food. The fox of day three, on the other hand, has no value except as sign, and a very powerful one at that. Gawain recognizes, at least implicitly, that kisses and words are primarily signs, and only secondarily things (are thus sublimations), and confines himself to such non-consequential significations of his identity.   In so doing he both avoids unpleasant consequences and asserts and accepts a qualified, more complex sense of who he is. As Arthur had accepted Gawain as a sublimation of— a substitute for—himself at Camelot, so Gawain here uses the kisses as sublimation and thereby accepts an attenuated version of himself as "courtly" knight.

On the third day of temptation though, the lady shifts her ground just enough to throw Gawain off his guard. Appearing to abandon hopes of the lovemaking, she asks for another sign: "Now dere, at þis departyng do me þis ese, / Gif me sumquat of þy gifte, þi glove if it were, / Þat I may mynne on þe, mon, my mournyng to lassen" (1798-1800). The glove is obviously a conventional token, and Gawain refuses to give it. He says that no honor would accrue to her to have it, that it does not, in other words, signify the putative Gawain of whom she has been speaking for three days. Whether this self deprecation is entirely earnest, or whether Gawain would prefer to avoid giving what would be a fairly obvious sign of more attachment than he feels or cares to admit is open to interpretation. But it is clear that to give the glove would be to signify himself as that Gawain he has chosen not to be, at least here with her. However, the lady's true intent is not to receive but give; she offers a ring, parallel to the glove as a conventional token, which Gawain refuses as such. She then offers the girdle, which Gawain also refuses, not, as she suggests, because it is paltry, but because it is a sign of her as his, a love token like the glove, and inappropriate for Gawain to accept as Bertilak's guest. Then why does Gawain change his mind? Because, I believe, the lady convinces him that the girdle is different from the ring, is not a token, a sign, but an instrument, a tool, to ward off harm. Intrigued by the possibility of the girdle as secret weapon, an object which has instrumental value and no sign value (the apparent opposite of Bertilak's fox, with which it will be associated), Gawain accepts.

If this poem and Gawain's experience up to this point teach anything, it is that all instruments and all actions are both what they are and also signs; shields, axes, holly bobs and girdles are all signs, both because, as Augustine held in *De trinitate*, everything is a sign of the Lord who created it and only God is pure entity (*res*) and not sign, and because, as noted earlier, medieval physical culture was highly and self-consciously codified.[19] There is nothing human which is purely *res*, no human act or instrument which is not also *signum*. In accepting the girdle and wearing it around his waist to meet the Green Knight, Gawain modifies his self once more, but because he believes the girdle is an instrument and not a sign and therefore does not wear it as a sign, he lies to himself and about himself. Once the Green Knight has shown Gawain that the girdle is in fact a sign (and only a sign, its instrumental value entirely bogus[20]) Gawain accepts it as such. There has been some confusion about Gawain's wearing of the girdle on his way to the Green Chapel. The note for line 2035 of the Tolkien, Gordon, Davis edition points out that "it is noteworthy (but not always noticed) that Gawain wears the girdle over his surcoat, in full view, not concealed under his armor... ,"[21] which is true. But at that point in the narrative, (2033-35) he wears it wrapped around his waist. As he accepts the girdle as a sign, a sign of himself, he shifts it from his waist to over one shoulder, "*Abelef as a bauderyk* bounden bi his syde, / loken vnder his lyft arme, þe lace, with a knot, / *In tokenyng* he watz tane in tech of a faute" (2486-88, emphasis added). Thus deployed as token, the girdle crosses Gawain's "cote," which he wears on his chest, and on which, as the poet has twice told us (637, 2026), Gawain wears his "cote-armeur," or "conysaunce," the pentangle.[22] The girdle thus forms a heraldic qualification of the pentangle, a "difference," in heraldic parlance, specifically a bend, as Gawain himself, handling the lace, tells Arthur: "þis is the bende of þis blame..." (2506).

The poet's heraldic train of thought is quite apparent here, in diction as well as imagery: "Abelef" (2486) is a heraldic term meaning "slantwise." Spelled thus, it appears in ME only in *Gawain* (a second time in 2517 to describe how the green girdle is worn by the members of the court). Spelled "embelif" it appears in heraldic contexts and as an astronomical term (see *MED*, s.v. embelif). Brault notes its use in blazon in the French romances *Lancelot del Lac*, the Vulgate Merlin Sequel, and *Durmart le Galois*.[23] Of the critics to speculate on the poet's heraldic intentions, Albert Friedman and Richard H. Osberg wonder whether "the diagonal wearing of [the girdle] represents the heraldic differencing of illegitimacy, the bend or bar sinister of nineteenth century novels," but the suggestion is unlikely: in the first place, the bend sinister as a difference of illegitimacy was a later development than our poem, and in the second place Gawain's bend is dexter, from right shoulder to (under the) left arm (2487). To W.R.J. Barron, the girdle's heraldic quality suggests "that Gawain no longer considers himself entitled to bear the symbol of trawþe."[24]

To the many patterns of repetition in the poem so frequently noted by its readers we may add another: a knight enters Camelot bearing strange arms, which he formally explicates for the court. The first is the Green Knight, with axe and holly bush, and the second Gawain, whose new arms may be blazoned as "gules a pentangle or, bend dexter verte." I believe Gawain's re-enactment of the Green Knight's action is meant to suggest Gawain's growth. He now wears (part of) the cognizance of the Green Knight, who had earlier shown keen awareness of the significant quality of his dress: "for I wolde no were, my wedez ar softer" (271); at the Green Chapel he tells Gawain, in reference to the girdle, "hit is my wede þat þou werez, þat ilke wouen girdel" (2358). Having worn the Knight's weed as instrument, in a fruitless attempt at guaranteeing his self-preservation, Gawain does well to wear it as "conysaunce," recognizing that every(thing) is significant, that metonomy is destiny.

Of course the green girdle indicates Gawain's sense of shame, and it may certainly be taken as a sign of humility, a virtue curiously missing from the sign of the pentangle. Gawain himself refers to it as a "token of untrawþe" (2509). But my point is not what specific vices or virtues the girdle signifies in itself, but rather that the pentangle qualified, differenced, by the girdle is a complex sign, as opposed to the pentangle alone which, for all its multi-pointedness, is most emphatically simple, which is to say singular. It is an endless figure or knot, indivisible, a fact the poet notes before and after his itemization of the particular virtues enfolded in the sign. In debating the relative importance or exact meaning of any of these virtues,[25] we may miss an essential point: the monosemous, unambiguous character of the pentangle as sign. Gawain's new sign, in contrast, is polysemous, complex, an acknowledgement of his new sense of himself. By this new sign, or cognizance, sign of the self, let me specify that I do not mean the girdle alone, which has so often been seen as replacing Gawain's pentangle,[26] but the entire arms of pentangle differenced by the girdle. It is easy to overemphasize Gawain's discovery that he is imperfect, as if he seriously entertained the notion that he was not. Nowhere in the poem does Gawain say in words that he is perfect, and in both Camelot and Bertilak's court he is in fact rather shamelessly self-deprecating. But he discovers that his conysaunce, the pentangle, does make such a claim, or something close to it.[27] With this sign Gawain has made himself known (conysaunce coming from *connaitre*) as singular, the integer of integrity. As his fault in accepting the girdle to protect himself, and his failure to yield it to Bertilak according to the rules of their game, and his qualifying conversations with the Green Knight and the Lady have demonstrated, his identity is not singular but complex, requiring a complex conysaunce, which he now possesses.

The Green Knight helps Gawain to see that he is flawed, not simple. But he also shows him the necessity of signifying that fact openly, making himself known as not duplicitous but complex. It has been argued that Camelot fails to understand Gawain on his return, and that the court shows a lack of seriousness in adopting Gawain's token as a sign of success,[28] but it seems to me that this wholesale adoption of the girdle as sign is entirely appropriate. Arthur had attempted to simplify the sign of the Green Knight, and Gawain had simplified the sign of the double lady. Now the court resists the temptation to simplify, to ignore the girdle while insisting upon the pentangle, and accepts complex, polysemous signs as befitting itself, doing so with heraldic explicitness, adopting the girdle as a "bende abelef." In other words, the court accepts Gawain's experience as part of its own experience, his badge as qualifying theirs individually as well as corporately. We may quarrel with the court's insistence that the girdle may be accorded to the "renoun" of the Round Table, but we cannot deny the justice of their claim to it as part of their experience.

One notes that the apparent dispute between Gawain and the court over the meaning of the girdle involves a dispute over who Gawain is, for it is his sign. Speaking of Gawain's understanding of the girdle as a sign of his specific sins, Ralph Hanna[29] has noted that "there is no inevitable connection between a symbol and its referent (signs are generally arbitrary), and the only measure of validity is public acceptance, whereby the symbol enters usage and passes as current." Hence Gawain is denied (by the court) the identity of "world's worst sinner." As Burrow puts it, the girdle "has no natural title to any particular moral signification: Gawain institutes it as a sign of untruth for purely personal reasons. This is *impositio ad placitum.* Hence it is open for the court to decide that it should be instituted a second time—as a sign of the 'renoun of þe Rounde Table'. Their significance runs counter to Gawain's; but this is always possible with an arbitrary sign: *'potest significare oppositum suae significationis'.*"[30] In a real sense the dramatized dispute over the meaning of the girdle reminds us that identity (unlike the locked pentangle) is not immutable, is always subject to negotiation.

In retrospect one can see that, at least from the perspective I have adopted here, the kinds of language most prominent in *Sir Gawain* are promises and namings. When Gawain makes his promises to exchange axe-blows and gifts, he is, in the terminology of speech-act theory, performing commissive illocutionary acts, whose fit is by definition from world-to-word. When he names himself and when he returns to Camelot wearing the green girdle, he is performing assertive illocutionary acts, whose fit is from word-to-world. An assertive may be assessed both in terms of truth and falsity and also in terms of felicity, since all assertives may be considered eliptical (e.g., "The book is a novel" implies "I state/believe that the book is a novel.") All assertions about the world and the self are subject, as it were, to rejection. As an instance of the assertive, the self-description ("I am a knight," "My name is Gawain") bears a striking similarity to the commissive, promising; assessing the promise involves understanding or hypothesizing about the character of the speaker, just as does assessing self-descriptions. There is little or no difference between "I will always love you" (a promise), and "I am in love with you" (an assertive). To interpret either statement, the auditor or recipient must evaluate the speaker. In Searle's terminology, the sincerity condition in the assertive is belief while in the commissive it is intent. But one's statements about oneself, I would argue, are always a mix of belief and intent. The self-speaker always hovers between belief and intention, promising to do what he believes he can do, asserting by promising that he is the person who will keep this promise. "This statement is false" is a paradox, but "I am untruthful" is not, because while the statement's falsity is fixed, the truthfulness or untruthfulness of a person is not. We can easily believe that someone has enough self-awareness to say "truthfully" that he is "untruthful," for a person is not reducible to one statement; he cannot—for example—know that he will be false tomorrow. As for fit, since the referent in "I am in love with you" is "I," and "I" can change, especially under the influence of the intentions of "I," the distinction between world-to-words and words-to-world has little force. In the final analysis the two kinds of language collapse into one. Naming oneself and keeping (or breaking) promises constitute one complex and inescapable action.

D. W. Robertson has taught us that medieval culture produced iconographic hierarchies, rather than antitheses.[31] Robertson's object was to argue against Romantic dialectical readings of medieval iconography, readings implying antitheses moving toward synthesis. Though there can be no quarrelling with the thrust of Robertson's argument, it would be a mistake to extrapolate from it a picture of a Middle Ages whose symbolism was therefore without tension; though iconography of the divinely ordered cosmos might, whatever its superficially tangled surface (like that of the pentangle), resolve itself finally into order, medieval iconography of humanity is not guaranteed to come inevitably to resolution and rest: like the late-medieval twin sarcophagi featuring lifelike effigy on one level and rotting corpse on the other,[32] medieval signs of humanity are often multifoliate, incapable of reduction to singularity without a quite unmedieval oversimplification. Unlike the commonplace debates between body and soul, the healthy body/rotting corpse dichotomy cannot be resolved hierarchically; the rotting corpse is man's physical end, but it is not superior (as is the soul to the body) to the healthy body. What was probably essential in such icons, didactically speaking, was that humanity recognize the impossibility of construing itself singly, with reference only to the here, the now, and the visible. The poet, I would argue, suggests that Camelot accept such antithetical images as the Green Knight and the Lady as more accurate and instructive, because complex, signs of its identity than its tapestries and candlesticks, or the undifferenced pentangle.

Notes

1.   A version of this paper was read first at the 18th International Congress on Medieval Studies in Kalamazoo in 1983, while a fuller version was read to the Medieval Studies Group of the Department of English of the University of Virginia in 1984.

2.   W. A. Davenport, *The Art of the* Gawain *Poet* (London: Athlone Press, 1978), p. 163.

3.   J. L. Austin, *How To Do Things With Words* (Cambridge, MA: Harvard University Press, 1962); John R. Searle, *Expression and Meaning: Studies in the Theory of Speech Acts* (Cambridge: Cambridge University Press, 1979).

4.   For the parallel workings of imposition in medieval heraldic practice, see Ross G. Arthur, *Medieval Sign Theory and* Sir Gawain and the Green Knight (Toronto: University of Toronto Press, 1987), pp. 54-57.

5.   "Semiotics and the Function of Culture," in *Essays in Semiotics*, ed. Julia Kristeva (The Hague: Mouton, 1971), p. 285. See further Maria Corti, "Structures idéologiques et structures sémiotiques dans les *sermones ad status* du xiiie siècle" in *Archéologie du Signe*, ed. Lucie Brind'amour and Eugene Vance (Toronto: Pontifical Institute of Mediaeval Studies, 1983), pp. 145-63.

6.   May McKisack, *The Fourteenth Century* (Oxford: Clarendon Press, 1959), p. 128.

7.   *Early Blazon: Heraldic Terminology in the 12th and 13th Centuries With Special Reference to Arthurian Literature* (Oxford: Clarendon Press, 1972).

8.   *Blazon*, especially pp. 37-52.

9.   Robert Hanning, "Sir Gawain and the Red Herring: The Perils of Interpretation," in *Acts of Interpretation: The Text in its Contexts, 700-1600, Essays on Medieval and Renaissance Literature in Honor of E. Talbot Donaldson*, ed. Mary J. Carruthers and Elizabeth D. Kirk (Norman, OK: Pilgrim Books, 1982), p. 14: "The Green Knight's sudden appearance forces the court, like the narrator and his audience, into an interpretive posture, and its response to the intruder becomes in turn the subject of further evaluation by the narrator."

10.   All citations of the poem are from *Sir Gawain and the Green Knight,* ed. J. R. R. Tolkien and E. V. Gordon, 2nd ed. rev. by Norman Davis (Oxford: Clarendon Press, 1967). Line numbers will be given, as here, parenthetically in the text.

11.   For the sources, cf. Larry D. Benson, *Art and Tradition In* Sir Gawain and The Green Knight (New Brunswick, N.J.: Rutgers University Press, 1965).

12.   Edited and translated by Daniel D. McGarry, *The Metalogicon of John of Salisbury* (Berkeley and Los Angeles: University of California Press, 1955), p. 11 (*PL* 199:827).

13.   *De vulgari eloquentia* bk. 1, ch. 3. (*Dante Alighieri opere minori* ed. Alberto Del Monte [Milan: Rizzoli], pp. 529-30).

14.   Ibid, p. 530.

15.   Davenport, *Art*, p. 160.

16.   Thus Davenport, *Art*, p. 190, "In the face of these challenges that he is failing to deserve a famous name, Gawain is required to define his own nature, to reply in effect: 'I am Gawain, but Gawain is other than you think'."

17.   Lines 1303, "I schal kysse at your comaundement, as a knyȝt fallez"; and 1501, "I am at your comaundement, to kysse quen yow lykez."

18.   *De doctrina Christiana*, I, 2, ii (*PL* 34:20), "Sunt autem alia signa quorum omnis usus in significando est, sicuti sunt verba; nemo enim utitur verbis nisi aliquid significandi gratia."

19.   *De trinitate* VI, 10, xii (*PL* 42:932). See also John Scot Eriugena, *Super ierachiam caelestem*, I.3 (*PL* 122:138-39). In his *De divisione naturae* (V.3), John wrote that "nihil enim visibilium rerum corporaliumque est, ut arbitror, quod non incorporale quid et intelligibile significet" (*PL* 122:865-66). Cf. Etienne Gilson, *History of Christian Philosophy in the Middle Ages* (London, Shead and Ward, 1955), p. 120. In the "N-Town Passion Play" Satan illustrates this point by referring to the red hose and piked shoes which allow a knave to "make comparycion" to a gentleman, and the "gret purvyauns" which permits "a beggerys dowtere" to "cownterfete a jentylwoman" and labelling a splayed collar trimmed with fur a "seyn to selle lechory" (ed. K. S. Block, *Ludus Coventriae or the Play Called Corpus Christi* [EETS e.s., 120; rpt. 1960], pp. 227-28, ll. 69-71, 101-02, 105-06). For further illustration of the medieval idea that "costume and gesture could actually create identity," see Diane Owen Hughes, "Earrings for Circumcision: Distinction and Purification in the Italian Renaissance City," in *Persons in Groups: Social Behavior as Identity Formation in Medieval and Renaissance Europe*, ed. Richard C. Trexler (Binghamton: Center for Medieval and Renaissance Studies, 1985), pp. 155-82.

20.   In *The Fortunate Fall of Sir Gawain: The Typology of* Sir Gawain and the Green Knight (Washington: University Press of America, 1982), Victor Haines argues that the girdle is potent but only to protect Gawain from being "tohewen," cut in pieces (pp. 141, 158-59).

21.   For example, Benson, *Art and Tradition* (pp. 219, 224) and Paul F. Reichardt, "Gawain and the Image of the Wound," *PMLA*, 99 (1984), 157, both write that Gawain conceals the girdle under his armor

22.   As J. A. Burrow, *A Reading of* Sir Gawain and the Green Knight (London: Routledge & Kegan Paul, 1965), p. 115, points out, the poet's efforts to bring the girdle into juxtaposition with the pentangle are quite noticeable.

23.   *Early Blazon*, p. 125.

24.   *Trawthe and Treason: The Sin of Sir Gawain Reconsidered* (Manchester: Manchester University Press, 1980), p.135. In a note (p. 145, n. 10) Barron adds that he is "not suggesting a formal heraldic distinction, since the normal use of a bend as

a difference was to distinguish the arms of members of the same family." Exactly what a "formal heraldic distinction" would be in this context is not clear to me; a device used to difference related parties could equally be used to alter a single individual's arms. The essential difference between Barron's reading and mine is that he appears to believe that the girdle negates the pentangle, the "symbol of trawþe" (though Gawain does still bear it), while I would emphasize that the two elements of pentangle and bend verte are combined into a new device.

25.   A particularly ambitious attempt to decode the pentangle point for point is Gerald Morgan's "Significance of the Pentangle Symbolism in *Sir Gawain and the Green Knight," Modern Language Review* 74 (1979), 769-90. One detects, however, a growing skepticism about the possibility or even appropriateness of such attempts, notably Kathleen Ashley, "'Trawthe' and Temporality: The Violation of Contracts and Conventions in *Sir Gawain and the Green Knight*, in *Assays Critical Approaches to Medieval and Renaissance Texts* 4 (1987): 3-24.

26.   For example, Burrow, *A Reading*, pp. 116 and 189; Lynn Staley Johnson, *The Voice of the* Gawain-*Poet* (Madison: University of Wisconsin Press, 1984), p. 89: "Rather than a shield which betokens the ideals of chivalry, he now wears a girdle which betokens the weaknesses of the flesh"; and P. B. Taylor, "Gawain's Garland of Girdle and Name," *English Studies* 55 (1974), 13: "… substitution of girdle for pentangle as emblem of worth is a reinforcement of his new-found name."

27.   Arthur, *Medieval Sign Theory*, argues that Gawain's pentangle is, in its geometric iconicity of endlessness, a typical sign of God, but that Gawain's use of the sign does not imply a claim to perfection but rather an aspiration.

28.   For example by P. B. Taylor, ("Gawain's Garland," pp. 13-14): "Uneasy before [Gawain's] puritanical sermon, they insist on taking too lightly the fault he takes too seriously," and more recently by Johnson (*Voice of the Gawain Poet*, p. 91): "captured by the court's laughter, is the sound of Camelot's fall."

29.   Ralph Hanna III, "Unlocking What's Locked: Gawain's Green Girdle," *Viator*, 14 (1983): 294.

30.   Burrow, *Reading*, p. 189.

31.   Most influentially in *A Preface to Chaucer* (Princeton: Princeton University Press, 1962, ch. 1).

32.   Like those of Alice de la Pole, Duchess of Suffolk, and Bishop Richard Fleming of Lincoln. For these and other examples, see T. S. R. Boase, *Death in the Middle Ages: Mortality, Judgment and Remembrance* (New York: McGraw-Hill, 1972), pp. 82-87.

BONDING AND SIGNIFICATION
IN *SIR GAWAIN AND THE GREEN KNIGHT*

The *Gawain*-Poet's brilliant use of imagery has nourished decades of critical prose. A recurrent motif in this criticism has been the difficulty of pinning down images whose chief trait is their tendency to subtle or to startling transformation—almost (one might say) to shiftiness. *Pearl* has been the locus for much analysis of imagery in the past, but recently Robert Hanning has examined the decorative images in *Sir Gawain and the Green Knight*, suggesting that:

> Society's decorative impulse wholly or partly conceals primary levels of experience or meaning beneath an artfully applied surface, be it of paint, rhetoric, game or ritual.[1]

Hanning's model makes an easy distinction between the "primary levels of experience" and the "artfully applied surface" above them; the difficulty for him lies in how to interpret the "decorative impulse." The ambiguities of the "civilized process of embellishment" both invite and thwart interpretation, Hanning argues, concluding that "the difficulty, or perhaps impossibility, of interpretation becomes not only a hallmark but a main theme of the poem."[2]

While I agree that interpretation itself becomes a theme of the poem, I disagree that we are meant to conclude that such interpretation is impossible. Instead, I would argue that the poem leads its reader to acknowledge ambiguity, and ultimately to understand the need for active *re* interpretation.

My essay takes as its subject the images of fastening, joining and enclosure which are ubiquitous in *Sir Gawain and the Green Knight* and examines these concrete physical connections as metaphors for relationships of all kinds. In a poem which scrutinizes the epistemological status of all connections and claims to meaning, the problematics of the signifier/signified bond can be epitomized by an analysis of the recurrent term "halche"[3]—defined by the *M.E.D.* as "to embrace, enclose, fasten together, or join." I will attempt to show that the poem systematically blurs our initial impression that nature and culture are separate realms. Robert Hanning's concept of "primary levels of experience or meaning" concealed beneath an "artfully applied surface" is not radical enough, for I would argue that the *Gawain*-Poet adopts a strategy which *transforms* "natural" to "conventional" bonding and signification.

At the beginning of the poem, Nature and Culture seem clearly distinguishable as the Green Knight—representing the mysterious forces of nature—bursts in on the cultured and artificed setting of Arthur's court. However, as Larry Benson has shown,[4] the description of the knight begins immediately to blur the distinction, for the intruder is alternatively described as an "aghlich mayster" (a monster or grotesque) and as a courtly figure, trim and well-dressed. The first two *descriptios* focus on the size and shape of the knight, first his hugeness which is fearsome and gigantic, and then his merry and well-shaped body (136-46). The second pair of *descriptios* focus on his color and costume, the image of a person "oueral enker grene" contrasting oddly with the courtly perfection of his clothing and equipment (151-72).

We are told that he wears a mantle with a fur lining and fur trim and a hood laid back on his shoulders (153-56), but the next descriptive passage reverts to the wildman image with the information that the Green Knight's busy beard and flowing hair half hid his arms since the latter came down to his elbows:

> Fayre fannand fax umbefoldes his schulderes;
> A much berd as a busk ouer his brest henges,
> Þat wyth his hiȝlich here þat of his hed reches
> Watz euesed al vmbetorne abof his elbowes,
> Þat half his armes þervnder were halched in þe wyse
> Of a kyngez capados þat closes his swyre. (181-86)

This image from rampant nature (a man's arms half-hidden under his bush-like hair) is cast into relief by the cloth mantle and fur we know he wears too, and by the comparison of his hair with a human artifact, the king's cape, in the simile: "half his armes þervnder were *halched* in þe wyse / Of a kyngez capados þat closes his swyre" (185-86). The word "halched" (enclosed) acts as a metaphorical hinge in this passage, connecting nature (the monstrously bushy beard) and culture (the king's cape). In fact, the comparison to the king's cloak, a civilized object, renders metaphorically ambiguous that image of the beard which had been clearly and literally described at first as a natural state.

The same deliberate confusion of the wild and the civilized is made in the description of the Green Knight's ax. The creature bears—ambiguously—a holly bob in one hand and in the other an ax, so onlookers are not sure when he enters whether his intention is seasonal jollity or menace. The ax is described first as "hoge and vnmete" (208) and seven lines follow which stress its huge length, the breadth and razor-sharpness of the blade, the strength of the handle wound with steel—all details conveying an impression of cruel functionality. However, the next five lines point out the decorative details of the ax handle, which is engraved in "gracios werkes" (216). It also has a lace wrapped around the handle, fastened at the head, and looped along the shaft with tassles and bright green buttons. The lace is "halched" to the ax shaft in a gay and ornate manner which totally undercuts the impression conveyed in the first description of its deadly potential as a weapon.

The art which has wound ("halched") the lace around the handle and attached ("tacched") the tassles and buttons seems the civilized opposite of the supernatural greenness and monstrous size of the man and his ax. The whole description of the Green Knight thus plays along the boundaries of nature (that over which man has no control) and culture (that over which he does). The result is that both terms in the equation are rendered ambiguous; or, to change our metaphor, the boundary is blurred, so that we have difficulty distinguishing that which is natural from that which is cultural.

One might argue that the romance is a machine for transforming that outside the human realm into something man can manipulate. When the knight rides forth into the unknown searching for adventure, the unforeseen challenge to test his mettle and his ingenuity, he hopes to overpower the challenger and gain mastery over that which seems opposed to civilized values. *Sir Gawain*, as the most sophisticated commentary on the romance genre surviving from the medieval period, takes the genre's key element and complicates it further. As the "meta-romance," *Gawain* reveals that what we took to be *natural* is—or can become—*conventional* and that even the civilized, the conventional, is open to redefinition. After all, before Gawain rides forth to his adventure, the Arthurian court had been invaded by the supernatural and its civilized values brought into question by their conjunction with "inhuman" forces.

These strategies of transformation are most clearly set forth in the central sign of this romance, the pentangle Gawain carried on his shield. The pentangle reads at first like a "natural" sign.[5] In the description of the pentangle, the connections and attachments are portrayed as endless and immutable:

> For hit is a figure þat haldez fyue poyntez
> And vche lyne vmbelappez and loukez in oþer
> And ayquere hit is endelez; and Englych hit callen
> Oueral, as I here, þe endeles knot. (627-30)

The endless knot symbolizes its bearer, as the poem emphasizes in a very long and ostentatiously allegorical passage during the arming scene (619-65). The narrator makes a point of lingering over the appropriateness of the pentangle to good Gawain, who is "Voyded of vche vylany, wyth vertuez ennourned in mote" (635). He is faultless in his five senses and his five fingers. Equally flawless is his faith in the five wounds of Christ, the five joys of Mary, and in the virtues of the fifth pentad: "clannes" and "cortaysye," "fraunchyse" and "felaȝschyp" and "pité." These last five were "harder happed" on this knight than on any other:

> Now alle þese fyue syþez, for soþe, were fetled on þis knyȝt
> And uchone halched in oþer, þat non ende hade,
> And fyched vpon fyve poyntez þat fayld never
> Ne samned neuer in no syde ne sundred nouþer,
> Withouten ende at any noke I oquere fynde,
> Whereever þe gomen bygan or glod to an ende. (656-61)

These virtues are fastened ("fetled") to the knight and each one linked ("halched") in the other so that their endlessness and continuity provoke the narrator to a series of negatives for emphasis: *non* ende hade, þat fayld *never*, *ne* samned *neuer* in *no* syde, *ne* sundred *nouþer*. The language of the passage is emphatic, the imagery unambiguous; the perfection of the endless knot unfailingly symbolizes the perfections of the virtuous Gawain. Just as the pentangle's lines and points are eternally locked, so Gawain's virtues are fastened to him, the poem asserts.

But, as we all know, Gawain does fail. He does reveal his survival instincts and compromise his oaths to Bercilak. When he does so, the pentangle's endless knot is no longer the appropriate symbol for the flawed knight. Its status as a natural sign, so insisted upon in the arming passage, is undermined and so too is our sense of the naturalness, security, and permanence of connections and meanings of all kinds. Significantly, Gawain has failed in loyalty just a little, in loving his life as the Green Knight points out (2366-68), though his other virtues remain intact; but even this little failure severs the naturalness and inevitability of connections ("uchone *halched* in other"). Bonds are not invulnerable.

Given the interrelationships of the *Gawain*-Poet's imagery, it should come as no surprise that a lace uncannily resembling that "halched" around the Green Knight's ax should be accepted surreptitiously by Sir Gawain from Bercilak's lady, to be worn "hemely *halched* aboute" when he goes to receive the return blow (1852). It becomes the symbol of his broken word to Sir Bercilak. Ironically, when Gawain had first arrived at Bercilak's court, the two men had expressed their social bond through a mutual embrace—"and ayþer *halched* oþer" (939)—but this social bond is threatened when Gawain breaks his exchange of winnings contract by not giving his host the lace he had won from the lady on the third day.

Perhaps even more ironic is the fact that Gawain accepts the lace as a magical talisman, full of intrinsic power ("þe costes þat knit ar þerinne," 1849) to protect him from death; yet the outcome of the adventure at the Green Chapel nullifies that putative power by revealing that the whole plot had been crafted by Bercilak, his lady, and Morgan le Fay—that what looked like the natural and the inevitable was actually the deliberately chosen, the crafted, the plotted. The escape from death is due not to the powers of the lace/girdle but to the amused mercy of Bercilak who has been playing with Gawain. Free choice, not natural destiny, and bonds which are made, not found, are at issue in this poem as we finally discover, disconcertingly.

The transformation of natural to conventional signification is enacted during the hunt for the wild boar which, despite daunting resistance, is dispatched and dismembered. The boar is cut up ("unlaced") along the backbone and gutted by a huntsman who is "wys vpon wodcraftez" (1605-13). But the two halves are then conjoined: "And 3et hem *halchez* al hole þe haluez togeder" (1613). The connection, the bond ("halching"), belongs entirely and unambiguously to the realm of human craft and culture. Indeed, the reconstruction of the boar after dismembering may stand as a central image for the poem's theory of signs. Although meaning may appear at first as intrinsic and natural, though the signified/signifier bond may appear inevitable, the poem systematically deconstructs all such bonds and connections. It then reconstructs them, emphasizing the role played by human choice and human art. The huntsman who is "wys upon wodcraftez" is a model the poem elevates. Man, the maker of civilization through his art and his artifacts, is a maker of meanings.

It is as free makers of meaning that I think we can understand the conclusion of the poem, which invites its readers to become resignifiers. As I have argued elsewhere, the Arthurian court's adoption of the lace as baldric constitutes a transformation of this symbol of failure and testifies to the redemptive possibilities of ambiguity.[6] Unlike most critics of the poem, I do read the ending as both comic and affirmative.

When Gawain realizes that the magical talisman that was to save him had in fact condemned him, he unloosens the knot of the lace and flings it away in loathing. However, the Green Knight offers it back to him as a token of his encounter at the Green Chapel, or his successful adventure. The Knight thus redefines what Gawain had rejected. Gawain in turn accepts the lace and promises to wear it as a token not of success but of sin. The series of reinterpretations of the lace's significance is brought to a conclusion by the Arthurian courtiers. Gawain's sign of sin, of "untrawþ," that he wears with such shame when he returns home, his fellows decide will be a badge of their brotherhood to be worn with honor. As joyful, not frivolous, interpreters, the Arthurian court expresses its sympathy for and solidarity with Gawain, who has been chastened by his encounter with the forces of the unknown and the uncontrollable.

The Green Knight and the court's reinterpretations of the lace assert man's power over the process of signification. The reader, too, has been instructed in the processes of resignification through the shifts and transformations in the poem's images of fastening and embracing. What the reader learns from the poem's play with an ambiguous sign system is not, as Hanning would have it, the perils and impossibility of interpretation but the pleasure and ultimate profitability of making connections—even in an uncertain world.

Notes

1.   "Sir Gawain and the Red Herring: The Perils of Interpretation" in *Acts of Interpretation: The Text in its Context, 700-1600*, ed. Mary J. Carruthers and Elizabeth D. Kirk (Norman, Oklahoma: Pilgrim Books, 1982), pp. 5-23.

2.   Hanning, "Herring," p. 5.

3.   I will use the edition by Theodore Silverstein, Sir Gawain and the Green Knight: *A New Critical Edition* (Chicago: University of Chicago Press, 1984).

4.   *Art and Tradition in* Sir Gawain and the Green Knight (New Brunswick, N.J.: Rutgers University Press, 1965), pp. 58-62.

5.   This is the argument J.A. Burrow makes, drawing on medieval speculative grammarians and their theory of signs. See *A Reading of* Sir Gawain and the Green Knight (New York: Barnes and Noble, 1966), "Appendix One," pp. 187-89.

GAWAIN'S SHIELD AS *SIGNUM* [1]

ROSS G. ARTHUR

he maker of *Sir Gawain and the Green Knight* [2] is a genial host: as even a cursory glance at the secondary literature on the poem reveals, he permits his guests to wander where they choose, without imposing directions on them. What is more, if we ask for clarification, he gives it, freely and abundantly. If we want to know about his pentangle, for example, he tells us what it is, what it means, and how it received that meaning. The difficulty is that he is too open-handed. He tells us not only that it is a "pentangel" (620, 623, 636, 664) but also that it is an "endeles knot" (630); as if that were not sufficient, he adds that it is a "gomen" (661). It betokens "trawþ" (626); that seems clear, but the dictionaries suggest rather more possible meanings than we would like for this short word. He tells us that Solomon "set" (625) it, but even this action becomes less than permanent because he also suggests that we be concerned about its use in a particular case ("quy þe pentangel apendez, 623). Further, although we would like to see it as a single sign with a single meaning, he insists on attaching referents to all its component parts, and we are confronted by the infamous five fives.

What the poet does not tell us is what he means by "meaning," or rather, what he means when he talks about the things we call "meaning." For that, we must look elsewhere. Generations of readers have turned to their own commonsense notions or to various formal theories, but very little has yet been done with the theory of signs current in the poet's own age. Dozens of tracts survive from the period which set forth the details of a powerful theory of meaning, one which dealt with problems of pure signification, meaning in propositional context, and even meaning in social context, but even though their ideas were all but universal in the fourteenth century, they have been only rarely mentioned in connection with the literature of the period and have never been fully applied. [3]

Medieval logicians recognized the arbitrary nature of signification by making a distinction between those signs which convey information to an audience naturally, such as the barking of dogs and the groans of the sick, and those which signify because of the consensus of a community, such as the words in human language. These latter signs, which signify *ad placitum*, are often said to have been imposed by a first institutor. If the word "dog" signified the barking animal naturally, then all people at all times would use the same word, but as it is, the consensus of various national groups has created "canis," "chien," "dog," "hund" and the like. This first institutor is rarely known by name when we are dealing with ordinary words, but more elaborate signs are often connected with stories of their imposition which preserve the name of their creator. This is especially the case when there is a reason behind his choice. Signs are arbitrary, but this does not mean that they are random. As Lambert of Auxerre says, the *voluntas* of the first institutor may act in accordance with right reason, so that there is a meaningful connection between a sign and its referent. The most widely known example is the Latin word for man, "homo," which was chosen for its resemblance to the word "humus," which means the earth from which the first man was created and to which our bodies will ultimately return. This is not a natural connection (or there would be no words "man," "anthropos" or "vir") but it is nonetheless a connection which teaches or reminds us of a natural truth.

Solomon is the first institutor of the pentangle as a sign. He did his work well, for, as we shall see, it teaches us much about its referent. The device itself has two names, each of which is connected with a different important property that it has. It is called a "pentangle" because of its five-fold nature; this would be understood by anyone who had paid attention in mathematics class or at Pentecost sermons. It is called an "endless knot" because it is a unified infinite figure, despite its composite nature. Even when considering it as a combination of elements, the reader is moved toward the idea of unified endlessness by the choice of the number. This a so-called circular number, for its square, cube and so on always end with the digit 5.[4] The pentangle itself is also endless in a geometrical sense, for new, smaller pentangles may be inscribed in the center pentagon of every pentangle, and the ratios of the line segments of the pentangle produce the ratio of the length and breadth of the self-replicating golden rectangle.

So far, so good. But there is a problem with the word "endless" since it could mean either spatial or temporal endlessness. A further problem is that the pentangle as an object is not really endless in either sense, for the shield on which it is painted could be destroyed and the figure itself is surely limited in area even if the line which contains it has no starting or stopping point. Why then the poet's insistence on endlessness?

The *significatio* of the pentangle is *trawþ*, not the word "trawþ," but *trawþ* itself. That is, when it is free from any propositional context, the pentangle causes the idea of trawþ to come into the mind of a beholder who knows the sign. In this connection, "trawþ" means "truth," for in the fourteenth century this word was replacing "sooth" in the senses of *OED truth*, "that which is true, real, or actual (in a general or abstract sense); reality; spec. in religious use, spiritual reality as the subject of revelation or object of faith." It is used as the English equivalent of

Latin *veritas* in such theologically charged passages as John 14:6, "I am weye truthe and liif," and John 8:32, "the truthe shal make ȝou fre,"[5] and contemporary vernacular works frequently refer to God as "souereyn trewþe"[6] or say that "God is trowthe, and all trowthe commeþ of hym."[7]

The pentangle, then, in the realm of pure signification, is a sign for absolute truth, *summa veritas*, which is both spatially infinite and temporally eternal, which is, in fact, God. In offering us such a sign, the *Gawain*-Poet is operating in the tradition which presents Hermes Trismegistus as the institutor of the infinite sphere with its center everywhere and its circumference nowhere as a sign for God,[8] or the shield which has the word "God" inscribed in its center and "Father," "Son" and "Holy Spirit" in its corners, linked to "God" by lines inscribed with the word "is" and to each other by the words "is not," as a sign for the Trinity. By placing such a device on Gawain's shield, the poet is not claiming that Gawain is God, any more that the cross on a crusader's shield means that he is the cross. Rather, it is a statement that Gawain believes in and relies on God as Infinite Truth.

Such an assertion seems immediately to contradict the experience of every modern reader of the poem. We all know that the pentangle means something about Gawain, and we can quickly point to lines 623 and 631ff. as proof. Yet there is no contradiction here, for the pentangle is capable of multiple meanings, as is the word "trawþ." In addition to being the equivalent for *veritas*, "trawþ" is also used where Latin texts use *fides*, and so also means "faith." Langland frequently uses the word in both senses, and the Middle English version of *St. Edmund's Mirror*[9] says that "trouthe es na noþer thyng bot trowyng of thyng þat may noghte be sene." This *fides*, however, is "shaped" exactly like *veritas*, for the soul in grace is once again in the image of God, with mind composed of properly interconnected reason, memory and will just as God is composed of the three Persons of the Trinity. With these words substituted for the words referring to God in three persons, the Shield of Truth becomes the Shield of the Soul.[10] The faith of the soul in grace is therefore appropriately symbolized by the pentangle, for, as Augustine reminds us,[11] our faith will become truth when we are given eternal life.

Absolute *trawþ* is both infinite and eternal, but human *trawþ* has a temporal beginning when the soul is created and is lost when the soul sins, only to be recreated again and again through the gift of grace in sacrament. The poet's pentangle, which is both composite and unified, which refers both to the eternal truth of God and to the mutable faith of humans (for even endless knots may be untied), is an appropriate image for a meditation on the most basic relationships between God and man. It is therefore an acceptable device not only for Gawain but for any Christian in a state of grace, that is, for anyone who has been perfected, however momentarily, by God.

Far from leading to confusion, then, the application of the theory of signification current in the poet's age to the excess of meaning in his description of the pentangle results in a fuller and more comprehensive understanding of his views. His knowledge of this theory allows him both to allow multiple meanings and multiple audience responses to come into being and to control such ideas within a theologically orthodox framework, and the potential for linguistic ambiguity is made to serve more unified ends. Our discovery of this method allows us to appreciate his curious use of the word "gomen" (661) as yet another name for the pentangle.

The medieval logicians were quite sensitive to the fact that the effect of a word in a proposition depends upon more than its *significatio*. In the first place, equivocal words (such as *trawþ*) may signify more than one thing. Yet even this does not exhaust the possibilities, for in certain propositional contexts words take on the added property of *suppositio*; they "stand for" referents quite different from their original signification, even though the rationale for their extension is quite clear. In "I am reading Cicero," the word "Cicero" stands for the man's books, but in "Cicero was a Roman consul," it stands for the man. When the pentangle shield is the Shield of the Trinity, it equates God and Truth, but when it is carried by Gawain, it means "Gawain is now faithful." The logical treatises, which have as their purpose the instruction of young men in the techniques of preventing ambiguity, are filled with examples of syllogisms which appear to be formally valid but are in fact fallacious because of their sloppy treatment of *equivocatio* and *suppositio* :

> quicquid currit, habet pedes
> Secana currit
> ergo Secana habet pedes.
>
> Whatever runs, has feet.
> The Seine runs.
> Therefore the Seine has feet.[12]
>
> canis est animal
> et celeste sidus est canis
> ergo celeste sidus est animal
>
> A dog is an animal.
> And a heavenly star is "the Dog."
> Therefore a constellation is an animal.[13]

In his use of the word "gomen" at line 661, the *Gawain*-Poet shows us his ability to use a word with multiple meanings in a context which allows many of its possible meanings to co-exist, without creating the sort of verbal strife which would force us to choose one from the set. If we hear it and think of *MED* 1a, "Joy, happiness; pleasure, delight, gaiety, mirth," then the fact that it is endless may move us to think of the eternal bliss which is promised to the elect, and which is called "endles gamen" in a contemporary sermon.[14] Such joy may quickly be contrasted with Gawain's own state of mind as he sets out on his journey, "þaʒ hym no gomen poʒt" (692). In another vein, if "gomen" makes us think of a game played according to rules and with fixed time limits, such as the game requested by the Green Knight ("gomen," 274, "game," 365, and "gomnes," 683) then the endlessness of spiritual bliss contrasts most poignantly with Gawain's own predicament as he sets forth, for he could foresee a most unhappy end to this game. The word *gomen* is also used to mean both the action of hunting (1894) and the object of the hunt (1635); both of these meanings appear in John Mirk's sermon on First Corinthians 9:24-6, which describes the duty of every Christian to strive for eternal life:

> To þis labour Seyunt Paule, yn hys pystyll of þis day, techeþe and saythe þus: "Sic currite, ut comprehendatys." "Rennyth soo þat ʒe may gripe þe gome." By þis gomen and rennynge ʒe schull undyrstond bysy labour. For he þat rennyþe for þe gamen, he enforsuþe hym yn all his myght to ren swyftly. So most yche good seruand enforse hym forto laboure yn þe degree þat God hath sette hym yn.[15]

Whichever of these interpretive paths we follow, then, the result is that we come face to face with Gawain's predicament, which is the predicament of all living humans. Our earthly lives have fixed beginnings and ends, but they should have as their goal the attainment of endless eternal joy. This is a state which may be known in advance, however fleetingly, only through grace, at those moments when our souls are in the image of God. At such times our faith is shaped like truth, but even this similarity may be shattered by a sinful act or thought.

The overabundance of meaning we find in the description of the pentangle and, for that matter, throughout the poem, is not, therefore, an indication that the poet is giving his audience carte blanche: his words allow (what words do not?) a multiplicity of interpretations, but they anticipate and even request a particular sort of structuring collaboration by the audience. The poet expected readers who would perceive the ambiguities not as evidence of confusion or indeterminacy but as a challenge to create for themselves a new example of the hierarchical pattern explicitly and much less interestingly expressed in so many other medieval texts; while there is nothing which requires us to *be* such readers, even the mere fact that a fourteenth-century poet could imagine such an audience is a fact worthy of future study.

Notes

1.   The material in this essay is discussed more fully and in fuller context in my *Medieval Sign Theory and* Sir Gawain and the Green Knight (Toronto: University of Toronto Press, 1987).

2.   Ed. J. R. R. Tolkien and E. V. Gordon: 2nd ed., rev. N. Davis (Oxford: Clarendon Press, 1967).

3.   The ideas discussed here are most readily found in Peter of Spain, *Tractatus,* called afterwards *Summule Logicales,* ed. L. M. de Rijk (Assen: Van Gorcum, 1972); Lambert of Auxerre, Logica (*Summa Lamberti*), ed. Franco Alessio (Firenze: La Nuova Italia, 1971); William of Sherwood, *Introduction to Logic*, trans. N. Kretzman (Minneapolis: University of Minnesota Press, 1966), and L. M. de Rijk, *Logica modernorum: A Contribution to the History of Early Terminist Logic* (Assen: Van Gorcum, 1962). Despite variations in detail, these works often present identically-phrased definitions and use identical examples, and their basic ideas were known to anyone with even the rudiments of a university education. Peter of Spain's tracts survive in hundreds of manuscripts, and Jean Gerson reports in *De examinatione doctrinarum* [*Oeuvres complètes* (Paris: Desclèe, 1973), p.475] that schoolboys memorized them while still too young to understand their contents.

4.   Boethius, *De arithmetica, PL* 63, col. 1137b: "Atque hoc usque in infinitum semper evenit."

5.   *The English Hexapala* (London: Samuel Bagster and Sons, 1841).

6.   *Dives and Pauper*, ed. P. H. Barnum, EETS 275, pp. 154, 232, 234.

7.   *Middle English Sermons from MS. Roy. 8B xxiii*, ed. W. O. Ross, EETS os 117, p. 45.

8.   Bartholomaeus Anglicus, *De Genuinis rerum coelestium, terrestrium, et inferarum proprietatibus*, ed. G. Pontanus (Frankfurt, 1601; rpt. Frankfurt: Minerva, 1964), p. 12.

9.   In *Religious Pieces in Prose and Verse,* ed. G. G. Perry, EETS os 26, p. 38.

10.   See Julian Franklyn, *Shield and Crest: An Account of the Art and Science of Heraldry,* (London: MacGibbon and Kee, 1967), p. 459; *Rolls of Arms: Henry III; The Matthew Paris Shields, c.1244-1259,* ed. T. D. Tremlett (London: University Press, 1967), p. 61; Ottfried Neubecker, *Heraldry: Sources, Symbols and Meaning* (New York: McGraw-Hill, 1976), p. 222; and Rodney Dennys, *The Heraldic Imagination* (London: Barrie and Jenkins, 1975), p. 48.

11.   Augustine, *De trinitate,* CCSL 50, IV, xviii (24).

13.   De Rijk, *Logica Modernorum*, p. 121.

14.   *English Metrical Homilies from Manuscripts of the Fourteenth Century*, ed. John Small (Edinburgh: William Patterson, 1862), p. 20.

15.   John Mirk, *Mirk's Festival*, ed. T. Erbe, EETS es 96, p. 65. This use of "gomen" to mean both the process and the goal is not unique. See also *Select English Works of John Wyclif*, Vol. 2, ed. Thomas Arnold (Oxford: Claredon Press, 1871), pp. 257-58.

SIR GAWAIN AND THE GREEN KNIGHT
AND THE FOURTEENTH-CENTURY INTERLUDE

VICTORIA L. WEISS

The opening scene in *Sir Gawain and the Green Knight* sets the stage, so to speak, for Sir Gawain's strange adventure. In so doing, it is not unlike the opening scene in many other medieval romances. King Arthur sits at court on a festive New Year's Day, declaring his intention not to eat until he is confronted with some adventure. As if on cue, a giant Green Knight appears with a huge ax in hand, challenging any of the knights present to play a "Crystemas gomen"[1]— that is, to give him a blow with an ax in exchange for the Green Knight's right to strike a similar blow a year later. When Gawain eventually steps forward to take up the challenge, he decapitates the Green Knight, who then retrieves his severed head, reminds Gawain of the terms of their agreement and leaves the court.

Though a vow like Arthur's often marks the beginning of Arthurian adventures, there is none that I know of which produces results and reactions as strange and mysterious as this one. Here the poet carefully registers the shock and dismay of court members, including King Arthur. Their realistic reactions to the strange tidings they've heard and the event they've witnessed are very much like our own— genuine puzzlement. We think back to Arthur's earlier invocation of one of his traditional customs—refusing to eat "er hym deuised were / Of sum auenturus þyng, an vncouþe tale, / Of sum mayn meruayle, þat he myȝt trawe, / Of alderes, of armes, of oþer auenturus, / Oþer sum segg hym bisoȝt of sum siker knyȝt / To joyne with hym in iustyng, in joparde to lay, / Lede, lif for lyf, leue vchon oþer, / As fortune wolde fulsun hom, þe fayrer to haue" (92-99). Surely the king did not expect to go hungry on this big feast day of the year. So what exactly was he expecting? When the king's declaration is followed so closely by the appearance of the Green Knight as if on cue, we might suspect that the King anticipated this performance. But after a bloody decapitation results from this "Crystemas gomen" (283) and Gawain suddenly finds himself under a deadly obligation, the King seems genuinely shocked. The poet tells us that the King himself "at herte had wonder" but "let no semblaunt be sene" (467-68). These lines seem to argue against Arthur's having had any previous knowledge of what was going to take place.

And yet in spite of what Arthur may have felt in his heart, he turns to his stunned court and suggest that what they have just seen was nothing more than the playing of an interlude:

'Wel bycommes such craft vpon Cristmasse,
Laykyng of enterludes, to laȝe and to syng.' (471-72)

After the King's explanation that what they have just witnessed is simply an interlude of the type appropriate to the season, we are told that everyone turned back to the feast in a spirit of completely restored merriment, "wyth alle maner of mete and mynstralcie boþe, / Wyth wele walt þay þat day, til worþed an ende in londe" (484-85).

This renewed merriment, following so closely on the heels of the decapitation and the Green Knight's ominous reminder as he departs, creates for us a kind of mood swing which is difficult to accept. A "Crystemas gomen" or interlude ought not to intrude in any lingering way on the real business of life. It ought to have a clear beginning and a clear end, so that there is no confusion about what is play and what is real.

But can we be sure that our views of the way games, plays, or interludes ought to behave were the medieval views? Unfortunately, for us the answer to this question remains hidden. No fourteenth-century interludes have come down to us, and the information available about the performance of secular plays by itinerant entertainers does not tell us much about the way English royalty might have expected to be entertained at feasts in the late fourteenth century.

In his edition of *Sir Gawain and the Green Knight*, Theodore Silverstein notes that the moment of the Green Knight's entrance into Arthur's court—between the first and second courses—is exactly the point at which the royal champion rode into the hall at English coronation feasts, challenging to battle anyone who denied the king's right to rule. Silverstein also notes that an interruption at the same spot in the banquet occurs in the *Perlesvaus* as a stranger enters bringing *nouvelles* or *mervailles* in Book One.[2] But interruptions occurred at other times that may have been predictable as well. In the "Poisoned Apple" episode of the Stanzaic *Morte Arthur*, Sir Mador interrupts what looks as though it is going to be Guenevere's last supper by appearing in the hall totally armed on horseback ready to fight after the third course of the meal.[3] And at this same spot in the banquet in Chaucer's *Squire's Tale*, a knight on a brass horse rides into Cambyuskan's court. This entrance occurs just after the third course when the King has turned from his meal to ask his minstrels to play.[4]

Even so, this third course business might be regarded as accidental or coincidental were it not for an interesting bit of etymology. The Low Latin term *intromissum* meaning "the third or middle course of a banquet" passed into French as *entremet*, developing the extended meaning of an extra dish or ornament designed to attract attention at a banquet, generally after the meat and before the dessert. Early on the term came to be associated with entertainment between courses.[5] This idea of an extra dish or ornament to fascinate and delight the guests at a banquet appealed to the English as well, developing into table devices known as "sotelties"—a boar's head, or a peacock still wearing all of its feathers, or four and twenty live blackbirds baked in a pie.[6] In France when these stuffed or confectionary figures finally became too large to set on the table, they were replaced by humans positioned on large, mechanized floats which were wheeled into the hall. These bigger devices were called "pageants" in England,[7] but the French continued to call even the big versions *entremets*.

The French word did come into English, first appearing around 1340 with the meaning of "entertainment between the courses of a meal."[8] The word and its English cognates have a fascinating history, but the point of this etymology lesson is that perhaps what look to us to be unexpected intrusions may have been scheduled instances of entertainments—that is, places where the banquet may have been customarily interrupted so that the host and guests might be surprised by the sudden entrance of a spectacle. These were not always restricted to the third course or even one course, as we see in a Dutch chronicle of an English event. In his *Spiegel Historiael*, completed in 1316, a Dutch priest, Lodewijk van Velthem, describes at some length events from the reign of the English King Edward I.[9] The ties between Lodewijk's native Brabant and Edward's England were particularly strong, cemented by marriage alliances. (Two of Edward's daughters married royalty of Brabant.)[10] The passage of most interest to us is Van Velthem's account of a Round Table which he claims took place in England at the time of Edward I's marriage to Eleanor of Castile.

Historians who have taken note of this chronicle roundly condemn it for its inaccuracies and point to Lodewijk's numerous compilations and translations of Arthurian romances to suggest that his interest in fantasy corrupted his sense of historical accuracy.[11] And yet Lodewijk claims to be presenting an historical account, and given Edward I's known fondness for Round Tables, no historians have been able to prove that his account is fiction.

In his description of this marriage feast, Van Velthem tells of a Round Table tournament in which knights assume the roles of King Arthur's knights. After a day of fighting during which the knight assuming the role of Sir Kay was knocked off his horse and provided much comic relief, the noblemen assembled for a banquet

'... oec daer mede,
Alse he feeste hilt, dat wi gelesen
Dicke hebben Gelijc oec desen
So dede Edeward nu, god weet (1274-78)

> ['... in courtly fashion,
> As King Arthur had done
> When he held a feast, as we have read
> Often. Exactly as he [Arthur] did,
> So now Edward did it, God knows.']

After the first course was served, the King had a page knock on a window with a rod to obtain silence. Then he announced:

> 'Bi mire cronen sweric dit word:
> Eer hier heden gerecht comt vord,
> So moetic niemare hebben vernomen!' (1294-96)
>
> ['By my crown, I swear the oath:
> Before the next course is served here,
> I will want to have heard tidings.']

Not long after this announcement, a blood-spattered squire rides in, and just as King Edward's vow recalls King Arthur's similar promise in *Sir Gawain and the Green Knight,* this bloody squire rides to the king's table and taunts him and his court just as the Green Knight does in *Sir Gawain* :

> 'Versaect coninc ende oec blode,
> Ende die hier sitten bi u, hoe node
> Souden si comen daer men soude striden!
> Ic sie wel, coninc, nu ten tiden
> Dat si sitten al versaect.' (1304-08)
>
> ['Cowardly king and all your relations,
> And those who sit here with you, how rarely
> They come where there is fighting!
> I certainly see, king, right now.
> That they all sit here cowardly.']

He goes on to ask God to destroy the King and his knights unless they take revenge on the Welsh for what they have done to him. The King himself responds to this challenge, promising to come to the squire's aid. After this, the knights present also promise to ride along with the king and aid him.

After the next course is served, the king again states that he would like to hear more tidings before he continues to eat. Once again his words are followed by the entrance of a squire, his hands and feet bound while riding on a mule. This challenger goes directly to the knight who has assumed the role of Lancelot and asks to be released from his bonds. Once freed, the squire gives "Lancelot" a letter from the King of Ireland, challenging him to a meeting with his troops on the coast of Wales. Van Velthem's "Lancelot," upon reading this message, sinks in fear and discouragement, but the knight acting the part of Gawain offers himself and the rest of the knights present to come to the aid of Lancelot. King Edward, too, offers his aid, telling "Lancelot":

> 'Ic sal elken hulpen wreken
> Sinen ween ende sinen scande.
> Gelijc dat Artur in allen lande
> Voer om die vander tavelronde,
> Al dier gelijc willic ter stonde
> Met elken ridder oec nu varen.' (1425-30)

> [' I shall help everyone to avenge
> His pain and shame.
> Just like Arthur in every country
> Rode out for the sake of those of the Round Table,
> Just so will I immediately
> Ride with every knight, too.']

It is interesting to note here, by the way, that though the other knights are referred to only by their assumed names as knights of the Round Table, Edward I throughout Van Velthem's account is referred to as Edward and simply makes connections between his behavior and Arthur's when he finds it appropriate to do so as he does here. As a consequence, we are never totally in the world of play acting.

After the next course, the King once again demands silence and then requests tidings. He has scarcely uttered his request when a third challenger, a loathly hag, enters. Van Velthem gives a lengthy account of her appearance—her foot-long nose, her donkey-like ears, her coarse braids like the mane of a horse, the goose-egg-sized goiter under her chin, her large protruding teeth. Making explicit reference to the story of Percival, Van Velthem relates that this hag specifically addresses first the knight who has assumed the role of Percival, requesting that he ride to Leicester to right injustices there. She then greets "Gawain" and urges him to do the same at "Cornuaelge" (perhaps Kenilworth?). Both knights promise to do what they have been asked. Van Velthem further tells us that while everyone was noisily speaking of the strange event which had just occurred, the hag slipped away and removed her "costume." For the hag was in actuality one of the King's own squires in make-up, and, like the other squires who had delivered challenges, had memorized a message taught to him by the King.

Then just at the point where at least one of the knights present was beginning to speculate that the Loathly Hag they had seen was an evil spirit, King Edward reveals to these unsuspecting knights that these interruptions have been staged by him as a part of the festival. But (and this is an important qualification), he intends to hold them to the pledges they made to these squire-actors. As Van Velthem puts it, Edward's knights, acting playfully as Arthur's knights, found

> Datsi moesten, sine weten hoe
> Hem hulpe doen van allen saken
> Die hem in sijn lant gebraken,
> Ende som oec jegen haers selfs mage. (1595-98)

> [That they had to, they did not know how,
> Help him in all kinds of things
> Which were wrong in his country,
> And some even against their own family.]

In other words, just as for Gawain, the consequences of their agree-ments to take up a challenge are serious and dangerous ones for these knights.

This account may indeed be bad history. No other chronicle of the period provides even a suggestion that such an event took place at this time.[12] In addition, Van Velthem's Edward I appears to be a king in the prime of life at this marriage feast whereas in 1254, when Edward I actually married Eleanor of Castile, he was a young man of sixteen, many years away from becoming king.[13] Also it is difficult to identify Van Velthem's town of "Cornuaelge," and neither Leicester nor Ireland was attacked in Edward's time.[14]

But while these errors might lead us to dismiss Van Velthem's account as enthusiastic fictionalizing by an avid Arthurian, historians have noted that Van Velthem does get some things right, and some of what he seems to get wrong can be accounted for. Thomas Chotzen, in a careful study of the Edwardian sections of Van Velthem's chron-icle, notes that for all the confused dating and unhistorical incidents, Van Velthem does appear to get right the big events of Edward's reign—his marriage to a Spanish princess, the baronial wars, the campaigns against the Welsh and the Scots.[15] Roger S. Loomis has noted that Van Velthem might have intended "Cornuaelge" to be Kenilworth and, hence, have intended the squire's challenge as a reference to Edward and his father's victory over the barons there in 1266. And while there was never an attack on Leicester, the Earl of Leicester, Simon de Montfort, was the leader of the rebellious barons and hence might account for this confusion. Loomis also notes the Van Velthem may have confused Ireland with Scotland, thereby making the other squire's challenge a feat Edward and his men attempted in their time.[16] At any rate, even those historians who are quick to point out his blunders are reluctant to dismiss his account altogether. While no one believes this Arthurian play occurred at Edward's marriage to Eleanor in 1254, the historians who take note of it believe it might have been a feature of one of the Round Tables known to have been held later in Edward's time.[17]

What historians seem to be saying is that even if Van Velthem's rendering of Edward's marriage feast is an inaccurate account of the event, he may not have had difficulty in passing it off as history since

Edward I and other noble tournament lovers of the period were known for their Round Tables and masquerades. Such events were popular enough in Edward's day to make historians reluctant to call this staged event a fictive episode.

While we may not judge for sure the veracity of Van Velthem's account, the chronicler makes a special attempt right at the outset to ward off any disbelief:

> Die gene diet dlatijn bescreef,
> Seide so vele van deser saken.
> Dat ongelorelije waer in spraken; ...
> Gine gelovets niet, sonder waen. (1115-17; 21)

> [The one who described it in Latin
> Said so much about this matter
> Which might be unbelievable in words; ...
> You won't believe it, I assure you.]

The vow of the king, the appearance of squires in costume, the challenges to the knights in attendance all correspond to similar features in the opening scene in *Sir Gawain and the Green Knight*. Like the real Arthurian knights in the romance, Edward's knights, even in their impersonated roles as knights of the Round Table, seem to take seriously the challenges put to them. While King Edward, unlike the Arthur of the romance, knows that his challengers are really actors, the drama or play to which the knights at the historical court have committed themselves leads to obligations which do not end when the play ends. Like Gawain after the Green Knight has left, these knights know that they cannot dismiss their promises as mere responses in a holiday game.

Both the romance and the chronicle, then, display a looseness of form, a mingling of the staged and the real. Interestingly, this same mingling seems to be a feature of the interlude when it emerges in full-blown form in the Tudor period. T. W. Craik, in his book on the Tudor interlude, notes a number of its features (in addition to its association with feasting) which may very well have been present in the interludes of an earlier day. Craik emphasizes that the dramatists worked hard to create "an atmosphere of informality" in these works, that the interlude was "constantly pretending to burst its artistic limits, skillfully affecting to be on the verge of extemporization." He also notes that there is "not a single Tudor interlude in which the audience is not brought into the action," that "continual contact with the audience is sought and maintained," and that "the spectators are encouraged to join in."[18]

The most remarkable instance of this "joining in" is to be found in our earliest complete text of a secular play, Henry Medwall's *Fulgens and Lucres*, written nearly one hundred years after *Sir Gawain*.

In this remarkable play, a debate (the device which was most often at the heart of Tudor interludes) receives minimal attention, and the subplot—a play within a play—becomes not only the major interest of the drama but actually interferes with the main plot and alters it. I wish to examine this play in some detail because it may reveal some interesting points worth considering for our understanding of *Sir Gawain*.

Like *Sir Gawain* where Arthur's vow primes the audience for some kind of entertainment, *Fulgens and Lucres* conveys the sense that it is now time for an entertainment. But unlike the Green Knight's grand entrance, this play begins without the audience even realizing that it is beginning. Two characters, referred to only as A and B, wander into the playing place in the hall. A appears to be a member of Cardinal Morton's entourage (the play was presented for the first time at the Cardinal's court), and he comes on asking Morton's guests why they stand so still and wondering why no recreation is taking place—some dancing girl or something. He even turns to one of the guests at the Cardinal's table to ask him, "Is it not so?"[19] Then B comes in, seeming to be but another attendant, and informs A that a play is about to take place. B appears to know the play and summarizes the plot for A and the audience. But as we soon see, the plot as B presents it is a bit different from the one we see enacted. In the course of this opening discussion, each character mistakes the other for a player in the play, and each denies it, taking the other's charge as an insult. What this remarkable opening scene does is blur the line between the audience and actor. These two nameless men who appear to be simply spectators are really the first, and soon to be principal, actors.

The main plot that B reveals to A and to the audience at the same time is a debate from classical times. In it, Lucres, daughter of the Roman Senator Fulgens, has narrowed her choice of a husband down to two men—a wealthy patrician, Publius Cornelius, and a valiant plebian, Gaius Flaminius. Having to choose between them gives rise to a debate over what makes for true nobility.

After A and B have retreated to watch the play, the Romans enter, and the rivalry between the two suitors is revealed. Then, all of a sudden, the patrician Cornelius decides his suit would be better advanced if he had the services of a servant / go-between, and he turns to the audience to find a volunteer:

> 'So many gode felowes as byn in this hall,
> And ther is non, syrs, among you all
> That wyll enterprise this gere?' (358-60)

At this request, B decides he will take the job, shrugging off A's claim that in doing so, he "wyll distroy all the play." In fact, B shrugs off A's criticism by urging him to "com in anone / with another pageant," convincing him that there is profit in it. A, then, quickly forgets about his earlier fears that such intervention would ruin the play and seeks out Gaius Flaminius, the other suitor, making a role for himself as he goes—lying to Gaius Flaminius that he has overheard a conversation between Lucres and a "fresshe galant" and convincing Gaius Flaminius that they have met before. In other words, the spectators, A and B, become part of the play's action, finding profit in the service of the two Roman suitors. Once inside the drama, they begin to mirror the main plot by competing for the affections of Lucre's maid, Jone. After a slapstick scene in which Jone soundly cudgels both A and B, the first half of the play ends with A telling B:

> 'Whe may not with oure long play
> Lett them fro theyre dyner all day;
> Thay have not fully dyned,' (1418-20)

A directs the ushers to serve good wine and promises that all will return "for to play the remanent / At my lordis pleasure" (1434-35).

The second half of the play is less interesting for our purposes except that Lucres herself chooses Gaius Flaminius as her husband, whereas in B's plot summary given at the beginning of the play, the decision was turned over to the Senate, and they made the choice for her. We see that once the two spectators become actors, the plot is altered.

A number of features in this play which can enhance our understanding of *Sir Gawain*. The antics of A and B—from their initial appearance as simply spectators in the hall to their eventual roles as participants—do an impressive job of confusing what is real and what is only spectacle, only entertainment. This fundamental confusion as to what is part of the play world and what is not is explored with delightful effect in Medwall's play. But it proves to be a frightening experience in *Sir Gawain*. There the trafficking between the play world and the world of the court becomes all the more confusing and frightening because, while we might be tempted to accept the attitude of Arthur and Gawain that this is a serious chivalrous challenge being put before the renowned Round Table, there are a host of features, just as there are in Medwall's play, that keep calling attention to the Green Knight's performance as a performance. The Green Knight appears as if on cue at exactly the moment when the king has refused to eat. As many have noted before me, what we have here is a figure looking like an actor from a folk play with all the spectacular features associated with such characters—the total greenness, the red rolling eyes, the wagging beard, the aggressive taunting of the audience.[20] Though we cannot be sure what the medieval versions of the mummers' plays (i.e., those plays growing out of the fertility rites of the folk) were like, the modern survivals continue to feature the beheading of a knight by a foreigner and the revival of the knight by a comic Doctor.[21] And the beheading idea from the folk play appears to have been current in the fifteenth century, for in the early morality play *Mankind,* written between 1465-70, Myschef offers to cure the wound of now-a-days by cutting off his head and setting it on again.[22] The point is that there are certainly enough echoes of theatrical or "staged" events in the Green Knight's performance to justify Arthur's reference to it as an "interlude."

It is clear that Medwall in *Fulgens and Lucres* has little if any interest in presenting the story of Lucres and her two suitors as a slice of Roman life—that is, a gripping drama in which the audience feels itself transported to the world of ancient Rome. In fact, as critics have shown, Medwall constantly interferes with the Roman story in such a way that any sense of the real world of these Romans is destroyed by the constant intrusion of those characters from the fifteenth century, A and B.[23] These two discuss the outcome of the play in advance, address the audience, announce intermission, give orders to the ushers. They worry about whether the play's conclusion will cause offense, and at the end B suggests that the play might be rewritten to please its audience:

> 'And glade wolde he be and ryght fayne
> That some man of stabyll brayne
> Wolde take on hym the labour and payne
> This mater to a mende.' (II, 914-17)

This same self-conscious sense of artifice, of a created entertainment, is suggested by the Green Knight's insistence in calling his challenge a "gomen," but the court is reluctant to accept it. This reluctance makes for the ambiguity and confusion which surround the court at first and continue to surround Gawain at the end of the poem. The playing out of the Green Knight's "game" even looks like a "Crystemas gomen," and yet it does not. It seems like an interlude in that it is divided into two parts, it is certainly spectacular in the ways that sotelties, entremets, and jousts with the king's champion were. It involves the audience and contains a spectacular special effect—much better than any four and twenty blackbirds baked in a pie. But the Green Knight calls into question the chivalry and prowess of the Round Table at the same time that he cheerfully urges his own beheading. And no one at court at the time of the challenge, least of all Arthur, is willing to regard this behavior with mirth.

This early contrast in attitude is sustained all the way through the romance, culminating in the final scene where Gawain, and this time, members of the court as well as the Green Knight take very different attitudes toward his behavior. As we have seen, an uneasy ending is also a marked feature of *Fulgens and Lucres* and Van Velthem's chronicle as well. In *Fulgens and Lucres*, A expresses his dissatisfaction with the play's ending: "And I wolde have thought, in vere dede, / That this matter sholde have procede / To som other conclusion" (II, 877-79). In Van Velthem's chronicle, Edward's men, as we have seen, are uneasily brought to the service of the king through game, many lamenting the necessity, now, of serving against their own families. In *Sir Gawain*, the outcome of the Green Knight's "Crystemas gomen," Arthur's suggested interlude, leaves both Gawain and Morgan le Fay unsatisfied. The enchantress' testing of the pride of the Round Table humbles Gawain but has not humbled the rest of the court nor frightened them or Guenevere to death. He insists on regarding the larger-than-life, the different-from-life Green Knight as an equal, just as he did when he decided to accept the green girdle. For Gawain, the Green Knight continues to be, not part of any interlude or game, but part of his real world.

What the *Gawain*-Poet seems to be aware of is the subtle power of a just emerging art form—the interlude, that form of feast entertainment which mingles the players with the audience, which seeks to merge the players' gratuitous, playful activities with the real lives of the audience and their activities at court. As secular drama developed, the lines between the players and the spectators became more sharply drawn and the two worlds more fully delineated. But back in the fourteenth century, the *Gawain*-Poet undoubtedly saw and recog-

Notes

1.   *Sir Gawain and the Green Knight*, ed., J. R. R. Tolkien and E. V. Gordon, rev. ed. Norman Davis (Oxford: Clarendon Press, 1967), 283. All subsequent references are made to this edition and will appear parenthetically in the text.

2.   *Sir Gawain and the Green Knight: A New Critical Edition*, ed. Theodore Silverstein (Chicago: University of Chicago Press, 1984), p. 5.

3.   Larry D. Benson, ed., *King Arthur's Death: The Middle English* Stanzaic Morte Arthur *and* Allliterative Morte Arthure (Indianapolis: Bobbs-Merrill, 1974), 1512.

4.   *The Works of Geoffrey Chaucer*, ed. F. N. Robinson, 2nd ed. (Boston: Houghton Mifflin, 1957), V (F), 81.

5.   See "intromissum" in Domino Du Cange, *Glossarium* (Paris: Librairie des sciences et des artes, 1938), IV, 407. See "entremet" in *Tresor de la langue francaise* (1979); Paul Robert, *Dictionnaire alphabetique et analogique de la langue francaise* (Paris: Presses universitaires de France, 1954); Institute de France, *Dictionnaire de L'Academie Francaise*, Septieme Edition (Paris: Librairie de Firmin-Didot et Cie, 1878), I.

6.   Glynne Wickham, *Early English Stages* (New York: Columbia University Press, 1959), I, 211.

7.   Enid Welsford, *The Court Masque* (Cambridge: Cambridge University Press, 1927), pp. 44-46.

8.   See "entremete" in *The Oxford English Dictionary* (1933; rpt. Oxford: Clarendon Press, 1978).

9.   Lodewijk van Velthem, *Voorzetting van den Spiegel Historiael (1248-1316)*, ed. Herman Vander Linden and Willem de Vreese (Brussels: Hayez, Drukker der Koninklijke Academie van Belgie, 1906), I., 295-321. I am grateful to Therese Decker of Lehigh University for the English translation, which appears in the text. Line references to this Dutch edition will appear parenthetically in the text.

10.   Roger S. Loomis, "Edward I, Arthurian Enthusiast," *Speculum* 28 (1953): 117-18.

11.   G. Huet, "Les traditions arturiennes chez le chroniqueur Louis de Velthem," *Moyen Age* 26 (1913): 173-79; Thomas Chotzen, "Welsh History in the Continuation of the 'Spiegel Historiael' by Lodewijk van Velthem," *Bulletin of Celtic Studies* 7 (1935): 47.

12.   Nicolaas Marais Hoogenhout, *Untersuchungen zu Lodewijk van Velthem's Spiegel Historiael* (Diss. Kaiser-Wilhelms-Universitat zu Strassburg. Leiden: Brill, 1902), p. 41.

13. Hoogenhout, *Untersuchungen*, p. 41; Huet, "Les traditions," p. 176.

14. Loomis, "Arthurian Enthusiast," p. 119.

15. Chotzen, "Welsh History," pp. 47-54.

16. Loomis, "Arthurian Enthusiast," p. 119.

17. Huet, "Les traditions," p. 176; Chotzen, "Welsh History," p. 50.

18. *The Tudor Interlude* (Leicester: Leicester University Press, 1958), pp. 2, 3, 25, 24.

19. *Fulgens and Lucres* in *The Plays of Henry Medwall: A Critical Edition*, ed. M. E. Moeslein (New York: Garland, 1981), Part I, Line 24. Subsequent references will appear parenthetically in the text.

20. Elizabeth M. Wright, "Sir Gawain and the Green Knight," *Journal of English and Germanic Philology* 34 (1935): 159.

21. Alan Brody, *The English Mummers and Their Plays* (Philadelphia: University of Pennsylvania Press, 1969), p. 5.

22. *The Macro Plays*, ed. Mark Eccles, EETS 262 (London: Oxford University Press, 1969), p. 168, ii, 434-35.

23. See Robert C. Jones, "The Stage World and the 'Real' World in Medwall's *Fulgens and Lucres*," *Modern Language Quarterly* 32 (1971): 131-42.

INDEX

Abraham, 40, 44, 50, 58, 95, 96, 106, 110, 111, 112, 113, 118, 121, 123, 124, 134, 134, 138, 140, 142
Acedia (Sloth), xviii, 163-74
Acheron, 187
Ackerman, Robert, 33, 53, 54
Acts, Book of, 123
Adam, 34, 41, 45, 65, 110, 118, 120, 139
Adoration of the Magi, 63, 65
Adrian and Ritheus , 144
Advent, 11
Aeneid , 186
Aenigma, 86, 90
Agnes, Saint, 76
Alain de Lille, 34
Albertus Magnus, 165, 169
Alcuin, 141, 142
Aldhelm, 57; *De virginitate,* 57
Alexander of Ashby, 34
"Alisoun," 89
Allegory, 14, 31-59
Allenbach, Jean, 191
Alliterative *Morte Arthure* , 143
Alypius, 14
Ambiguity, 199, 204, 214-18, 224, 238
Ambrose, Saint, 56, 115, 144,146; *Commentariorum in Ezechie-lem Prophetam,* 56, 58, 59
Amos, Book of, 56, 121
Amplificatio, 33, 34, 36
Ancrene Wisse, 80, 88
Anderson, J. J, 74, 159
Andrew, Malcolm, 3, 173, 184, 192
Angelome of Luxeuil, 57, 141

Animals/ Animal Imagery, 17-29, 54, 134-41, 144, 180, 186, 192, 205
Annunciation, 64, 76
Anselm, Saint, 37
Anti-Christ, 50-51, 179
Apocalypse, Book of, 7, 47, 67, 74
Aquinas, Thomas, Saint, 34, 35, 55, 57, 73, 164, 165, 170, 174, 200; *Summa theologicae,* 55, 57
Archetypes, 121
Aristotle, 4, 52, 89
Ars conciondandi, 55
Ars praedicandi, xiii, 31-59
Arthur, King of Britain, 195, 197, 198, 199, 200, 201, 202, 203, 204, 207, 214, 229, 230, 232, 233, 236, 237, 238, 239
Arthur, Ross G., xvii, xviii, 210, 212
Ascension, xviii, 63
Ashley, Kathleen, 212, 219
Astrology, 8-9, 11-12, 15
Atkins, J. W. H., 138
Attwood, E. Bagby, 74
Augustine of Hippo, Saint, 4, 6, 14, 15, 37, 49, 53, 56, 57, 74, 81, 82, 89, 90, 102-03, 105, 114, 115, 138, 141; *De civitate Dei,* 114, 138, 141, 142; *De doctrina Christiana,* 56, 74, 81, 82, 89, 211; *De magistro,* 89; *De sacramentis,* 115, 116; *De spiritu et lettera,* 56 *De trinitate,* 205, 211, 226; *De utilitate credendi,* 56; *Enarrationes in Psalmos,* 56; *Sermones de Scriptures,* 15,